Worth More than Many Sparrows

Studies in Ancient Religion and Culture

Series Editors:

Philip L. Tite, University of Washington

Michael Ng, Seattle University

Studies in Ancient Religion and Culture (SARC) is concerned with religious and cultural aspects of the ancient world, with a special emphasis on studies that utilize social scientific methods of analysis. By "ancient world," the series is not limited to Greco-Roman and ancient Near Eastern cultures, though that is the primary regional focus. The underlying presupposition is that the study of religion in antiquity needs to be located within cultural and social analysis, situating religious traditions within the broader cultural and geopolitical dynamics within which those traditions are located.

This series also encourages cross-disciplinary research in the study of the ancient world. Due to the historical development of various academic disciplines, there has arisen a set of largely isolated and competing fields of study of the ancient world. Often this fragmentation in academia results in outdated or caricatured scholarly products when one discipline does use research from another discipline. A key goal of this series is to help facilitate greater cross- and inter-disciplinary work, bringing together those who study ancient history (especially social history), archaeology (of various methods and geographic focuses, as well as theorists in archaeology), ancient philosophy, biblical studies, early patristics/church history, Second Temple and formative Judaism, and Greek and Roman classics, as well as philologists.

Given the focus on the social and cultural context within which religion functions, the series also publishes studies which explore the various social locations in which real people in antiquity practiced or interacted with their religious traditions. Examples include the domestic cult, food production and consumption, temple worship, funerary practices/monuments, development of social networks, military cult, and ancient medicine.

Finally, the series encourages a broader application of theoretical and methodological tools to the study of the ancient world. While the main perspective is social-scientific (understood broadly), specific analyses from the reservoir of critical theory, narrative theories, economic theory, bio-archaeology, gender analysis, anthropology of religion, and cognitive theory are welcome.

Worth More than Many Sparrows

Essays in Honour of Willi Braun

Edited by
Sarah E. Rollens and Patrick Hart

SHEFFIELD UK   BRISTOL CT

Published by Equinox Publishing Ltd.

UK: Office 415, The Workstation, 15 Paternoster Row, Sheffield, South Yorkshire S1 2BX

USA: ISD, 70 Enterprise Drive, Bristol, CT 06010

www.equinoxpub.com

First published 2023

© Sarah E. Rollens, Patrick Hart and contributors 2023

All rights reserved. No part of this publication may be reproduced or transmitted in any form or by any means, electronic or mechanical, including photocopying, recording or any information storage or retrieval system, without prior permission in writing from the publishers.

British Library Cataloguing-in-Publication Data

A catalogue record for this book is available from the British Library.

ISBN-13 978 1 80050 196 6 (hardback)
978 1 80050 197 3 (paperback)
978 1 80050 198 0 (ePDF)
978 1 80050 245 1 (ePub)

Library of Congress Cataloging-in-Publication Data

Names: Braun, Willi, 1954- honouree. | Rollens, Sarah E., 1984- editor. | Hart, Patrick, editor.
Title: Worth more than many sparrows : essays in honour of Willi Braun / edited by Sarah E. Rollens and Patrick Hart.
Description: Sheffield, South Yorkshire ; Bristol, CT : Equinox Publishing Ltd, 2023. | Series: Studies in ancient religion and culture | Includes bibliographical references and index. | Summary: "In an effort to honor Braun's work and mentorship, this volume is focused on exploring, probing, and theorizing ancient religious data as reflections of human interests and activities"-- Provided by publisher.
Identifiers: LCCN 2022007094 (print) | LCCN 2022007095 (ebook) | ISBN 9781800501966 (hardback) | ISBN 9781800501973 (paperback) | ISBN 9781800501980 (epdf) | ISBN 9781800502451 (epub)
Subjects: LCSH: Bible--Criticism, interpretation, etc. | Theology. | Church history.
Classification: LCC BS511.3 .W669 2022 (print) | LCC BS511.3 (ebook) | DDC 220.6--dc23/eng/20220513
LC record available at https://lccn.loc.gov/2022007094
LC ebook record available at https://lccn.loc.gov/2022007095

Typeset by ISB Typesetting, Sheffield, UK

Contents

	Introduction *Sarah E. Rollens and Patrick Hart*	1
1.	Partaking in the Great Supper of God: Figuring Birds in the Apocalypse of John *Sarah E. Rollens*	13
2.	Authority and Canon: I Fight Authority, but does Authority Always Win? *Patrick Hart*	31
3.	Ornitheology *Francis Landy*	48
4.	Shipwrecked on a Desert Island: The Barren Isolation of "Christian Origins" *William Arnal*	63
5.	The Ontological and Zoomorphic Semiotics of Two Hellenistic Savior Deities *Darlene Juschka*	78
6.	From Liturgy to Polemic and Back: Social Identity Issues in the Use of Two Psalms *Steven Muir*	93
7.	'The Spirit Descended Like a Dove': Bird Divination, Carrier Pigeons, and the Baptism of Jesus *Jennifer Eyl*	113
8.	Syriac Dialogue Hymns and New Comedy *Robyn Faith Walsh*	131
9.	Diamonds and Rust: *Q*, Mythic Marcion, and the (De)Contextualization of Divine Wisdom *Glen J. Fairen*	152
10.	The Past as Simulacrum: Shifting Our Focus in Studying "Religion" in the Ancient World *Vaia Touna*	166

11. The Corinthian Funerary Cultural Context and Baptism on behalf
    of the Dead Ritual 181
    Mark Wheller

12. Reconstructing Socio-Cultural Institutions in the Gospel of Mark 200
    Allan Wright

13. "After This, Nothing Happened": Historical Vulnerability and the
    End of (Cultural) Time in the Gospel of Mark 220
    John W. Parrish

14. Farm to (School)table: The Cultivation of *Paideia* in the
    Gospel of Thomas 238
    Ian Phillip Brown

15. Transgressing New Testament Classrooms with Thecla 256
    Anna Cwikla

    Index of Subjects 274
    Index of Modern Authors 277

Introduction

Sarah E. Rollens and Patrick Hart

This Festschrift came about as many do, through informal discussions between students about an esteemed mentor, with an idealized vision of the perfect collection of essays and someone finally concluding, "We should really do this!" Of course, planning such collections takes a great deal of time and energy, but we are thrilled with the quality of essays that we have collected in honor of Willi Braun.

Overview of Willi Braun's Scholarship

Willi Braun received his PhD degree at the University of Toronto in 1993. He was initially under the supervision of Heinz Guenther, but when Guenther unexpectedly[1] retired, John S. Kloppenborg took over the role. Kloppenborg, whose own list of former graduate students reads as a "who's who" of scholars on early Christianities (including Rollens and several other contributors to this volume), remembers Willi as a student who "didn't need much guidance—he wrote very well, it was always well argued and researched, and required very little adjustment once he had submitted it."[2] Kloppenborg also describes Willi as "one of those scholars who you can depend upon to come up with something that is serious, carefully nuanced, and really worthwhile thinking about."[3] Willi's dissertation, "The Use of Mediterranean Banquet Tradition in Luke 14.1-24," examined the way that Luke combined Greco-Roman social practices with Jesus traditions for the purposes of social formation. This work went on to be published with Cambridge University Press as *Feasting and Social Rhetoric in Luke 14*.

Yet notwithstanding the focus of his doctoral studies, Willi's expertise and erudition have hardly been confined to the area of early Christianities

---

1. We emphasize the *unexpected* nature of his retirement. As Willi tells it (perhaps with some exaggeration? It's hard to know!), he arrived in person to submit a draft of his project to Guenther, who accepted it and immediately turned it back over to him, announcing that he was retiring. After Willi recovered from the understandable trauma, he was happily able to find a new supervisor in John S. Kloppenborg.
2. John S. Kloppenborg, email correspondence with Sarah Rollens, July 15, 2020.
3. John S. Kloppenborg, email correspondence with Sarah Rollens, July 15, 2020.

(a plural that Willi has strenuously and rightly insisted upon). In addition, his interests and scholarly contributions relate to social theories of history and myth in the study of religion, and—more broadly—method and theory in the study of religion. Willi's intellectual contributions to this latter area are amply evidenced by his tenure as one of the editors of *Method & Theory in the Study of Religion* (*MTSR*). Joining the fledgling publication in 1991, Willi's involvement with *MTSR* proved pivotal to the growth of the journal as a vital haven for critical scholarship in the field of Religious Studies. In fact, by the time Willi departed the *MTSR* editorial team in 1997, his impact was already well-established, as attested to by his fellow editors: "Though [Willi] has consistently shunned what little limelight *MTSR* has provided for its editors and authors, readers should know that he is directly responsible for much of *MTSR*'s success over the past several years."[4]

In addition to this, Willi, along with his frequent collaborator Russell McCutcheon, assembled and edited the well-known *Guide to the Study of Religion*, or simply "the *Guide*," as it is affectionately referred to by many Religious Studies students. Comprised of 31 essays, the *Guide* addresses a wide variety of topics related to the scientific study of religion, e.g., Definition, Classification, Myth, Discourse, Ideology, etc. Since its initial release in 2000, the *Guide* has been reprinted (twice), and has gained renown as a frequently cited and highly regarded anthology in the critical study of religion. Indeed, as noted by one reviewer (and contributor to this volume), "[t]he *Guide* is a truly remarkable text and a must for all students and scholars of religion."[5]

Willi has also edited a number of other volumes—either alone, or with one or both of his perennial brothers-in-arms, William Arnal and Russell McCutcheon: *Rhetoric and Reality in Early Christianites* (Waterloo: Wilfrid Laurier University Press, 2005), *Introducing Religion: Essays in Honor of Jonathan Z. Smith* (London: Equinox, 2008), *Failure and Nerve in the Study of Religion: Essays in Honor of Donald Wiebe* (London: Equinox, 2012), and *Reading J.Z. Smith: Interviews & Essays* (New York: Oxford University Press, 2018).

Beyond his significant editorial work in the academy, Willi has also been a prolific essayist throughout his career. In fact, the above scarcely scratches the surface of Willi's own substantive contributions to the study of religion, and more specifically, the study of early Christianities. Underlying all of this work is Willi's unwavering fidelity to a certain critical ethos: "that the

---

4. *Method and Theory in the Study of Religion* 10 (1998): 2.

5. Darlene Juschka, review of *Guide to the Study of Religion*, ed. Willi Braun and Russell T. McCutcheon, *SR/SR* 29.3 (2000): 346.

proper object of the scholar's study consists of the 'religious' behaviours of people, a study that consists of description and explanation in general anthropocentric terms."[6] Put more concisely, Willi would sometimes summarize his own approach with reference to the words of Alexander Pope: "Know then thyself, presume not God to scan; The proper study of mankind is Man."[7] Alternatively, one might say that Willi's approach to the study of religion aligns with the words of the pre-Socratic philosopher Protagoras: "Where the gods are concerned, I am not in a position to ascertain that they exist, or that they do not exist. There are many impediments to such knowledge, including the obscurity of the matter and the shortness of human life."[8]

In any event, Willi's anthropocentric approach to the study of religion has been the unequivocal hallmark of his "attitude," one that "signals not an arrogant stance of being deeper in the know, but an intellectual alignment."[9] Fortunately for all of us Braun-iacs, this attitude is now accessible to us in the form of a collection of Willi's essays, entitled *Jesus and Addiction to Origins: Towards an Anthropocentric Study of Religion* (London: Equinox, 2020).

Yet despite his vast erudition and significant contributions to the field, those who know Willi know also that he has always maintained a casual and unassuming demeanor, steadfastly exuding a level of humility that stands in stark contrast to what one would be inclined to expect of an academic with his tremendous intellect and accomplishments. Nonetheless, there is no doubt that Willi's contributions to the academy are highly regarded. As evidence of this, one need look no further than the dedication written by his close friends and collaborators, William Arnal and Russell McCutcheon, in *The Sacred is the Profane: The Political Nature of "Religion."* There, Arnal and McCutcheon describe Willi as *"il miglior fabbro,"* i.e. the best craftsman.[10] Indeed, this is an apt and much-deserved description of Willi and his contributions to the academy.

---

6. Willi Braun, "Disciplinary Anxieties in the Study of Religion," *Temenos* 43.2 (2007): 225.
7. See for example, Braun, "Disciplinary Anxieties," 225; Willi Braun, "Introducing Religion," in *Introducing Religion: Essays in Honor of Jonathan Z. Smith*, eds. Willi Braun and Russell T. McCutcheon (London: Equinox, 2008), 482; and William Arnal and Willi Braun, "The Irony of Religion," in *Failure and Nerve in the Academic Study of Religion: Essays in Honor of Donald Wiebe* (London: Equinox, 2012), 233.
8. Robin Waterfield, trans., *The First Philosophers: The Presocratics and Sophists* (Oxford: Oxford University Press, 2000), 211.
9. Braun, "Introducing Religion," 485; and Braun, "Disciplinary Anxieties," 228–9.
10. There is some history to the use of this phrase. It appears first in Dante's *Divine*

List of Selected Publications

Willi is widely published both in the study of early Christianity and also in Religious Studies more broadly conceived. We provide here a list of his most important and influential publications (sometimes selfishly listing the ones that we were most influential on *us*), including those published works that involved collaborators:

Braun, Willi, *Feasting and Social Rhetoric in Luke 14*. SNTMS 85 (Cambridge: Cambridge University Press, 1995). Reprinted in paperback in 2005.
—ed., *Rhetoric and Reality in Early Christianities*. Studies in Early Christianity and Judaism/Études sur le christianisme et le judaïsme, 16 (Waterloo: Wilfrid Laurier University Press, 2005).
—"Disciplinary Anxieties in the Study of Religion," *Temenos:* 43.2 (2007): 223–42. https://doi.org/10.33356/temenos.7913
—ed. Braun, Willi, William Arnal and Russell T. McCutcheon, eds., *Failure and Nerve in the Study of Religion: Essays in Honor of Donald Wiebe* (London: Equinox, 2012).
—Braun, Willi and Russell T. McCutcheon, eds., *Introducing Religion: Essays in Honor of Jonathan Z. Smith* (London: Equinox, 2008).
—"'Wir haben doch den amerikanischen Jesus'. Das amerikanische Jesus Seminar: Eine Standortbestimmung." *ZNT* 16.8 (2005): 30–40.
—"The Past as Simulacrum in the Canonical Narratives of Christian Origin." *Religion & Theology* 8 (2001): 213–28. https://doi.org/10.1163/157430101X00107
—"Socio-Mythic Invention, Graeco-Roman Schools, and the Sayings Gospel Q." *Method & Theory in the Study of Religion* 11 (1999): 210–35. https://doi.org/10.1163/157006899X00032
—"Symposium or Anti-Symposium? Reflections on Luke 14:1-24." In John S. Kloppenborg and Leif E. Vaage, eds., *Scriptures and Cultural Conversations: Essays for Heinz Guenther* at 65. *TJT* 8.1 (1992): 70–84. https://doi.org/10.3138/tjt.8.1.70
—"The Historical Jesus and the Mission Speech in Q 10:2–12." *Foundations & Facets Forum* 7.3-4 (1991): 279–316.
—Braun, Willi and William Arnal, "The Irony of Religion." In William Arnal, Willi Braun and Russell T. McCutcheon, eds., *Failure and Nerve in the Academic Study of Religion: Essays in Honor of Donald Wiebe* (London: Equinox 2012), 230–38.
—"The First Shall Be Last: The Gospel of Mark After the First Century." In Panayotis Pachis and Donald Wiebe eds., *Chasing Down Religion in the Sights of History and the Cognitive Sciences: Essays in Honor of Luther H. Martin* (Thessaloniki: Barbounakis, 2010), 41–57.
—"'Our Religion Compels Us to Make a Distinction': Prolegomena on Meals and Social Formation." In Zeba Crook and Philip A. Harland, eds., *Identity and Interaction in the Ancient Mediterranean: Jews, Christians, and Others* (Sheffield: Sheffield Phoenix Press, 2007), 41–55.

Comedy, where Dante uses it in reference to the troubadour Arnaut Daniel. Centuries later, in *The Waste Land*, T. S. Eliot would employ the same phrase in a dedication to Ezra Pound.

—"Rhetoric, Rhetoricality and Discourse Performances." In Willi Braun, ed., *Rhetoric and Reality and in Early Christianities*. Studies in Christianity and Judaism / Études sur le christianisme et le judaïsme, 16 (Waterloo: Wilfrid Laurier University Press, 2005), 1–26.

—"The Schooling of a Galilean Jesus Association (The Sayings Gospel Q)." In Ron Cameron and Merrill Miller, eds., *Redescribing Christian Origins*. SBL Symposium Series (Atlanta, GA: Scholars Press; Leiden: Brill, 2004), 43–66.

—Braun, Willi and William E. Arnal, "Social Formation and Mythmaking: Theses on Key Terms." In Ron Cameron and Merrill Miller, eds., *Redescribing Christian Origins*. William E. Arnal SBL Symposium Series (Atlanta, GA: Scholars Press; Leiden: Brill, 2004), 459–69.

—"Fugitives from Femininity: Greco-Roman Gender Ideology and the Limits of Early Christian Women's Emancipation." In David B. Gowler, Gregory L. Bloomquist and Duane Watson, eds., *Fabrics of Discourse: Essays in Honor of Vernon K. Robbins* (Harrisburg, PA: Trinity Press International, 2003), 317–32.

—"Religion." In Willi Braun and Russell McCutcheon, eds., *Guide to the Study of Religion* (London: Cassell, 2000), 3–18.

—"Argumentation and the Problem of Authority: Synoptic Rhetoric of Pronouncement in Cultural Context." In Thomas H. Olbricht and Stanley E. Porter, eds., *The Rhetorical Analysis of Scripture: Essays from the 1995 London Conference*. JSNT Supplement, 146 (Sheffield: Sheffield Academic Press, 1997), 185–99.

—"Socio-Rhetorical Issues: Context." In William E. Arnal and Michel Desjardins, eds., *Whose Historical Jesus?* Studies in Christianity and Judaism/Études sur le christianisme et le judaïsme (Waterloo: Wilfrid Laurier University Press, 1997), 92–7.

Influence on Emerging Scholars

Perhaps as equally valuable as his scholarship on early Christianity and the study of religion is Willi's patient guidance and unwavering support of junior scholars, both those who were officially his students, as well as those who simply happened to come into his orbit by being involved in the scholarly projects, conferences, and seminars that he frequented. In some ways, his way of being a scholar—his "attitude," as mentioned above—has been just as influential on emerging scholars as the content of his research has been.

Anyone who knows Willi appreciates how he has always moved effortlessly between systematic thinking about his specific area of research (early Christianity) and more general endeavors to synthesize and theorize the data that he encounters in that topical area, all the while maintaining a kind of sober corrigibility or epistemic humility that is entirely consistent with his anthropocentric approach. Unsurprisingly, these characteristics are alluded to numerous times within the contributions to this volume. For instance, Francis Landy observes in Willi's scholarship "the necessity for patience, for determination, for seeing all sides of the data...a kind of relentless curiosity." John Parrish points to his "undoubted mastery of his specialized data domain" that "allows him to draw upon these data to provide 'e.g.'s' illustrating the concepts and fleshing out the categories that his rigorous and insightful theoretical work calls forth." Comparably, Sarah E. Rollens identifies how Willi's body of work engages in both wide-angled theoretical analyses of the study of religion that take place from a bird's eye view, as well as research that is narrowly focused, requiring "systematic examination of small details in ancient texts to uncover new meaning." Conversely, yet still consistent with Willi's overall ethos, Patrick Hart's essay begins by making note of a somewhat crude but amply-warranted observation by Willi about the scholarly plight: that "we're all in the middle of the shitpile." Capturing the comprehensive animus behind the statements of both Hart and Rollens, Willi's longtime friend and colleague William Arnal rightly states that "the consistent thread of Willi Braun's scholarship has been an effort to humanize the ancient literary artifacts that constitute our area of inquiry." In short, Willi is the best of all worlds: he is a specialist in his chosen discipline, skilled in the theory that helps him access many different perspectives on that subject matter, yet also a scholar whose work exhibits a persistent appreciation for the ancient Greek aphorism *gnōthi seauton*, or "know thyself," which also appears at the beginning of the aforementioned quote by Alexander Pope. That is, as an anthropocentric-minded scholar, Willi always keeps two feet planted firmly on the ground.

Bearing all of this in mind, it is also unsurprising, as any of Willi's students will know, that he instilled in us a great level of humility when engaging with our scholarly predecessors. Willi never let us get away with overly brazen dismissal of the generations of thinkers that came before us (a tactic that most graduate students try out at least once). Instead, he insisted that we present their ideas in a fair manner and critique them with attentiveness and respect, no matter how much we disagreed with them. Indeed, Willi's approach to the critical enterprise was itself integral to his pedagogical efficacy. As Willi himself so articulately puts it, he does not use the word criticism "as a synonym for negation or refutation," but rather "in the old Greek sense, meaning the will and ability to distinguish and decide (*krinein*) between options on the basis of standards (*kritēria*) that are themselves the precipitates of a critical (*kritikos*) process that now, as in ancient Greek societies, is not esoteric but exoteric, that is, public."[11] This approach enculturated in us a sense of place in our intellectual lineage and an appreciation of how ideas develop and build on one another over time. In order to "saturate" us in our research, moreover, he often allowed us to work with him to create directed reading classes tailored to our research interests. At the same time as he created focused graduate-level work for us, Willi also allowed us a

---

11. Braun, "Introducing Religion," 490.

great deal of autonomy and let us follow our interests down different paths. Here again, we would claim that his modus operandi as a supervisor was as important as the content that he relayed to us as students.

One of the academic initiatives that Willi has been most influential in has been the Redescribing Christian Origins seminar of the Society of Biblical Literature. This seminar originated in the 1990s at the behest and under the guidance of Burton Mack, Ron Cameron, and Merrill Miller, among others. Willi was an early participant in the seminar and contributed an essay on the Sayings Source Q to the first round of proceedings from the seminar. Equally as important as the scholarship generated in the seminar, Willi (along with other early participants) viewed this intellectual space as a venue to mentor the work of emerging scholars whose work arguably did not "fit" into the mainstream scholarship of the discipline. Like those who came before them, participants were asking questions that others thought irrelevant (even irreverent!) or too difficult to answer. Many of Willi's graduate students presented some of their early work within the seminar, and it was always received with an ethos of generosity and curiosity. Willi also made sure that the seminar's work was consistently on the reading lists for his graduate students. In this way, he gently nudged the field in a different—and arguably more interesting and more productive—direction. While there has been an obvious and expected turnover of participants within the seminar, Willi regularly shows up to hear our papers, our responses, and our discussions, and continues to offer his own much-valued feedback and critique.

Another academic enterprise that Willi has long been involved with is the North American Association for the Study of Religion (NAASR). Started by some of his own academic mentors (E. Thomas Lawson, Luther H. Martin, and Donald Wiebe), NAASR is yet another venue for scholars whose work does not fit with the "mainstream" study of religion and who are asking more critical—and less reverent—questions about their objects of study. While not focused on early Christianity specifically, there have been several joint conference panels between NAASR and the Redescribing seminar. Willi has regularly given papers at NAASR panels and has contributed to their many publications. Importantly, he has also encouraged his students to do the same, drawing no distinction between the intellectual contributions of established scholars and emerging ones. In this way, he has fostered in his students the ability to frame their questions about Christian origins within the wider academic study of religion and to adopt the critical methodologies of Religious Studies proper.

In addition to the above, much of Willi's support for emerging scholars comes not in specific advice, but rather in the way that he is a model for collaborative scholarship with his peers. He has jointly published numerous articles and books with his aforementioned intellectual "partners in crime," William Arnal and Russell McCutcheon. Modeling this scholarly collaboration is increasingly important, in our view, because as the job market tries to force us to be more competitive with one another and to articulate our individual, unique contributions to our discipline, we risk losing the intellectual gains made when we collectively think through our questions and problems. Willi discouraged any sort of cutthroat competition among his students. By modeling collaborative scholarship, he deliberately encouraged us to engage with fellow scholars' work and to collaborate if there was an intellectual payoff.

One cannot help but notice that among Willi's collaborative works are many that deal with teaching the study of religion. This is because Willi has also been continually interested in producing work that will act as tools for his peers and for emerging religionists. Take for example *The Guide for the Study of Religion*. Willi's own contribution to this anthology was in fact to consider the lofty term "religion"—no mean task. In keeping with the goals of the volume, he systematically articulates the crucial issues that must be borne in mind when deploying the term "religion." As many in the intellectual lineage of Willi know, this term is too often used as if its referent were self-evident. True to form, instead of writing a singularly definitive essay on the matter, Willi's discussion of the concept of "religion" is a *guide* to the major issues one must be wary of when studying and teaching in this discipline.

Overview of the Contributions in the Volume

The co-editors of this volume were both Willi's graduate students at the University of Alberta—Rollens for her MA degree, and Hart for both his MA and PhD. We both knew Willi as students in his classes (mostly graduate seminars), as well as through his one-on-one guidance of our research. Other contributors to this collection range from other former students, to emerging scholars who have benefited from Willi's scholarship or mentorship, to admiring friends and colleagues. The only requirement we asked when inviting contributors was that the essays had to deal with studying religion in antiquity. Needless to say, contributors were only too happy to join in this project.

Despite the rather open topic of religious discourse in antiquity, some other common themes nevertheless emerged among the essays. For one, in the spirit of Willi's careful and systematic reading, many contributors have looked closely at textual imagery and how certain ideas are manifested and put to use at the level of discourse. For another, readers will also notice that another group of essays focuses on the Gospel of Mark and its myth-making efforts in Christian origins. This focus is understandable, given Willi's long-standing fascination with Mark as one of the earliest occasions for the followers of Jesus to try to make sense of their identity and social experience. Several of these papers emerge from students who took one of his graduate seminars on Mark (which often and appropriately featured Burton Mack's *A Myth Innocence: Mark and Christian Origins* centrally). And finally, though the contributors engage with a range of texts, traditions, and approaches, a delightful number of these essays honor Willi's curiosity with all things avian, and thus opt to explore ornithological imagery within ancient religious texts.

Sarah E. Rollens' essay acknowledges Willi's beloved passion for birding and considers the avian imagery in the Apocalypse of John. Despite there only being four major references to birds (five, if a minor reference to eagle wings in Rev. 12.14 is counted), this imagery is laden with significance. Representations of birds appear at opportune moments in the unfolding revelation, she observes, and in some cases, act as agents of divine violence. Birds in the Apocalypse, Rollens concludes, are "paradoxical," being associated simultaneously with "movement, life, and the heavenly realm, while also being harbingers of violence, destruction, and death."

Patrick Hart's contribution uses a casual and somewhat irreverent observation of Willi's as a launch point for a discussion on canonical (and more specifically Pauline) authority. After giving some attention to the historical use and development of the term "canon," and through consideration of Paul's own struggles with authority vis-à-vis some of his *ekklēsiai*, the nuanced and even paradoxical nature of authority is made vividly apparent.

Also engaging with the avian theme, Francis Landy's essay explores, in his characteristic poetic fashion, birds in the Hebrew Bible. As he shows, they are symbols full of rich signification. They embody numerous sentiments, from the raven's association with death and destruction, to the dove's association with the feminine, to the ostrich's association with folly. Yet, as Landy demonstrates, despite the diversity of bird metaphors, many are mobilized to communicate something about the nature of the divine, whence comes the neologism in his essay's title: orintheology.

William Arnal interrogates the scholarly use of the term "Christian" and argues that in addition to being anachronistic, it also has a profound distorting effect on the ancient data that we study. He pushes back against those who see the presence of Jesus in these texts as the all-determining feature."The simple presence of Jesus in our earliest Christian textual artifacts," he argues, "does not in itself require us to read those writings as somehow separate and distinct from the kinds of issues and problems that would have been of interest to other citizens of the ancient world." Continuing this theme of not isolating early Christian texts as somehow special, Darlene Juschka's essay focuses on two Hellenistic savior deities (Jesus and Mithras) to expose the "shared sensibilities" that animate the traditions associated with them. Often overlooked because of the assumption of Jesus' uniqueness, Juschka shows that both Jesus and Mithras share similar ontological myths, bodily comportment, and zoomorphic associations. Such observations, she notes, point to "a shared context, shared imaginative conceptualizations and shared semiotic systems, all of which shaped the parameters of their mythographies."

In his contribution, Steven Muir examines the lives and afterlives of Psalm 82 and Psalm 110. Unlike many commentators on the Psalms, he carries his exploration through to the Orthodox tradition, arguing that the meanings of these Psalms change with time and are adaptable to new context. They are "striking case studies in the multi-generational and multi-community appropriation of texts, with radical shifts at each stage."

Returning again to avian imagery, Jennifer Eyl analyzes the dove in the story of Jesus' baptism, exploring how the imagery would be understood in its Graeco-Roman context. She examines the dove's associations with divination practices and moral virtue, finding many affinities with non-Christian literature. Modeling her intellectual curiosity on that exemplified by Willi, she argues that 'one of Christianity's most enduring visual symbols—the white dove—arises as a product of the Mediterranean world of bird divination, courier pigeons, and an allegory of moral perfection."

Robyn Faith Walsh's chapter looks at the affinities between Syriac dialogue hymns and the literature of New Comedy in antiquity, focusing on such common motifs as "the spurned love," "the penitent harlot," and "the jilted love." Like other contributions that laud Willi's methodological approach, she too refuses to treat early Christian literature as special or somehow intellectually isolated from its surrounding cultural influences. After her analysis, Walsh concludes that the hymn writers "were at the very least aware of these stock characters [in New Comedy] and how to use them to great effect in their dialogues." Through these tactics, "the hymnist was able to give new life to their subjects."

Glen Fairen's essay tackles the gospel attributed to Marcion, which, similar to the Q source, is hypothetical but can be reconstructed from passages in Luke. For this reason, Q and Marcion's gospel (as they have been reconstructed) end up having some overlaps in content. Fairen's analysis of these overlaps reveals, among other things, that "any assumption of Marcion's anti-Judaism should be seen as academically naive at best." For him, this highlights the way that Q can be a kind of tool for undoing scholarly presuppositions. In his words, "[t]he value of Q in deconstructing the theological/academic assumptions about Marcion is hardly overstated."

Vaia Touna's essay then examines the theoretical issues involved in studying the category of religion in the ancient world. She offers numerous strategies to correct this assumption, including recognizing one's positionality and that the categories that one uses for analysis are products of this positionality. In addition, she advises always bearing in mind that the reconstructed past is a simulacrum, which requires attention to "artificiality and... representation that are present at every step of the historical production."

Inspired in no small part by Willi's own socio-historical approach to the study of early Christianities, Mark Wheller looks at the funerary practices present in Corinth at the time when Paul wrote to his *ekklēsia* there. Buttressed in part by the Catherine Bell's theory of ritual, Wheller argues that the Corinthians melded the Christ-hero with cultural funerary practices that were already familiar to them, resulting in a novel means of addressing their mortuary and ancestral concerns.

Allan Wright's contribution also deals with the socio-cultural context of Mark as a post-War intellectual project. Instead of focusing on Mark as only a response to or struggle with the upheaval and trauma of war, he expands the lens to view Mark's effort to engage in restitution of his perceived crises. "Mark offers specific discourses," Wright suggests, "that rectify his chaotic world" and envision news forms of identity construction.

John Parrish's essay continues the focus on Mark and treats the phenomenon of apocalyptic time in the Gospel of Mark in the context of the aftermath of the Jewish War with Rome. Parrish explains Mark as grappling with a specific kind of cultural trauma and dissonance among the early followers of Jesus, a "doubly-deracinated group of Judean refugees." The Gospel, he concludes, "is an attempt to bring some 'good news' to a group of people who were experiencing a loss of identity from a position of exile."

Ian Brown's contribution compares the *Gospel of Thomas* to Graeco-Roman schools in relation to their use of agricultural metaphors on the subject of education, or *paideia*. In doing so, Brown makes the case that there is a genealogical relationship between the two, as the *Gospel of Thomas* makes use of metaphors for education and virtue drawn from Graeco-Roman schools.

Last, but certainly not least, Anna Cwikla's essay explores the extent to which Thecla represents a liberated female figure in antiquity, especially when some elements of her legacy actually reinscribe patriarchal assumptions. In particular, she is interested in how to present this issue in the classroom when the female characters that students encounter in early Christian texts are already so limited. Her discussion suggests that while

"Thecla may not be a fully transgressive figure in her narrative world...she can become our transgressive accomplice in the classroom if we situate her story properly."

We intend this collection to serve as a testament to Willi's intellectual influence. One of the most rewarding things about the pedagogical enterprise is that the teacher gets to impart knowledge and skills into numerous eager students and then send them out into the world to make their own impact. Occasionally, these students are able to come back and offer something in return. It is in this spirit—and with great gratitude and appreciation—that we offer this volume to Willi.

Sarah E. Rollens is the R. A. Webb Associate Professor of Religious Studies at Rhodes College. She holds a MA from University of Alberta (2008) and a Ph.D. from University of Toronto (2013). Her research focuses on the social history of the early Jesus movements, and she has published on such facets as text production and source use among early Christians, the social experiences and identities of early Jesus people, affinities between Pauline groups and other ancient voluntary associations, and, most recently, the use of imagery of violence and persecution by early Christian authors. Characteristic of many of Braun's students, she is also deeply interested in theoretical and methodological issues involved in studying ancient religion, and has published several articles that engage with this topic. She is currently the English language Book Review Editor for *Studies in Religion/Sciences Religieuses*.

Patrick Hart is a contract instructor at the University of Alberta and practicing lawyer. He obtained his MA, PhD, and LLM from the University of Alberta, and his JD from Queen's University. His research interests include the study of Paul and early Christianities, religion and philosophy, method and theory in the study of religion, and the intersection of law and religion. His doctoral research was published as *A Prolegomenon to the Study of Paul* (Brill, 2020), and he has had various articles published in religious studies journals and legal journals.

Chapter One

Partaking in the Great Supper of God: Figuring Birds in the Apocalypse of John

Sarah E. Rollens

And should the word "joy" shock, so be it, for here too the issue is the need for a translation capable of bringing the meaning of what we as humans know of joy into conjunction with the miracle of that escape from gravity that birds epitomize in their upward soaring; capable too, perhaps, of precipitating a retroactive effect, with the meaning and sensation of flying, thrust very deep into the imaginary realm, opening space up, as though from within, so that our contemplation is impregnated by it and our thinking is flooded by the radiant and dilated sense of what opens up and is nothing but opening up.

-Jean-Christophe Bailly[1]

When a bird flies through the air,
no evidence of its passage is found;
the light air, lashed by the beat of its pinions
and pierced by the force of its rushing flight,
is traversed by the movement of its wings,
and afterward no sign of its coming is found there.
-Wisdom of Solomon 5.11[2]

Introduction

This essay examines the small collection of avian imagery present in the Apocalypse of John. Though less visually commanding than the monstrous beasts and composite creatures that populate much of the Apocalypse's imagery, there exist a handful of easily overlooked references to birds that help animate the unfolding conflict in John of Patmos' revelation. Upon closer inspection, the imagery of birds turns out to be consistently aligned with the agency and activity of the divine. In addition to this connection, birds are also figures with communicative power, which the Apocalypse treats as nothing other than ordinary. And finally, when one reads carefully, it becomes clear

---

1. Jean-Christophe Bailly, "Animals are Masters of Silence," in *Animots: Postanimality in French Thought*, eds. Matthew Senior, David L. Clark and Carla Freccero, Yale French Studies 127 (New Haven, CT: Yale University Press, 2015), 84–94, here 89.
2. All Bible verses are NRSV unless otherwise noted.

that birds help usher in the divine violence that plays out in the text; sometimes they even carry such violence out directly. Far from being merely ornamental in the story or peripheral to the eschatological visions, these feathered figures are complex and intriguing characters in the Apocalypse.

Why Birds?

As readers will no doubt observe, several essays in this volume engage with the theme of birds and ancient religious material. This is no happy coincidence: in addition to being a wise sage when it comes to ancient religion, culture, and society, Willi Braun is also, endearingly, a bird aficionado. Anyone who is friends with Willi on social media will have no doubt had their mindless scrolling interrupted by one of his magnificent and perfectly-timed photographs of birds. Some of these masterful portraits came together in a small children's book that Willi created called *B is for Birds*.

During the second year of my doctoral program, I emailed Willi with exciting news that I'd had an article accepted into *Method & Theory in the Study of Religion*. He sent back a photograph that he had taken of a "wise owl" (which was actually, he specified, a Northern Hawk owl). About the photo, he explained, "I offer it to you as a symbol of my congratulation."[3] Suffice it to say that when I (and many others) think of Willi, we cannot help but think of his ornithological interests. Thus, there is no better way to honor his academic influence on me and others than by writing about the animals that fascinate him so.

Birds in Ancient Mediterranean Literature

My idea for writing this essay is fortuitously timed; it comes on the heels of two important publications: Jeremy Mynott's 2018 comprehensive study of birds in the ancient world and Patricia Cox Miller's more narrowly focused 2018 study of the zoological imagination in patristic writings.[4] With both of these studies available to me, much of the hard, contextual work of examining avian imagery in ancient discourse has already been done, and so I build on these studies with much deference and gratitude.

---

3. Willi Braun, personal communication, February 27, 2009.
4. Patrica Cox Miller, *In the Eye of the Animal: Zoological Imagination in Ancient Christianity* (Philadelphia, PA: University of Pennsylvania Press, 2018); Jeremy Mynott, *Birds in the Ancient World: Winged Words* (Oxford: Oxford University Press, 2018).

Birds are, to use the increasingly tired phrase coined by Claude Lévi-Strauss, useful to "think with" in ancient literature.[5] It was routine for ancient authors to treat "birds as thoughts"[6] and to use aspects of their appearance, mannerisms, and behaviors to discuss moral, cosmic, and other concerns. And this was for good reason. As Jeremy Mynott explains:

> Wherever you were, there were birds—feeding, displaying, fighting, vocalizing, mating, and engaging in a whole range of social behaviors that seem instantly recognizable to human observers. No surprise, then, that birds did not just present themselves as physical objects of curiosity and study, but also populated people's minds and imaginations and then re-emerged in their language, legends, and patterns of thought in some symbolic form.[7]

In short, birds are richly fertile items of discourse, "ideally constructed, both physically and symbolically, to be the bearer of signs and meanings, the links between gods and men."[8] Within early Christian writings, bird imagery is often closely tied to Christological language. Consider the well-known scene of Jesus' baptism in which the Holy Spirit descends upon him in the form of a dove. In this instance, the dove is a vessel of the divine, a conduit that allows a divine figure to invade Jesus' human body. Or take the *Infancy Gospel of Thomas*, wherein the creative power contained in the young Jesus manifests for all to see when he playfully brings clay doves to life. Elsewhere, Jesus' providential (and curiously, maternal) care is articulated through the use of hen imagery to describe his relationship to Jerusalem (Luke 13.33-34//Matt 23.24). Avian imagery can be deployed in early Christian texts to evoke the miraculous or the divine even when not talking about God or Jesus specifically. The parable of the mustard seed, for instance, imagines the kingdom of God as a tiny seed that grows into a robust shrub capable of providing shelter for the birds that take refuge in its branches (Mark 4.30-32).[9]

Birds are associated with all manner of positive qualities and phenomena in antique literature. Above all, they are connected with various forms of knowledge acquisition: wisdom, perception, prophecy, and the like. The

---

5. Note that this widely used phrase appears to be a slight mistranslation of the original French: James K. Stanescu, "Animals are More than Good to Think with, Part 1," *Critical Animal*, 16 July 2012, http://www.criticalanimal.com/2012/07/animals-are-more-than-good-to-think.html.
6. Miller, *In the Eye of the Animal*, 17.
7. Mynott, *Birds in the Ancient World*, 245.
8. Mynott, *Birds in the Ancient World*, 359.
9. In the Parable of the Sower (Mark 4.1-8), birds are depicted as dangers to the sown seeds; indeed, when Jesus interprets the metaphors, the birds represent Satan, who takes away "the word" once it has been taught to people.

ability to decode information embodied by birds was a form of divination, a skill recognized by nearly everyone and "rather like forecasting the weather."[10] The goal was not necessarily to learn specific items of knowledge, but rather to gauge propitiousness of possible actions or to get a sense of the correct way to proceed. There are a myriad of examples in ancient literature of birds acting as omens, indicators, or guideposts for action; one need only peruse Homer for numerous instances of birds acting as both positive and negative signs (Homer, *Iliad* 12.200-08; 24.315-21; *The Odyssey* 2.164-180; 15.179-90). This tight association between birds and knowledge carries over into the Roman world, wherein augury becomes a prestigious occupation with a specialized vocabulary.[11] Ancient people did not just use birds to discern the order of the world, though. They also employed them in hopes of *changing* it, and so we routinely find them involved in various ritual practices aimed at intervening in the workings of the world or at influencing the gods or fate.[12]

Interestingly, the Hebrew Bible pushes back a bit on the association of knowledge with birds. The Book of Job, for instance, comments that birds, like most humans, cannot find wisdom (Job 28.7). Indeed, wisdom is "concealed even from the birds of the sky" (Job 28.21). However, Job 12.7 is of a different piece and presents the "birds of the air" as among those creatures that *are* able to discern the wisdom of nature. Similarly, Jeremiah 8.7 contrasts storks and doves, which are able to discover the will of God, with humans, who are not as perceptive. This inconsistency is what we might expect from a collection of books stemming from various times, places, and authors. At least in Israelite traditions, then, birds can occupy an interesting paradoxical space, both connected to and apart from knowledge.

Following from the capacity of birds to reveal information, in many cases information related to the gods and their machinations, we also observe that birds are uniquely connected to the divine realm and fate. They were the "principal agents through which the gods revealed their will to humans."[13] As the philosopher Celsus explains regarding augury and its connection with the divine realm:

---

10. Mynott, *Birds in the Ancient World*, 251.

11. Mynott, *Birds in the Ancient World*, 251, 261. Note, of course, that there are always dissenters. Cicero was famously skeptical of various forms of divination (*On Divination* 2.115).

12. Mynott, *Birds in the Ancient World*, 267-84. Mynott discusses this under the classification of "Magic and Metamorphosis" apart from "Religion." However, any respectable student of Willi would never opt to take over such an uncritical distinction, and so I cannot.

13. Mynott, *Birds in the Ancient World*, 249.

> Well then, men learn this from other animals, especially from birds; and those who understand the indications which they give are diviners. If then the birds and all other prophetic animals which are given foreknowledge by God teach us by means of signs, they seem to be naturally so much nearer in communication with God and to be wiser and dearer to God.[14]

To discern the plans of the gods, the flight patterns and vocalizations of birds were studied.[15] The assumed "naturalness" of birds' connection to the divine, we might suppose, follows from the realization that birds inhabit "the heavens" alongside God. Their connection to divinity was based on their vertical movement and their ability to progress toward the divine realm, leaving humans behind on earth.[16] It is important to note that this connection was more one of mediation, rather than one of embodiment or symbolism.[17]

Bird imagery is also related to liberation, and this connection has carried over to the modern period. Indeed, as Miller observes, "For modern and ancient thinkers alike, birds embody a liberating sense of openness," derived surely from their freedom in flight.[18] The notion of the flights of birds being both tethered to fate and thus embodying a kind of knowledge about the mechanics of the world, while also simultaneously being open to possibility creates an intriguing paradox. This paradox is encapsulated in their movement: on one hand, they embody unrestrained freedom, constant movement, and necessary change, but on the other, if their flight is indeed

---

14. This translation comes from Miller's *In the Eye of the Animal*, 39. As Miller goes on to explain, Origen, in whose writings Celsus' words are preserved, was not a fan of augury: "Origen argues that divination by birds is neither prophetic nor genuine. If birds really had prophetic souls, he reasons, they would not get trapped in nets set for them by human beings and they would know ahead of time where archers trying to shoot them were located and so avoid those spots…[B]irds have no idea of God at all and thus cannot act even as intermediaries between divine intention and human life. The very idea, Origen says, is repellent" (39-40). Such opposing views surrounding augury are critical to keep in view, because it is often easy to make sweeping statements about what a culture did or did not believe or practice, especially when texts are our only evidence. Origen and Celsus' views illustrate the diversity of beliefs that existed within the very same cultural context.

15. Mynott, *Birds in the Ancient World*, 250.

16. Miller, *In the Eye of the Animal*, 19. For later Christians who began to think of themselves as alienated from their proper, celestial home, birds became an especially fruitful metaphor. For instance, Augustine interprets the dove, which was thought to make noises akin to mourning, as a symbol of "an eschatological hope for 'flight' to our 'native country,' the heavenly realm" (Miller, *In the Eye of the Animal*, 36).

17. Although in some ancient stories, there are some instances of embodiment, such as Zeus transforming himself into a swan to pursue Leto.

18. Miller, *In the Eye of the Animal*, 19.

indicative of the interworkings of fate or the divine, then their flight is *not* open or random: the conclusions of augury suggest that the cosmos imbues their actions with restricted meaning. A curious modality, to be sure.

Ancient authors regularly treated birds as a unique class of animals, neither of the sea nor of the land, and certainly different from swarming animals, despite the flocking habits of many species of birds. Classifying birds as a unique type of animal helped these authors to map their cosmos, to locate and arrange different realms of space, and to systematize the space that they inhabited. Birds were relegated an entire domain, differently expressed as "the air," "the skies," or "the heavens." Fish have the sea, hoofed animals have the land, and birds have the air—together with remaining oddities, such as swarming insects, the cosmos is complete. Even Paul echoes this cosmic classification in his bricolage-esque explanation of how the physical resurrection works, explaining that each type of creature has a unique fleshly constitution: "Not all flesh is the same: People have one kind of flesh, animals have another, birds another and fish another" (1 Cor. 15.39). Whenever an author wanted to describe something that affected life on earth on a comprehensive scale, it was important to include the domain of birds.

Birds were also involved in mapping cultural space as well. That is, they were indicative of some cultural proclivities; the best example here is how they function in the levitical food laws in Israelite traditions. As a species of animal that can be clean or unclean, birds offer an object through which cultural identity can be explored and expressed. In this sense, they contain yet another method of communication, for they signal where one lies in the complex terrain of cultural practices, most clearly, food preferences. They become one possible site to communicate information about one's cultural affiliations. The so-called "unclean" birds in the Hebrew Bible essentially fall into three categories: "birds of prey, water birds, and [two] perching birds."[19] "Bird of prey" is a classification that includes both eagles and vultures, both of which eat flesh; vultures especially are and were known to eat carrion (as in Luke 17.37//Matthew 24.28). Almost certainly for the clear association of these birds with the consumptions of flesh and blood, these birds are categorized as "unclean" in the Hebrew Bible.

There is far more to say about the import of birds to ancient people,[20] but the nuances drawn out so far will suffice to set the stage for discussing the avian imagery in the Apocalypse of John. Though brief, the discussion

---

19. Peter Goodfellow, *Birds of the Bible: A Guide for Bible Readers and Bird Watchers* (Oxford: John Beaufoy Publishing Limited, 2013), 30.

20. Jeremy Mynott's *Birds in the Ancient World* will likely become recognized as the standard study for such interests.

already highlights the rich symbolism and semantic range associated with birds. In short, knowing some of the ideas that birds evoked in ancient audiences will help us appreciate better their imagery in the Apocalypse of John.

Birds in the Apocalypse of John

There are four references to birds in the Apocalypse of John: Revelation 4.5-8; 8.13; 18.1-3; and 19.17-21.[21] We will consider each in turn. The first two references employ the Greek term ἀετός, usually rendered as "eagle," while the latter two use ὄρνεον, a more generic term for bird. This is curious, because different vocabulary aside, eagles or birds of prey seem to be what is presupposed in most of the references. At the very least, then, all the birds discussed in the Apocalypse fall into the "unclean" category in terms of Israelite reckoning of food laws. But, as we will see, what might be unclean for eating might also be the most regal of birds in the heavens and therefore the closest to God.

Revelation 4.5-8 (The Eagle-Like Creature Covered in Eyes)

The first avian reference in the Apocalypse of John comes in the throne room scene. At the beginning of the story, the seer, John, is on the island of Patmos when he encounters a vision of "one like a son of man" (Rev. 1.13), who gives him messages for the Christ groups in Asia; afterward, he sees an open door leading to heaven; a voice invites him to come "up" and hear about future events. The text does not state explicitly that he accepts the invitation, nor does it describe his physical movement into heaven; John simply states that he was immediately "in the spirit" and found himself before an elaborate throne. The description of the throne is at once beautiful and terrifying, fueling Christian imagination and imagery for centuries:

> Coming from the throne are flashes of lightning, and rumblings and peals of thunder, and in front of the throne burn seven flaming torches, which are the seven spirits of God; and in front of the throne there is something like a sea of glass, like crystal. Around the throne, and on each side of the throne, are four living creatures, full of eyes in front and behind: the first living creature like a lion, the second living creature like an ox, the third living creature with a face like a human face, and the fourth living creature like a flying eagle. And the four living creatures, each of them with six wings, are full of eyes all around and inside. Day and night without ceasing they sing, "Holy, holy, holy, the Lord God the Almighty, who was and is and is to come." (Rev. 4.5-8)

---

21. There are actually five if we count the minor reference to "eagle wings" in Rev. 12.14.

The four creatures surrounding the throne—the so-called tetramorph—are each individually important to early Christian theology, art, and imagination,[22] but since our present focus is birds, we will only focus on the fourth. John sees this fourth creature as something "like an ἀετός" (usually translated as eagle) among the creatures that surround the throne. Like the other creatures, its "living" (ζῷον) quality is emphasized (though admittedly more so in the English rendering than in the original Greek). Whereas the other creatures are living but static, the ἀετός is the only one to have a qualifying adjective that signals dynamic movement of flight: πετομένῳ.

The eagle-like creature's proximity to the throne implies its connection to God. This, as we have seen, is a common association with birds in antiquity, due in part to their vertical movement through the heavens. Indeed, later commentators who associated the four creatures of the tetramorph with the canonical evangelists also assumed their close connection with the divine, often expressing the relationship in terms of inspiration. At the same time as they are *close* to the throne, we note that they are also simultaneously *subordinate* to its occupant. They sing his praise and worship him continually, often by prostrating themselves or producing song or music. Together with twenty-four elders (who each have their own thrones) and an indeterminate number of angels, the scene depicts a raucous, even slightly hectic, royal court.

Artists who have wished to depict these creatures have tended to overlook their composite nature: they are all covered in eyes and have six wings each. Thus, what John sees is not just something *like* an eagle, but something *more than* an eagle: it is a six-winged, googly-eyed monster. Such composite beasts are common in apocalyptic and prophetic literature, and the Apocalypse, as many have noted, is obviously drawing its imagery from Ezekiel's throne vision in Ezekiel 1.[23] In the present setting, we might also surmise that these countless eyes, both in front and back of the eagle, evoke a kind wisdom, which is what one gains with proximity to God.

---

22. As is well known, later Christian thinkers connected the four canonical evangelists to these four creatures: Luke to the ox, Mark to the lion, Matthew to the human-like creature, and John to the eagle.

23. Isaiah 6 also informs the Apocalypse's imagery. The imagery in Ezekiel differs from the Apocalypse of John in important ways. For one, Ezekiel sees four composite beings, each identical. The four beings each have human bodies, four wings, and four different faces. These four faces that appear on each creature (a human face, an ox face, a lion face, and an eagle) are taken over by the author of the Apocalypse of John and turned into individual creatures. Ezekiel's beings, moreover, are not covered in eyes. Rather, the throne is propelled by some rather complex wheels, and it is they that are covered in eyes.

The avian creature is vocal, imbuing the scene with auditory as well as visual intrigue. It sings hymns to God and offers formulaic statements of praise that describe God's immortal and creative characteristics. Interestingly, the ἀετός and the other creatures communicate in a language that John can apparently understand, though no comment is made regarding how this is possible. Mynott observes the intriguing frequency with which birds are thought to communicate with humans. Ancient peoples had a:

> fascination with the capacity of birds to mimic human voices… [though] it may be just mindless repetition…. But the possibility of more genuine forms of communication with animals was considered by some later philosophers, in connection with the related question of whether animals could be said to be *rational* in any real sense.[24]

The sounds that the eagle in the throne room produces is not mere parroting, but neither is it complex, rational communication; its repeated praise and hymnal performance lie somewhere in between.

The ἀετός's function in this scene is not entirely clear at first. Part of its purpose is to offer ceaseless praise to the throne's occupant, and like many of the inhabitants of heaven, it will stand by as a witness to the eschatological violence to come. Upon closer examination, however, it becomes clear that the eagle is no passive observer; rather, it is active in the unfolding violence of the Apocalypse. After taking in the throne scene and observing that its occupant is holding a scroll, John begins to weep, as he thinks that there is no one worthy to open it. Immediately, a lamb "standing as if it had been slain" (Rev. 5.6) (curiously, also called a lion in the previous verse) appears; this is Christ embodying a duality of animal symbolism: the lamb is a sacrificial victim, thus recalling Christ's sacrificial death, while the lion indicates his descent from the tribe of Judah. The ἀετός and the other creatures encircle the lamb and begin singing to it. Their song confirms that the lamb is indeed worthy to open the scroll. In that sense, the ἀετός helps facilitate the onslaught of apocalyptic violence to follow. The ἀετός's role in the violence is made even clearer in Revelation 6, where the four horses and riders emerge after the opening of the first four seals of the scroll. Which living creatures are involved in calling which horse and rider is not entirely obvious, but if we are to assume that the creatures beckon the horses in the order that they were initially presented in Revelation 4.7, then the ἀετός ushers in the pale horse, ridden by Death, with Hades in tow (Revelation 6.7-4). This particular horse and rider are allowed to kill a quarter of the earth's inhabitants. Thus, not only does the ἀετός, long with the other animals, confirm that the lamb can open the scroll, it participates in inviting the apocalyptic violence.

---

24. Mynott, *Birds in the Ancient World*, 329.

At this point, it is useful to comment on the nuances of the particular type of bird in view in this passage: the ἀετός. The term ἀετός is usually translated as eagle, but it could theoretically be other sorts of birds of prey, too. Different species of birds of prey are not always kept straight in ancient literature, which complicates matters somewhat. Eagles are regularly associated with "regal characteristics,"[25] as well as honor, strength, and power.[26] Because they hunted live prey, they are also associated with violence, warfare, and the like. Mynott explains the close association of birds of prey with imagery of violence:

> Raptors, and particularly eagles, were the species most often referred to in military contexts.... [R]aptors were predators, who conveyed the necessary sense of power and physical violence; and since they were often carrion eaters they had a literally visceral relationship with animal entrails.... Raptorial birds (defined more generally) tended to have a special relation to the gods, too...the eagle was the bird of Zeus (king of the gods), the falcon and raven were the messengers of Apollo (god of prophecy), while the little owl (*Athene noctua*) was the eponymous bird of Athena (goddess of war).[27]

Curiously, ἀετός (and similarly the Herbrew term *nešer*) can sometimes stand for vulture, and probably should be rendered as such more often. The propensity to translate it as eagle "reflects the contempt for the vulture that is deeply rooted in the Western tradition but has no equivalent in the worldview of the ANE and Bible, which the vulture is generally held in high esteem."[28] Indeed, vultures could also be associated with kingship.[29] Even so, vultures, which are carrion eaters, were associated more with death, "doom and gloom," and other ominous sentiments.[30] While the ἀετός in Revelation could theoretically be either a vulture or an eagle, convention leans toward an eagle. As we will see, vultures are likely in view with the third and fourth avian references in the Apocalypse, even though, curiously, the text only uses the generic term ὄρνεον for both.

Revelation 8.13 (The Eagle in Heaven Pronouncing Woes)

Avian imagery recedes into the background until Rev. 8, which begins with the opening of the seventh and final seal of the scroll. Afterward, an angel fills a censer with fire and coal from the altar in heaven and hurls it upon the

---

25. Goodfellow, *Birds of the Bible*, 128.
26. Goodfellow, *Birds of the Bible*, 130–1.
27. Mynott, *Birds in the Ancient World*, 254–5.
28. Christoph Berner, "Eagle" *EBR* 7: 105.
29. Christoph Berner, "Bird of Prey" *EBR* 3: 1211.
30. Goodfellow, *Birds of the Bible*, 128.

earth. A new series of disasters is initiated, this time each following an angel sounding a trumpet. After the fourth trumpet, a single eagle appears in the skies, pronouncing woes on the inhabitants of the earth:

> Then I looked, and I heard an eagle crying with a loud voice as it flew in midheaven, "Woe, woe, woe to the inhabitants of the earth, at the blasts of the other trumpets that the three angels are about to blow!" (Rev. 8.13)

Like the bird described in the throne room, this, too, is an ἀετός, and therefore, likely an eagle or vulture. Here it is worth pausing to remember that birds of prey (eagles, raptors, ravens, vultures, and the like) are not "kosher" according to Israelite food laws, yet they are closely connected to the heavens, to messages from God, and, as demonstrated in the previous passage, to God himself. We thus recall an intriguing connection: the birds commonly connected with the heavenly realm and its knowledge are also a class protected from base consumption in the Jewish cultural context.

Similar to the eagle-like creature in the throne room, this bird is vocal as well; it cries out with a loud voice and speaks in language that humans can understand, again reflecting the ancient tendency to presume some manner of communication between humans and birds. What's more, its dynamism is evident as well: it calls out in the midst of flight, just as the creature in the throne room gave the appearance of being in flight. Rev. 8.13 specifies that this bird is at some distance from the divine realm, only flying in "midheaven" (μεσουρανήματι). Perhaps its location in mid-heaven is important for its mediating purpose: it acts as a conduit from the divine realm to the inhabitants of the earth. It knows the wrath of God that is yet to come and is tasked with announcing it before it takes place.

Since the ἀετός imparts a message to the inhabitants of the earth, it also seems to participate in the frequent associations of birds with wisdom or knowledge. This knowledge is eschatologically oriented: the woes that it pronounces are not based on what *has* happened already in the apocalyptic destruction but on what *will* happen. The ἀετός thus has prescience and is prophetic. While not the *agent* of destruction, it is certainly the *herald*. This is therefore a classic example of birds being "gods' messengers" or "privileged intermediaries."[31]

The intervention of the ἀετός as this specific point in the systematic destruction following each trumpet initially appears random, but it is, I propose, not accidental. Before its pronouncement, the earth suffers several calamities: "hail and fire, mixed with blood" (Rev. 8.7); the transformation of one third of the sea to blood, killing a third of the sea creatures and

---

31. Mynott, *Birds in the Ancient World*, 249.

destroying a third of its ships (Rev. 8.8-9); the poisoning one third of the fresh rivers and waters (Rev. 8.10-11); and the blotting out of one third of the light of the moon, stars, and sun (Rev. 8.12). All of this destruction is aimed at the "natural" (that is, non-human[32]) world, but what follows the ἀετός's announcement is violence aimed directly at humans. The monstrous locusts that are loosed from the bottomless pit are specifically commanded to harm only humans. A calvary numbering two million then unleashes plagues, which kill one third of humanity (Rev. 9.18). Contextualized thus, we observe that the function of the ἀετός in Revelation 8.13 is to signal the transition for the violence to move from damaging the cosmos to damaging humans. In short, despite seeming at first glance to be only a passing reference, the avian imagery here marks a significant transition.

Revelation 18.1-3 (The Birds that Populate the Fallen City of Babylon)

Avian imagery recedes once again until Revelation 18, which contains the third avian reference. Revelation 18 describes the fate of the city of Babylon, which is generally agreed to be a cipher for Rome.[33] The chapter begins with a description of what remains for the city:

> After this I saw another angel coming down from heaven, having great authority …. He called out with a mighty voice, "Fallen, fallen is Babylon the great! It has become a dwelling place of demons, a haunt of every foul [lit. "unclean"] spirit, a haunt of every foul [lit. "unclean"] bird, a haunt of every foul [lit. "unclean"] and hateful beast." (Rev. 18.1-3)

The Greek term for bird in this passage is ὄρνεον, which is a rather generic term for bird. Given that the reader is supposed to classify this variety of bird as unclean (ἀκαθάρτου), we might suppose that it is a bird of prey (such as the vulture or eagle, both of which may have been in view so far in the Apocalypse), some kind of water bird, or one of the two perching birds that the Hebrew Bible says are unclean.[34] In distinction to the first two avian references so far, this imagery thus relies strongly on cultural mapping of attitudes toward birds that stems from the Israelite tradition.

Why do birds make an appearance in this passage? Their primary function seems to be to signal the desolation and judgment of Babylon/Rome. Babylon's fallen state is evident by what lives in her, these undesirable animals

---

32. Notice, however, that birds are immune from all of the apocalyptic destruction throughout the Apocalypse.

33. On this argument, see Sarah E. Rollens, "The Viability of Materialist Approaches to Persecution: Revelation as a Test Case," *Annali Di Storia Dell'esegesi* 36.1 (2019): 75-93, here 77.

34. Goodfellow, *Birds of the Bible*, 30.

and spiritual entities. These creatures, in turn, represent her suffering, which was a consequence of her moral baseness (Rev. 18.4-8). The residents of the city are called out of its environs, leaving behind all the unclean animals and spirits. For this reason, they are *indicative* of judgment and suffering, but not their cause. Nor are they agents or heralds of divine punishment as the first two ornithological references were, but rather, they are *symbols* of it—their purpose in the scene is to communicate loss and abandonment to the reader. Babylon is devoid of creatures emanating life and virtue. Later, we learn that everything reflecting urban civilization has also ceased (Rev. 18.21-23), which implies that the desolation of the urban civilization is complete; the infestation of the birds suggests that the city has been returned to nature.

The Apocalypse almost certainly wants the reader to agree that the fate of Babylon is tragic and undesirable, but some counterpoints could be marshaled against a solely negative interpretation of the ornithological inhabitants. For one, the presence of "unclean" animals is not automatically a bad thing, especially if consumption of them is already entirely out of the question. Suppose that the unclean animal that Revelation 18.2 has in view is the eagle. While eagles indeed fall into the category of "unclean" in the Hebrew Bible, it makes little sense for the presence of this bird to be indicative of moral rot, since this bird may also be in view in heaven in close proximity to the throne of God. On the flip side, if the unclean bird is a carrion eater, such as a vulture, it may have been regarded as a welcome scavenger who helped rid the city of waste. In that sense, vultures could be indicative of future revival of the city, cleansed of its moral failings. Another possible counter-point to a singularly negative interpretation involves shifting the perspective to that of the natural world. Decentering the human from this scene affects its negative valences: for animals to reclaim an urban space from its human inhabitants could be considered a "success" from the perspective of nature's flourishing.

Some positive qualities and interpretative scenarios not withstanding though, the connection of birds of prey with forsaken cities is widespread in the Hebrew Bible and tends toward negative connotations of judgment. This association comes out even more strongly in Rev. 19.17-21.

Revelation 19.17-21
(The Birds that Eat Flesh of the Conquered Enemies of God)

Finally, we arrive at Revelation 19.17-21, a passage that is often overlooked in favor of the imagery that precedes it: that of Jesus riding a white horse and leading the armies of heaven. That Jesus dominates the imagery in this chapter is for good reason, though, since he dons a cloak dipped in blood and has a sword coming out of his mouth as he leads his armies to victory.

After this victory, the remainder of the chapter features a "clean up" process, which is where the birds come in:

> Then I saw an angel standing in the sun, and with a loud voice he called to all the birds that fly in midheaven, "Come, gather for the great supper of God, to eat the flesh of kings, the flesh of captains, the flesh of the mighty, the flesh of horses and their riders—flesh of all, both free and slave, both small and great." Then I saw the beast and the kings of the earth with their armies gathered to make war against the rider on the horse and against his army. And the beast was captured, and with it the false prophet who had performed in its presence the signs by which he deceived those who had received the mark of the beast and those who worshiped its image. These two were thrown alive into the lake of fire that burns with sulfur. And the rest were killed by the sword of the rider on the horse, the sword that came from his mouth; and all the birds were gorged with their flesh. (Rev. 19.17-21)

This passage contains some of the goriest imagery in the Apocalypse, rivaled, to my mind, only with Rev. 14.14-20. In Rev. 19.17-21, the birds of heaven devour the dead flesh of all manner of defeated peoples. Goodfellow assumes that the "birds that fly in midheaven" must be vultures, because they feed on what has already been killed.[35] The Greek term that the text uses is ὄρνεον, but the interpretation of vultures or some other carrion eater makes the most sense, given their actions in this scene.[36] Indeed, vultures are often associated with war scenes due to their eating habits.[37] While the vultures themselves are not the bringers of death here (Jesus alone is [v. 21]), they continue the destruction that he began. And, whereas their immediate role in violent deeds was ambiguous in some previous passages, the birds here are *active* agents of divine violence: they are specifically commanded by an angel to take part in this military skirmish.[38] Their victims are kings, captains, riders and their horses, and slave and free people—in other words, anyone and anything that allied itself with the beast and the false prophet.

The Apocalypse describes these vultures' feast with vivid language; they are "gorged" (ἐχορτάσθησαν) on dead flesh. Middleton notes that although

---

35. Goodfellow, *Birds of the Bible*, 35.

36. As the reader might be concluding, the vocabulary for birds that the author of the Apocalypse uses is precisely opposite of what one would expect: ἀετός is used for seemingly more generic birds, while ὄρνεον is used for what is clearly a bird of prey. There is no easy explanation for this, but it might be due in part to participating in the Apocalypse's rhetoric of reversal. That is, in the "world upside down" presupposed by the text, the reversal of expected vocabulary for even something as common as birds makes sense.

37. Christoph Berner, "Bird of Prey" *EBR* 3: 1212.

38. The claim that eagles were agents of divine violence is not unique to Christianity; Zeus' eagle, for instance, carried out the unending torture of Prometheus. Mynott, *Birds in the Ancient World*, 297.

the image of "the Word" doing the killing could be taken as metaphorical, the birds cannot be; they are "a graphic representation of the slaughter that John envisages."[39] Such an image underscores the complete destruction of the enemies, initiated first by Jesus and his heavenly army, but completed definitively by the vultures at the angel's command. They devour and digest the opponents of the heavenly army. This "garbage disposal" function is an accurate interpretation of vultures in the ancient context. Ancient people relied on carrion eaters to consume the animal scraps left over from a slaughter or sacrifice (e.g., Gen. 15.11 where vultures swarm around the multi-animal sacrifice that Abram has prepared), essentially keeping villages clear of vermin and wild dogs that would descend on these scraps if the vultures did not.[40] Thus, the cleanup work that the birds carry out in this passage, gruesome as it may sound, was frequently welcomed.

At the same time, having birds dispose of the enemy's bodies serves another purpose. It deprives the dead of a dignified burial and threatens to disturb their afterlife experience. As is widely known, ancient Near Eastern, Greek, Roman, and other similar cultures greatly valued care of the dead. Proper burial was an especially important practice for the living descendants to carry out, as was regular maintenance of the grave site.[41] If a person died without receiving a proper burial, then they were unable to rest in the afterlife, no matter how such a space was conceived.

The importance of proper burial is reflected in two classic scenes from Greek and Roman epic literature. First, while in the Kingdom of the Dead (Homer, *The Odyssey* Book 11), Odysseus encounters Elpenor, his former shipmate who died after drunkenly falling off a roof. Odysseus' crew left him behind in haste, neglecting to bury him, and the shade of Elpenor requests that they return to perform the proper burial rites to grant him rest. Later in the Roman period, *The Aeneid* contains a similar account. A certain Misenus drowns and is not suitably buried. Before Aeneas is able to visit his deceased father in the Underworld, he has to carry out the appropriate rites for Misenus (Virgil, *The Aeneid* Book 6). Elsewhere, *The Aeneid* makes it a point to emphasize that those who have not received proper burial rites are unable to cross the river Acheron to enter the Underworld (Book 6). It is likely early readers of the Apocalypse were exposed to both Jewish and Hellenistic cultural forms and recognized that Jesus' enemies in Revelation

---

39. Middleton, *The Violence of the Lamb*, 123.
40. Goodfellow, *Birds of the Bible*, 138.
41. Gabriela Ingle, "Funerary Dining Scenes in Roman Tombs: Ensuring Happiness in the Afterlife," in *Imagining the Afterlife in the Ancient World*, ed. Juliette Harrisson (Abingdon: Routledge, 2018), 83–97.

19 would be deprived of an honorable burial. We might surmise, then, that the effect of these birds' actions on the enemies of Jesus was far more than initially meets the eye: whereas Jesus deprived them of present life in battle, the carrion eaters deprived them of their afterlife.

The involvement of the birds in this post-battle scene is described in terms of them attending a "great supper" or banquet. The facets of this analogy are manifold. Overall, the banquet is a victory feast, a celebration of conquest, albeit grotesque. This echoes language of a divine banquet described elsewhere in the New Testament. For instance, the Gospel of Luke looks forward to Jesus convening a future banquet in which the followers of Jesus can eat, drink, and pass judgment with Jesus on the twelve tribes of Israel (Luke 19.28-30). Luke elsewhere uses the metaphor of a great banquet to depict those who reject Jesus and those who are chosen to replace them (Luke 14.15-25). Luke 14 makes much of the sought-after nature of this invitation; one should accept it with enthusiasm, lest one be replaced. The angel's invitation to the birds once again signals proximity to and an intimacy with the divine. They are invited to this victory banquet, a divine communion, while others are excluded.

It is important to note, of course, that the imagery of animals feasting on the victims of conquest is found much earlier in Jewish texts. This "macabre" imagery, to use Paul Middleton's phrasing, ultimately derives from Ezekiel 39.17-20.[42] Other Israelite prophecies of destruction routinely feature the threat of birds of prey feeding upon the dead, too. For instance, in 1 Kings 14.10-11, Ahijah prophecies to Jeroboam's wife that there will be a "disaster on the house of Jeroboam....and [that] the birds will feed on those who die in the country." A psalm reflecting on the destruction of Jerusalem by the Babylonians echoes this imagery: "O God, the nations have invaded your inheritance; they have defiled your holy temple, they have reduced Jerusalem to rubble. They have left the dead bodies of your servant as food for the birds of the sky, the flesh of your own people for the animals of the wild." This language goes back to Deuteronomy 28.25-26, where it is a generic punishment for disobedience: "The Lord will cause you to be defeated before your enemies...Your carcasses will be food for all the birds and the wild animals, and there will be no one to frighten them away." In sum, birds consuming the conquered dead has a long history in Israelite traditions, and in its setting in Revelation, it likewise contributes to an unsettlingly violent vignette of victory. This is just par for the course, however, when considered within the wide-ranging violence of the text as a whole.

---

42. Middleton, *The Violence of the Lamb*, 183.

Concluding Remarks

While some of Willi Braun's work deals with theoretical analyses of the study of religion (from a "bird's eye view," so to speak), others, such as his careful analysis of Luke 14, engage in carefully focused, systematic examination of small details in ancient texts to uncover new meaning; it is the latter method which I wanted to imitate here (I suspect that we will get ample theory in this Festschrift!).

Some closing observations: birds in the Apocalypse are paradoxical. They are associated with movement, life, and the heavenly realm, while also being harbingers of violence, destruction, and death. They appear at key moments in the unfolding apocalyptic violence, yet are curiously insulated from it, even though other animals suffer it (e.g., Rev. 8.9). And finally, while it is common to think of birds as neutral entities that simply inhabit space or convey beauty while expressing little intentionality, they can be found doing deliberate work in the Apocalypse of John, both heralding in and engaging in forms of destruction. While this analysis shows that birds are good to "think with" to learn more about early Christian literature, I am not sure that I would have thought of them in relation to the Apocalypse of John without the opportunity here in Willi's Festschrift to do so. Perhaps the consequences of his life, like the consequences of birds in the Apocalypse, are even more far-reaching than we thought.

Author biography

Sarah E. Rollens is the R. A. Webb Associate Professor of Religious Studies at Rhodes College. She holds a MA from University of Alberta (2008) and a Ph.D. from University of Toronto (2013). Her research focuses on the social history of the early Jesus movements, and she has published on such facets as text production and source use among early Christians, the social experiences and identities of early Jesus people, affinities between Pauline groups and other ancient voluntary associations, and, most recently, the use of imagery of violence and persecution by early Christian authors. Characteristic of many of Braun's students, she is also deeply interested in theoretical and methodological issues involved in studying ancient religion, and has published several articles that engage with this topic. She is currently the English language Book Review Editor for *Studies in Religion/Sciences Religieuses*.

References

Braun, Willi. Personal Communication. February 27, 2009.
Berner, Christoph. "Eagle" *EBR* 7: 105–113.

—"Bird of Prey" *EBR* 3: 1210–22.
Goodfellow, Peter. *Birds of the Bible" A Guide for Bible Readers and Bird Watchers*. Oxford: John Beaufoy Publishing Limited, 2013.
Miller, Patricia Cox. *In the Eye of the Animal: Zoological Imagination in Ancient Christianity*. Philadelphia, PA: University of Pennsylvania Press, 2018. https://doi.org/10.9783/9780812295221
Mynott, Jeremy. *Birds in the Ancient World: Winged Words*. Oxford: Oxford University Press, 2018.
Rollens, Sarah E. "The Viability of Materialist Approaches to Persecution: Revelation as a Test Case." *Annali Di Storia Dell'esegesi* 36.1 (2019): 75–93.
Stanescu, James K. "Animals Are More than Good to Think with, Part 1." *Critical Animal*, 16 July 2012. http://www.criticalanimal.com/2012/07/animals-are-more-than-good-to-think.html.

Chapter Two

Authority and Canon:
I Fight Authority, but does Authority Always Win?[1]

Patrick Hart

Introduction

Many years ago I had a discussion with Willi Braun that, in hindsight, surely contributed to my descent down a rabbit hole on the topic of authority (and by extension, epistemology). Broadly speaking, our discussion concerned the formation of the Christian "canon," the issue of biblical authority, and the nature of authority in general. At the time, I imagine that our chat was occasioned by my own preoccupation with metaphysics, and with the nature of authority in connection to the search for absolute truth—a confession that would perhaps make Braun squeamish.[2] Nonetheless, what I distinctly remember in that conversation was Braun's pithy and suitably irreverent summation of matters concerning authority, epistemology and the human condition: "we're all in the middle of the shitpile," he said.[3]

---

1. The latter part of this title is a play on the lyrics in John Mellencamp's "Authority Song." I use them here as a nod to Braun's past affinity for referencing (in print and conversation) Mellencamp's lyrics from "Small Town," in which Mellencamp sings of being "taught to fear Jesus in a small town" (or "taught the fear of Jesus in a small town," depending on which version of the lyrics one looks at). See Willi Braun, "Religion," in *Guide to the Study of Religion*, ed. Willi Braun and Russell T. McCutcheon (London: Continuum, 2000), 4.

2. In this regard, I recognize that some of my own more philosophical-oriented research interests in the study of religion do not align well with Braun's injunction that "the proper object of the scholar's study consists of the 'religious' behaviours of people, a study that consists of description and explanation in general anthropocentric terms." Willi Braun, "Introducing Religion," in *Introducing Religion: Essays in Honor of Jonathan Z. Smith*, ed. Willi Braun and Russell T. McCutcheon (London: Equinox Publishing Ltd., 2008), 482.

3. While I will provide some account of how canonical or Pauline authority is understood or constructed later in this essay, I should note an important caveat here: in recognizing or giving credence to Braun's remark, there was—and is—a sense in which I am viewing his assertion *itself* as authoritative. In fact, throughout this article, I will of course be citing various "authorities." Given that this study is concerned with the concept of authority, the paradox or irony of all of this is not lost on me. Yet while this

Braun's observation serves as something of a launch point for what I wish to explore here. In what follows, the fundamental issue that I am interested in is the operation of *authority* in canon, using the Christian canon, and specifically the Pauline canon, as an example.[4] In doing so, my focus lies in reminding us, as scholars of religion, to remain attuned to how nuanced, and perhaps even paradoxical, the concept of authority is, in terms of how it is constituted, reconstituted, adopted, and adapted.

The Concept of Canon

The notion of a "canon" is something that ranges from being a passing curiosity for some, to a point of vital theological importance for others. Indeed, despite divergent views about its relevance, on a variety of levels—e.g., theological, historical, literary, or socio-political—the Judeo-Christian bible,[5] or the Christian canon, remains deeply entrenched in the western psyche.[6]

The word "canon" is derived from the Greek term *kanōn*, which referred literally to "a straight rod," and in turn came to denote more generally a criterion, standard or rule. The term had a broad range of uses in the ancient world, and was by no means reserved exclusively to the ecclesiastical context. Aristotle, for example, advocated for an understanding of *kanōn* that

---

irony is relevant to any examination of the phenomenon of authority on a broad level, it is not something that I will be addressing here. That is, what I am *not* examining here is the operation of authority as it pertains to the study of religion, or more generally, the operation of authority in rhetoric. These are certainly important areas of investigation, but they are not my focus in this study.

4. For some, the very notion of a "canonical Paul" might appear curious on its face. But the label is amply warranted, given the wealth of non-canonical Pauline material that exists (e.g. the Acts of Paul, the Correspondence Between Paul and Seneca, the Epistle to the Laodiceans, the Third Epistle to the Corinthians, the Prayer of the Apostle Paul, and the Apocalypse of Paul).

5. I am referring here to "bible" in a generic sense, recognizing of course that its precise contents are by no means agreed upon universally by various Christianities. For the purposes of this particular study, however, the issue need not be dwelled on, as all iterations of the present-day Christian bible include the same Pauline material that I will be referring to here.

6. In making this assertion, I believe I am echoing a sentiment similar to that stated by Burton Mack, who expresses some surprise at this state of affairs: "[o]ne might have thought that the western history of intellectual enlightenments, social revolutions, scientific discoveries, and industrialized technologies would have outgrown an archaic myth-ritual system created in a bygone age of cultural class and experimental social formations. That, however, has not happened." Burton L. Mack, *The Christian Myth: Origins, Logic, and Legacy* (New York: Continuum, 2001), 178.

was distinct from the concept of *nomos*, or law. In Aristotle's view, a *kanōn*, or rule, was something more malleable than law:

> [T]here are some cases for which it is impossible to lay down a law, so that a special ordinance becomes necessary. For what is itself indefinite can only be measured by an indefinite standard, like the leaden rule used by Lesbian builders; just as that rule is not rigid but can be bent to the shape of the stone, so a special ordinance is made to fit the circumstances of the case.[7]

This use of the term is particularly interesting, as Aristotle's conception of a mutable *kanōn* of course stands in stark contrast to the contemporary understanding of the biblical canon as something utterly incapable of being modified, and thus ultimately closed.

Yet even in the context of early Christianities, the term *kanōn* had a range of applications, being used to refer to particular ecclesiastical rules or norms, to clergy who were associated with certain churches or *ekklēsiai*,[8] and eventually to a list of authoritative writings.[9] However, as Bruce Metzger notes, this last use of the word was "late in developing; so far as

---

7. Aristotle, *Nicomachean Ethics*, trans. H. Rackham (Cambridge, MA: Harvard University Press, 1926), 1137b. For an interdisciplinary overview of the varied historical functions of "canon," see Jan Gorak, *The Making of the Modern Canon: Genesis and Crisis of a Literary Idea* (London: Athlone, 1991).

8. In the Pauline letters, the word "church" is generally used to translate the Greek term *ekklēsia* (ἐκκλησία), though the latter is more literally translated as those who are "called out." The word appears frequently in the Pauline letters, particularly in reference to the intended recipients of the letters (e.g. 1 Cor. 1.2; 2 Cor. 1.1; Gal. 1.2; 1 Thess. 1.1; 2 Thess. 1.1). Regardless, while the word "ecclesiastic" and its cognates obviously derive from the word *ekklēsia*, it is worth contrasting the meaning of "ecclesiastic" in the modern sense with the term *ekklēsia* as it was used in the classical period, where the term could be taken to refer to the Athenian public assembly. As R.K. Sinclair, notes, "[t]he Athenian Ekklesia decided on a vast range of matters from high matters of state to minor administrative details. It was open to all adult males of citizen birth: membership was not dependent on a property qualification such as pertained in oligarchic states. The Demos as embodied in the assembly held sovereignty or power (*kratos*)." R.K. Sinclair, *Democracy and Participation in Athens* (Cambridge: Cambridge University Press, 1988), 19. Insofar as many of us (as contemporary readers) possess a deep-rooted and anachronistic preconception of the word "church," I will employ the term *ekklēsia* here, in the interests of trying to sidestep this preconception. In making this decision, however, I am both conscious of and sympathetic to the utility of simply employing the term "association" as a taxonomic category in the study of early Christianities. See, for example, Richard Ascough, Philip A. Harland, and John S. Kloppenborg, *Associations in the Greco-Roman World: A Sourcebook* (Waco, TX: Baylor University Press, 2012).

9. Bruce M. Metzger, *The Canon of the New Testament: Its Origin, Development, and Significance* (Oxford: Clarendon Press, 1987), 290–2. Notably, the word only appears twice in the New Testament, with both occurring in the Pauline correspondence: Gal. 6.16 and 2 Cor. 10.13-16.

we have evidence, it was not until the second half of the fourth century that κανών [standard or rule] and its derivatives κανονικός [regular or usual] and κανονίζειν [to regulate] were applied to the Scriptures."[10] Ultimately, however, it is this latter chronological sense of *kanōn* that is of primary relevance here. For it is *this* notion of *kanōn* that bears the closest synonymity with the contemporary use of the word canon as referring to "the definitive, closed list of the books that constitute the authentic contents of scripture."[11]

Canonical Authority

To be sure, there are of course multifarious iterations of authority that can be observed in various religions, and a variety of canons. For my purposes here, however, I am concerned with authority in the Christian canon, and more specifically, some of the layers and operation of authority in the Pauline canon.

As Adolf Jülicher writes, "[t]he canon is the norm to which everything in the Church accommodates itself; to canonize means to recognize as part of this norm. The Christian of *c*. 400 felt at the mention of the word 'canonical' precisely as we do when we say divine, holy, infallible, absolutely authoritative."[12] A. van de Beek expresses a similar sentiment:

> According to the church, the canon has *divine* authority. In these books it is not only our forebears in culture and faith who are speaking, but in their words the word of God comes to us. Judaism, Islam, and Christianity technically agree with one another that there is a canonical book, which is the word of God for mankind. This book is even the normative Word of God,

---

10. Metzger, *The Canon of the New Testament*, 292. Harry Gamble concurs on this point, noting that "the word 'canon' did not begin to be applied to Christian *writings* until the mid-fourth century. The earliest known use of the term in this connection is furnished by Athanasius, bishop of Alexandria, in his *Decrees of the Council of Nicaea*, written soon after 350. There he describes the document known as *the Shepherd of Hermas* as 'not of canon' (*mē ōn ek tou kanonos*)." Harry Y. Gamble, *The New Testament Canon: Its Making and Meaning* (Philadelphia, PA: Fortress Press, 1985), 17.

11. Eugene Ulrich, "The Notion and Definition of Canon," in *The Canon Debate*, ed. Lee Martin McDonald and James A. Sanders (Peabody, MA: Hendrickson Publishers Inc., 2002), 34. However, as Lee Martin McDonald suggests, it is also worth noting that "the term 'canon' was not regularly used in reference to a closed collection of scriptures until David Ruhnken used it thus in his 1768 *Historia critica oratorum Graecorum*." Lee Martin McDonald, *The Formation of the Christian Biblical Canon* (Peabody, MA: Hendrickson Publishers, Inc. 1995), 16.

12. Quoted in *New Testament Apocrypha, Vol. 1*, ed. Wilhelm Schneemelcher, trans. Robert McLachlan Wilson (London: Lutterworth Press, 1963), 23–4. See Adolf Jülicher, *Einleitung in das Neue Testament*, 7th ed. (Tübingen: Mohr, 1931), 555.

so that other words stand under its critique, and may even be discounted in advance.[13]

What follows, for those who adhere to this particular view of canon, is a necessary allegiance to a particular hermeneutic: the contents of the canon cannot be severed in any manner, nor is there any relative authoritative weighting to its individual books. All of it is equally and absolutely authoritative and immutable.[14] To put it in terms of an admittedly pejorative expression, this sort of stance might be summarized thus: "the bible says it, I believe it, and that settles it."[15]

In less pejorative terms, however, this understanding of canon aligns entirely with one aspect of Bruce Lincoln's polythetic definition of religion:

> [Religion involves] *a discourse whose concerns transcend the human, temporal, and contingent, and that claims for itself a similarly transcendent status*...Insofar as certain propositions or narratives successfully claim such status, they position themselves as truths to be interpreted, but never ignored or rejected.[16]

---

13. A. van de Beek, "Being Convinced: On the Foundations of the Christian Canon," in *Canonization and Decanonization*, ed. A. van der Kooij and K. van der Torn (Leiden: Brill, 1998), 332.

14. With respect to this latter assertion, the closing remarks in Revelation (and ultimately the Christian bible) are worth considering: "I warn every one who hears the words of the prophecy of this book: if any one adds to them, God will add to him the plagues described in this book, and if any one takes away from the words of the book of this prophecy, God will take away his share in the tree of life and in the holy city, which are described in this book" (Rev. 22.28-19). In its immediate context, the injunction is obviously restricted in scope, referencing only the text in Revelation, not the canon as a whole. Yet functionally, by virtue of its position in the Christian bible, it becomes a pronouncement with far broader application, conveying both the legitimacy and immutability of the canonical contents in their entirety.

15. Despite my reference to this pejorative expression, my intention is not to patronize those who are engaged in apologetic or overtly theological hermeneutic endeavours. While I have no interest in these approaches myself, I am not inclined to pass judgment on the merit of pursuing them (in their proper context), or the frequently ancillary desire—tacit or otherwise—to employ canonical texts (and more specifically, the Pauline texts) to adjudicate contemporary matters. In this regard, I concur with Paula Fredriksen, who writes that "[t]heological readings of foundational religious texts are intrinsically anachronistic...Systematic rereading is how these ancient Jewish eschatological texts that are Paul's letters retain—or, rather, *obtain*—contemporary meaning. There is no dishonor in this. It is theology's project." Paula Fredriksen, "Historical Integrity, Interpretive Freedom: The Philosopher's Paul and the Problem of Anachronism," in *St. Paul Among the Philosophers*, ed. John D. Caputo and Linda Martín Alcoff (Bloomington, IN: Indiana University Press, 2009), 71-72.

16. Bruce Lincoln, *Holy Terrors: Thinking About Religion After September 11* (Chicago, IL: University of Chicago Press, 2009), 5–6.

The texts of the Christian canon can most assuredly be classified as this kind of discourse. What is fascinating, however, is that by and large, it is not that the texts claim for themselves a transcendent status.[17] Rather, it is the *collection* of that discourse, or its formation into a canon, that metamorphizes mere writing, or "scripture" (i.e. *graphē*), to "Scripture." For example, the words in 2 Tim. 3.16 ("All scripture is inspired by God and profitable for teaching, for reproof, for correction, and for training in righteousness") do not expressly make the claim that 2 Timothy is itself "Scripture." Rather, that reinscription occurs later—it is only at the point of canonization that the reference to "scripture" in 2 Timothy is augmented into something that is self-referential.[18]

Another point of interest in the operation of canonical authority relates specifically to the Pauline corpus. Irrespective of their occasional nature, Adolf Deissmann rightly notes that "the letters of Paul have come into our possession with the venerable halo of canonical dignity."[19] As such, this canonical setting of the Pauline correspondence serves as a critical backdrop for the way in which readers cognize or construct Paul and his letters as authoritative.

Yet paradoxically, when one focuses on the *context* of the Pauline correspondence, we find instances within the letters where Paul is contending with the destabilization of his authority. In other words, we find evidence of a tension between Paul and some of his audiences, as Paul is distressed and agitated by the threat of his *ekklēsia* viewing others as greater authorities than Paul himself. In 2 Corinthians, for example, Paul writes of his concern in this regard:

---

17. To be clear, I am speaking here of the *discourse* or the *writings*, and less in relation to the authoritative status of *Paul himself* (though the authoritative status of Paul will be addressed further below). That said, I recognize that it is difficult to demarcate a clear distinction between the two, a point that Jerome McGann affirms: "[a]s the very term 'authority' suggests, the author is taken to be—for editorial and critical purposes—the ultimate locus of a text's authority, and literary works are consequently viewed in the most personal and individual way." Jerome J. McGann, *A Critique of Modern Textual Criticism* (Chicago, IL: University of Chicago Press, 1983), 81. Yet further blurring the relation between the authority of the text and the authority of the author, McGann also writes, "[b]ecause literary works are fundamentally social rather than personal or psychological products, they do not even acquire an artistic form of being until their engagement with an audience has been determined." McGann, *Modern Textual Criticism*, 43–4.

18. As Gregory Fewster writes, "canon authorizes itself by elevating the authorial figure in a way that co-opts authorial authenticity and intention in service of the canonical apparatus." Gregory Fewster, "Archiving Paul," *Archivaria* 81 (2016): 117.

19. Adolf Deissmann, *Paul: A Study in Social and Religious History*, 2nd edition, trans. William E. Wilson (New York: Harper & Row, 1957), 15.

> But I am afraid that as the serpent deceived Eve by his cunning, your thoughts will be led astray from a sincere and pure devotion to Christ. For if some one comes and preaches another Jesus than the one we preached, or if you receive a different spirit from the one you received, or if you accept a different gospel from the one you accepted, you submit to it readily enough. I think that I am not in the least inferior to these superlative apostles. (2 Cor. 11.3-5)

More telling is the Galatian correspondence, in which Paul harangues his audience for "turning to a different gospel" (Gal. 1.6), spews invective in the direction of those who apparently "bewitched" the Galatians (Gal. 3.1, Gal 5.12), and belabours to his delinquent *ekklēsia* his credentials as an authority figure (Gal. 1.11–2.21).

Yet despite the debatable status of Paul's authority *within* these letters, there is a tendency on the part of Pauline readers—and certainly Christian readers—to compartmentalize Paul's palpable socio-historical struggles for authority over his *ekklēsiai*. That is, by virtue of the canonical locale of the correspondence, there is a hermeneutic tendency to press Paul's struggles over his own authority into service for a host of alternative purposes—e.g. utilizing them in arguments related to orthodoxy (Paulinism) and heresy (anything non-Pauline), or using them as examples of (or proof-texts for) pastoral care or doctrinal admonishment. Employing the letters for these purposes, any question over Paul's authority recedes into the background for the contemporary reader.

In fact, in contemporary readings, it is not only Paul's dubious authoritative relationship over these *ekklēsiai* that is minimized. What is also often forgotten or disregarded is the patent lacuna in this correspondence: we only have *Paul's* side of the discourse, not the side of his *ekklēsiai*. In other words, we very easily forget that we do not possess any account or narrative by Paul's *ekklēsiai*, except for what we can glean out of Paul's own letters.[20]

---

20. I should emphasize here that while this move is *frequently* seen in scholarship, I hardly intend to suggest that it is universal. To be sure, there is unequivocally scholarship that, contrary to this assertion, engages precisely in the task of examining the socio-historical setting of the letters, and more precisely the *Sitz im Leben* of Paul's *ekklēsiai*. See, for example, Gerd Theissen, *The Social Setting of Pauline Christianity* (Philadelphia, PA: Fortress Press, 1982); Bruce W. Winter, *After Paul Left Corinth: The Influence of Secular Ethics and Social Change* (Grand Rapids, MI: Eerdmans, 2001); Richard S. Ascough, *Paul's Macedonian Associations: The Social Context of 1 Thessalonians and Philippians* (Tübingen: Mohr-Siebeck, 2003); Joseph A. Marchal, ed., *The People Beside Paul: The Philippian Assembly and History from Below* (Atlanta, GA: SBL Press, 2015); Richard Last, *The Pauline Church and the Corinthian Ekklēsia: Greco-Roman Associations in Comparative Context* (Cambridge: Cambridge University Press, 2016); and Mark Wheller, "Christ as Ancestor Hero: Using Catherine Bell's Ritual Framework to Analyze 1 Corinthians as an Ancestor Hero Association in First Century CE Roman Corinth," (Ph.D. diss., University of Alberta, Canada, 2017).

Consequently, owing in large part to the canonical milieu in which we encounter the letters, there appears to be an odd augmentation of Paul's authority, despite the fact that internally, there are certain letters that point in the *opposite* direction when it comes to Paul's authoritative standing. That is, contrary to the implied authority of the *canonical* Paul, certain letters in fact evidence that Paul's authoritative standing was, to some of his *ekklēsiai* at least, very much a precarious matter.

Theorizing Authority

The operation of Paul's authority described above can be theorized in multiple ways. One way of doing so involves consideration of two specific modes of authority: executive authority and epistemic authority.

Executive authority, as defined by Richard De George, "is the right or power of someone (X) to do something (S) in some realm, field, or domain (R), in a context (C)."[21] In the aforementioned discussion of Paul one can locate, on multiple levels, a kind of executive authority in him or his writings. With Paul himself, his status as the recipient of revelation or as an apostle can conceivably imbue him with a level of executive authority. Indeed, if the contemporary reader takes Paul at his word when he claims that he did not receive his gospel "from man," but rather "through a revelation of Jesus Christ" (Gal. 1.11-12),[22] then it would indeed appear that Paul makes a legitimate claim to having executive authority.[23] Further, and as

---

21. Richard T. De George, *The Nature and Limits of Authority* (Lawrence, KS: Kansas University Press, 1985), 17.

22. In stating this, however, I recognize that I am unduly giving curt treatment to the word *apokalupsis*, i.e. "revelation." As Bernard Brandon Scott notes, "'[r]evelation' as a translation has the disadvantage of reading into Paul's account the vivid image of the in-breaking of the supernatural world in the form of the blinding light and dramatic voice addressing Saul that occurs in the Acts account. 'Insight' and 'to make known' sidestep Acts's dramatic image and imply that it might not be a single, dramatic moment, but may have occurred over a period of time. But it risks downplaying that, for Paul, the event is from God." Bernard Brandon Scott, *The Real Paul: Recovering His Radical Challenge* (Salem, MA: Polebridge Press, 2015), 32.

23. While I will not address it in detail here, ancillary to the notion of authority being derived from revelation is the identification of biblical texts as "inspired" writings (e.g. 2 Tim. 3.16: "[a]ll scripture is inspired by God"). This leads Ben Witherington, for example, to call for an investigation into a "theory of inspiration and its relationship to the authority of the apostle and his letters." Ben Witherington, "Contemporary Perspectives on Paul," in *The Cambridge Companion to St. Paul*, ed. James D.G. Dunn (Cambridge: Cambridge University Press, 2003), 267–8. I have no interest in examining the issue further here, but recognize that the notion of "inspiration" and authority bear some link to "revelation" and authority. For some discussion of this, see Søren Kierkegaard,

alluded to above, the writings attributed to Paul possess an additional level of executive authority, simply on account of their canonical status.

Epistemic authority, on the other hand, relates to an authoritative status conferred on account of expertise or knowledge that a person or text exhibits (or appears to exhibit, at least) in a particular field of knowledge.[24] This notion of authority aligns with what H. L. A. Hart describes as "theoretical authority":

> To be an authority on some subject matter a man must in fact have some superior knowledge, intelligence, or wisdom which makes it reasonable to believe that what he says on the subject is more likely to be true than the results reached by others through their independent investigations, so that it is reasonable for them to accept the authoritative statement without such independent investigation or evaluation of his reasoning.[25]

In the case of the Christian canon, apologetic readers, at least, might view the individual authors of the texts—or rather the purported authors of the texts—as authoritative figures who possess a kind of epistemic authority. The position is most certainly a curious one, given that the authorship of the texts within the Christian canon is by and large unknown, at least from the perspective of critical scholarship. In the New Testament, for example, the true authors of the gospels are themselves unknown; in most scholarship, authorship of the gospels is rarely associated with their eponymous composers.[26] Comparably, the non-Pauline epistles in the New Testament (i.e. James, Peter, Jude, and John) are generally identified as being written by persons other than their purported authors. Notably, Paul is the one figure that would seem to be on solid footing when it comes to associating at least some New Testament texts with their putative author(s). In fact, among biblical

---

The Book on Adler, trans. Howard V. Hong and Edna H. Hong (Princeton, NJ: Princeton University Press, 1998).

24. Bruce Lincoln, *Authority: Construction and Corrosion* (Chicago, IL: University of Chicago Press, 1994), 3–4. See also De George, *The Nature and Limits of Authority*, 22. To be clear, however, De George frames the issue somewhat differently than I am here. De George's primary distinction is between executive authority and *non-executive* authority. Epistemic authority is a particularly notable subcategory of the latter, though it is not the only one. See De George, *The Nature and Limits of Authority*, 22–3. Further, in the case of Lincoln, I do not intend to suggest that his view of authority is such that it is simply accounted for through distinguishing between executive and epistemic authority. Indeed, Lincoln is partially concerned with transcending that distinction. See Lincoln, *Authority*, 3. I will return to this point below.

25. H. L. A. Hart, "Commands and Authoritative Legal Reasons," in *Authority*, ed. Joseph Raz (Oxford: Basil Blackwell Ltd., 1990), 108.

26. Raymond Brown, *Introduction to the New Testament* (New York: Doubleday, 1997), 109.

scholars at least, it is fair to suggest that Paul is the *only* biblical character who has been able to withstand modernity's deconstruction of traditional or apologetic assumptions concerning the authorship of the canonical texts.[27]

Irrespective of such concerns, it remains the case that from a theoretical perspective, one's views on *who* authored a given canonical text can function to augment the epistemic authority of the text. For example, in the case of Paul, one might be inclined to give weight to his views not merely on account of any executive authority that he has, but also on account of him being identified as a "gifted exegete"[28] or "genius."[29]

None of this is intended to suggest, however, that these two categories of authority are mutually exclusive. Rather, as Lincoln notes, "[e]pistemic and executive authority are not necessarily opposed to one another, but can be complementary. Often the two articulate in hierarchic fashion, such that epistemic authority supplies advice, expertise, and the like to executive authority, while the latter retains final decision-making power."[30] Accordingly, I should make it clear that I do not intend to suggest that canonical authority or Pauline authority lie unequivocally in the realm of either epistemic or executive authority. To be sure, there is overlap and interplay between these two, and it would prove exceedingly difficult to fully detach one from the other. For example, Paul's epistemic authority might itself be tied to the claim that he was given a revelation. Yet at the same time, as the recipient of a revelation, Paul is also an executive authority. In other words, as a recipient of a divine

---

27. The realization of this carries significant implications, on multiple levels. Perhaps most important is the fact that an erroneous association between a text and a putative author very much impacts this issue of epistemic authority. That is, if we genuinely (but mistakenly) attribute a text to an author we hold in high regard, this of course affects the epistemic weight that we are inclined to grant to that text. A secondary concern on the issue of authorship, or more specifically pseudonymity, is outlined by Donald Penny. As Penny puts it, "the concern about pseudepigraphy has been related primarily to the ethical question. How can the fact of pseudonymous writings within the New Testament be reconciled with canonical inspiration or with a sense of morality, honesty, and integrity?" Donald Penny, "The Pseudo-Pauline Letters of the First Two Centuries," (Ph.D. diss., Emory University, Atlanta, GA, 1979), 29.

28. See Jacob Jervell, "Paul in the Acts of the Apostles: Tradition, History, Theology," in *The Unknown Paul: Essays on Luke-Acts and Early Christian History* (Minneapolis, MN: Augsburg Publishing House, 1984), 76.

29. See Deissmann, *Paul*, 79; Calvin J. Roetzel, *The Letters of Paul: Conversations in Context*, 5th edition (Louisville, KY: Westminster John Knox Press, 2009), 19; and David G. Horrell, *An Introduction to the Study of Paul*, 3rd edition (London: Bloomsbury T&T Clark, 2015), 1.

30. Lincoln, *Authority*, n. 168. Similarly, De George acknowledges that "there may be some instances of authority which fall clearly on neither one side nor the other." De George, *The Nature and Limits of Authority*, 22.

revelation, Paul's thought is imbued not only with a type of executive authority (on account of the divine's omnipotence), but also a level of epistemic authority (on account of the divine's omniscience).[31]

Building on this, it is worth noting that locating Pauline authority firmly in one category or another also proves difficult in relation to his canonization. On the one hand, one might be inclined to argue that Paul's writings were to some degree valued on account of their epistemic authority, and that this valuation occasioned their reinscription as canonical authorities, i.e. executive authorities. On the other hand, one might otherwise insist that the Pauline writings possessed executive authority from the very outset, on account of Paul's apostolic authority, or again, on account of his claimed status as the recipient of a revelation.[32] Consequently, while I think it is worthwhile to reflect upon the ways in which the authority of Paul and the letters might be framed in terms of executive or epistemic authority, I do not intend to suggest that all modes of Pauline authority can be subsumed exclusively under one category or the other.

The Final Authority

Admittedly, all of this discussion about executive and epistemic authorities skirts around a fundamental issue. What has been absent thus far is due consideration to how authority is conferred, or more precisely, *who* confers it. This issue is touched on by Hans-Georg Gadamer:

> [T]he authority of persons is based ultimately, not on the subjection and abdication of reason, but on an act of acknowledgement and knowledge—the knowledge, namely, that the other is superior to oneself in judgment and insight and that for this reason his judgment takes precedence, i.e., it has priority over one's own.[33]

---

31. Strictly speaking, however, Paul's executive authority is actually one step removed from God. Accordingly, one might be inclined to think of the situation here as involving three, rather than two categories, as outlined by Joseph Raz: "To have authority is, sometimes, (1) to have (a right created by a) permission to do something (which is generally prohibited). It is also (2) to have the right to grant such permissions, and finally, it is (3) to be an expert who can vouch for the reliability of particular information." Joseph Raz, "Introduction," in *Authority*, ed. Joseph Raz (Oxford: Basil Blackwell Ltd., 1990), 2. The first and second categories described by Raz are both aspects of executive authority. Paul's executive authority might be placed into subcategory (1), as his authority is one permitted by the divine.

32. Regardless of how one theorizes this particular issue, I would at the very least maintain that the canonization of Paul reifies him and his epistles as executive authorities.

33. Hans-Georg Gadamer, *Truth and Method*, 2nd edition, trans. Joel Weinsheimer and Donald G. Marshall (New York: Continuum, 1999), 281.

Taking this notion further, it is worth turning again to Lincoln, who asserts that irrespective of the distinction between executive and epistemic authority, the concept of authority in general "is best understood in relational terms as the effect of a posited, perceived, or institutionally ascribed asymmetry between speaker and audience that permits certain speakers to command not just the attention but the confidence, respect, and trust of their audience, or—an important proviso—to make audiences act *as if* this were so."[34] In this framework, the role of the audience is critical—indeed, the audience has an integral role in the identification of the "ascribed asymmetry" that Lincoln notes.

Consequently, any recognition of canonical authority, or authority in the Pauline corpus, is ultimately a product of our own cognition. It is actually we, the readers or interpreters of Paul, who are the arbiters of authority. In this regard, R.G. Collingwood's analysis of the historian's role applies equally to readers of the canon, and more specifically, Paul:

> Throughout the course of his work the historian is selecting, constructing, and criticizing; it is only by doing these things that he maintains his thought upon the *sichere Gang einer Wissenschaft* [secure course of a science]. By explicitly recognizing this fact it is possible to effect what, again borrowing a Kantian phrase, one might call a Copernican revolution in the theory of history: the discovery that, so far from relying on an authority other than himself, to whose statements his thought must conform, the historian is his own authority and his thought autonomous, self-authorizing, possessed of a criterion to which his so-called authorities must conform and by reference to which they are criticized.[35]

This leads Collingwood to conclude that "[f]or the historian there can never be authorities, because the so-called authorities abide a verdict which

---

34. Lincoln, *Authority*, 4. While De George specifically makes the remark in connection to epistemic authority, his thought reflects a sentiment similar to Lincoln's, as he observes that the analysis of epistemic authority involves "defining an epistemic authority in terms of those for whom he is an authority...It emphasizes the relation of an authority to those for whom he is an authority, and so it underlines the functional aspect of being an authority." De George, *The Nature and Limits of Authority*, 27.

35. R. G. Collingwood, *The Idea of History: With Lectures 1926-1928*, ed. Jan van der Dussen (Oxford: Oxford University Press, 2005), 236. Collingwood appropriates the phrase *sichere Gang einer Wissenschaft* [secure course of a science] from the preface of Kant's *Critique of Pure Reason*. See Immanuel Kant, *Critique of Pure Reason*, ed. and trans. Paul Guyer and Allen W. Wood (Cambridge: Cambridge University Press, 1998), 106–20.

only he can give."[36] Or as Johann Gottlieb Fichte puts it, "[a]uthority is trust in our power of correct observation and in our veracity."[37]

While there is much to be said about these assertions, I would offer just a couple of closing observations. First, when we as readers (or audiences) are relying on "our power of correct observation," we are of course hardly dispassionate observers. On the contrary, we bring with us a conceptual matrix, or a fundamentally necessary bias. In sociological terms, this is sometimes referred to as "framing," which denotes "'schemata of interpretation' that enable individuals 'to locate, perceive, identify, and label' occurrences within their life space and the world large."[38] This framing is by no means something that can be discarded or bracketed. It is simply the lens through which we experience, interpret, and make sense of the world.

The second and related point is that our biases, or framing, engenders "a systematic preference for evidence that supports one's decisions or standpoints, and in turn, [neglects] conflicting information."[39] This, in short, is a description of what is commonly referred to as "confirmation bias," which is inextricably connected to the way that we filter data, and the way that we locate and adjudicate authorities. Nonetheless, we can—and certainly should—endeavour to be "relentlessly self-conscious"[40] of our biases or preferences.

In any event, what is critical for the purposes of this particular investigation is simply this: the true grounding of all canonical authority, and all

---

36. Collingwood, *The Idea of History*, 238. See also Gadamer, *Truth and Method*, 281.

37. Johann Gottlieb Fichte, *Attempt at a Critique of All Revelation*, ed. Allen Wood, trans. Garrett Green (Cambridge: Cambridge University Press, 2010), 52.

38. David A. Snow, E. Burke Rochford, Jr., Steven K. Worden and Robert D. Benford, "Frame Alignment Processes, Micromobilization, and Movement Participation," *ASR* 51 (1986): 464. In Gadamer's thinking, this has been referred to as the "positivity as prejudice." As Gadamer writes, "[p]rejudices are not necessarily unjustified and erroneous, so that they inevitably distort the truth. In fact, the historicity of our existence entails that prejudices, in the literal sense of the word, constitute the initial directedness of our whole ability to experience. Prejudices are biases of our openness to the world. They are simply conditions whereby we experience something—whereby what we encounter says something to us." Hans-Georg Gadamer, *Philosophical Hermeneutics*, ed. and trans. David E. Linge (Berkeley, CA: University of California Press, 1976), 9.

39. Peter Fischer, Nilüfer Aydin, et al., "The Cognitive Economy Model of Selective Exposure: Integrating Motivational and Cognitive Accounts of Confirmatory Information Search," in *Social Judgment and Decision Making*, ed. Joachim I. Krueger (New York: Psychology Press, 2012), 23.

40. I am appropriating this phrase from Jonathan Z. Smith's often-quoted dicta concerning the foundation of the religious studies discipline, i.e. that "[r]eligion is solely the creation of the scholar's study." Jonathan Z. Smith, *Imagining Religion: From Babylon to Jonestown* (Chicago, IL: University of Chicago Press, 1982), xi.

Pauline authority lies with *us*, the readers and interpreters of the canon. Given this, it would seem that John Mellencamp might not be correct in proclaiming, "I fight authority, authority always wins." Rather, I think we are better served by giving consideration to the question posed by the sage lyrical prophet and self-styled "anti-myth rhythm rock shocker,"[41] Zack de la Rocha:

> With this mic device, I spit non-fiction
> "Who got the power?", this be my question
> The mass of the few in this torn nation?
> The priest, the book, or the congregation?[42]

Insofar as we are ultimately our own authorities, and that we in fact possess our own criteria to which any other so-called authorities must conform, it would appear that in spite of the ostensible authority of the priest (e.g. Paul), or the book (e.g. the Christian canon), it is indeed in the *congregation* (e.g. the *ekklēsia*, or the audience) where the foundation of authority truly resides.

Author biography

Patrick Hart is a contract instructor at the University of Alberta and practicing lawyer. He obtained his MA, PhD, and LLM from the University of Alberta, and his JD from Queen's University. His research interests include the study of Paul and early Christianities, religion and philosophy, method and theory in the study of religion, and the intersection of law and religion. His doctoral research was published as *A Prolegomenon to the Study of Paul* (Brill, 2020), and he has had various articles published in religious studies journals and legal journals.

---

41. Rage Against the Machine, "Mic Check" and "Calm Like a Bomb."
42. Rage Against the Machine, "Mic Check." As noted earlier, I realize that I am side-stepping the irony or paradox involved in *citing* various authorities in order to make an argument *about* canonical or Pauline authority. Citing lyrics from a (semi-)contemporary rock band involves yet another curious iteration of the same conundrum. While this, too, is a topic deserving of further discussion, I would limit myself here to offering up a small visceral hunch: given that pop culture references tend to be more pervasive or ubiquitous among audiences than the work of esoteric academics, there can be some rhetorical utility in appealing to these sources, as they resonate as being more "familiar" or accessible to a broader range of audiences—depending, of course, on who one's intended audience is. This hunch of course aligns with the foregoing argument, i.e., that the interpreters, readers, or audience play a pivotal role in the ascription of authority.

Bibliography

Aristotle. *Nicomachean Ethics*. Translated by H. Rackham. Cambridge, MA: Harvard University Press, 1926. https://doi.org/10.4159/DLCL.aristotle-nicomachean_ethics.1926

Ascough, Richard, Philip A. Harland, and John S. Kloppenborg. *Associations in the Greco-Roman World: A Sourcebook*. Waco, TX: Baylor University Press, 2012.

Ascough, Richard. *Paul's Macedonian Associations: The Social Context of 1 Thessalonians and Philippians*. Tübingen: Mohr-Siebeck, 2003.

Braun, Willi. "Religion," 3–18 in *Guide to the Study of Religion*. Edited by Willi Braun and Russell T. McCutcheon. London: Continuum, 2000.

Braun, Willi. "Introducing Religion," 480–98 in *Introducing Religion: Essays in Honor of Jonathan Z. Smith*. Edited by Willi Braun and Russell T. McCutcheon. London: Equinox Publishing, 2008.

Brown, Raymond E. *An Introduction to the New Testament*. New York: Doubleday, 1997.

Collingwood, R.G. *The Idea of History: With Lectures 1926-1928*. Edited by Jan van der Dussen. Oxford: Oxford University Press, 2005.

De George, Richard T. *The Nature and Limits of Authority*. Lawrence, KS: Kansas University Press, 1985.

Deissmann, Adolf. *Paul: A Study in Social and Religious History*, 2nd ed. Translated by William E. Wilson. New York: Harper & Row, 1957.

Fewster, Gregory. "Archiving Paul." *Archivaria* 81 (2016): 101–28.

Fichte, Johann Gottlieb. *Attempt at a Critique of All Revelation*. Edited by Allen Wood. Translated by Garrett Green. Cambridge: Cambridge University Press, 2010.

Fischer, Peter, Aydin Nilüfer, Julia Fischer, Dieter Frey, and Stephen E.G. Lea, "The Cognitive Economy Model of Selective Exposure: Integrating Motivational and Cognitive Accounts of Confirmatory Information Search," 21–39 in *Social Judgment and Decision Making*. Edited by Joachim I. Krueger. New York: Psychology Press, 2012.

Fredriksen, Paula. "Historical Integrity, Interpretive Freedom: The Philosopher's Paul and the Problem of Anachronism," 61–73 in *St. Paul Among the Philosophers*. Edited by John D. Caputo and Linda Martín Alcoff. Bloomington, IN: Indiana University Press, 2009.

Gadamer, Hans-Georg. *Philosophical Hermeneutics*. Edited and translated by David E. Linge. Berkeley, CA: University of California Press, 1976.

Gadamer, Hans-Georg. *Truth and Method*. 2nd ed. Translated by Joel Weinsheimer and Donald G. Marshall. New York: Continuum, 1999.

Gamble, Harry Y. *The New Testament Canon: Its Making and Meaning*. Philadelphia, PA: Fortress Press, 1985.

Gorak, Jan. *The Making of the Modern Canon: Genesis and Crisis of a Literary Idea*. London: Athlone, 1991.

Hart, H. L. A. "Commands and Authoritative Legal Reasons," 92–114 in *Authority*. Edited by Joseph Raz. Oxford: Basil Blackwell Ltd., 1990.

Horrell, David G. *An Introduction to the Study of Paul*, 3rd edition. London: Bloomsbury T&T Clark, 2015.

Jervell, Jacob. "Paul in the Acts of the Apostles: Tradition, History, Theology," pages 68–76 in *The Unknown Paul: Essays on Luke-Acts and Early Christian History*. Minneapolis, MN: Augsburg Publishing House, 1984.

Jülicher, Adolf. *Einleitung in das Neue Testament*, 7th ed. Tübingen: Mohr, 1931.
Kant, Immanuel. *Critique of Pure Reason*. Edited and translated by Paul Guyer and Allen W. Wood. Cambridge: Cambridge University Press, 1998. https://doi.org/10.1017/CBO9780511804649
Kierkegaard, Søren. *The Book on Adler*. Translated by Howard V. Hong and Edna H. Hong. Princeton, NJ: Princeton University Press, 1998.
Last, Richard. *The Pauline Church and the Corinthian Ekklēsia: Greco-Roman Associations in Comparative Context*. Cambridge: Cambridge University Press, 2016. https://doi.org/10.1017/CBO9781316179130
Lincoln, Bruce. *Authority: Construction and Corrosion*. Chicago: University of Chicago Press, 1994. https://doi.org/10.7208/chicago/9780226682518.001.0001
Lincoln, Bruce. *Holy Terrors: Thinking About Religion After September 11*. Chicago: University of Chicago Press, 2009.
Mack, Burton L. *The Christian Myth: Origins, Logic, and Legacy*. New York: Continuum, 2001.
Marchal, Joseph A., ed. *The People Beside Paul: The Philippian Assembly and History from Below*. Atlanta, GA: SBL Press, 2015. https://doi.org/10.2307/j.ctt189tt2d
McDonald, Lee Martin. *The Formation of the Christian Biblical Canon*. Peabody, MA: Hendrickson Publishers, Inc. 1995.
McGann, Jerome J. *A Critique of Modern Textual Criticism*. Chicago, IL: University of Chicago Press, 1983.
Metzger, Bruce M. *The Canon of the New Testament: Its Origin, Development, and Significance*. Oxford: Clarendon Press, 1987.
Penny, Donald. "The Pseudo-Pauline Letters of the First Two Centuries." Ph.D. diss., Emory University, Atlanta, GA, 1979.
Raz, Joseph. "Introduction," 1–19 in *Authority*. Edited by Joseph Raz. Oxford: Basil Blackwell Ltd., 1990. https://doi.org/10.1093/acprof:oso/9780199562688.003.0001
Roetzel, Calvin. *The Letters of Paul: Conversations in Context*, 5th ed. Louisville, KY: Westminster John Knox Press, 2009.
Schneemelcher, Wilhelm, ed. *New Testament Apocrypha, Vol. 1*. Translated by Robert McLachlan Wilson. London: Lutterworth Press, 1963.
Scott, Bernard Brandon. *The Real Paul: Recovering His Radical Challenge*. Salem, MA: Polebridge Press, 2015.
Sinclair, R. K. *Democracy and Participation in Athens*. Cambridge: Cambridge University Press, 1988. https://doi.org/10.1017/CBO9780511552694
Smith, Jonathan Z. *Imagining Religion: From Babylon to Jonestown*. Chicago, IL: University of Chicago Press, 1982.
Snow, David, A. E. Burke Rochford, Jr., Steven K. Worden and Robert D. Benford. "Frame Alignment Processes, Micromobilization, and Movement Participation." *ASR* 51 (1986): 464–81. https://doi.org/10.2307/2095581
Theissen, Gerd. *The Social Setting of Pauline Christianity*. Philadelphia, PA: Fortress Press, 1982.
Ulrich, Eugene. "The Notion and Definition of Canon," 21–35 in *The Canon Debate*. Edited by Lee Martin McDonald and James A. Sanders. Peabody, MA: Hendrickson Publishers Inc., 2002.
van de Beek A. "Being Convinced: On the Foundations of the Christian Canon," 331–49 in *Canonization and Decanonization*. Edited by A. van der Kooij and K. van der Torn. Leiden: Brill, 1998. https://doi.org/10.1163/9789004379060_024
Wheller, Mark. "Christ as Ancestor Hero: Using Catherine Bell's Ritual Framework to

Analyze 1 Corinthians as an Ancestor Hero Association in First Century CE Roman Corinth." Ph.D. diss., University of Alberta, Canada, 2017.

Winter, Bruce W. *After Paul Left Corinth: The Influence of Secular Ethics and Social Change*. Grand Rapids, MI: Eerdmans, 2001.

Witherington, Ben. "Contemporary Perspectives on Paul," 256–69 in *The Cambridge Companion to St. Paul*. Edited by James D.G. Dunn. Cambridge: Cambridge University Press, 2003. https://doi.org/10.1017/CCOL0521781558.019

Chapter Three

Ornitheology

Francis Landy

In one of his more apodictic statements in the introduction to *The Guide to the Study of Religion*, Willi Braun says, "the *Guide* advises that whoever has 'an intimate personal knowledge' of the *ontos*... of religion is 'requested to read no further.'"[1] The target of Willi's polemic, and what I have learned from him in our many years of teaching together, is the idea that religion is something special, "sui generis," that it can be isolated from the other discourses of the human sciences, that to study it requires a particular sensibility, what he calls a "privileged, intuitive knowledge" of the "being" or "ontos" of religion beyond all its manifestations, what Eliade famously calls "hierophanies."[2] Religious Studies displaces Theology as the queen of the sciences, but it is then only theology in disguise. Its practitioners—again one thinks of Eliade, but there are scores of others—are shamans manqués, guiding the initiate to the heart of the mystery.

I've always resisted this story, which made our teaching together, and our friendship, especially valuable for myself and for our students. I don't really want to examine our differences here, at least not directly, in part because they are differences of temperament, and in part because in many respects I agree with the critique. But most of all because I want to talk about something else: birds, or what I fancifully call ornitheology, and my first love, the Hebrew Bible, and birds and YHWH in the Hebrew Bible.

Willi loves birds. His photographs of birds, as we all know, are models of patience, resourcefulness, and an aesthetic sense of what is perfect. Every photograph is an epiphany, a momentary appearance of a particular birdiness in our field of vision, where it stays for ever. Willi may be a mystic of birds, like all his fellow ornithologists, and he is of course a member of the community of bird lovers, a fellowship like those he writes about in his

---

1. Willi Braun, "Religion" in Willi Braun and Russell T. McCutcheon, eds., *Guide to the Study of Religion* (London: Cassell, 2000), 3–18 (9).
2. The problem is the idea that there is a special "ontos" of religion, as if being could somehow be parcelled up into different domains, as well as that there is some privilege in knowing that "being".

so-called academic work.[3] Why the fascination for birds I don't know; I've never asked. I fancy it is because birds are so beautiful, and so a-human. I wish to invoke Otto's mysterium tremendum et fascinans, or Blake's "fearful symmetry," but it doesn't somehow seem appropriate to most of the birds Willi studies and portrays. Is the love and lore of birds related to the interest (or disinterest) in religion? To the transactions between the human and non-human, and thus to the emerging discipline of post-humanism? The eye of a bird looking at one and at its world, with its own consciousness, its interests, its fierceness, like the owl who stole Willi's car keys. The sharpness of the encounter. Mysticism?

Hélène Cixous, in her *Three Steps on the Ladder of Writing*, a book I return to ever and again, writes of the association between "birds, women, and writing," before turning to the list of abominable birds in Leviticus, why birds may be abominable, and the "imundity" (shamefulness, but also otherworldliness) of birds, women and writing, for what she, following her beloved Clarice Lispector, calls "those He-Bibles."[4] Cixous is obviously unfair and uncomprehending, especially of what the text means by *to'evah*, "abomination." But she points to something important: what do birds mean in the biblical imagination, or to what extent are they symbols of the imagination?

The Bible is full of birds, not surprisingly, since birds were part of the biblical landscape. Like all symbols, they hover between the real and the imaginary. The Israelites/writers of the Bible knew birds intimately, either as domestic fowl, or as things they saw flying around, heard spookily or mellifluously, representatives of that which is outside the human family. Birds could be sacrificial, permitted but non-sacrificial, or prohibited; they spanned the sacred as well as alimentary economy. As denizens of the air, they mediated between heaven and earth, the divine realm and its terrestrial counterpart. For that reason, they acquired powerful symbolic connotations, derived sometimes from folklore (silly doves etc),[5] sometimes from observation, because of the pressure of any literary work to saturate its contents with meaning. We are dealing with literary birds, not real ones.

It should be clear what I mean by a symbol. A symbol is a node to which is attached all sorts of significations, through metaphor and metonymy, which accumulate through life and/or the literary work. A prime example

---

3. It is not that I wish to denigrate Willi's academic work. It is just that I am suspicious of the categorization separating academic from non-academic research, bird watching from the study of religion.

4. Hélène Cixous *Three Steps on the Ladder of Writing*, trans., Sarah Cornell and Susan Sellers (New York: Columbia University Press, 1993), 111–13.

5. Hosea 7.11.

of a symbol is "I," which cannot be separated from its experiences and relationships. Neuroscientifically, the "I" is the product of immensely complicated feedback loops, invested with intense feelings and attachments.[6] The "feelingfulness" is what I want to stress here. Symbols are not concepts in the sense of ideas; they are hard-wired triggers of conscious and unconscious processes. Think of snakes.

The most important symbol of Israelite identity is its deity, YHWH. YHWH means many things; the Hebrew Bible is evidence of its growth and transformation. As a symbol, it is attached to innumerable objects, personalities, and narratives, whose limitlessness is suggested by aniconism. YHWH is hybrid, the plethora of images combining with imagelessness. It is as if the images for YHWH, as well as his representatives, carry an implicit message, that they are not YHWH. What YHWH "is" is inseparable from the question of what a person is, or what being is.[7] We are back to "ontos," being-in-itself, as something we intimately know, but cannot fix. Insofar as YHWH is a mystery, hidden away in darkness, revealing itself in dribs and drabs, it is not very different from the rest of us. Among the many symbols for YHWH are birds, particularly eagles. YHWH is winged; he flies (II Sam. 22.11 = Ps. 18.11); he shelters people, like Ruth, under his wings (Ruth 2.12);[8] he carries the Israelites on eagles' wings to the encounter at Sinai; he nurtures them like an eagle with its fledglings; he has pinions, with which he transports them (Deut. 32.11).[9] At the beginning of the creation story, God "hovers" over the face of the waters, the same verb (*RHP*) as is used in Deut. 32.11 for the eagle hovering over its nest (Gen. 1.2). One of the faces of the creatures that emanate from the divine in Ezekiel's vision is that of an eagle (Ezek. 1.10). The divine retinue is likewise winged; the invisible presence of YHWH above the Ark of the Covenant is flanked by two winged cherubim; the seraphim who stand around YHWH in Isaiah's vision are six-winged. They are similarly hybrid. In Ezekiel's vision the cherubim combine four creaturely domains; in Isaiah's they are fiery humanoid serpents.[10]

---

6. Douglas Hofstadter, *I am a Strange Loop* (New York: Basic Books, 2007) and Antonio Damasio, *The Strange Order of Things: Life, Feeling, and the Making of Cultures* (New York: Pantheon Books, 2018) are my principal neuroscientific resources here.

7. There is an interminable debate on the meaning of YHWH. I take it to be derived from HWY, "to be."

8. The image is very frequent in Psalms.

9. I follow Koehler-Baumgartner Hebrew and Aramaic Lexicon of the Old Testament (Leiden: Brill, 2001) in translating 'ebrâ as *pinions*, as opposed to David J.A. Clines, ed., *The Concise Dictionary of Classical Hebrew* (Sheffield: Sheffield Phoenix, 2009), which has *wings*.

10. For the cherubim as griffins, see William H. Propp, *Exodus 19-40* (AB 2A; New York: Doubleday, 2006), 386–92, 517–19, with a very pretty illustration from a Megiddo

The imagery is metaphorical, as indicated morphologically by the comparative particle *kĕ*, "like," or by the context, such as the Israelites' journey in the wilderness. Only selected features of the comparanda are evoked, for example the swiftness of the eagle, its care for its young, its status as an apex bird. One may imagine a real eagle, the product of ornithological observation, but also a cultural construction, notably as the king of the birds. As with all metaphors, particularly those relating to the deity, it raises questions of divine corporeality, and the relationship between the two components of the metaphor. If God's care is like that of an eagle, is an eagle's like God's? Is an eagle a theophany? Ezekiel's vision would suggest so. What is the relationship between the creatures in the vision and the deity? The text often blurs the distinction between "angels" and YHWH. Are angels—cherubim, seraphim etc—simply manifestations of YHWH?

Are the wings of YHWH then real or metaphorical? They are metonymies, pointing to an absent body, a space for thought, as if YHWH were pure wing. In the background are ancient Near Eastern winged deities as emblems of imperial conquest, like Assur. But here it is something else, transformed into a figure of compassion, a maternal impression. What is it like to be nestled by a giant bird, like a roc? At issue is the nature of metaphorical thinking, which, as the cognitive school has shown, is at the basis of all thinking. If we have an invisible, imageless deity as the originator and thinker of the world, how can we imagine it? As Maurice Merleau-Ponty has said, what is at stake is "knowing," that we can only know tactilely, sensually.[11] All that is real then is the eagle.

The simile is a distraction. It pretends to be talking about God but it is really talking about eagles. Fictional eagles, of course. This is true of all images about God. I have argued, for instance, that in Isaiah's vision we are immediately diverted from the transgressive vision of God to the seraphim and thence to their extremities.[12] Isaiah sees YHWH, he tells us, but we cannot see him or even know what Isaiah sees, as if it is unbearable. That

---

ivory. See also Tryggve N.D. Mettinger, "Cherubim" in Karel van der Toorn, ed., *Dictionary of Deities and Demons in the Bible* (Leiden: Brill, 1999), 299–302. We do not exactly know what the cherubim consisted of, and the image might have changed over time. For the seraphim as flying, burning serpents, see Num. 21.6-9, Deut. 8.15, and Isa. 30.6, as well as the description in Isa. 6.2, in which they are the divine retinue. The root ŚRP means "burn," and they are probably equivalent to the uraei, or sacred cobras (*Eg. śrrf*), which surmounted Pharaoh's crown.

11. Maurice Merleau-Ponty, *The Visible and the Invisible*, ed., Claude Lefort trans., Alphonso Lingis (Evanston, IL: Northwestern University Press, 1968), 129.

12. Francis Landy, "Strategies of Concentration and Diffusion in Isaiah 6," *BibInt* 6 (1999), 58–86, reprinted in Landy, *Beauty and the Enigma and Other Essays on the Hebrew Bible* (LHB/OTS 312; Sheffield: Sheffield Academic Press, 2001), 298–327.

the seraphim cover their faces with their wings suggests that it is. The imaginative eye is fascinated by the scotoma, the edge of vision. Moreover, the metaphorical distance is insistently blurred by ambiguity and by doubling. In Deut. 32.11b, for instance, the subject maybe the eagle or YHWH or both; they blend into each other. The simile of the eagle is paired with one comparing Israel to the pupil of God's eye; we have to reflect on the tension between the two. Similarly, hybridity, such as that of the cherubim and seraphim, suggests both the fantastic (and grotesque) breach of norms and the radical collision of categories; every hybrid is a metaphor (griffins, sphinxes, etc.).

What does it mean for YHWH to be surrounded by these strange flying creatures? In Ezekiel's vision, they come and go (*rāṣô' wāšôb*), absorbed and re-emerging from the cloud, fire and the mysterious *ḥašmal* at its center (Ezek. 1.14). They, like the seraphim, seem to represent all the orders of being. They thus articulate the relation between creation and creator. The first mention of birds in the Hebrew Bible is in the creation account (Gen. 1.20-23). The birds, like all other creatures, are materialized ideas in God's mind. They are paired with the *tannînim*, the sea-monsters, air creatures complementing water ones (Gen. 1.21). They are described, euphonically, as *'ôf kānāf*, literally "bird wing," the rhyme emphasizing the hendiadys. A bird is a winged creature; one follows the line of the wing flying off one doesn't know where, disappearing beyond sight. Birds and sea-monsters couple together extremities of existence, but also of the imagination. God thinks birds into being.

Kěnaf, "wing," has other significations, as it does in English.[13] It means "edge" or the hem of a garment. Sometimes the different meanings are used strategically, as in Ruth.[14] They indicate the edge of things, points of transition, as when the wings of the cherubim stretch up to infinity.

There are other images of birds, including avian imagery for YHWH; the Hebrew Bible could be seen as a bird book. In Isa. 31.5 YHWH defends Jerusalem "like flying birds," "protecting and delivering, swooping over and saving." It is a beautifully realized image of a swarm of birds mobbing a predator, ironically juxtaposed with one in which YHWH is the predator himself (31.4). Typically of Isaiah, YHWH takes on both roles at once. In Ps. 68.14, "the wings of a dove are overlaid with silver, its pinions with greenish gold." We do not know to what this refers, it appears totally out of context, but given the preceding phrase: "If you lie among the sheepfolds,"

---

13. One thinks of "left wing," the "wings of a theatre" etc.
14. In Ruth the wings of YHWH under which Ruth has come to shelter are manifest in the "wing" of Boaz's skirt with which he covers her in 3.9. See further Francis Landy, "Ruth and the Romance of Realism, or Deconstructing History," *JAAR* 62 (1994): 285–317, reprinted in *Beauty and The Enigma*, 218–51 (esp. 234–5).

it might suggest that the dove is lit up by the setting sun. Justin Walker suggests that this is a symbol for the goddess, but equally it could be YHWH, a brilliant figure of luminescence on the edge of vision.[15]

Other birds are associated with death. In Isa.8.19, the ghosts and familiar spirits "chirp and twitter"; in Isa. 29.4, besieged Jerusalem's voice is like a ghost, and from the dust it chirps (*těṣafṣēf*); the onomatopoeia intensifies the sinister lambency. Karel van der Toorn argues that cross-culturally in the ancient Near East, the spirits of the dead take the form of birds; in Egypt, for example, the Ba is represented as a soul-bird. He suggests that in Isa. 28.10 and 13, necromancers ventriloquized birds; their strange sounds, *qu qu* and *ṣu ṣu*, are oracular calls which they interpreted, possibly in a state of semi-consciousness.[16] In Isa. 38.14, the sick Hezekiah writes that he chirped like a swift and thrush (*kěsus 'agûr*), and cooed like a dove; in his morbid state he already prospectively, imaginatively, inhabits the world of the dead.[17]

Death is the great enemy of YHWH. The cult of the ancestors and death is insistently prohibited in the Hebrew Bible; the purity code is designed to keep death, except in the form of sacrifice, away from the sanctuary. They also have an affinity. Agents of death, like Resheph, are part of YHWH's entourage. YHWH is experienced as a predator, for example in Amos and Job. Death is an ultimate horizon, a limit term to human existence, and thus like YHWH. Sometimes one cannot tell YHWH and Death apart. In Hos. 13.14, a series of vertiginous puns suggests that YHWH is an agent of death as well as the one who abolishes death. YHWH kills and gives life (Deut. 32.39). Death, like YHWH, is unrepresentable; yet, like YHWH, it is the subject of thought, drawn into the circle of human discourse, not least as personified in the deity Mot. Birdsong, seductive or plaintive, bears messages from another world. It is outside the domain of human language, addressing us in its strangeness, about our mortality, the fragility of the human world. One can imagine the ancestors whispering incomprehensibly just on the fringes of consciousness, with their greed, their loss, their

---

15. M. Justin Walker, "The Wings of the Dove are Covered in Silver: The (Absent) Presence of the Goddess in Psalm 68," *UF* 47 (2016): 301–42. Walker argues that goddess imagery was transferred to Israel.

16. Karel van der Toorn, "Echoes of Judean Necromancy in Isaiah 28,7-22," *ZAW* 100 (1987): 199–216. See also Joseph Blenkinsopp, *Isaiah 1-39* (AB 19A; New York: Doubleday, 2000), 245, who comments that in Enkidu's dream in Gilgamesh 7.34-51, the dead "are clothed in feathers, chirp like birds, and are nourished on dust and clay."

17. For the identification of these birds (though he adopts the emendation of *sus* to *sis*, following BHS) see Göran Eidevall, "Sad as a Bird: On Avian Metaphors in Biblical Descriptions of Human Suffering," in Blaženka Scheuer and David Willgren Davage, eds., *Sin, Suffering, and the Problem of Evil* (Tübingen: Mohr Siebeck, 2021), 85–96.

concern. In Isa. 28.10 and 13 they may articulate the covenant with Death that the rulers/aphorists hope to forge in 28.15, ironically so as to escape death.[18] In 8.19 they are deities, perhaps identical with the Ugaritic *rpu'm*, "the healing ones," with an insistent claim on the living: "should not a people inquire of its gods, on behalf of the living to the dead?" They are powerful and feeble at the same time. Comparably, doves are figures of lament; Hezekiah "moans" (*'ehgeh*) like a dove (Isa. 38.14); the community in Isa. 59.11 likewise moans like doves.[19] Doves evoke mourning, a ritualized ululation below the threshold of language.

Birds inhabit the wilderness, the region of death. The dystopia of Isa. 34.13-15 is an aviary of fateful, sometimes unidentifiable or mythical, birds: owls, ostriches, vultures, culminating in Lilith. In Ps. 102.7-8, the psalmist writes "I am like the pelican of the wilderness, I have become as the screech owl of ruins; I watch and become like a lonely sparrow on a roof."[20] Here birds are associated with solitude, ruins, and desolation, as images of the isolation and desperation of the poet. The self, foregrounded through the repeated "I am like," inhabits a waste world, made more intolerable by the press of people surrounding and persecuting it. In the case of owls, their hooting and screeching intensifies the eeriness; the psalm, with its dense but passionate ordering of words, reverberates with their shrieks, a whirl of sound that cannot be accommodated.[21] I am an outcast,

---

18. Christopher B. Hays, *A Covenant with Death: Death in the Iron Age II and Its Rhetorical Uses in Proto-Isaiah* (Grand Rapids: Eerdmans, 2015), 294–303, argues that there is a punning reference to the Egyptian goddess Mwt, who is symbolized by a vulture.

19. See also Ezek.7.16 and Nah. 2.8. For a detailed reading of these two texts, see Eidevall, "Sad as a Bird."

20. No one knows what these birds really are. "Pelican" follows the versions and sounds nice, but they are associated with water. Koehler-Baumgartner Hebrew and Aramaic Lexicon of the Old Testament suggests "scops owl" among others. Similarly, there are various guesses as to the identity of *kos*, which I translate "screech owl"; others have "little owl." Tova Forte, *"Like a Lone Bird on a Roof": Animal Imagery and the Structure of* Psalms (University Park, PA: Eisenbrauns, 2018), 76, cites Tristram that in Arabic the little owl is known as "the mother of ruins" (Henry Baker Tristram, *The Survey of Western Palestine: The Fauna and Flora of Palestine* [London: Palestine Exploration Fund, 1885], 93). Tristram writes, "his low wailing note is sure to be heard at sunset, and he himself seen bowing and keeping time to his own music."

21. Susanne Gillmayr-Bucher, "'Ich Wachte und War Wie ein Einsamer Vögel auf dem Dach' (Ps102,8): Ps 102 als examplarischer Identitätsdiskurs," in J. van Oorschot et al., eds., *Individualität und Selbstreflexion in den Lituraturen des Alten Testaments* (Leipzig: EVA, 2017), 279–96 (288), comments on the mournful cry of the owl, quoting this charming Akkadian birdcall text: "The owl is the bird of Ea. Its cry is 'Lament, lament'" (*tuk-ku, tuk-ku*) (288 n. 40).

it seems to say. Where once there were people, a social world, there are just ruins, intolerable nostalgia. The simile of the sparrow on the roof is equally disconcerting.[22] A bird on a roof is one thing, a lonely bird another. If it is an image of the poet, looking at himself looking out, it suggests exclusion from both domestic and social space.[23] The house is not a shelter but a look out point. The vigilance is also a vigil over a disintegrating self; round him are mocking enemies (v. 9), his heart is dessicated like grass (v. 5), he is skin and bones (v. 6). The bird suggests dissociation, the poetic voice mourning over itself. It looks, tiny, fragile, anxious, over a hostile landscape, equivalent to the desert ruins of the owl and the pelican, the verb *šaqādtî*, "I watch," connoting intensity, wariness, and persistence.[24]

Doves,[25] often paired with turtle doves,[26] are among the most widely distributed of biblical birds, figuring in narratives, such as that of Noah's Ark, in ritual, and poetry. They also have an extraordinary wide range of associations, from the erotic to the lugubrious. Cross-culturally, doves are emblems of goddesses of love, and messenger birds.[27] It is this latter characteristic that gives the dove its import in the Flood story, perhaps as an etiology of its domestication. Returning twice to Noah, once with the olive leaf in its beak, it is the homing bird, with its message that the flood is receding (Gen. 8.8-11).[28] Even when it finally flies off, never to return (8.12), it is a messenger to the returning world, preceding by a verse or two the exit of Noah and all

---

22. For the *ṣippôr* as sparrow, see Eidevall, "Sad as a Bird," 10. He notes that a solitary sparrow would be easy prey.

23. Gillmayr-Bucher, "Ich Wachte," 289 comments that the lyric "I" is thrown back on itself, it is no longer part of a flock.

24. ŠQD is most often used for YHWH's hostile watching over Israel, or that of evildoers. It may also refer to the defence of a city (Ps. 127.1) or watching at the door of wisdom in Prov.8.34. Gillmayr-Bucher, "Ich Wachte," 288, observes that the nocturnal cries of the owl are transferred to the bird, suggesting that it too wakes at night.

25. It is not clear to what member of the dove family the word *yônâ* refers. It may be a pigeon.

26. The turtle dove (*tûr*) is a migratory bird, flying annually between Europe/the Mediterranean and southern Africa. Hence its arrival in Song of Songs 2.13 is a sign of spring. Unfortunately, it is critically endangered; its numbers have dropped by about 80% since the 1990s. Its name has nothing to do with turtles, but is an onomatopeia (*turtur* in Latin). It is clear, however, from its pairing with *yônâ* that it was also domesticated. James W. Watts' suggestion that it is a chicken is surely to be rejected (*Leviticus 1-10* [HCOT; Leuven: Peeters, 2013] 218–20).

27. J. Fossum, "Dove" in van der Toorn ed., *Dictionary of Deities and Demons in the Bible* (Leiden: Brill, 1999), 263–4. See also Walker, "The Wings of the Dove," esp. 317–22.

28. The same pairing of dove and raven is found in the Gilgamesh/Atrahasis Flood Story, but in reverse order and with the addition of the swallow.

the creatures in the Ark. In contrast, the raven[29] flies back and forth, awaiting the reappearance of dry land; it has no intention of returning to Noah, feels no attachment to him. Dove and raven are opposed as tame to wild; ravens depend on YHWH for their food (Ps. 147.9; Job 38.41), as evidence of his care for all creatures.[30] Ravens feed Elijah with bread and meat morning and evening while he is hiding in Wadi Kerit (1 Kgs 17.2-6). The story, the first in the Elijah-Elisha cycle, establishes Elijah's affinity with the wilderness, what Laura Feldt calls the "fantastic' element in the narrative;[31] it foreshadows his miraculous sustenance by an angel in 1 Kgs 19.5-8. The ravens are commanded by YHWH; one can imagine them listening to his imperative, in raven-talk perhaps, and acting very uncharacteristically. One hesitates to think what the meat consisted of; ravens and crows are notorious carrion eaters. Maybe it had a kosher label? In the previous chapters, the descendants of Jeroboam and Baasha are condemned to be devoured by dogs in the city and birds in the country, in entirely formulaic phrases (1 Kgs 14.11, 16.4).[32] Does Elijah literally eat the food of kings?

Ravens, together with eaglets, figure rather gruesomely also in Prov. 30.17: "The eye that scorns its father and despises the authority of its mother, ravens of the brook will peck it out, and eaglets consume it."[33] Ravens pecking out eyes may be based on observation or repute,[34] but the proverb also evokes a terrifying fantasy, a sort of biblical version of Alfred Hitchcock's film *The Birds*. But these are also moral birds, acting out a grim karma on the eye that wickedly disparages its parents. However, one suspects that it is not meant entirely seriously, given the humorous context of Prov. 30, which consists largely of riddles. A parent might well say this to an errant child.

---

29. As in French, no distinction is made in Hebrew between the raven and the crow.

30. In the Ancient Near East, ravens have extensive mythological associations. Like doves, they are messengers of the gods. In Assyria a star or constellation is called the Raven. In the "god description text" it is identified with the divine mole (Bob Becking, "Raven" in van der Toorn, ed., *Deities and Demons*, 688–9).

31. Laura Feldt, *The Fantastic in Religious Narrative from Exodus to Elisha* (London: Equinox Publishing, 2012). Feldt points out that the story of the ravens parallels the miraculous provision of food in the wilderness narrative (199, 222).

32. For this rather standard trope, see also Isa.18.6, Ezek. 39.4.

33. Tova Forti, *Animal Imagery in the Book of Proverbs* (Vetus Testamentum Supp.158; Leiden: Brill, 2008), 79–84, has a detailed discussion of the proverb. The word *yiqqĕhat*, "obedience, homage," is somewhat obscure.

34. The more sensationalist newspapers are full of stories of ravens attacking newborn lambs e.g. "Death from Above: The Ravens Slaughtering New Born Lambs," *Daily Telegraph*, May 1st, 2016, which calls them "these notorious birds of darkness." "Rise in Shocking Attacks of Ravens on Sheep," *Daily Mail Online,* May 13th, 2017 etc.

Doves and turtledoves feature in a rather minor capacity in the sacrificial code, as substitutes for major beasts by poor people, or as components of relatively minor offerings, like those which reintegrate parturients, sufferers from flux, and lepers into the community. They play no part in the regular cycle of daily and festival offerings, nor can they be used for *shelamim*, the well-being offerings which celebrate the restoration of the divine-human relationship, or simply express gratitude, in the form of a carnivorous meal shared between the worshipper, his or her family, the priest and God. It isn't that God doesn't like pigeon, but they have a fairly small place in the pastoral sacred economy and imagination.

There is one exception, the ritual that I call "At-Swim-Two-Birds," after Flann O'Brien's novel. When a leper[35] recovers from his or her sickness, and the recovery is confirmed by a priest, two wild birds are taken;[36] one is slaughtered over an earthenware pot above a running stream, and the other dipped in the blood, together with the standard purificatory bundle of cedarwood, scarlet cloth and hyssop. Then the blood is sprinkled seven times on the recovered patient, and the living bird allowed to fly free (Lev. 14.1-7). This is only the first stage in the purificatory process, which is completed after eight days with the former leper's readmission to the sanctuary. As throughout the sacrificial system, blood is life-substance, communicated to the patient through sprinkling; thereby death, including the living, social death of leprosy, is transformed into life. Running water, which in Hebrew is literally "living water," likewise washes away impurity; contaminated clothes, cooking utensils, and persons have to be cleansed through immersion. The life of the dead bird is transferred to the sufferer; the water washes away the infection; the asperging bundle ensures the safe transmission of the vital fluid. The living bird, likewise dipped in blood, carries away the miasma. The impurity is released into the open fields; the cured patient begins the process of restoration to normal life. It is a typical liminal rite, in which the stream itself may represent transition. But it happens outside the human domain; the disease remains an ever-present threat. Similarly, in the

---

35. It should be noted that biblical "leprosy" has nothing to do with Hansen's disease. No one knows quite what it is, but it is evidently some kind of psoriasis or eczema. A somewhat abbreviated and adjusted form of the ritual is applied to "leprous" houses (Lev. 14.48-53).

36. It is not clear who captures the birds. Perhaps it doesn't matter. The species is not specified either, except that they are *těhōrôt*, "pure birds," in other words that they do not belong to the list of impure birds, such as eagles and owls, which may not be eaten, according to Lev. 11.13-20 and Deut. 14.12-18. For the translation as "wild," see Jacob Milgrom, *Leviticus 1-16* (*AB* 3; New York: Doubleday, 1991), 832. The rabbis identified the birds as sparrows.

ritual for the Day of Atonement the two goats enact the two parts of the purgative process. One is offered to YHWH, while the other carries the sins of the people into the wilderness.

That the birds are wild renders the drama anomalous; it is not sacrificial, since sacrifice may only be performed with domestic animals, symbolically or actually possessed by the donor.[37] Otherwise it would not be a gift. The slaughtered bird is not offered to YHWH. The analogy with the scapegoat ritual, where the goat is delivered to the goat-god Azazel, suggests that the free bird goes to some maleficent power, whence comes leprosy and all the dangers to human existence. Only the priest acts as the representative of YHWH, exorcising the malady by sprinkling blood, at the boundary between the symbolic order, the closed world of the priestly writers, and the outside. Leprosy itself is a symptom of symbolic breakdown, associated with sacrilege, a pathology of the skin and thus of the body and the body politic. The integrity of the body is itself the source of extreme anxiety, especially for the priestly writers. The small birds, twittering at the edge of consciousness, with their echoes of the world of the dead, are trapped; one dies and the other is let go. As with every liminal rite, it reasserts symbolic order when it is most imperiled.

Several characters have bird names: Jonah, the dove, who flees to the end of the earth only to return home and find it unfamiliar; Zipporah, the sparrow, hopping round the feet of Moses and averting catastrophe; Agur, the thrush, the melancholy would-be mystic of Prov. 30.1-9. The names suggest an affinity between birds and humans, a metaphorical aspiration. What would it be like to be a dove, a sparrow, a thrush?

In the Song of Songs, corresponding to its role as an emblem for the mother- and love-goddess in the Ancient Mediterranean, the dove is a metaphor for the woman (2.14, 5.2, 6.9), as well as for her eyes (1.15, 4.1). "My dove" is linked to other epithets: *'aḥōtî ra'yātî yônātî tammātî*, "my sister, my friend, my dove, my pure one" in 5.2; "my dove, my pure one" in 6.9. The Song of Songs is full of endearments, especially from the male lover. Thereby he draws her into his relational circle: she is a sister, a companion, a pet, with their full affective range. *Tammātî*, "my pure one," has no implication of continence;[38] it conveys flawlessness, which presumably is physical but also suggests an innocence and simplicity of character, perhaps

---

37. Adriana Desto and Mauro Pesce, "Sacrifice - The Ritual for the Leper in Leviticus 14," in Philip Esler, ed., *Ancient Israel: The Old Testament in its Social Context* (Minneapolis, MN: Fortress, 2006), 69, insist that it is sacrificial. I cannot see why. They also err in assuming that the blood is mixed with the water (71).

38. *Ṭāhôr* would be the common word if that were the case.

even inexperience.[39] The dove may be a simple bird, tame, affectionate, so the juxtaposition suggests. Both lovers have fantasies of mutual possession (e.g. 2.16, 6.3). In 1.15 and 4.1 the image of the dove-like eyes is associated with beauty: "Behold, you are beautiful, my love, behold, you are beautiful, your eyes are doves." The eyes are beautiful because of their shape, so the metaphor suggests, and maybe because of their color; it also tells us that doves are beautiful, as we might guess from Ps. 68.14. In the eyes is concentrated the entire beauty of the person; we go from the whole to the part, which in 4.1 introduces the itemized description of the lovers. The eyes are hidden for the moment behind a veil.[40] Like all the metaphors of fauna in the Song, it links the human and animal domains; sexuality is what they have in common. Humans and animals share the natural world between them, in an idealized portrait of spring. The "voice of the turtle dove" in 2.12 heralds the spring, but it also has its own amatory message, as if all the lovers need to say is "tur tur." In 2.14 the voice of the dove is again evoked: "My dove in the clefts of the rock, in the secret places of the cliffs, let me see your face, let me hear your voice, for your voice is sweet and your face is lovely." The dove is imagined as remote, inaccessible, shy, a creature of the wilderness, a reversal of roles, since the woman is in the house and the man wooing her from outside (2.8-17). Intimacy implies distance.

In 5.12, the man's eyes are compared to doves: "his eyes are like doves by watercourses, washed in milk, sitting by brimming pools."[41] As usual in the Song, the simile takes off on its own, forms its own delicate little poem, but we need not follow it. What matters is that the man and woman share the figure of the dove between them. One remembers that doves are messenger birds. As metaphors for the eyes, they pass backward and forwards between the lovers. The eyes are expressive, opening up an interiority, as in the clefts of the rock, but they communicate in their own sensual language, which comprises the entire vernal world that they see.

Birds are wondrous, as Willi knows. One of the things that is too wonderful for me, according to the proverb immediately after the one about the raven, is "the path of the eagle in the sky" (Prov. 30.19). I want to turn, however, to one particular wondrous bird, the ostrich.

> The wings of the ostrich flap,
> if the pinions of the stork and the falcon?[42]

---

39. Both Jacob (Gen. 25.27) and Job (Job 1.1, 8, 2.3) are described as *tam*, before anything happens to them.
40. If that is what the word *ṣammâ* means.
41. I have adopted Cheryl Exum's beautiful translation (J. Cheryl Exum, *Song of Songs: A Commentary* [OTL; Westminster/John Knox, 2006, 184).
42. Edwin M. Good, *In Turns of the Tempest: A Reading of Job* (Stanford: Stanford

> For she leaves her eggs on the ground,
> and she warms them in the dust;
> forgetful of feet that can shatter them,
> and the beasts of the field that can squash them.
> She neglects[43] her young, as if they were not hers,
> She frets not that her effort's for nothing.
> For God has deprived her of wisdom,
> And gave her no share of understanding.
> Time comes, on high she spreads her wings,[44]
> She laughs at the horse and its rider. (Job. 38.13-18).

The ostrich is proverbially foolish, and a bad mother (e.g. Lam. 4.3). Its carelessness, however, is related to its laughter. It does not have a care in the world. Birth and freedom are the major themes of God's speech from the whirlwind. Although it is flightless, it flaps its wings (if that is the meaning),[45] perhaps for pleasure, perhaps to terrify its enemies. She laughs at the horse and rider, presumably because she can run faster than they, and is in her element; all their wisdom is for nought. She represents something indomitable in nature and in creation, like the wild ass and ox of the previous descriptions (39. 5-12). She is contrasted with the stork, whose name means "the kindly one" in Hebrew, and whose house is among cypresses, according to Ps. 104.17, but also with all birds who build nests and care for their young. She is absurd, with an absurdity that matches that of the divine vision from the whirlwind.

Perhaps Willi's love of birds is absurd, too, without reason. I am reminded of another of my favorite essays of Willi's, the one on "Introducing Religion" in the J.Z. Smith Festschrift, one that I also find incomprehensible.[46] In it, Willi writes about "riding (a theory) like a bat out of hell"[47]—now, if I were a bat, I would want to go straight back into hell, where it is nice

---

University Press, 1990), 160 comments on the second half of verse: "Anyone who can find meaning in that is welcome to do so." Edward L. Greenstein, *Job: A New Translation* (New Haven, CT: Yale University Press, 2019), 173, translates, with considerable emendation, "Does she fly (like the) stork and the falcon?"

43. *Hiqšiaḥ* is usually translated "treat harshly" (see Koehler-Baumgartner Hebrew and Aramaic Lexicon of the Old Testament), but it seems to me that "neglect" better fits the context, both here and in the only other instance in which the word occurs, Isa. 63.17. I cannot account for the change of gender.

44. Another very obscure line. My translation is adapted from Good and Greenstein.

45. *Ne'elāsâ* defeats commentators. It may also mean "to be joyful," a variant on 'LZ and 'LṢ.

46. Willi Braun, "Introducing Religion," in Willi Braun and Russell T. McCutcheon eds., *Introducing Religion: Essays in Honor of Jonathan Z. Smith* (London: Equinox Publishing, 2008), 480–98.

47. Braun, "Introducing Religion," 488.

and cozy and dark. And "riding one's theory 'hell-bent for leather'." I'm not sure that Willi does that, that he has a single strong theory, and in any case in my view anyone who rides "hell-bent for leather" is sure to crash, but it seems to me to touch on something very important, the necessity for patience, for determination, for seeing all sides of the data, what he calls "monomaniacal theorizing," by which he means a kind of relentless curiosity which is "not beholden to an *a priori* foundational premise" (490). This is what I love about Willi, and why we got on so well in the classroom. Willi is a wise owl.

Author biography

Francis Landy was Willi Braun's colleague for many years at the University of Alberta. The two taught the advanced/graduate course in Method and Theory in the Study of Religion, and learned from each other as much as they taught the students.

Bibliography

Becking, Bob. "Raven" in Karel van der Toorn, ed., *Dictionary of Deities and Demons in the Bible* (Leiden: Brill), 688–9.

Blenkinsopp, Joseph. *Isaiah 1-39* (*AB* 19A; New York: Doubleday, 2000). https://doi.org/10.5040/9780300261301

Braun, Willi. "Religion" in Willi Braun and Russell T. McCutcheon, eds., *Guide to the Study of Religion* (London: Cassell, 2000), 3–18.

—"Introducing Religion" in Willi Braun and Russell T. McCutcheon, eds., *Introducing Religion: Essays in Honor of Jonathan Z. Smith* (London: Equinox Publishing, 2008), 480–98.

Cixous, Hélène. *Three Steps on the Ladder of Writing* trans. Sarah Cornell and Susan Sellers (New York: Columbia University Press, 1993).

Damasio, Antonio. *The Strange Order of Things: Life, Feeling, and the Making of Cultures* (New York: Pantheon Books, 2018).

Eidevall, Göran. "Sad as a Bird: On Avian Metaphors in Biblical Descriptions of Human Suffering" in Blaženka Scheuer and David Willgren Davage, eds., *Sin, Suffering, and the Problem of Evil* (Tübingen: Mohr Siebeck, 2021), 85–96.

Exum, J. Cheryl. *Song of Songs: A Commentary* [OTL; Westminster/John Knox, 2006).

Feldt, Laura. *The Fantastic in Religious Narrative from Exodus to Elisha* (London: Equinox Publishing, 2012).

Forti, Tova. *Animal Imagery in the Book of Proverbs* (VTSupp 158; Leiden: Brill, 2008). https://doi.org/10.1163/ej.9789004162877.i-196

—*"Like a Lone Bird on a Roof": Animal Imagery and the Structure of Psalms"* (University Park, PA: Eisenbrauns, 2018).

Fustom J. "Dove" in van der Toorn, ed., *Dictionary of Deities and Demons in the Bible* (Leiden: Brill), 263–4.

Gillmayr-Bucher, Susanne. "'Ich Wachte und War Wie ein Einsamer Vögel auf dem

Dach' (Ps102,8): Ps 102 als examplarischer Identitätsdiskurs" in J. van Oorschot et al., eds., *Individualität und Selbstreflexion in den Lituraturen des Alten Testaments* (Leipzig: EVA, 2017), 279–96.

Good, Edwin M. *In Turns of the Tempest: A Reading of Job with a Translation* (Stanford, CA: Stanford University Press, 1990).

Greenstein, Edward L. *Job: A New Translation* (New Haven, CT: Yale University Press, 2019). https://doi.org/10.12987/9780300163766

Hays, Christopher B. *A Covenant with Death: Death in the Iron Age II and Its Rhetorical Uses in Proto-Isaiah* (Grand Rapids, MI: Eerdmans, 2015).

Hofstadter, Douglas. *I am a Strange Loop* (New York: Basic Books, 2007).

Landy, Francis. "Ruth and the Romance of Realism, or Deconstructing History". *JAAR* 62 (1994): 285–317, reprinted in Landy, *Beauty and the Enigma and Other Essays on the Hebrew Bible* (LHB/OTS 312; Sheffield: Sheffield Academic Press, 2001), 218–51.

—"Strategies of Concentration and Diffusion in Isaiah 6," in *BibInt* 6 (1999), 58–86, reprinted in Landy, *Beauty and the Enigma*, 298–327. https://doi.org/10.1163/156851599X00245

Merleau-Ponty, Maurice. *The Visible and the Invisible,* ed. Claude Lefort, trans. Alphonso Lingis (Evanston: Northwestern University Press, 1968).

Mettinger, Tryggve N.D. "Cherubim" in Karel van der Toorn, ed., *Dictionary of Deities and Demons in the Bible* (Leiden: Brill), 299–302.

Propp, William H. *Exodus 19-40* (*AB* 2A; New York: Doubleday, 2006). https://doi.org/10.5040/9780300261103

Tristram, Henry B. *The Survey of Western Palestine: The Fauna and Flora of Palestine* (London: Palestine Exploration Fund, 1885). https://doi.org/10.5962/bhl.title.7594

van der Toorn, Karel. "Echoes of Judean Necromancy in Isaiah 28, 7-22," *ZAW* 100 (1987): 199–216. https://doi.org/10.1515/zatw.1988.100.2.199

Walker, M. Justin. "The Wings of the Dove are Covered in Silver: The (Absent) Presence of the Goddess in Psalm 68". *UF* 47 (2016): 301–42.

Watts, James W. *Leviticus 1-10* (HCOT; Leuven: Peeters, 2013).

Chapter Four

Shipwrecked on a Desert Island:
The Barren Isolation of "Christian Origins"

William Arnal

The consistent thread of Willi Braun's scholarship has been an effort to humanize the ancient literary artifacts that constitute our area of inquiry. Effort is required, because at least part of the mystification that so easily attaches to ancient writings is by virtue of their categorization as *religious*, and particularly as *Christian*. The following chapter, then, is inspired by and in aid of that effort, arguing that at least some of the texts that comprise our earliest evidence for Christianity were not written by people who were *Christians* in any meaningful way. In some respects, this is a very easy argument to make: the term "Christian" is a second century coinage, appearing only three times in the entire New Testament and there in literature (Acts, 1 Peter) best understood as quite late. It is widely recognized that in the first century most of the people we would retroactively designate as "Christian" thought of themselves, in fact, as Jews. Unfortunately, this observation, beyond offering a correction of terminology, does not seem to change our perspective or advance our understanding very much. The issue is somewhat deeper, and not to be resolved through a slight adjustment of nomenclature. The point is rather more far-reaching: when we categorize some of our earliest texts as "Christian," we are profoundly inhibiting our understanding of what the authors of these documents were doing and why they were doing it. Identifying our texts as Christian, or even, if we try to be more careful, calling them the products of "Jesus people," isolates them from the culture and population that generated them. Consider, as an example, an excellent volume called *Religions of the Ancient world: A Guide*.[1] An incredibly useful reference book, it nonetheless has a rather peculiar organization. After opening with a section on method, the next segment of the book traces the religious histories of various regions in the ancient Mediterranean and Near East. The areas listed are: Egypt, Mesopotamia, Syria and Canaan, Israel, Anatolia, Iran, Minoan and Mycenaean civilizations,

---

1. Sarah Iles Johnston, ed., *Religions of the Ancient World: A Guide* (Cambridge, MA: Harvard University Press, 2005).

Greece, Etruria, Rome, and ... early Christianity. One almost gets the sense that "early Christianity" was a place—perhaps an island somewhere in the Mediterranean. The effect is to present early Christianity as a thing distinct from all of the other (regional) cultures of the ancient world; that it was not a part of Syria, or Greece, or Rome, and did not emerge from any of those regions. Such assumptions—usually unstated but all the more powerful for that—seem to frame far too much scholarship on antiquity. In the same volume, Harold Attridge claims that: "As Christianity expanded, it adapted in various ways to the *ambient culture*."[2] "Christianity," it seems, is an independent thing that can expand and adapt; it is distinct from and perhaps adversarial to the "ambient culture." It is not an aspect of that culture so much as an *infiltration* of it.

Precisely the opposite is true. The earliest writings dealing with Jesus, in or out of the New Testament, that we so casually designate "Christian," did not *interact* with the culture and conversations of the time: they were *part* of the culture and conversations of the time. Like other literature from the same period, they were efforts to comment on the issues and problems that mattered for people living under Rome in the first and second centuries. This is how we should think about them. The fact that they mention Jesus, or use Jesus as a character, symbol, or argumentative device, should not lead us to think that these texts were *about* Jesus in some kind of freestanding or independent way. What they were really about, rather, were the concerns and issues shared with other people in the same time and place, including people who happen not to have used the figure of Jesus to make their arguments. Our textual data speaks, not to the uniquely peculiar interests of an isolated cult, but to big questions of the day. Two distinct examples can help illustrate what I mean.

The Gospel of Thomas

The *Gospel of Thomas* is not part of the canon of the New Testament, and had in fact been lost to us until 1945, when a single complete copy of it (translated from Greek into Coptic) was discovered in upper Egypt. The manuscript itself can be fairly precisely dated to the middle 300s, but the date of the original composition of the gospel is hotly contested. Based on its content, and references to it by other writers, serious arguments for a date anywhere from the middle of the first to the middle of the second century

---

2. Harold Attridge, "Early Christianity" (233–9 in Sarah Iles Johnston, ed., *Religions of the Ancient World: A Guide* (Cambridge, MA: Harvard University Press, 2005), 237, emphasis added.

CE have been proposed. More precision than this is unnecessary for my purposes here. What is of consequence is the format *Thomas* takes. This gospel is actually a list of sayings, with each new saying introduced by the phrase "Jesus said," or something similar. There is no biography, almost no narrative detail at all, Jesus' crucifixion is not recounted, he does not rise from the dead; he is not even called "Christ" or "Messiah" in the text. All he does is pronounce rather mystifying sayings to his disciples or unspecified audiences. For example: "Jesus said: If two make peace with each other in a single house, they will say to the mountain: Move from here! and it will move" (48). This style of communication continues rather monotonously for approximately 114 sayings, culminating in the following (114): "Simon Peter said to them: Let Mary leave us, for women are not worthy of life. Jesus said: Behold, I will lead her to make her male, so that she too may become a living spirit resembling you males. For every woman who makes herself male will enter the kingdom of heaven."

The obscure character of *Thomas*'s individual sayings turns out to be a unifying feature of the document as a whole: the first few sayings indicate that it is *supposed* to be difficult to interpret. It opens with a description of its content as "the secret sayings of the living Jesus," and goes on to promise that whoever can figure them out will be rewarded with eternal life. The next saying describes the extended process the interpreter must endure: "Jesus said: Let the one who seeks not stop seeking until he finds, and when he finds, he will be troubled, and when he is troubled he will marvel, and he will rule over everything." The opaque nature of Jesus' teaching in the sayings that follow is therefore intentional, and in fact the gospel employs several relatively crude methods to heighten the obscurity of this teaching. These techniques of mystification include such things as taking closely-related sayings and dispersing them to different parts of the gospel. Or again, several different and unrelated ideas will be bundled together into a single saying, leaving the reader to pick them apart. Sayings in *Thomas* will make allusions to other writings—especially the biblical book of Genesis—without indicating where the allusions come from. The sayings also use terminology in contradictory ways, or will use a variety of quite different words to describe the same concept. To give a sense of how this works, consider saying 7: "Jesus said: blessed is the lion that the human will eat, so that the lion becomes human. And defiled is the human that the lion will eat, and the lion will become human." Considered by itself, this utterance is rather baffling and apparently self-contradictory. But when we set it side by side with a scattering of other sayings in which references to food and consumption lead to references to death, then to bodies and materiality, the point becomes clearer: allowing oneself to be consumed by this material world is degrading and fatal, and we should avoid this if we want to cultivate our better selves.

So we are left with a mysterious record of mysterious teachings, which opens by pointing out how very mysterious it all is, and then challenges the reader to make sense of it. As it happens, however, unraveling the meaning of the material is actually not very difficult at all. In spite of its artificial obscurity, all one really needs to do to get a coherent message from *Thomas* is to read it often enough and carefully enough to more or less memorize it. Once the text becomes familiar, it is easy enough to start to recognize similar sayings, changing uses of vocabulary, and allusions to literature with which one is already conversant. And what is the payoff, in the end? What momentous revelation can be puzzled out from this artificially arcane text? Having pieced together the meaning of Jesus' teachings, we learn that the material world is a bad place, that it seeks to consume us in change and death. Happily, our intellectual spirits are made in God's image, and when we come to recognize that our true identity consists of the divine spirit, our bondage to the world is ended. In the ancient world, especially among even moderately educated people, such ideas are about as mysterious or controversial as online cat memes are for us today. They are clichés of the commonplace Middle Platonism of the first and second centuries, and would have been familiar to anyone who was awake to any intellectual discourse at all.

Explaining the nature of the *Gospel of Thomas* has been easy for scholarship. This text, so the reasoning might go, is a gnostic writing. Gnostics are here understood as heretical Christians who thought that the world was created by a malevolent and inferior deity, and that Jesus had come to reveal the unworldly, spiritual spark within us, a vestige of the true Father who exists in an entirely non-material realm. There are two major problems with this explanation of the *Gospel of Thomas*. First, the Gospel is actually not very "gnostic" at all. It lacks, for instance, the developed mythology of a series of emanations from the mind of God, the fall of one of those emanations, and the accidental generation of an ignorant and malevolent creator God, the demiurge, who fashions the imprisoning world of matter. Nothing of this sort is present in *Thomas*—the material world is inferior, but there is no suggestion at all that it is a product of anything like a gnostic demiurge. More importantly, calling *Thomas* "gnostic," even if it were an accurate characterization, merely describes its ideological content, but does not in the least explain why someone would produce a text like this. In particular, the invocation of "gnosticism" fails to explain why this Gospel so deliberately and crudely aims to impede straightforward understanding of its banal content. This artificial mystification is sometimes vaguely waved off as "typical gnostic mumbo-jumbo," but we are still left wondering why real flesh and blood would produce such a text, what benefit they would derive from doing so, what effect they hoped this would have on their readers.

It turns out, however, that there *are* clear ancient analogues to the sort of thing we see in *Thomas*, and we don't need to turn to "gnostic" sources, nor even Jewish or Christian ones, to find them. The most interesting parallels come from Plutarch, a second century Greek historian and moral philosopher, and his obscure and baffling quotations from Pythagoras, a much earlier Greek philosopher. These Pythagorean *symbola* or "signs" include such important advice as: "do not wear a tight ring," "do not sit on a peck measure," "do not put food in a slop-pail," and "abstain from beans." Plutarch describes aristocratic dinner parties in which learned guests reinterpret these senseless commands as moral allegories: do not allow your freedom to be constrained; do not be idle but work for your daily bread; do not use rhetoric to pretty up a base character; avoid politics (*Moralia* I 727; cf. 12). As with the *Gospel of Thomas*, the payload of the interpreted material is surprisingly banal, consisting of conventional moralisms and advice that hardly require the cloak of secrecy. Plutarch is hardly the only example from the Roman period. As Plutarch appeals to the mystical wisdom of the great sage Pythagoras, so also the Hermetic texts put an Egyptian spin on things, attributing their not-very-profound insights to the ancient sage Hermes, son of Thoth. The Jewish Platonist, Philo of Alexandria does the same thing with Moses: in every place where Torah appears baffling, archaic, crude, or meaningless, Philo rescues the text by some contrived interpretive mechanism which yields some self-evident truth showing Moses to be, in fact, a Platonic philosopher.

Clearly, then, the point of these textual puzzles does not lie in their content, but in the act of interpretation itself, the puzzling out of sensible meaning from apparently senseless words. The appropriation of dense, obscure, or archaic traditions to contemporary moral truisms serves to demonstrate the interpreter's distinction, wit, and moral integrity. Plutarch's discussion of the Pythagorean *symbola* does not attest to any great moral debate in antiquity, nor to factions or rifts in the Pythagorean school; it shows, rather, that Plutarch is a respectable character, that he is intelligent, refined, and has conventional morals, and that therefore he is to be entrusted with his culture's cherished traditions. The implications for the *Gospel of Thomas* should be obvious: those who produced and transmitted this text were simply repeating and imitating what practically everyone else was doing at the same time: that is, they were *exercising cultural capital through the interpretation of obscure traditional texts*. In this sense, they were doing nothing specifically Christian, but rather emulating elite and sub-elite behaviors from all over the Roman world, behaviors which applied to Jewish texts, Greek traditions, Egyptian traditions, and others besides. The sage may be different, but the form of the material, its content, and the textual and hermeneutic technologies involved are identical.

Yet this simple and straightforward explanation is not completely satisfying. There are several features of the *Gospel of Thomas* that differentiate it from the utterances of Pythagoras or the laws of Moses. Among them is the artificiality of the putative tradition here, reflected in the use of Jesus as the speaker—a rather marginal and *nouveau* sage in the pantheon of antiquity. Whatever they might originally have meant, the *symbola* of Pythagoras were centuries old by the time Plutarch and his friends came across them. Torah, likewise, was centuries old before Philo came along, and was said to have been authored by a hero of many centuries past, Moses. Moreover, Torah was closely associated with age-old traditions of a specific ethnic group, a nation: the Judeans. The obscurity of such ancient writings is actually a function of their age: Torah fails to make literal sense to Philo of Alexandria precisely because it was written centuries before in a completely different social environment. So also the Pythagorean *symbola*. The act of contrived interpretation is necessary in these cases to rescue ancient tradition from irrelevance in a new world. The *Gospel of Thomas* is quite different, and more like the Hermetic writings in this respect: the author or editor of the text has created it *in order* to be obscure. It represents no high-status, long-standing, or ancient tradition—indeed, it is a wonderful example of the outright fabrication of tradition. But if everyone was already interpreting obscure ancient texts, why invent a new one, and why attribute it to a sage of such marginal standing as Jesus?

This question brings me to my final point about the *Gospel of Thomas*. This is a text which aims to imitate an elite cultural practice. To do so, the author must have the skills associated with such practices, and they clearly do: they are literate, have literary aspirations, are acquainted with Jewish interpretive traditions around Torah, and are familiar with the philosophical currents of antiquity at a basic level. This was a person who shared, albeit with a lower degree of sophistication, the literary and cultural competencies of a Philo or a Plutarch. Yet he evidently did not share Philo or Plutarch's high economic class or unquestionable social standing, a fact reflected in *Thomas*'s critique of wealth (63, 64), his sneering at the official guardians of tradition (39), his assertions that the kings and rulers of this world do not know the truth (78). This all makes perfect sense, since if the author of *Thomas* had been active in the highbrow intellectual currents of his day, he would not have needed to invent a document to be highbrow *about*. I would suggest, then, that texts like the *Gospel of Thomas*, and, later, the non-Christian Hermetic writings, are simply a social effect of the expansion of literacy in urban settings in the first and second centuries. As the bureaucracy of empire expanded, it required more and more literate people to staff it, especially in the cities. Since literacy had in the past generally been restricted to the elites, it was strongly correlated with high social standing and cultural prestige. But of course as writing competencies expanded, they expanded beyond the classes to which they were originally restricted: what had once been a rare sign of status was now available to more and more people, and for fairly menial administrative purposes. Education did not become the ticket to a rapid social ascent, and if those who had newly acquired this skill wanted to participate in the cultivation exhibited by the true elites, they would have to invent the occasion—and the tradition—for themselves. One such occasion, and a ready-made tradition to go with it, was provided by the composition of the *Gospel of Thomas*. Around such a text, culturally ambitious city-dwellers could pretend to elite cultivation by interpreting, to one another, their own tradition: the secret sayings of Jesus.

The Gospel of Mark

In some ways, it is a little too easy to use the *Gospel of Thomas* as an example of the earliest Christians not being especially Christian. The *Gospel of Thomas* is non-canonical, it is alleged to be heretical, it fails to conform to our expectations of what earliest Christianity was all about. None of this can be said, however, about the Gospel of Mark, a work that has been much more central, historically, to the Christian tradition, and that possesses most of the characteristics we associate with core Christian beliefs. Mark is the first of the canonical gospels to be written, and was the major literary source for Matthew and Luke, and probably John as well. The date of composition is important: Mark's references to the destruction of the Jerusalem Temple, and his concern with the dramatic events of the first Jewish rebellion against Rome, make it almost certain that Mark was composed shortly after that war's conclusion in 70 CE. Unlike *Thomas*, Mark is a narrative: Jesus is presented as a teacher, but what is really important about him is the story of his adult life, culminating in his horrific and shameful crucifixion in Jerusalem during the Passover.

To try to make sense of Mark as a relatively ordinary cultural product of the later first century, we need first to consider a completely different author, Flavius Josephus, a Jewish aristocrat and military leader who participated in the rebellion against Rome, but surrendered to the enemy, and lived to write histories of his people that remain to this day important sources of information about the ancient world. The earliest of Josephus's writings is referred to as *The Jewish War*, and represents an effort to explain and account for the rebellion against Rome and, ultimately, its failure. Among many anecdotes in Josephus' history, there is one about a man named Jesus—a common enough name, and not the figure described in the Christian gospels. Josephus writes:

> Four years before the war, when the city [Jerusalem] was enjoying profound peace and prosperity, there came to the feast at which it is the custom of all Jews to erect tabernacles to God, one Jesus, son of Ananias, a rude peasant, who, standing in the temple, suddenly began to cry out: "A voice from the east, a voice from the west, a voice from the four winds; a voice against Jerusalem and the sanctuary, a voice against the bridegroom and the bride, a voice against all the people." Day and night he went about all the alleys with this cry on his lips. Some of the leading citizens, incensed at these ill-omened words, arrested the fellow and severely chastised him. (*JW* VI.300-301)

Josephus goes on to describe how this Jesus would not cease prophesying against the temple in spite of beatings, and when brought before the governor would only shout "woe to Jerusalem" even when flogged. Eventually, he was written off as a madman, and left to wander about the city shouting "woe to Jerusalem" for the next seven and a half years. The war comes, the Romans lay siege to the city, and the story of Jesus son of Ananias ends thus (*JW* VI.308-309): "While going his round and shouting in piercing tones from the wall, 'Woe once more to the city and to the people and to the temple,' as he added a last word, 'and woe to me also,' a stone hurled from the *ballista* struck and killed him on the spot. So with those ominous words still on his lips he passed away."

The whole thing sounds like a tragic farce, but Josephus is very clear about why he tells this story and what he thinks it means. He refers to this entire set of events as an "alarming portent" (VI.300), and it was hardly the only one. Josephus complains that the people "disregarded the plain warnings of God" (VI.288) and so failed to recognize that the city of Jerusalem and its temple were doomed. Among the warnings, he mentions a comet shaped like a sword that hung over the city of Jerusalem (289); a light that shone around the sanctuary (290); a cow that gave birth to a lamb (292); and images of chariots and armies seen in the sky (299). Even more ominous are indications of divine *abandonment*. Josephus recounts that:

> ... at the feast which is called Pentecost the priests on entering the inner court of the temple by night, as their custom was in the discharge of their ministrations, reported that they were conscious, first of a commotion and a din, and after that of a voice as of a host, saying "We are departing hence." (300)

In the same context, he also describes one of the gates to the temple's inner court, fastened by bars and bolted into the ground, as mysteriously opening without any visible agency, adding that:

> This again to the uninitiated seemed the best of omens, as they supposed that God had opened to them the gate of blessings; but the learned understood that *the security of the temple was dissolving of its own accord* and that the opening of the gate meant a present to the enemy, interpreting the portent in their own minds as indicative of coming desolation. (300, emphasis added)

These omens are indications that God has abandoned the temple. Although Josephus is describing earlier events, he is actually writing after the temple was destroyed by the Romans in the year 70. To at least some degree, he is trying to explain how it was possible that the Romans, mere mortals and Gentiles to boot, could prevail over the God of Israel. His answer is that they did not prevail over the God of Israel, that God allowed them to destroy his house, because he had already abandoned that house. Thus the defeat to the Romans in the Jewish War was not a defeat of Israel's God, but a sign of that God's judgment against his own people.

Josephus also provides reasons for that judgment and abandonment: the impious and sacrilegious behavior of a certain faction of Jewish rebels, the Zealots, who in his view had already desecrated the temple before the Romans arrived to destroy it. These insurgents, Josephus thinks, are guilty of murder, and specifically the murder of Jewish noblemen. By using the temple as a refuge, they stain it with guilty blood, and reduce it to little more than a fortress. Josephus blames the Zealot rabble for murder and impiety, leading God to abandon the temple to Roman destruction. Jerusalem could not have fallen had God not forsaken it first.

The Gospel of Mark makes almost precisely the same argument. Like Josephus's account, it was written after the Jewish War but set before the War, and like Josephus's account it tries to link earlier events to the catastrophe of the year 70. For the author of Mark, the earlier event in question was the murder of an innocent man—the crucifixion of Jesus, the anointed one sent by God. God sent his holy messiah to Israel where he performed miracles, taught wisdom, and was joyfully received by the people, but the wicked leadership of Judea opposed God, killed his son, and their guilt led God to abandon his temple and city, allowing, eventually, the Romans to destroy both. As with Josephus, omens of this future disaster are given out in advance, but are not understood.

That this is the core message behind Mark's narrative is nowhere more clear than in his presentation of Jesus' activities on the temple grounds themselves. On his second day in Jerusalem, Jesus stalks about the temple court, engaging in arguments with the chief priests, the scribes, and the elders (11.27), who are trying to trap and trick him. He actually predicts his own death to the very people eventually responsible for it, the accusation itself serving them with motive. Jesus goes on to harangue representatives of various other powerful factions: first the Pharisees and Herodians, then some Sadducees, then a scribe. He then sits down by the temple treasury and criticizes the wealthy. Finally, he departs, which Mark describes thus: "As he came out of the temple, one of his disciples said to him, 'Look, teacher, what large stones and what large buildings.' Then Jesus asked him, 'Do you see these great buildings? Not one stone will be left upon another. All will be thrown down'" (13.1-2). So from his entry into the temple until his exit from it, Jesus uses this space to engage in hostilities with the Jewish leadership, tells a parable predicting catastrophic destruction as punishment for hostility to God's son, and concludes with an explicit statement that the temple would be demolished. But all of this has come from Jesus' second day at the temple. It follows close on the heels of his first day there:

> They came to Jerusalem. And he entered the temple and began to drive out those who were selling and those who were buying in the temple, and he overturned the tables of the money changers and the seats of those who sold doves; and he would not allow anyone to carry anything through the temple. He was teaching and saying, "Is it not written, 'My house shall be called a house of prayer for all the nations?' But you have made it a 'den of robbers.'" And when the chief priests and the scribes heard it, they kept looking for a way to kill him. (11.15-18)

There are several things worth noting here. First, Jesus' actions should be taken not as a "cleansing" of the temple, as it is so often described, but as a judgment and symbolic destruction of it. The doves being sold in the court were being sold as sacrifices; and the money changing was undertaken so that appropriate coinage could be used to pay the temple tax. Jesus thus does not restore the temple to its original purpose, but actively prevents it from being used for that purpose. Why? Because, second, Mark condemns the temple as having ceased to maintain its holy status. In fact, precisely as Josephus claims, this desacralization is essentially military in nature—the problem, the thing that sabotages the temple's holiness, is not commerce but the use of the building as a hide-out for bandits. The Greek word used by Mark is λῃστής, a term used of bands of robbers, pirates, and also insurrectionists. Josephus uses this same term to describe some of the most prominent of the rebels against Rome. For Josephus, the temple ceased to be a sacred place because it was literally used as a hide-out or fortress for bandits, i.e., the insurrectionists against Rome. For Mark, the bandits in this case are metaphoric: the chief priests and scribes whom Jesus so vociferously denounced. Perhaps of even greater interest, the specific terminology "den of robbers" is taken from the book of Jeremiah (7.11)—Jeremiah is the prophet known, preeminently, for predicting the Babylonian destruction of the first, Solomonic, Jerusalem temple, and the doomsday preaching of

Jesus ben Ananias as recounted by Josephus also invokes terminology from the book of Jeremiah; in fact, from the same chapter that Mark uses ("bridegroom and bride," Jer 7.34). Jesus predicts the destruction of the temple; but he also clearly presents this event as the judgment of God for the impiety of Israel's leaders.

Their ultimate act of impiety is of course the crucifixion of Jesus, undertaken, Mark claims, illegally and unjustly. That Jesus is innocent is underscored in a variety of ways. An armed band arrests him by night, even though he puts up no resistance. Jesus complains that "you have come out as against a robber, with swords and clubs to arrest me" (14.48)—the word "robber" here is again Greek λῃστής: bandit, insurrectionist. And if the arrest is stealthy and implicitly criminal, the trial is even more so. It also takes place in secret and by night. It is undertaken by precisely the same people identified as Jesus' enemies up to this point: the chief priests, elders, and scribes (14.53). Even a show trial fails to produce grounds for conviction: "The chief priests and whole council sought testimony against Jesus to put him to death; *but they found none*. For many bore false witness against him, and their testimony did not agree" (14.55-56). The charge on which Jesus is finally accused is that of blasphemy. He claims to be God's son:

> The high priest asked him, "Are you the Christ, the son of the Blessed?" And Jesus said, "I am; and you will see the Son of man seated at the right hand of Power, and coming with the clouds of heaven." And the high priest tore his garments, and said, "Why do we still need witnesses? You have heard his blasphemy. What is your decision?" And they all condemned him as deserving death. (14.61-64)

Thus the only true statement made in the entire trial—that Jesus is God's son—turns out to be the basis for Jesus' conviction. Even the Roman prefect, Pilate, recognizes that Jesus is innocent of any crime (15.14).

Stressing Jesus' innocence, and so the guilt of those who condemned him, is also, in my view, the point of Mark's version of the resurrection story. In spite of our tendency to view the resurrection as the absolutely central facet of the Christian message, Mark's account is astonishingly brief and incomplete. Jesus predicts his resurrection earlier in the Gospel, but only as a complement to predictions of his murder. And the event itself is not part of Mark's narrative, nor does the resurrected Jesus appear to his disciples as he does in all of the other canonical gospels. The text of Mark has been amended by later copyists to rectify this omission, but as the most ancient and reliable manuscripts attest, the gospel originally ended at Chapter 16, verse 8, with the women at the empty tomb. The resurrection is attested by an angel in the tomb who announces that Jesus has been raised, but it is not sufficiently important to Mark to merit narration or additional reflection. It is simply a vindication of Jesus by God, an assertion that his execution was in fact illegitimate, that he *was* truly the son of God, that his murder was an act of sacrilegious injustice which God himself saw fit to rescind.

The real climax of Mark's gospel is the death on the cross, which is described in appalling detail. Weaving together a series of allusions to Psalms 22 and 69 with a realistically horrifying description of one of the worst deaths imaginable, complete with torture, mockery, and public humiliation, Mark could provide no sharper or more moving contrast to the triumphant proclamations and healings of the earlier parts of the Gospel. The culminating moment is described thus: "And Jesus let out a great cry, and breathed his last. *And the curtain of the temple was torn in two, from top to bottom*" (15.37-38). And so at the moment of Jesus' death, God deserts his house, leaving it empty and undefended from whatever depredations might ensue. We cannot fail to recall Josephus' description of great voices shouting "we are departing hence." Mark establishes what he has been claiming all along: that the price of killing God's beloved one is the temple itself, that the leaders of the people are responsible for an act of impiety that has brought God's abandonment and judgment against them, a judgment that is finally enacted 40 years later when the Romans bring Jesus' dark forecast to completion.

The Gospel of Mark, then, just like Josephus's *Jewish War*, is a writing that aims to explain how the Romans were able to destroy the national temple of the Judeans. Both authors answer the question in very similar ways. For Josephus, Jewish acts of impiety, culminating in murder, desecrate the temple, leading God to abandon it, an abandonment signaled via a variety of omens, predictions, and allusions to the book of Jeremiah. For Mark, the impiety of the Jewish leadership in failing to recognize God's son, and culminating in murder, leads God to abandon his house, an abandonment predicted and foreshadowed by omens, veiled predictions, and allusions to the book of Jeremiah. Josephus blames the rabble for the catastrophe: bandits and insurrectionists who angered God by their blasphemy and opposition to the Jewish leadership, and who led the disastrous charge to revolution. Mark blames the aristocracy for the events, identifying them as the real bandits and lawbreakers whose injustice led God to give up his house to the Gentile armies. But in both cases, what we see is an effort to make sense of an historical event with shocking implications. The Roman destruction of the great national temple and the holy city could be taken as evidence that Israel's God had been defeated as well. Was Roman military power stronger than God himself? Was God unable to defend his own house? Was Israel a defeated people? For Mark and for Josephus, themselves Jews, these questions revolved around the Roman victory of 70 CE, and hence pertained to Jewish identity. But the same kinds of questions in different forms and in different circumstances would have been raised by all of the many peoples who came under Roman rule. A Briton, a Greek, an Egyptian, might all have asked: Have the Romans defeated our gods? Or have our gods abandoned us? What does the future hold? Mark uses the figure of Jesus as martyr to answer these kinds of questions in a specifically Jewish way. But all of the nations defeated by Rome would have been beset by similar doubts, and would have constructed their own responses.

Conclusion

The examples could be multiplied. There are similar cases to be made for Paul, for the author of the Gospel of Matthew, and for other writers. The simple presence of Jesus in our earliest Christian textual artifacts does not in itself require us to read those writings as somehow separate and distinct from the kinds of issues and problems that would have been of interest to other citizens of the ancient world, including non-Christians and non-Jews. They, too, struggled with issues of literacy and social status. They, too, wondered about the relationship between their ancestral gods and the Romans. They, too, wanted their barbarian cultural traditions to have universal and cosmopolitan applicability. It just so happens that some people in the first century, mostly Jews at first, found in the figure of Jesus a helpful instrument for making sense of those problems, for organizing their thoughts, and even for providing tentative solutions. He could serve as a wise teacher, or a heroic martyr, or a resurrected spirit-man, as circumstance and need dictated. *Jesus was good to think with*. Other people took different approaches to the same issues, and used different techniques to think about them, varying according to their class, their ethnic backgrounds, their proximity to power. But all were participating in broader socio-cultural conversations and living in the same world that provided the conditions of those conversations. The mere whisper of the name of Jesus was not sufficient to propel a discourse or subject-matter into isolation and incomprehensibility.

In a sense, none of this is especially different from the way we behave today. There are important issues that animate all of us, and we discuss them using stock characters, events, and historical figures that resonate with us, that serve our arguments well, or that help us break down and represent what we think is happening. One of the most straightforward analogues concerns the United States, a country which, even a decade ago, before the Trump presidency and all that entailed, was deeply divided. One of the ways of making sense of these rifts is to turn to the past, and think imaginatively and analytically about the present in terms of a past paradigmatic moment of American division, the

Civil War. It is remarkable that in the year 2012 alone, at least three separate films were released with an American Civil War setting, and that two of these three had Abraham Lincoln as their central protagonist. One of these treatments, Steven Spielberg's "Lincoln," is very serious, and actively proposes specific models for addressing such division. Quentin Tarantino's "Django Unchained" is only semi-serious. The other, Timur Bekmambetov's "Abraham Lincoln, Vampire Hunter" is not very serious at all, but in its way, just as earnest. But all three films speak, in different ways, to contemporary concerns about freedom, unity, morals, and American identity. These films are not the competing products of a controversy-ridden Abraham Lincoln-cult.

Starting in the second century, and then only gradually, Christianity began to develop as a more encompassing and ready-made identity. The first securely-datable uses of the term "Christian" appear in the second decade of the second century; it is only by the end of the second century that anything like an identifiable Christian material culture emerges. But even at these later stages, the self-conscious development and contestation of Christian identity simply generated a more or less stable set of symbols and positions and references, not a totalizing perspective on all elements of the world, nor a unique one. The invention of Christianity over the course of the second, third, and fourth centuries meant simply that a specific arsenal of cultural tropes and symbols had coalesced somewhat, so that the entire system could be invoked metonymically simply by referring to one of its elements. The slow development of a Christian identity meant, in the end, that Christianity did eventually come to be a discernible and distinct entity, the apparent coherence of which was imposed, retroactively, onto earlier cultural artifacts. But this is an effect of later decisions about canon, not an indication of the agenda behind the production of these works. When we allow these kinds of anachronistic assumptions to govern our approach to earlier texts, we radically foreclose the interpretive possibilities, the wide range of comparative points of reference, and especially the ordinariness of the points those texts make. By insisting on their extraordinary Christianity, or extraordinary religiosity, we risk denying these cultural artifacts their mundane, but profound, humanity.

Author biography

William E. Arnal is Professor of Religious Studies at University of Regina. He is the author of *Jesus and the Village Scribes* (Fortress) and *The Symbolic Jesus* (Equinox).

References

Attridge, Harold. "Early Christianity," 233–9 in Sarah Iles Johnston, ed., *Religions of the Ancient World: A Guide*. Cambridge, MA: Harvard University Press, 2005. https://doi.org/10.4159/9780674264823-026

Sarah Iles Johnston, ed. *Religions of the Ancient World: A Guide*. Cambridge, MA: Harvard University Press, 2005.

Chapter Five

The Ontological and Zoomorphic Semiotics of Two Hellenistic Savior Deities

Darlene Juschka

Found in the ancient Greco-Roman world were savior deities, deities who had an interest in individual humans and were willing to assist them in this world and the next world, however that was defined.[1] Hellenistic savior deities, deities who assisted followers during and after death, were well defined in the early Greco-Roman period, and numbered such deities as Isis, Demeter and Persephone, Dionysus, Orpheus, Mithras and Jesus among others. The extant mythographies of these deities link them with the chthonic underworld insofar as they can move across the boundaries between the living, the dead and the deities and therefore are able to "light" the way for their followers. To access the light of the savior deity, one had to devote oneself to their mysteries, as the *The Golden Ass* by Apuleius[2] tells its reader, a developed ritual process parts of which were undisclosed. Demeter and Persephone, Isis and Osiris had their mysteries along with Mithras and Jesus. The ritual play of the mysteries changed aimless wanderers into followers allowing them to survive the vicissitudes of life and the uncertainties of death.

Jesus and Mithras were two such hellenistic savior deities whose ritual practices were engaged by increasing numbers beginning in the mid first century CE and the late first century CE[3] respectively, and lasting until the fourth century CE wherein most mithraea had fallen into disuse[4]. A few mithraea were overlaid by third-century Christian ritual space as evidenced by the Basilica of Saint Clemente in Rome underneath of which is a second century CE mithraeum. Their respective followers shared social, political, economic, mythic, ritual, semiotic and imaginistic space, something

---

1. Luther H. Martin, *Hellenistic Religions: An Introduction* (Oxford: Oxford University Press, 1987).
2. Sarah Ruden, *The Golden Ass* (New Haven, CT: Yale University Press 2011).
3. Manfred Clauss, *The Roman Cult of Mithras: The God and His Mysteries*. Translated by Richard Gordon (New York: Routledge, 2001), 21.
4. David Walsh, *The Cult of Mithras in Late Antiquity: Development, Decline and Demise c. A.D. 270-430* (Late Antique Archaeology. Supplementary Ser. v. 2. Brill, 2019), 49.

reflected in the mythographies of Jesus and Mithras. Certainly there are important differences between the deities of Jesus and Mithras, and while these also provide insight into these two hellenistic savior deities, the general intention of this chapter is to pay attention to their shared sensibilities. By comparing the ontological, somatic and zoomorphic mythemes of these two savior deities I hope to further understanding of savior deities.

Comparison

J. Z. Smith provided a map for comparison in his multiple works and showed how, as he wrote, "in comparison a magic still dwells."[5] The imaginistic horizons of the two deities, Jesus and Mithras, share a context and may even have shared practitioners over the centuries. Their mythographies, both written and visual in the case of Jesus but largely visual in the case of Mithras (aside from a few inscriptions and an unassigned liturgy[6]), reflect their shared context. For example, the prevalent view of the healing powers of water was shared throughout this period and in evidence in the mythography of both Mithras and Jesus, along with other hellenistic savior deities whose teachings and ministrations provided healing and direction for the lost. In *The Golden Ass*, a third-century novel written by Apuleus, Lucius, the protagonist, has been changed into the form of a donkey and wanders lost with confused purpose seeking to be returned to his human form. He is ultimately saved by Isis, who arranged for his transformation back into that of a human. Once a human he joined hers and Osiris' mysteries securing both his future in life and death:

> Sometime during the first watch of the night, I awoke in sudden terror. The full orb of the Moon was shining with an immoderate brilliance as it emerged from the sea swell.... All bodies in the earth, sky, and sea grew in accordance with her [Isis] additions and then were diminished in deference to her losses..... Devote yourself obediently to our sect and take on the voluntary yoke of service. For when you become the goddess's slave, you will know a still greater enjoyment of your freedom.[7]

Sharing in the ontological narrative of humans lost and adrift in a hostile world,[8] much as Lucius, the ritual practices concerning Mithras and Jesus

---

5. Jonathan Z. Smith, *Imagining Religion: from Babylon to Jonestown* (Chicago, IL: University of Chicago Press, 1982), 19–35.
6. Called the "Mythraic Liturgy," this brief text, an ascension spell, is found in the Greek Magical Papyri. See Hans Dieter Betz, *The Greek Magical Papyri in Translation, Including the Demotic Spells* (2nd ed., Chicago, IL: University of Chicago Press, 1992).
7. Sarah Ruden, *The Golden Ass* (New Haven, CT: Yale University Press, 2011), 248, 58.
8. Martin, *Hellenistic Religions*, 37.

provided structure, clarity, and concreteness in a world seemingly fraught with the fickleness of powers that ruled human life and death. Sharing in the provision of light by which to guide their adherents, much like Isis, the figures of Jesus and Mithras also shared in attributes that spoke of healing, sacrifice and ritual eating, overcoming death and the realm of the stars making them viable mythic figures to compare. Drawing primarily on visual representations of Mithras and visual and textual representations of Jesus, this chapter compares ontological and zoomorphic features of aspects of these two hellenistic deities of the Greco-Roman world of the first century CE until the fourth century CE.

Mythic ontologies Jesus and Mithras

The mythographies of Jesus and Mithras create a sense of specialness, of difference from the norm, for their respective deities. Like any of the hellenistic savior deities, one or both of the parents are themselves deities. In mythography of Jesus his mother, named Mary, is represented as human, while his other parent is represented as a masculine deity. Born in an undisclosed house in Bethlehem in Matthew's origin myth, Jesus' life is already at risk, as an angel warns his foster father Joseph to take the child to Egypt. It is only later, like the savior deity Dionysus, that Jesus the child returns "home" to "the land of Israel" (Mt. 2.1-23). The origin myth in the text of Luke varies slightly and locates the birth of the infant deity in a manger since "there was no place for them in the inn" (Luke 2.7). Eight days later the infant deity was circumcised and named, and thereafter presented to the Temple, being a first born male, while a sacrifice of two birds was made by the human parents of the infant deity (Luke 2.21-23). In the Lukan mythography of Jesus the reader is presented with the deity's life as he grew showing himself to be prodigious (2.47-50) and upon reaching maturity the myth reveals his divine savior status. In the mythography of *The Infancy Gospel of James*, Mary the mother Jesus is depicted as retreating to a cave to give birth. At this point a dark cloud overshadows the cave and then a "great light" appears and the infant deity is born (19.3-5). Shortly thereafter, the deity Jesus is hidden away in a cow stable to prevent his murder by Herod who, in the myth, was seeking to kill infants and children under the age of two. In these origin myths of Jesus, he appears on the surface to be unremarkable, but hinted at is an "as yet to be realized" power contained within the infant who will, upon maturity, take up the role of savior. Others entities, however, angels, shepherds, wise men and women and midwives were able to recognize the extraordinary child.

In the iconography of the fourth-century fresco in the catacomb of the Sts Mark and Marcellian and the late third-century Catacomb of Priscilla, the infant of Jesus is depicted with his mother Mary and both are adored by the Magi.[9] As with the mythic texts, others recognize the power of this being and worship the heroic infant deity. On a fourth century sarcophagus a donkey and an ox (along with two shepherds with their crooks) gaze down on the wrapped infant deity recognizing the significance of the tiny hero in the manger.[10] As with many birth scenes, the child is announced, but in the instance of the birth of the infant deity Jesus, this announcement went beyond humans and included non-human animals again signifying the singularity of the birth event.

In the iconography of Mithras, he is typically depicted emerging from a large single rock or a pile of smaller circular rocks, and in a few representations, rocks shaped like pine cones and in another a tree,[11] while inscriptions also reference Mithras as "rock born."[12] The rock born motif in mythography of Mithras locates the deity as chthonic as do the cave, stylized cave, or grotto, which served as ritual space for adherents to the mysteries. Mythemes wherein a rock or a collection of rocks (e.g., cairns) are marked as significant flourished in the ancient Mediterranean world wherein pillars protected homes,[13] while the omphalos at Delphi marked the center of the world, along with having been served up to Kronus by Rhea in leu of Zeus. Mithras, born as a naked male human infant/child/youth from a rock, emerged clutching a dagger (or sword) in one hand and a torch (or shelfs of grain) in the other. Robert Turcan, following Reinhold Merkelbach, relates a myth of Mithras wherein the heroic deity born from a rock vanquishes the "demons of the shadows" who threaten world and as such saves the world from evil and serves as the guardian of the cosmos, ruling and protecting it.[14]

The ontological myths of Mithras and Jesus depict them as emerging from the feminine; a female human body in the instance of Jesus and an earth-bound rock or pile of rocks in terms of Mithras.[15] The link to the feminine in the context of hellenism meant a relationship with the chthonic and the terrestrial as played out in the Platonic-Aristotelian-Ptolemaic model

---

9. Thomas Mathews, *The Clash of Gods: A Reinterpretation of Early Christian Art* (Princeton, NJ: Princeton University Press, 1993), 82–3.

10. Mathews, *The Clash of Gods*, 49.

11. See Clauss, *The Roman Cult of Mithras*, 63–71, Figures 21-30 for rock birth, pile of rocks; 71, Figure 33 for tree birth; and 126, Figure 92 for pine cone shaped rocks birth.

12. Clauss, *The Roman Cult of Mithras*, 62.

13. Jennifer Larson, *Ancient Greek Cults: A Guide* (New York: Routledge, 2009), 87.

14. Robert Turcan, *The Cults of the Roman Empire* (Cambridge MA: Blackwell Publishers, 1996), 221–3.

15. Clauss, *The Roman Cult of Mithras*, 62–8.

of the cosmos,[16] a model that divided the cosmos into realms; the terrestrial and sublunar ruled by the chthonic and elemental powers along with the moon and the superlunar realm that included the realm of the stars and the heavens above Olympus.[17] In this paradigm, the female/feminine, although unstable, was a site of fecundity, life and death. The power of creation located in the chthonic/terrestrial realm was a power of fundamental origin, but this power had its limitations bound to the earth as it was. The moon as well shared in the properties of the feminine being cold and humidifying, as Ptolemy, the organizer of the new geocentric paradigm, wrote in his *Tetrabiblos*: "The day, in its heat and aptitude to action, is masculine:—the night, in its moisture and appropriation to rest is feminine" (I: VII) and "The moon principally generates moisture…" (I: IV). Classical Greek deities had come in feminine (Hera), masculine (Zeus), and transgendered (Dionysus) reflected the normative dichotomous thinking found in much of Greek thought[18], and this oppositional thinking continued to be an aspect of how the world was thought in hellenistic systems of belief and practice. Played out fully on the canopy of the sky in hellenistic systems of belief and practice, gender ideology defined the parameters of existence. Saviors were gendered male/masculine such as Mithras and Jesus, female/feminine such as Isis and Demeter, and both/neither seen in the figure of the Anatolian Agdistis, who had, like Mithras, links to Phrygia.[19]

Emerging from the feminine, the masculine signified savior deities Jesus and Mithras entered existence as vulnerable beings and not as mature beings. However, the extant written and visual myths of both deities do not emphasized their childhood other than they are precocious: Mithras was born with emblems of power clenched in his tiny fists sporting a Phrygian cap, while Jesus in the *Infancy Gospel of Thomas* evinced remarkable powers afflicting and healing, and killing and raising from the dead any who offended him. This precociousness marks these figures as beyond the human pale; beings who may look human but certainly were not. This otherness, reflected in

---

16. Wolfgang Hübner, "The Ptolemaic View of the Universe," *GRBS* 41.1 (2000): 66–7.

17. Martin, *Hellenistic Religions*; Olaf Pedersen, and Alexander Jones, *A Survey of the Almagest* with Annotation and New Commentary by Alexander Jones, 1st edn. (New York: Dordrecht, Heidelberg, London: Springer, 2011).

18. G. E. R. Lloyd, *Science, Folklore and Ideology* (Cambridge: Cambridge University Press, 1983).

19. Giovanni Casadio, "The Failing Male God: Emasculation, Death and Other Accidents in the Ancient Mediterranean World," *Numen* 50.3 (2003): 232; Jan Bremmer, however, questions Phrygia as the origin site of the Hellenistic Attis/Agdistis myth suggesting its origins were in Greece. "Attis: A Greek God in Anatolian Pessinous and Catullan Rome," *Mnemosyne* 57.5 (2004): 542.

their births and precociousness, acted as the basis of their power, sourced as it was in the metaphysical realm, the realm to which both returned via a blood sacrifice. Although their mythographies demonstrate some variance in the ontological narratives, such as both are born of the female/feminine, how that female/feminine was represented shows difference. This difference could represent variation in influences of both mythographies with the origin myth of Jesus showing some Greek mythic influence wherein the hero, for example, Herakles or Theseus, was fathered by a deity and mothered by a human female. Mithras' birth from a rock, however, suggests influence from both Greek and Anatolian mythographies with the mytheme of the fecundity of the earth/rock being well attested in both geographical locations.[20] Jan Bremmer relates a fourth-century BCE version of the birth of the Anatolian Agdistis from a rock that Zeus impregnated:

> From stones taken from the rock Agdus in Phrygia, Deucalion and Pyrrha made the Great Mother. When Zeus unsuccessfully attempted to rape her, he poured out his semen on a rock. This produced the fierce, hermaphroditic Agdistis. In order to tame him, Dionysos lured him to a spring with wine, and tied his testicles to a noose. When Agdistis awoke from his hangover and tried to get up, he unwittingly castrated himself.[21]

The discursive formations that mapped both savior figures overlapped showing a shared context, that of hellenization, which is unsurprising. But what is interesting is that both mythological formations backbench the feminine principle, and indeed both mythic narratives eschew the female/feminine once the savior deity is born: Mithras' primary interlocutors in his myths are predominantly male/masculine and it is only the moon that holds the female/feminine principle, while Jesus' primary interlocutors in his myths are predominantly male/masculine and the female/feminine evidenced in the figures of the Marys (Mt. 28.1; Mark 16.1-8; Luke 24.1-8; John 20.1). In Greco-Roman systems although the male/masculine might hold more authority than the female/feminine, for example, in the myths of Juno and Jupiter, and Hera and Zeus, there was a heterosexual pairing that linked the powers of both gendered principles ensuring a necessary balance that then sustained creation. In the hellenistic mythographies of Jesus and Mithras there is no effort toward heterosexual pairing of deities and their power: instead the female/feminine principle is subsumed (Mary and Luna) allowed it to serve the needs of the male/masculine savior deities who alone in their masculinity provide for their followers.

---

20. Jan Bremmer, "Attis: A Greek God in Anatolian Pessinous and Catullan Rome," *Mnemosyne* 57.5 (2004): 544.
21. Bremmer, "Attis," 544.

Body morphology

In their origin mythographies both deities are born vulnerable; that is they first appear as beings in need of care due to age or not having realized their potential as savior deities. The vulnerable flesh birth into the Terrestrial (and Sublunar) realm trace the birth narrative of the tragic heroix and their associated cultic practices. The male/masculine heroix lived a life of greatness although that greatness was overshadowed by anguish, pain and often times death.[22] Achilles and Herakles, born of deity and human, lived outside the norm that shaped the lives of the ordinary humans and suffered as no other, deity or human, has suffered. Formed of both flesh and spirit, the hero served as a threshold being who marked the doorways to the living, the dead and the deities. Suppliants who visited their altars/tombs sought their power in order to effect change in their lives, while poleis integrated their worship into their festival calendars, such as with Orestes at Sparta.[23] The twining of greatness and pain that shaped the mythography of the hero bound the flesh of the hero's body. The body of the hero, like those of ancestors, served the needs of the living and marked a passage way allowing communication between the environs of the living, dead, and the divine.[24]

Mithras and Jesus, like the hero of Greek and hellenistic systems of belief and practice, were born into fleshy existence and continued in the form of human males growing in stature and age. Once grown both take up the mantle of the savior and enact a ritualized drama of sacrifice that served as the core to their mythographies. As adults, Jesus and Mithras are shown as young men verging on maturity. Luke 3.23 presents Jesus as thirty years, while the mythographies of Matthew, Mark and John assume Jesus to be of a mature age. Representations of Jesus depict him as newly mature and unshaven, often with a *lituus* or augur's wand, the later used to mark the templum or space marked off in order to take the auspices or to designate

---

22. The female/feminine hero, born of human and deity, also lived turbulent and painful lives, although death was not a typical outcome, for example, Helen and Medea. Human female/feminine hero, however, tended to come to an untimely end as seen with Antigone and Clytemnestra.

23. Margaret Visser, "Worship Your Enemy: Aspects of the Cult of Heroes in Ancient Greece," *HTR* 75.4 (1982): 418–19, n. 48.

24. Dennis Hughes, "Hero Cult, Heroic Honours, Heroic Dead," in Robin Hägg, ed., *Ancient Greek Hero Cult: Proceedings of the Fifth International Seminar on Ancient Greek Cult, Organized by the Department of Classical Archaeology and Ancient History, Göteborg University, 21-23 April, 1995* (Stockholm: Paul Åströms Förlag, 1999), 170–74.

space for particular cultic use.[25] In a stone relief from the mid-4th century CE housed in the Museo Pio Cristiano, Vatican Museum, is a representation of a beardless Jesus with wand in his left hand performing a healing and filling wine jugs,[26] while in the catacomb of Callistus a beardless Jesus is shown standing with wand in his left hand and his right hand raised as Lazarus emerges from the tomb.[27] A 340 CE sarcophagus in the Lateran Musei Vaticani, Rome also depicts the beardless Jesus with wand in his left hand raising Lazerus from the dead.[28]

Mithras is depicted holding a dagger, sword, bow and arrow, torch, or grain. He is not depicted with a wand, but like the wand, his arrows have a magical quality and are able to bring water forth from a rock. The Mithraic water scene is one of supplication[29] and Mithras uses his arrow to assist the supplicant kneeling by the rock. In these scenes Mithras is also an unbearded male, one verging on maturity. Like Jesus, his vigor, that is bodily wholeness and strength, is evidenced by his youthfulness and his having just arrived on the cusp of maturity. Unbearded, Mithras, like Jesus, has an abundance of hair and even if their hair is typically depicted as shorn, it is full and rich.

Born into flesh, both Jesus and Mithras are depicted as definitively male/masculine, but the depiction of their masculinities vary in some measure. As infants, both are cherubic, but as adults their masculinity varied. Mithras' male corporality is depicted as svelte suggesting an military masculinity. Indeed, Mithras slim and trim physique and his ease of chasing down, overcoming and carrying the bull as depicted in part on a jamb of the Neuenheim complex relief[30] and the marble statue in the Pokrajinsku Muzej, Ptuj, speak to his strength. Here Mithraa is represented as holding the bull by his rear legs, while lifting and dragging the bull to the grotto where the bull is to be

---

25. Varro, *On Latin Language* VII.8-10 in Mary Beard, John North and Simon Price, eds., *Religions of Rome: Volume 2: A Sourcebook* (Cambridge: Cambridge University Press, 1998), 86; Ulrike Egelhaaf-Gaiser, "Roman Cult Sites: A Pragmatic Approach," in Jörg Rüpke, ed., *A Companion to Roman Religion* (Oxford, UK: Blackwell Pub., 2007), 205.

26. Lee M. Jefferson, *Christ the Miracle Worker in Early Christian Art* (Minneapolis, MN: Fortress Press, 2014), 185.

27. Jefferson, *Christ the Miracle Worker*, 197.

28. Mathews, *The Clash of Gods*, 55. Interestingly, although Mithras is not depicted with a wand, the Pater or Father of the Mithraic community is depicted holding the implements of Mithras. Reinhold Merkelbach, *Mithras: Ein persisch-römischer Mysterienkult* (Verglag Wiesbaden: Albus, 1998), 276.

29. Clauss, *The Roman Cult of Mithras*, 71–3.

30. Clauss, *The Roman Cult of Mithras*, 75.

sacrificed.[31] Such strength is also signified again in the famous bull sacrifice scene found in multiple mithraea. In this representation, Mithras is depicted as straddling the sacrificial bull from behind, and lifting the bull's head with his left hand he plows the dagger/sword in his right hand into the bull's shoulder. Such a scene speaks to the vigor, youthful maturity and strength of Mithras in his capacity to overcome and sacrifice the bull. Jesus' fleshy masculine physique, on the other hand, although equally svelte does not signify herculean strength: No bull is caught, carried and/or dragged and then sacrificed.

The figuring of Jesus does not reflect the masculinities of the warrior; instead the masculinities of the healer, magician and teacher mapped out the contours of his somatic representation. As healer, Jesus is represented as fully robed with *lituus* in hand, while power exudes from him as we learn in Mark 5.29-34 when power leaves him upon the touch of the hemorrhaging woman; a scene depicted in the Catacomb of Peter and Marcellinus in Rome.[32] In the mythography of Jesus as robed magician, he is represented as calming the seas and rebuking the wind with only his words (Mark 4.39), while he also exhibits knowledge of the future (Mark 10.33-34)—knowledge that overwhelmed him bringing about "sweat…like great drops of blood falling on the ground" (Luke 22.44). As teacher, Jesus is a mystical guide whose magical language and riddles provide an opaque window on the truths. Called crazy by his family (Mark 3.21) and declared demonically possessed by the scribes from Jerusalem (Mark 3.22), the savior deity spoke in a specialized speech of parables so that his message might be appreciated by those who had the capacity to understand his truth. As a healer with power over disease, death and demons his masculinity is providentially apropos, while as a magician with power over the natural and supernatural worlds—water, winds and demons—of the terrestrial and sublunar environs, his masculinity exudes the authority of the celestial environ.

The ontological representations of Mithras and Jesus share the mythemes of infantile birth into the cherubic human flesh and of an infant having emerged from the female/feminine. The female/feminine, having served as the threshold or limen, is backgrounded until such time as needed to witness the savior deities' sacrifice, Luna in the instance of Mithras and Mary(s) in the instance of Jesus. Achieving maturity as young beardless deities, the masculinities of Mithras and Jesus vary with Mithras' speaking to a warrior masculinity of strength and agility, dagger or sword in hand, and Jesus' masculinity speaking to the authority embodied by that of the

---

31. Clauss, *The Roman Cult of Mithras*, 78.
32. Jefferson, *Christ the Miracle Worker*, 188, Figure 9.

healer-magician-teacher who with *lituus* in hand overcomes disease, death and demons.

Zoomorphic associations: Jesus and Mithras

Both mythographies of Mithras and Jesus have non-human animals associated with their roles as savior deities in the ancient Greco-Roman world. Mithras, of course, was linked to the bull that he is depicted hunting and then sacrificing. But also associated with Mithras were a plethora of non-human animals, many of which represent the constellations, while one of which, the raven, also acted as messenger of Mithras. In his mythographies Jesus is linked to cows (Mt. 22.4), a dove (Luke 3.22), pigs (Mark 5.11-13) and a donkey and colt (Mt. 21.2), but all are incidental to his mythography and serve either as detail such as the donkey, colt and cows, or as non-human animals the forms of whom are used to mask or contain a supernatural being: the dove masks the holy spirit (Luke 3.22), while the pigs were used by Jesus as receptacles to hold the "unclean" demons driven out of a deranged man Jesus healed (Mark 5.13).

In Mithraic mythography non-human animals are closely related to the work of the savior and they are represented as benefiting from the sacrifice. In the tauroctany, or bull slaying, a dog and serpent are shown lapping up the blood flowing from the wound Mithras has just inflicted on the bull, while a scorpion is depicted grasping the bull's testicles. As celestial signs, the dog (Major and Minor Canis), scorpion (Scorpius) and serpent (Hydra, Serpens and Draco) constellations, along with the Raven and Taurus constellations mark the skyways and ascensions of the Mithraic mysteries.[33]

The death of the bull and the death of Jesus speak to the act of sacrifice; and in both cases a necessary sacrifice. In the mythography of Jesus John the Baptist recognizes Jesus as the sacrifice when, "The next day he saw Jesus coming toward him and declared, "Here is the Lamb of God who takes away the sin of the world!" (John 1.29), while in the Mithraic mythography those who observe the sacrifice do so with benevolence and approval. Both the sun Sol and the moon Luna gaze down on Mithras' slaughter of the bull benignly as the sacrifice bought "about not merely life on earth, but also the creation of the cosmos as a whole."[34] Once the sacrifice is complete a ritual meal, another frequent scene that decorated mithraea and its altars, with Mithras and Sol seated on the bull's hide, as depicted on the sandstone

---

33. Roger Beck, *The Religions of the Mithras Cult in the Roman Empire: Mysteries of the Unconquered Sun* (Oxford: Oxford University Press, 2007), 160, 194–7.
34. Clauss, *The Roman Cult of Mithras*, 84.

complex relief from Rückingen at the Museum Hanau, Schoß Philippsruhe Geschichtsverein in Germany[35] takes place. Joined by the flesh of the sacrificial bull Sol and Mithras gaze contentedly upon existence.

Reversing the order of the ritual meal and sacrifice as depicted in mithraea, the mythography of Jesus represents a ritual meal, Passover, taking place prior to the sacrifice of Jesus. Rather than the twelve zodiac signs or constellations who attended Mithras, are the twelve male/masculine followers, all of whom fell under the verbal spell of Jesus when he called them and they came (Mark 1.16; Mt. 4.18-22). At the feast a ritual formula was established in order to understand the sacrifice of Jesus, that was to follow (Mark 14.22-25; Mt. 26.26-29; Luke 22.19-20).

The sacrifice of the savior deity Jesus first required that he be maimed.[36] Until his sacrifice Jesus is a healthy, strong and coherent figure, much as Mithras. Unlike Mithras, but like the sacrificial bull of Mithras' mythography that was be chased down and incapacitated, Jesus must be maimed in order that the sacrifice may take place (Mark 15.16ff). Weakened and debilitated after his maiming, the savior deity Jesus was sacrificed and the acceptance of the sacrifice, its appropriateness, was signified by signs from the natural world, which went dark, while "[t]he earth shook, and the rocks were split" (Mt. 27.51) and the metaphysical world when the "curtain of the temple was torn in two, from top to bottom" (Mark 15.38; Mt. 27.51). Sacrificed, like the sacrificed Mithraic bull, the deaths of the bull of heaven and the lamb of heaven establish a link and pathway to the environ of the celestial realm.

Analysis of comparison

When compared, the ontologic, morphologic and zoomorphic significations that comprise the mythographies of Mithras and Jesus demonstrate interesting similarities. Brought into existence through the lumen of female/feminine, they appear as an infant, which marks them as corporeal rather than incorporeal, much as the origins of the hero (and ancestors) are differentiated from deities in Greek and hellenistic mythography. Baby and child heroes populated Greek and hellenistic myth, such as the murdered children of Medea.[37] Other child heroes who succumbed death were Linos, the infant torn apart by a shepherd's sheepdogs,[38] the children of Herakles[39] murdered

---

35. Clauss, *The Roman Cult of Mithras*, 111, Figure 71.
36. Casadio, "The Failing Male God," 233.
37. Corinne Ondine Pache, *Baby and Child Heroes in Ancient Greece* (Urbana and Chicago, IL: University of Illinois Press, 2004), 10.
38. Pache, *Baby and Child Heroes*, 68.
39. Pache, *Baby and Child Heroes*, 49–50.

by their father or Demophon, an infant hero killed by Demeter.[40] Demophon, in a variant myth found in the *Homeric Hymn to Demeter*,[41] however, approximates more closely the figure of the infant Jesus when he also survives the threat that would end his human existence. The infants and children who fail prey to suffering and death were subsequently immortalized in ritual practices. Mithras and Jesus are both represented as receiving worship as infants, although neither succumb to death as infants. It was a near thing, however, in the case of infant Jesus who had to be hidden from child killer Herod the Great (Mt. 2.12-15).

Mithras does not appear to have been threatened as an infant, and instead emerges from rock or stones with torch and dagger in hand and Phrygian cap on his head. Any threat or difficulties Mithras has in the visual mythography come when he is an adult and subdues the bull or struggles with Sol whom Mithras overcomes and then raises up (much like Enkidu and Gilgamesh). The Mithraic relief in the Poetovio museum depicts Mithras with a bull's haunch lifted over the head of the kneeling Sol in a gesture of domination or even aggression (Abb.137: V 1579).[42]

As adult males, the penis of both savior deities is not typically exposed in representation. This is the opposite of the representation of these savior deities when infant or child. In his ontological representation, Mithras is shown emerging bereft of all clothing but his cap, and while Jesus' penis is not visually exposed, as with Mithras, it is referenced in the mythography of Luke when is said to have been circumcised on the eight day (2.21). Their male/masculine genitalia although ontologically signified as infants are then masked beneath their garb once they are morphed into adult male humans. Masked, however, the penis must be nonetheless represented and so substitute sign-symbols were engaged: the dagger/sword serving to represent Mithras' penis now phallus, and the *lituus*, or augur's wand, served as a visible sign for the unseen penis now phallus of Jesus. As adults both savior deities evince masculine strength and vigor on the cusp of maturity, and although beardless neither are feminized: their phallic power, military in the case of Mithras and brimming with authority in the case of Jesus, although masked was signified by their weapons of sacrifice and healing.

In the mythography of both savior deities, non-human animals were put in their service acting as messengers, witnesses, supporters and sacrifices. As in much mythography, non-human animals can cross the boundary between

---

40. Pache, *Baby and Child Heroes*, 75.
41. Martin L. West, Hymn to Demeter in *Homeric Hymns. Homeric Apocrypha. Lives of Homer* (Cambridge, MA: Harvard University Press, 2003), l. 262–7 in Pache, *Baby and Child Heroes*, 75.
42. Merkelbach, *Mithras*, 373.

the physical and metaphysical worlds serving as messengers of the deities depicted by the figures of the dove and the raven linked to Jesus and Mithras respectively. As witnesses, they give evidence to the power of the savior deities, and as supporters they assist the savior deities toward accomplishing their tasks. In sacrifice, the sacrifice of the bull of heaven, or Taurus, by Mithras created and recreated the cosmos[43] with its blood nourishing the constellations and its flesh nourishing Sol and Mithras in their feast. Jesus, however, is not the sacrificer in his mythography, instead he served as sacrifice. Named a lamb by John the Baptizer, who acts as a human animal witness, Jesus was maimed and then slaughtered, much as the Mithraic bull. And like the Mithraic bull of heaven, it was the flesh and blood of Jesus, the lamb of heaven, that created and recreated the cosmos. Unlike the military Mithras who is represented as subduing and dominating existence in the form of the bull, Jesus, similar to the first human Purusha or the frost giant Ymir,[44] was dominated and subdued in order that existence may be realized.

Semiotics of the male/masculine savior deity

In the mythography of both savior deities, maleness and masculinity is central to their ontology and morphology. Both are represented as evincing a particularly masculinity, military in the case of Mithras and authoritative in the instance of the healer-magician-teacher Jesus; and although differing, both are commanding masculinities and therefore both are appropriately masculinity. And even if their penis/phallus is masked beneath their garb and while no beard relays a message of proper masculinities, the hard cold dagger in the right hand of Mithras and a rigid *lituus* or wand in the left hand of Jesus reminds the reader phallic power is present. With his dagger Mithras took life from the bull to provide life and create the cosmos, while Jesus with his *lituus* healed, raised the dead and gave up his own life to refresh the cosmos.

In this chapter I hope I have shown how in comparison a magic still dwells. Comparing the figures of Mithras and Jesus I have sought to make apparent similarities that exist in their mythographies; similarities that point to a shared context, shared imaginative conceptualizations and shared semiotic systems, all of which shaped the parameters of their mythographies. Equally, my comparison is meant to demystify and destabilize the so-called

---

43. Bruce Lincoln, *Discourse and the Construction of Society: Comparative Studies of Myth, Ritual, and Classification* (Oxford: Oxford University Press, 1989).

44. Bruce Lincoln, *Myth, Cosmos, and Society: Indo-European Themes of Creation and Destruction* (Cambridge, MA: Harvard University Press, 1986).

historical Jesus, the latter a conceit that has plagued the study of this figure. In the study of systems of belief and practice our efforts should never be to authenticate a system of belief and practice, but rather to be curious about it particularly in terms of how it relates to other systems of belief or practice, ancient and modern.

Author biography

Darlene Juschka is Associate Professor in the Department of Gender, Religion, and Critical Studies at the University of Regina. Her most recent book is *Contours of the Flesh: The Semiotics of Pain* (Equinox).

References

Beard, Mary, John North, and Simon Price, eds., *Religions of Rome: Volume 2: A Sourcebook.* Cambridge: Cambridge University Press, 1998.
Beck, Roger. *The Religions of the Mithras Cult in the Roman Empire: Mysteries of the Unconquered Sun.* Oxford: Oxford University Press, 2007. https://doi.org/10.1093/acprof:oso/9780199216130.001.0001
Betz, Hans Dieter. *The Greek Magical Papyri in Translation, Including the Demotic Spells.* 2nd edn. Chicago, IL: University of Chicago Press, 1992.
Bremmer, Jan. "Attis: A Greek God in Anatolian Pessinous and Catullan Rome." *Mnemosyne* 57.5 (2004): 534–73. https://doi.org/10.1163/1568525043057892
Burkert, Walter. *Ancient Mystery Cults.* Cambridge, MA: Harvard University Press, 1987.
Casadio, Giovanni. "The Failing Male God: Emasculation, Death and Other Accidents in the Ancient Mediterranean World." *Numen* 50.3 (2003): 231–68. https://doi.org/10.1163/156852703322192400
Clauss, Manfred. *The Roman Cult of Mithras: The God and His Mysteries.* Translated by Richard Gordon. New York: Routlege, 2001.
Coogan, Michael D. *The New Oxford Annotated Bible*: New Revised Standard Version with the Apocrypha: an Ecumenical Study Bible. Fully revised fourth ed. Oxford: Oxford University Press, 2010.
Coogan, Michael D., et al., ed., *The New Oxford Annotated Bible with the Apocrypha: New Revised Standard Version.* Oxford: Oxford University Press, 2001.
De Jong, Albert. "A New Syrian Mithraic 'Tauroctony.'" *Bulletin of the Asia Institute* 11 (1997): 53–63.
Egelhaaf-Gaiser, Ulrike. "Roman Cult Sites: A Pragmatic Approach". In *A Companion to Roman Religion,* eds., Jörg Rüpke (Blackwell Publishing, 2007), 205–21. https://doi.org/10.1002/9780470690970.ch15
Hübner, Wolfgang. "The Ptolemaic View of the Universe." *GRBS* 41.1 (2000): 59–93.
Hughes, Dennis. *Hero Cult, Heroic Honours, Heroic Dead,* 167–75 in *Ancient Greek Hero Cult: Proceedings of the Fifth International Seminar on Ancient Greek Cult, Organized by the Department of Classical Archaeology and Ancient History, Göteborg University, 21-23 April, 1995.* Edited by Robin Hägg. Stockholm: Paul Åströms Förlag, 1999.

Jefferson, Lee M. *Christ the Miracle Worker in Early Christian Art.* Minneapolis, MN: Fortress Press, 2014. https://doi.org/10.2307/j.ctt22nm6x5

Kouremenos, Theokritos. "Aristotle on Geometric Perfection in the Physical World." *Mnemosyne* 56.4 (2003): 463–79. https://doi.org/10.1163/156852503769173066

Larson, Jennifer. *Ancient Greek Cults: A Guide.* New York: Routledge, 2009.

Lincoln, Bruce. *Discourse and the Construction of Society: Comparative Studies of Myth, Ritual, and Classification.* Oxford: Oxford University Press, 1989.

Lincoln, Bruce. *Myth, Cosmos, and Society: Indo-European Themes of Creation and Destruction.* Cambridge, MA: Harvard University Press, 1986. https://doi.org/10.4159/harvard.9780674864290

Lloyd, G.E.R. *Science, Folklore and Ideology.* Cambridge: Cambridge University Press, 1983.

Martin, Luther. *Hellenistic Religions: An Introduction.* New York: Oxford University Press, 1987.

Mathews, Thomas F. *The Clash of Gods: A Reinterpretation of Early Christian Art.* Princeton, N.J: Princeton University Press, 1993.

Merkelbach, Reinhold. *Mithras: Ein persisch-römischer Mysterienkult.* Verglag Wiesbaden: Albus, 1998.

Pache, Corinne Ondine. *Baby and Child Heroes in Ancient Greece.* Urbana and Chicago: University of Illinois Press, 2004.

Pedersen, Olaf and Alexander Jones. *A Survey of the Almagest with Annotation and New Commentary by Alexander Jones*, 1st edn. New York: Dordrecht, Heidelberg, London: Springer, 2011.

Ashmand, J., Ranger, and Francis Bacon Library. *Ptolemy's Tetrabiblos: Or, Quadripartite; Being Four Books of the Influence of the Stars: Newly Translated from the Greek Paraphrase of Proclus, with a Preface, Explanatory Notes, and an Appendix Containing Extracts from the Almagest of Ptolemy and the Whole of His Centiloquy, Together with a Short Notice of Mr. Ranger's Zodiacal Planisphere and an Explanatory Plate by J. M. Ashmand.* London: W. Foulsham & Co. Ltd, 1917.

Ruden, Sarah. *The Golden Ass.* New Haven, CT: Yale University Press, 2011.

Smith, Jonathan Z. *Imagining Religion: from Babylon to Jonestown.* Chicago, IL: University of Chicago Press, 1982.

Visser, Margaret. "Worship Your Enemy: Aspects of the Cult of Heroes in Ancient Greece." *HTR* 75.4 (1982): 403–28. https://doi.org/10.1017/S0017816000031539

Walsh, David. *The Cult of Mithras in Late Antiquity: Development, Decline and Demise Ca. A.D. 270-430.* 2019. Late Antique Archaeology. Supplementary Ser. v. 2. Leiden; Boston: Brill. https://doi.org/10.1163/9789004383067

West, Martin L. *Hymn to Demeter. Homeric Hymns. Homeric Apocrypha. Lives of Homer.* Cambridge, MA: Harvard University Press, 2003.

Chapter Six

From Liturgy to Polemic and Back:
Social Identity Issues in the Use of Two Psalms[1]

Steven Muir

> The whole life of the community was conditioned by [its] interpretation of Scripture. It has been said that the history of doctrine is the history of exegesis, in that the whole development of ... doctrine is based on the interpretation of a certain number of passages in Scripture *in the light of particular needs...*[2]

It is a pleasure to contribute to this Festschrift honoring my colleague and friend, Willi. I have known Willi for more than twenty years: first through our mutual membership and work in projects of the Canadian Society of Biblical Studies, and latterly through my service on the examination committee for many of his students at the University of Alberta. I am always impressed by Willi's keen attention to methodological and theoretical issues and lively interest in many aspects of Christian origins and religious communities. He has passed on these interests to his students, and truly models the role of an engaged scholar-teacher. As a friend, I also know and appreciate his dry humor and thoughtful, kind manner.

My contribution to this volume matches some of Willi's research interests. In his 1995 monograph *Feasting and Social Rhetoric in Luke 14*, Willi's analysis is helpfully informed by social science theory (in particular, honor-shame in Mediterranean cultures). In this essay, I use and adapt Social Identity theory to track and explain changes in the reception history of two Psalms. In his chapter in his 2005 edited volume *Rhetoric and Reality in Early Christianities*, Willi argues convincingly that the social context of a text must be understood if one is to correctly assess its message and persuasive power to a particular audience. I prove this position, by demonstrating how the same text (set of words) can be given very different meanings,

---

1. A version of this article was presented to the 2014 meeting of The Context Group, a team of scholars that specializes in combining historical exegesis of the Bible and religious communities with theories and methodologies from the social sciences.

2. Manilo Simonetti, *Interpretation in the Early Church: An Historical Introduction to Patristic Exegesis*, trans. by J. A. Hughes (Edinburgh: T&T Clark, 1994), 1, emphasis mine.

depending upon the various social-cultural contexts in which the text was encountered and used.

What follows is a reception history analysis of elements in Psalms 82 and 110 through various phases: pre-Exilic and post-Exilic Israelite, Rabbinic, New Testament, and later Christian, including the Orthodox Tradition. The choice of Orthodox Christianity in my analysis is deliberate. I wanted to include a later Christian community in which the Psalms had a lively, liturgical usage—as they presumably once had in ancient Israel. The rather creative interpretations of these Psalms within Orthodox Christianity demonstrate the adage *Lex orandi, lex credendi* (Latin: "the law of what is prayed [is] the law of what is believed"). For Orthodox Christianity, I assume that the relevant liturgical material is not readily available to many readers. I have included that material in Appendix 1.

I focus on the received text of the Psalms which is post-Exilic, and offer creative and I hope informed speculation on their pre-Exilic contours. I use Social Identity Theory (SIT) in an explanatory way, to give insight into social causes which likely were the foundation for the rich array of interpretations of the same two texts by different groups.

Social Identity Theory

SIT is a branch of social psychology which proposes that a significant component of a person's identity comes from social settings.

> … social identity will be understood as that *part* of an individual's self-concept which derives from his knowledge of his membership of a social group (or groups) together with the value and emotional significance attached to that membership.[3]

For a person to derive positive value or emotional significance from their group, it should compare favorably with other groups.[4] Brown states,

> SIT is essentially a theory of group differentiation: how group members can make their ingroup(s) distinctive from, and wherever possible, better than outgroups. Self-evidently, therefore, groups which discover themselves to be similar to each other should be especially motivated to show intergroup differentiation.[5]

---

3. Henri Tajfel, "Social Categorization, Social Identity and Social Comparison," in *Differentiation between Social Groups: Studies in the Social Psychology of Intergroup Relations,* ed. Henri Tajfel (London: Academic Press, 1978), 61–76, here 63.

4. Rupert Brown, "Social Identity Theory: Past Achievements, Current Problems and Future Challenges," in *Euro. J. Soc. Psychol.* 30 (2000): 745–78, here 746–7.

5. Brown, "Social Identity Theory," 757. See also Rupert Brown, "The Role of Similarity in Intergroup Relations," 603–23 in *The Social Dimension: European*

Similarity can be attitudinal (e.g., values and ideologies) or relating to status (e.g., some dimension of group value or prestige).[6] Here, I am examining two cases of attitudinal similarity—how various groups use the same text and yet differentiate themselves by their interpretations of the text. Brown notes that among the variables influencing intergroup differentiation,

> ... the situation should permit evaluative intergroup comparisons, the outgroup must be sufficiently comparable (e.g., similar or proximal) and that pressures for distinctiveness should increase with comparability.[7]

Thus, we see a double-edged sword: for intergroup comparisons to be meaningful, the groups must have some point or points of similarity—yet for positive estimations to occur, these similarities must be downplayed or re-conceptualized in favor of the ingroup. According to SIT, group members tend to exaggerate differences between their group and other groups to create an aura of distinctiveness, superiority and to establish a social boundary between groups. Under the category of "ethnocentrism," the American sociologist William Graham Sumner noted as early as 1906:

> Each group nourishes its own pride and vanity, boasts itself superior, exalts its own divinities, and looks with contempt on outsiders. Each group thinks its own folkways the only right ones, and if it observes that other groups have other folkways, these excite its scorn.[8]

The next point to consider is that ideas and beliefs may serve both as points of comparison and social boundary markers. Bar-Tal defines group beliefs as convictions that group members (a) are aware that they share and (b) consider as defining their "groupness. ... the contents of group beliefs typically pertain to group identity, myths, goals, values, ideology, norms, tradition, or history."[9] I modify Bar-Tal's list by using the phrase "symbol set" (SS) as a generic descriptor for myths, stories, sacred texts, creedal statements or images.

There can be advantages for a group in appropriating the SS of another group. This SS may be well-developed and have the prestige of antiquity and tradition.[10] It can be the repository of years of thought and practice. In

---

Developments in Social Psychology, vol. 2, ed. Henri Tajfel (Cambridge: University Press, 1984): 603–23, here 608–9.
  6. Brown, "The Role of Similarity," 603.
  7. Brown, "Social Identity Theory," 747.
  8. William Graham Sumner, *Folkways: A Study of the Sociological Importance of Usages, Manners, Customs, Mores and Morals* (New York: Mentor Books, 1960), 28.
  9. Daniel Bar-Tal, *Group Beliefs: A Conception for Analyzing Group Structure, Processes, and Behavior* (New York: Springer-Verlag, 1990), 36.
  10. A striking example is the adoption of the *fasces* symbol from ancient Rome by the totalitarian governments of Germany and Italy during the 1930s and 1940s.

ancient societies which valorize tradition and are suspicious of innovation, borrowing a SS lets a new group piggy-back on a well-developed status identifier. However, when two distinct groups have a common SS, there may be a perception of unstable social boundaries between groups. Members could ask, "since we are alike in this way, why are we separate?" Are the boundaries legitimate? Are they stable?

To deal with this uncertainty, a nuanced form of social differentiation comes into play. Where there is a shared SS, members of each group may develop distinctive interpretations and understandings of it. It will be these interpretations (rather than the SS itself) which is distinctive to the group. SIT calls these positive distinctiveness strategies. Group members will apply positive descriptors to their understanding and interpretation of the SS: e.g., progressive, elite, true, enlightened, orthodox or correct. Group members use negative descriptors for the understanding of outgroups: e.g., superficial, unenlightened, old-fashioned, heretical.[11] In textual interpretation, debates over literal vs. allegorical, historical vs. typological interpretation reveal this process at work. The English sociologist Roy Wallis follows a similar line of thought. He argues that sects and subgroups often are characterized by what he calls "epistemological authoritarianism." According to Wallis, these groups,

> …lay a claim to possess unique and privileged access to the truth or salvation. Their committed adherents typically regard all those outside the confines of the collectivity as 'in error'.[12]

By their nature, Psalms are focal points of social identity issues. Hymns and group prayers are a collective activity: in their liturgical performance and through their words they express and help to enact group identity. The worshipping group is a bounded group, in both the physical worship setting and the conceptual space of the community. Those not participating in the worship are the outgroup. The worshipping group is aware of them and denounces them as it distances itself from them. On this issue, Holladay makes an astute observation about the recurring motif of "us vs. them" throughout the Psalms.[13] Many Psalms speak of the God of Israel's relationship to a protagonist, be that the king (representative of the people),

---

11. An example of this line of thought is in Paul's comment in 2 Corinthians 3.12-16, where he contrasts the "veiled" perception by Israelites of Moses and Torah with the "unveiled" understanding among Christ-followers.

12. Roy Wallis, *The Road to Total Freedom: A Sociological Analysis of Scientology* (New York: Columbia Press, 1977), 17.

13. William L. Holladay, *The Psalms through Three Thousand Years* (Minneapolis, MN: Fortress, 1993), 48–9.

the group, or an individual voice from the ingroup. The protagonist feels oppressed, embattled, and threatened. The protagonist appeals to God for help against these foes or foresees the defeat of those foes due to God's intervention. Two points emerge in my analysis.

First, a perception of unity gives group members a sense of stability and security. The group will use texts which are part of the group's tradition. Use of these texts affirms continuity with the group's past (or past generations of the group). The fact that texts from the past are meaningful to a group of a later period gives a sense of timelessness and masks the contingent, constructed nature of the current group. I suggest that when we see a very creative, symbolic or imaginative new interpretation (e.g., in contradiction to the plain meaning of the text) we might suspect a profound need in a group to feel continuity with its past—even at the expense of common-sense interpretation or ignoring substantial issues of change between then and now. We will see radical shifts in interpretation in the reception history of Psalms 82 and 110.

Second, groups similar to the group but which are not part of the group threaten the group. The group will want to feel superior to its rivals. By appropriating elements from its cultural tradition and giving them a unique interpretation, the group demonstrates its status vis-à-vis others. Texts which speak of the superiority of the group (and/or the group's representative or god) over other groups (or the representatives or gods of those groups) will be prized and rehearsed in public settings. Inter-group rivalry is a timeless phenomenon—the particular groups may vary but the issue persists. Thus, texts which speak to the inter-group rivalry issue have the capacity to meet the needs of many generations—particularly when we allow for the creative interpretation of the traditional texts.

Psalm 82

Pre-exilic outlines

Form criticism identifies several Ancient Near East (ANE) motifs which appear to have contributed to Psalm 82: an assembly of gods with a presiding divine figure, the assigning of various territories and peoples to each god, and the ascension to supremacy of one god in the pantheon.[14] A credible pre-Exilic sketch of what emerges in finished form as Psalm 82 is as follows:

---

14. Frank-Lothar Hossfeld and Erich Zenger, *Psalms 2: A Commentary on Psalms 51-100* trans. Linda M. Maloney (Minneapolis, MN: Fortress, 2005), 329. William F. Albright, *Yahweh and the Gods of Canaan: A Historical Analysis of Two Contrasting Faiths* (Garden City, NY: Doubleday, 1968), 190–92 discusses the Divine Council motif

> *The god of Israel appears in an assembly of gods, understood as being the gods of other nations or regions. He critiques or judges them, strips them of power or immortality, and thereby establishes his supremacy.*[15]

A strong element here is the ascension of the God of Israel to power, whether this was understood as being a new development or a re-assertion of power.[16] This episode would be attractive to pre-Exilic Israelites. It portrays their god as powerful enough to judge or dominate other gods. Arguably, the psalm in its rudimentary form could even be pre-monarchic, reflecting struggles of Israelites against their Canaanite neighbors.[17]

Since there is a connection between a god and the territory/people under his administration, the account of the ascension of the God of Israel over other gods is also an implied portrait of Israel as a nation dominating or superior to its neighbors. The element of the rivalry between nations, personified by their gods, has been discussed by scholars.[18]

Post-exilic features

The theme of judgment is a recurring element in the Psalm we see. Variations on the Hebrew word *shâphat* ("judge, pronounce sentence, govern") occur four times in this short psalm (1c, 2a, 3a, 8a). The God of Israel calls the other gods to judgment. They have not judged well; they should judge better. The psalm closes with a plea for the God of Israel to step in and judge the world fairly. Thus, the problematic judgment of the other gods becomes

---

in various Canaanite and Ugaritic texts. Also see James M. Trotter, "Death of the *Elohim* in Psalm 82," *JBL* 131.2 (2012): 221–39, here 222. Mitchell Dahood, *Psalms II, 51-100* (Garden City, NY: Doubleday, 1968), 269 classes Ps 82 very early (pre-monarchic) based on ANE influence. Sigmund Mowinckel, *The Psalms in Israel's Worship*, trans. D. R. Ap-Thomas, (Nashville, TN: Abingdon Press, 1962), vol 2: 132 also identifies a New Year festival, at which the destiny of the coming year was determined by the council of gods. See also the interesting discussions in Min Suc Kee, "The Heavenly Council and its Type-scene," *JSOT* 31.3 (2007): 259–73 and Dragoslava Santrac, "God and 'Gods'—Poetic Ambiguity and Wordplay: A Proposal towards a Better Understanding of Ps 82," *JATS* 27.1 (2016): 37–54.

15. Psalm 58 is similar in theme. See Mowinckel, *The Psalms*, 1.208; Trotter, "Death," 231; Dahood, *Psalms II*, 268–71.

16. Mowinckel, *The Psalms*, 1.150-51 and 2.64, 132 speculates that there was a Festival of Divine Enthronement in pre-Exilic Israel, and that this psalm was used liturgically at that festival. This hypothesis is based on parallels in ANE context. However, this element of Mowinckel's form critical work has been debated by scholars, who do not see strong evidence for such a festival in Israel.

17. So, Holladay, *The Psalms*, 22.

18. Hans-Joachim Kraus, *Psalms 60-150: A Commentary*, trans. Hilton C. Oswald, (Minneapolis, MN: Augsburg, 1989),155–8; cf. Hossfield and Zegner, *Psalms 2*, 328–37.

the basis for the judgment against them, the reason for their downfall and the catalyst for the ascension of the God of Israel.[19]

The location and status of the God of Israel in the divine assembly is deliberately left ambiguous in the text.[20] The God of Israel is not called YHWH, but rather *elohim*.[21] Thus Israel's *elohim* appears in the Council of *El* and judges the other *elohim*. This sort of nomenclature is retained in the Septuagint.[22] The issue of the location of the God of Israel (presiding/judging *over* the assembly vs. appearing *in the midst* of the assembly as an accuser) had been debated by scholars.[23] I estimate that the initial ambiguity of the scene is a literary technique to make the ascension to power of Israel's God more dramatic. The ability to pronounce judgment (or a death sentence) reveals that the *elohim* of Israel has superiority over other *elohim*.

The theme of sonship is evident. At this point, the most credible interpretation is that the "sons of the Most High" in verse 6 is a poetic parallel phrase to accompany "gods". However, this feature offers a foundation for later interpretations which consider the text to be speaking of God's adoption of humans to some sort of elevated status, as "sons."[24]

I estimate that the most likely candidate for any addition/emendation to the basic model from the pre-Exilic phase is the development of the social justice critique, so often seen in the later literary prophets (e.g., Amos, Isaiah, and Ezekiel). While this could have been present in some form in pre-Exilic material, it is a somewhat unusual basis for critique of ANE gods, since it is not clear that there were ever expectations of social justice from them in their involvement in earthly affairs.[25] However, social justice clearly is consistent with what was established in the Hebrew Scriptures (HS) canonical segment The Prophets (*Nevi'im*), and here may reflect some adjustment to fit that theme. Indeed, we might imagine that a portrait of the God of Israel acting as a social critic would have greatly appealed to those writing in the literary-prophetic vein.

---

19. As we will see, the judgment theme here will lead to further interpretations, namely that human judges are being critiqued.

20. Hossfield and Zegner, *Psalms 2*, 329 ns.3, 333, 335.

21. Unlike the otherwise similar Psalm 58, which uses both *Elohim* and YHWH in verse 6, in parallel structure. Trotter, "Death", 222–4.

22. *Ho theos en synagōēi theōn... en mesō theous.* God appears among them and judges the gods. The assembly (synagogue) aspect in Greek here is interesting and would have had a special resonance with Judeans of the Diaspora.

23. See Trotter, "Death", 225–8.

24. On the issue of sonship/adoption, see discussion below.

25. Trotter, "Death", 231–2.

Considering the Exile experience, Psalm 82 may have undergone some changes.[26] Israel had faced heightened contact with other nations. The supremacy of their god likely was questioned. The explanation of the literary prophets was that Israel failed in its responsibility for social justice (and covenantal monotheism) and was judged by God. Bringing in or heightening the theme of social justice here allows for a blurring in understanding of exactly who is being critiqued—supernatural gods, rulers acting on behalf of those gods, or a combination of the two.[27]

Rabbinic treatment

Here we see the above blurring taken a step further. It appears that a growing discomfort with polytheistic perspectives of the past leads to a rather bold (or forced) interpretation—that the beings being critiqued were in fact humans. Related to this move, a shift takes place in the social location of the critique, from outside (inter-community) to inside the community (intra-community). Again, we might suspect the influence of The Prophets and the exilic and post-exilic experiences. Several streams of Rabbinic interpretation emerged.[28] I focus on two.

One stream identified the beings called "gods" as judges or rulers of Israel. We see this in Midrashim and Targum literature.[29] This is in some ways an understandable interpretation: there is a similar critique applied to human judges/rulers of Israel in Isaiah 3.13-15 and Ezekiel 28.1-10. The Rabbinic desire to see all of scripture as a continuum and/or the use of certain exegetical methods[30] probably allowed the rabbis to interpret Psalm 82 in light of or in conversation with The Prophets. Since literature of the ANE

---

26. Hossfield and Zegner, *Psalms 2*, 335.
27. Trotter, "Death", 230, Hossfield and Zegner, *Psalms 2*, 331.
28. Jerome H. Neyrey, "I said: You are Gods": Psalm 82:6 and John 10," *JBL* 108.4 (1989): 63–4. Neyrey 647 notes four: angels, Melchizedek, judges, Israel at Sinai. Also see George R. Beasley-Murray, *John: Word Biblical Commentary* (Waco, TX: Word Books, 1987): 175–7. The Melchizedek line of interpretation of Psalm 82 is developed in the DSS document 11QMelchizedek, noted in Carl Mosser, "The Earliest Patristic Interpretations of Psalm 82, Jewish Antecedents, and the Origin of Christian Deification," *JTS* NS 56.1 (2005): 30–74, here 60–62.
29. Trotter, "Death," 228; cf. James S. Ackerman, "The Rabbinic Interpretation of Psalm 82 and the Gospel of John," *HTR* 59.2 (1966): 186–91, here 186 n. 1; Raymond Brown, *Gospel According to John* (Garden City, NY: Doubleday, 1966-70): 409–10.
30. For example, *gezerah shavah*—in which issues which apply to one passage apply to other passages where the same words are used (here, "judge"). Noted in Mosser, "Earliest Patristic," 46.

often portrays human rulers as having divine or semi-divine status, this sort of interpretation may have had some validity.[31]

As a result of acting on behalf of God regarding social justice, the human administrators became god-like—in a functional or derivative way. In their failure to bring justice, Israel's God appears and judges the judges. Rabbinic discomfort over polytheism leads to a convoluted interpretation, one which does damage to the plain sense of the text.[32] The beings in question are stripped of immortality ("you will die like any [human] prince"), so the statement only makes sense if those beings originally were immortal (that is, fully divine rather than 'functionally' god-like human beings). Nonetheless, the interpretation held in some Rabbinic circles.

Another Rabbinic interpretation was that those who were called "gods" were the Israelites as a collective at Mount Sinai (Exodus 19ff).[33] Again, their god-like status is understood as being derivative and coming from God. To grant them immunity from contact with the supreme holiness of Torah, God gave them immortality. Perhaps we see a return to Eden, albeit a temporary one. This special condition was lost in what has been termed a "Second Fall" narrative—namely the Golden Calf incident (Exodus 32). According to the rabbis, God rescinded his gift of immortality to punish this apostasy. The advantage to this interpretation is that it takes seriously the immortality motif and attempts to work it into the interpretation. The disadvantage is that it is a rather rococo elaboration on the story in Exodus. Ackerman calls this interpretation an act of "myth-creating."[34]

New Testament treatment

Jesus' allusion to Psalm 82 arises in an episode in the Gospel of John where Jesus is accused of blasphemy, of "making" himself God or claiming to be God. Jesus' answer is somewhat short (unusual for John) and cryptic (usual for John). Jesus' reference to the Psalms as "the law" (*nomos*) presents a view (of John's community certainly, and likely in first-century Judaism) that The Writings were approaching canonical status as "scripture" (*graphē*, "writings" however that term was understood). Therefore, the authority of the text is itself a component of Jesus' argument. A straight-forward reading

---

31. Trotter, "Death," 233.
32. Hossfield and Zegner, *Psalms 2*, 330.
33. See Neyrey, "You are Gods," 648–9; Urban C. Von Wahlde, *Gospel and Letters of John*, vol. 2 (Grand Rapids, MI: Wm B. Eerdmans, 2010F), 474; Brown, *Gospel*, 410–11.
34. Ackerman, "Rabbinic," 186 n. 1, see also Neyrey, "You are Gods," 654–9. Neyrey, "You are Gods," 647 speaks of "ingenious interpretation and exegetical principles."

of the argument is that Jesus is arguing that a precedent exists for calling humans "gods," that this identification was based on divine initiative, and that he (Jesus) is consistent with the will of God which had established that precedent. The Gospel of John appears to incorporate the view that the beings called "gods" by God was the community at Sinai which received the law (v. 35), though it is possible to read the "judges administering the law" aspect into the text.

There is a situation of conflict in and behind the text. The Johannine community sees itself as distinct from its Judean neighbors, so whether this is an internal conflict or an external one is a matter of interpretation. Regardless, a polemical use of this Psalm is evident.

Later Christian

Psalm 82:6 becomes one of the principal proof-texts used in support of a theological principle in Orthodox Christianity, namely the process of becoming god-like through the grace of God. The doctrine of *theosis* or deification is a central tenet of Orthodox Christianity. This doctrine very much goes to the heart of Orthodox group identity, and it has proved controversial (at least to some Protestant audiences). At times, the fact that Jesus said something along these lines appears sufficient to establish it within Orthodox theology. For example, in Timothy Ware's erudite and accessible *The Orthodox Church* (which I use as the textbook for my Greek Orthodox class), the following striking statement is made:

> 'In My kingdom, said Christ, I shall be God with you as gods.' Such, according to the teaching of the Orthodox Church, is the final goal at which every Christian must aim: to become god, to attain theosis, 'deification' or 'divinization.' For Orthodoxy our salvation and our redemption mean our deification.[35]

Here, Ware cites the Canon for Matins of Holy Thursday, Ode 4, Troparion 3.[36] As a Biblical scholar, I find it interesting that Ware's principal defense for a key theological doctrine is a liturgical proclamation rather than scripture, and that the liturgy differs substantially from scripture.[37]

The underlying issue is explained by Ware in the section on "Sources of Orthodox Faith."[38] Ware ranks the sources as follows: the Bible, The Creed

---

35. Timothy Ware, *The Orthodox Church* (London: Penguin, 1991), 231.
36. Psalm 82 is also found in the Communion Hymn for Holy Wednesday (The Liturgy of Presanctified Gifts). See Appendix 1.
37. Compare the liturgical "In My kingdom, said Christ, I shall be God with you as gods," with either Psalm 82.6 or John 10.34.
38. Ware, *Orthodox*, 204–5.

(and other documents of the Seven Ecumenical Councils), (documents of) Later Councils, (writings of) The Fathers, The Liturgy, Canon Law, and (the visual aspects, use and concepts in) Icons. It is the use of the Liturgy to which I want to draw attention. Many liturgical features are not expressly stated in definitive Ecumenical Councils; rather, they arose in popular use. Notwithstanding, through use in worship these features have, in an organic manner, become established not only in practice but as teaching points in Orthodoxy. Ware notes, "*Lex orandi lex credendi*: our faith is expressed in prayer," and then says:

> Nor is it merely the words of the services which are a part of Tradition; the various gestures and actions... all have a special meaning, and all express in symbolical or dramatic form the truths of the faith.[39]

A brief explanation of *theosis* in Orthodox theology is in order. According to St. Gregory Palamas, God is entirely transcendent, in his essence unknowable. However, Palamas asserts that God may be known or experienced in his "energies" or transmissions. The process of *theosis*[40] is thought to involve the grace of God in awakening the divine potential (i.e., image of God) within humanity. Conceptually, this process is a sort of return to Eden. Thus, *theosis* involves a second-order divinization. It is not thought that humanity can become god-like in essence, only in energy. However, paradoxically Orthodox theologians also assert that while God's energies are distinct from his essence, the energies nonetheless are themselves fully divine and that the God known through his essences is in fact, God in his full divinity.

Orthodox theology is built upon Greek Patristic texts. Mosser's essay on early Patristic exegesis of Psalm 82 is excellent and detailed and gives insight into the origins of the doctrine of *theosis*. Mosser argues that the use of Psalm 82 in support Orthodox doctrine of *theosis* is not (as some have characterized it), "... a bald proof-text that lacks warrant even by the usual canons of ancient exegesis"[41] but in fact has a logical (albeit tendentious) early Patristic pedigree which bears some relation to second-Temple views. I summarize a few of Mosser's points here, ones of relevance to my paper. Three early Patristic writers are examined: Justin Martyr (*Dialogue with Trypho*), Irenaeus (principally *Adversus haeresus*) and Clement of Alexandria (*Protrepticus* and *Paedogogus*). All three writers make a similar exegetical move to that which we saw in Rabbinic Judaism, namely to identify the "gods" and "sons of the Most High" of Psalm 82 as being the believing community. Here, Christians rather than the Israelites at Sinai are in view.

---

39. Ware, *Orthodox*, 205.
40. Early Patristic writers called it *theopoiēsis*, making god-like.
41. Mosser, "Earliest Patristic," 33.

Whereas Justin Martyr sees the issue of sonship along Johannine/begotten lines, Irenaeus and Clement draw upon Paul's concept of adoption for their understanding of sonship. But an interesting common thread is the return to Eden motif we saw in Rabbinic understanding. Here it is developed in Christological ways. Christ, the new Adam, re-establishes the purity and immortality of the original state of humanity. Those in relation to him participate in this process. Finally, it is interesting that Justin and Irenaeus develop their exegesis in light of conflict and controversy with inter-group and intra-group opponents (for Justin, Judeans and for Irenaeus the followers of Valentinus). Justin and Irenaeus are citing a common text and using it in different ways from their opponents.

The liturgical use of Psalm 82 in the Orthodox tradition has interesting aspects.[42] The Psalm is quoted in services for Passion Week (Holy Wednesday and Holy Thursday). The theme of judgment in the text fits well with the Lenten mood. At first, the statement of the falling gods seems odd in this seasonal setting. I suggest that it fits well with the anticipated triumphal note of Easter—victory of Christ over Satan and the forces of evil. Thus, we see a radical and yet successful adaptation of an old theme from the Israelite tradition—the victory of God over those supernatural forces opposed to him.

Psalm 110

Pre-exilic outlines

There is near universal consensus among HS scholars that Psalm 110 is best understood as a psalm celebrating the kingship of a king of Israel.[43] Similar texts are well attested in ANE literature.[44] While there is debate as to whether the psalm may be linked to a particular festival or festivals (e.g., coronation/enthronement oracle, New Year festival, etc.), the political imagery is evident. It may an act of romanticism to identify this Psalm as one said at the coronation of King David (assuming the historicity of such a figure), yet we are surely not amiss to suppose a Psalm of this type was said

---

42. See Appendix 1.
43. See the surveys of Herbert W. Bateman, "Psalm 110:1 and the New Testament," *BibSac* 149 (October 1992): 438–53; Barry C. Davis, "Is Psalm 110 a Messianic Psalm?" *BibSac* 157 (2000): 160–73; Kraus, *Psalms 60-150*, 343.
44. Established in form-critical analysis by Hermann Gunkel, *The Psalms: A Form-Critical Introduction*, trans. Thomas M. Horner (Philadelphia, PA: Fortress Press, 1967), 24; cf. Mowinckel, *Psalms*, 2.132; 2.47, 54, 63–4. Also W. R. G. Loader, "Christ at the Right Hand—Ps. CX.1 in the New Testament," *NTS* 24 (1978): 199–217, here 199, Dahood, *Psalms II*, 112–20. Perceptive analysis of this issue is offered by Helen Genevieve Jefferson, "Is Psalm 110 Canaanite?", *JBL* 73.3 (1954): 152–6.

to subsequent kings of the united kingdom or of Judah to affirm their divine mandate and their Davidic connection. I propose that a credible sketch of the Psalm in its pre-Exilic stage is as follows.

An official acting as liturgical celebrant and prophet announces that YHWH has installed the king "at YHWH's right hand." YHWH promises to defeat the enemies of the king.

The phrase "at his right hand" is to be understood here not in terms of location (i.e., heaven) but as a metaphor for divine support in granting the human king power and authority in the earthly realm.[45] There likely is a motif of adoption understood at this point.[46] Thus, the king is announced as having been granted divine mandate for his rule and access to divine power for his actions.[47] Because of God's support, the king will have superiority over his (the king's) rivals (i.e., the kings of other nations).[48]

If there was some sort of attribution to David at this point of the psalm's life, it would serve to strengthen the claim to political authority of subsequent kings, who would inherit the mantle of authority given to that mythic/historical and idealized king. For that reason, we may assume a location in Jerusalem, whether that is part of the united kingdom or of Judah. Many HS scholars agree that that primary connotation of the phrase "my lord" at this point would have been a human, contemporary king rather than a future messiah figure.[49]

Post-exilic features

Here we likely see addition of the superscription "to David" as the collection is assembled and structured into canon. We get indication of the community view that the text was linked to David in some fashion. The absence of a viable human king in the early post-Exilic community gives this text both a nostalgic air and a hopeful (perhaps proto-eschatological) one, laying the groundwork for later messianic speculation. Eventually, Hasmonean rulers appear, yet they cannot claim Davidic background. One wonders if such a psalm would have been part of their coronation ceremony. Perhaps

---

45. Mowinckel, *The Psalms*, 2.54–5, Kraus, *Psalms 60-150*, 348, Dahood, *Psalms III*, 114.
46. Kraus, *Psalms*, 1.73, 2.350. The wording of the Hebrew text, "YHWH said to my lord (*adonai*)" makes clear the qualitative difference between the two figures and thus necessitates an adoption/elevation process (however that would be understood).
47. So, Loader, "Christ," 199, Brown, *Gospel*, 442–3, Kraus, *Psalms* 1.67; 2.346.
48. This victory is announced in verses 5-6, which prophetically announce the crushing defeat of those kings.
49. For example, Mowinckel, *The Psalms*, 2.48–9.

a Hasmonean interest in establishing the legitimacy of their rule as priest-kings led to the development (or emphasis) of the Melchizedek interpretation of verse 4.[50] The Herodian line of rulers had even less claim to Davidic legitimacy. If the psalm was used in their context, its Davidic aspect would have been downplayed.

The obscurity of phrases in the middle section of the Psalm (verses 3-6, see Appendix 1) has led to considerable debate among scholars as to the meaning of the text. That obscurity gives flexibility in translation and application by various groups.

At some point, we likely see a transition in practice and the received text. The practice of substituting the divine name YHWH with *Adonai* is eventually reflected in the Septuagint's rendition of the phrase *ho kyrios… kyriō mou*. While those in the Judaic context understood the first agent to be God/YHWH, a change has happened with respect to the second agent. In the Hebrew text, clearly there is a substantial difference between the two figures, divine vs. human. Now in liturgical practice and in the Greek text, the same word "Lord" (*kyrios*) suggests some sort of similarity between the two figures—one of shared lordship, authority, and possibly nature.

Rabbinic treatment

The attribution to David aspect has now taken on a life of its own. Perhaps to parallel the Moses/Pentateuch segment of HS, the Davidic authorship of all the Psalms emerges as a strong conviction among the rabbis.[51] The implications of that view for Psalm 110 lead to a somewhat convoluted situation: a Psalm formerly said to David now is seen as a Psalm said by David. The referent of "my lord" changes from a human king another figure—probably some sort of messiah. Entailed in this is the issue of rank and status. The person speaking to "my lord" is signaling a lower social status with respect to the referent (an oracular priest to a king, for example). But how can David speak of someone other than YHWH who is his (David's)

---

50. David M. Hay, *Glory at the Right Hand: Psalm 110 in Early Christianity* (Nashville, TN: Abingdon, 1973), 24. The Hebrew text here is difficult and obscure. See Holladay, *Psalms*, 23–4. The phrase has been translated (a) as "You are a priest forever according to the order of Melchizedek" or (b) … "…forever, a rightful king by my edict." DSS texts such as 11QMelchizedek give evidence of the first trajectory, as does the Epistle to the Hebrews. Due to the complexity of the Melchizedek issue generally, its difficulty in the HS text of Ps 110, and constraints of space, I refrain from extensive analysis of it here.

51. Not restricted to the ancient world. Brown, *Gospel*, 444–5 optimistically asserts the issue, as part of a Christian-typological apologetic.

lord? A related issue is how a messianic figure might have been understood. The usual designation for a messiah would be "son of David"—and sonship does not imply superiority, but rather a lesser status.[52] Thus, the logic of David calling a future messiah "his lord" implies a figure greater than David—which will be precisely the point of the Synoptic writers.

New Testament treatment

A popular motif in the literature of the Jesus movement is the assertion that the Messiah would be a figure greater than David. In the parallel versions in the Synoptics, Psalm 110 is cited on this point.[53] We also find Psalm 110 several times in Acts,[54] a bit in Paul (Romans) and echoes of it throughout Hebrews.[55] Its multiplicity of locations indicates a widespread idea in early Christianity. I will confine my comments here to the Synoptics.

As recounted in Mark 12, the saying focuses on the superiority of the Messiah to David. This assertion fits well with Mark's Christology, in which the concept of messiah is stripped of political implications and filled with the portrait of a figure of power (Son of God) and then of a suffering/victorious figure (Son of Man). The element of controversy is downplayed in Mark—"the crowd heard him gladly." Matthew 22 retains the teaching point but sharpens the controversy and debate aspect. In Matthew, Jesus provocatively poses the question, leads his opponents into a logical trap, refutes their logic, and silences them. We may assume that Matthew's audience delighted in this scenario. Both Mark and Matthew demonstrate a conviction that David (in composing the Psalms) was inspired by the Spirit of God—and by extension here was prophetically describing the future Messiah. Luke 20 does not develop the controversy. For him, the teaching point of the superiority of the Messiah over David is sufficient. Interestingly, despite Luke's interest in the activity of the Holy Spirit, he does not mention David's inspiration. Instead, Luke gives us an early attestation to the view that the Book of Psalms was part of the final segment of the HS.[56]

---

52. So, the logic of "The son is not greater than the father," John 14.28.
53. Matthew 22.41-46; Mark 12.35-37; Luke 20.41-44.
54. Here, see the insightful analysis of Eva Mroczek, "'David Did not Ascend into the Heavens' (Acts 2.34): Early Jewish Ascent Traditions and the Myth of Exegesis in the New Testament," *J. Anc. Jud.* 3 (2015): 219–52.
55. Loader, "Christ," 203–5.
56. We have seen a similar understanding of the Psalms as authoritative scripture in Gospel of John, discussed above.

Later Christian treatment

As with Psalm 82, the use of Psalm 110 in Orthodox liturgy has some interesting aspects. Strikingly, it is used as an antiphon for the celebration of Christ's nativity (December 25). See Appendix 1. The liturgist takes full advantage of the difficulty in the Hebrew text of verses 3-6 to construct a tendentious and effective citation of the Psalm. A creative adaptation of the Hebrew of 82.3b allows the Psalm to speak of incarnation and Jesus' birth signaled by a star. The "Melchizedek" translation is favored to allow the Psalm to echo the theology of the Epistle to the Hebrews. In general, a lovely yin-yang liturgical motif is constructed: the celebration of Jesus' incarnation and earthly nativity is set against the glorious motif of Christ's ascension to heaven and enthronement in eternal power: Christmas anticipates Easter.

Finally, the most widespread and influential use of Psalm 110 is to be found in the Apostles and Nicene Creeds. While the context of the Apostles' Creed is a bit obscure, the context of the Nicene Creed is very clear—namely, one of intra-group conflict. At Nicea, the views of heterodox groups are refuted in the official doctrine of the emerging Church. We see the following:

> He ascended into heaven
> and is seated at the right hand of the Father.
> He will come again in glory to judge the living and the dead,
> and his kingdom will have no end.

While the phrase "being at the right hand" is not unique to Psalm 110 in the HS or New Testament, the popularity of Psalm 110 in various New Testament texts and its use in messianic claims likely has led to its entrenchment in the creedal statements of the church. It is interesting that in the section above we also hear an echo of Psalm 82. The image of the figure in heaven judging others perhaps echoes Psalm 82. Thus, we see the two Psalm streams coalescing in these powerful creedal statements—definitions of group self-identity for millennia of Christians.

Conclusion

There have been other treatments of the reception history of the Psalms, but my study ventures into new territory by considering liturgical elements within the Orthodox Christianity—a bookend approach to early Israelite tradition which keeps the functional worship elements of the Psalms in view. Psalms 82 and 110 are striking case studies in the multi-generational and multi-community appropriation of texts, with radical shifts at each stage. These shifts, often linked to group identity issues, are well served by having Social Identity

Theory as a background point of reference. What emerges is a picture of the utility of texts which speak of group conflict situations—those texts can be adapted to fit a variety of conflict situations. I often wish that human society was not so conflict-ridden… but then I would have far less to study.

Author biography

Steven Muir is a Professor of Religious Studies at Concordia University of Edmonton. His publications focus on the social-scientific study of the New Testament and Early Christianity in their Greco-Roman context.

Appendix 1—Orthodox Liturgy

Communion Hymn for Holy Wednesday—Liturgy of Presanctified Gifts[57]

REFRAIN: Oh taste and see that the Lord is good. Psalm 33.8

VERSE 1: Blessed is the man who hopeth in Him. Psalm 33.8

VERSE 2: Oh fear the Lord, all ye his saints // for there is no want to them who fear in Him. Psalm 33.8

VERSE 3: Judge for the orphan and the poor man // do justice to the humble and the pauper. Psalm 81 (82).3

VERSE 4: Rescue the poor man and the needy // from the hand of the sinner deliver him. Psalm 81 (82).4

VERSE 5: They have not known, nor understood; they walk in darkness. // Let all the foundations of the earth be shaken. Psalm 81 (82).5

VERSE 6: I said, you are gods, and all of you sons of the Most High, // But like men ye die, and like one of the rulers do ye fall. Psalm 81 (82).6,7

Nativity of Our Lord Jesus Christ (December 25), Liturgy of St. John Chrysostom[58]

Third Antiphon—Psalm 110

110.1a The Lord said to my Lord: "Sit at my right hand!"

Thy Nativity, O Christ our God, has shown to the world the light of wisdom! For by it, those who worshipped the stars, were taught by a star to adore Thee, the Sun of Righteousness, and to know Thee, the Orient from on high. O Lord, Glory be to Thee!

110.1b Until I make thine enemies Thy footstool!

Thy Nativity…

---

57. Psalm 110 is also in the Canon Matins for Holy Thursday, Ode 4 Troparion 2.
58. *Service Books* vol 1, 135–7.

110.2 The Lord sends from Zion Thy mighty scepter. Rule in the midst of Thy foes.

Thy Nativity…

110.3a Authority shall be with Thee on the day of Thy power, among the splendor of Thy Holy Ones![59]

Introit of the Little Entrance

110.3b-4 Out of the womb, before the morning star, have I begotten Thee![60] The Lord has sworn and will not change His mind. Thou art a priest forever after the order of Melchizedek. Thy Nativity…

Bibliography

Ackerman, James S. "The Rabbinic Interpretation of Psalm 82 and the Gospel of John." *HTR* 59.2 (1966): 186–91. https://doi.org/10.1017/S0017816000009676

Albright, William F. *Yahweh and the Gods of Canaan: A Historical Analysis of Two Contrasting Faiths.* Garden City, NY: Doubleday, 1968.

Bar-Tal, Daniel. *Group Beliefs: A Conception for Analyzing Group Structure, Processes, and Behavior.* New York: Springer-Verlag, 1990. https://doi.org/10.1007/978-1-4612-3298-8

—"Group Beliefs as an Expression of Social Identity," 93–113 in *Social Identity: International Perspectives.* Edited by S. Worchel et al. Thousand Oaks, CA: Sage, 1998. https://doi.org/10.4135/9781446279205.n7

Bateman, Herbert W. "Psalm 110:1 and the New Testament," *BibSac* 149 (1992): 438–53.

Beasley-Murray, George R. *John: Word Biblical Commentary.* Waco, TX: Word Books, 1987.

Braun, Willi. *Feasting and Social Rhetoric in Luke 14.* SNTS Monograph series 85. Cambridge: University Press, 1995. https://doi.org/10.1017/CBO9780511520303

—"Rhetoric, Rhetoricality, and Discourse Performances," 1–26 in *Rhetoric and Reality in Early Christianities.* Edited by Willi Braun. Waterloo, ON: Wilfred Laurier University Press, 2005.

Brown, Raymond. *Gospel According to John.* Garden City, NY: Doubleday, 1966–70.

Brown, Rupert J. "The Role of Similarity in Intergroup Relations," 603–23 in *The Social Dimension: European Developments in Social Psychology*, vol. 2. Edited by Henri Tajfel. Cambridge: University Press, 1984. https://doi.org/10.1017/CBO9780511759154.012

—"Social Identity Theory: Past Achievements, Current Problems and Future Challenges," *European Journal of Social Psychology* 30 (2000): 745–78. https://doi.org/10.1002/1099-0992(200011/12)30:6<745::AID-EJSP24>3.0.CO;2-O

Chrysostom, John. *Service Books of the Orthodox Church, vol. 1: The Divine Liturgy of St. John Chrysostom.* South Canaan, PN: St. Tikhon's Seminary Press, 1984.

---

59. Free translation of a difficult Hebrew passage.
60. Free translation of a difficult Hebrew passage.

Dahood, Mitchell. *Psalms II, 51-100* (Anchor Bible). Garden City, NY: Doubleday, 1968. https://doi.org/10.5040/9780300261264

—*Psalms III, 101-150* (Anchor Bible). Garden City, NY: Doubleday, 1970.

Davis, Barry C. "Is Psalm 110 a Messianic Psalm?" *BibSac* 157 (2000): 160–73.

Geertz, Clifford. *The Interpretation of Cultures: Selected Essays.* New York: Basic Books, 1973.

Gunkel, Hermann. *The Psalms: A Form-Critical Introduction.* Translated by Thomas M. Horner. Philadelphia, PA: Fortress Press, 1967.

Hay, David M. *Glory at the Right Hand: Psalm 110 in Early Christianity.* Nashville, TN: Abingdon, 1973.

Holladay, William L. *The Psalms through Three Thousand Years.* Minneapolis, MN: Fortress, 1993.

Hossfeld, Frank-Lothar and Erich Zenger. *Psalms 2: A Commentary on Psalms 51-100.* Translated by Linda M. Maloney. Minneapolis, MN: Fortress, 2005.

—*Psalms 3: A Commentary on Psalms 101-150.* Translated by Linda M. Maloney. Minneapolis, MN: Fortress, 2011.

Jefferson, Helen Genevieve. "Is Psalm 110 Canaanite?" *JBL* 73.3 (1954): 152–6. https://doi.org/10.2307/3261728

Kee, Min Suc. "The Heavenly Council and its Type-scene." *JSOT* 31.3 (2007): 259–73. https://doi.org/10.1177/0309089207076356

Kraus, Hans-Joachim. *Psalms 1-59: A Commentary.* Translated by Hilton C. Oswald. Minneapolis, MN: Augsburg, 1988.

—*Psalms 60-150: A Commentary.* Translated by Hilton C. Oswald. Minneapolis, MN: Augsburg, 1989.

Loader, W. R. G. "Christ at the Right Hand—Ps. CX.1 in the New Testament," *NTS* 24 (1978): 199–217. https://doi.org/10.1017/S0028688500007840

Mosser, Carl. "The Earliest Patristic Interpretations of Psalm 82, Jewish Antecedents, and the Origin of Christian Deification," *JTS* NS 56.1 (2005): 30–74. https://doi.org/10.1093/jts/fli002

Mowinckel, Sigmund. *The Psalms in Israel's Worship.* Translated by D.R. Ap-Thomas. 2 volumes. Nashville, TN: Abingdon Press, 1962.

Mroczek, Eva. "'David Did Not Ascend into the Heavens' (Acts 2:34): Early Jewish Ascent Traditions and the Myth of Exegesis in the New Testament." *J. Anc. Jud.* 3 (2015): 219–52. https://doi.org/10.1484/J.JAAJ.5.103822

Neyrey, Jerome H. "I said: You are Gods": Psalm 82:6 and John 10," *JBL* 108.4 (1989): 647–63. https://doi.org/10.2307/3267185

Santrac, Dragoslava. "God and 'Gods'—Poetic Ambiguity and Wordplay: A Proposal towards a Better Understanding of Ps 82," *JATS* 27.1 (2016): 37–54.

Simonetti, Manlio. *Interpretation in the Early Church: An Historical Introduction to Patristic Exegesis.* Translated by J.A. Hughes. Edinburgh: T&T Clark, 1994.

Sumner, William Graham. *Folkways: A Study of the Sociological Importance of Usages, Manners, Customs, Mores and Morals.* New York: Mentor Books, 1960 [1906].

Tajfel, Henri, ed. *Differentiation between Social Groups: Studies in the Social Psychology of Intergroup Relations.* London: Academic Press, 1978.

—"Social Categorization, Social Identity and Social Comparison," 61–76 in *Differentiation between Social Groups: Studies in the Social Psychology of Intergroup Relations.* Edited by Henri Tajfel. London: Academic Press, 1978.

Trotter, James M. "Death of the *Elohim* in Psalm 82," *JBL* 131.2 (2012): 221–39. https://doi.org/10.2307/23488222

Turner, J. "Social Comparison, Similarity and Ingroup Favouritism," 235–50 in *Differentiation between Social Groups: Studies in the Social Psychology of Intergroup Relations*. Edited by Henri Tajfel. New York: Academic Press, 1978.

Turner, J.C., Michael A. Hogg, Penelope J. Oakes, Stephen D. Reicher, and Margaret S. Wetherell, eds. *Rediscovering the Social Group: A Self-Categorization Theory*. Oxford: Basil Blackwell, 1987.

Von Wahlde, Urban C. *Gospel and Letters of John*, vol. 2. Grand Rapids, MI: Wm B. Eerdmans, 2010.

Wallace, David. "The Use of Psalms in the Shaping of a Text: Psalm 2:7 and Psalm 110:1 in Hebrews 1," *Restoration Quarterly* (2003): 41–50.

Wallis, Roy. *The Road to Total Freedom: A Sociological Analysis of Scientology*. New York: Columbia Press, 1977.

Ware, Timothy. *The Orthodox Church*. London: Penguin, 1991.

Chapter Seven

"The Spirit Descended Like a Dove":
Bird Divination, Carrier Pigeons, and the Baptism of Jesus

Jennifer Eyl

In the four canonical gospels, the baptism of Jesus is marked by the arrival of a dove, *peristera* in Greek, who is accompanied by a divine voice indicating that Jesus is the son of the Judean deity. While the earliest gospel writers associate the dove with Jesus' baptism, conferral of the divine *pneuma*, and the adoption of Jesus as God's son, the dove will eventually find its place in Christian art as a symbol of the "Holy Spirit"—a later theological formulation, in hypostasized form, of the Christian Trinity. Indeed, one need only look upward in numerous basilicas beginning in late antiquity to see the wings of a white dove outspread in the ceiling of a cupola or adorning the apse. Doves show up in early Christian art by the third century, as in the sarcophagus in Santa Maria Antiqua which depicts Jesus' baptism in bas-relief (dated c. 275 CE) and in the third- and fourth-century catacombs of San Sebastiano, San Lorenzo, San Callisto, and others. In early Christian art, the dove is by far the most common bird portrayed.[1] By the tenth century, the dove is affiliated as immediately with one part of the Trinity as with Jesus' baptism scene. The dove, as Holy Spirit, will eventually stand for itself, and the ancient associations which first prompted Mark to utilize the bird will recede from Christian memory.

How would an ancient audience have encountered the gospels' use of the *peristera*? Why this bird? Why not a falcon, eagle, or sparrow? Indeed, why a bird at all? This essay will reason that Mark's *peristera* story, copied by the other biographers, is best understood in three contexts: ancient practices of bird divination (ornithomancy), widespread uses of the *peristera* as the ideal messenger among all species of birds, and the moral virtues appended to the bird by the first century. Birds were widely understood as bearing divinatory meaning in antiquity; the *peristera* makes sense since delivering messages is often what that species was bred to do. Equally, the bird would eventually be associated with wisdom and moral perfection—which the

---

1. Paul Corby Finney, ed., *Eerdman's Encyclopedia of Early Christian Art and Archaeology* (Grand Rapids: Eerdmans, 2017), 66.

gospel authors wish to parlay to Jesus. Given Willi Braun's abiding interest in the diverse world of winged creatures, as well as Willi's brilliance as a scholar of ancient Christianity and theoretical insights into the construction of 'religion,' it seems most appropriate to honor him by explaining the presence of this bird by its historical significance in antiquity.

Canonical Gospel Accounts

The author of the Gospel of Mark first recounts the baptism of Jesus in the Jordan river by John the Baptist, claiming, "...as he was coming up out of the water, he saw the heavens part and the *pneuma* descending like a dove to him (τὸ πνεῦμα ὡς περιστερὰν καταβαῖνον εἰς αὐτόν). And a voice came from the heavens, 'You are my son, the beloved; with you I am well pleased'" (Mk 1.10-11). [Σὺ εἶ ὁ υἱός μου ὁ ἀγαπητός, ἐν σοὶ εὐδόκησα.].[2] Lacking the birth narratives later invented by Matthew and Luke, this moment in Mark operates as Jesus' "birth" as the son of a god. Mark gives little indication that Jesus is special in some way prior to this baptism scene. Likewise, Mark's description makes it difficult to disentangle the divine pneuma, the verbal declaration of adoption, and the bird itself.[3] Was there an *actual* bird, according to Mark, or is he describing some wispy, otherworldly swirl of pneumatic material in the shape of a dove that descended to Jesus, while a voice bellowed from the sky above? The Greek does not help answer this question.

Matthew and Luke copy Mark's story, altering it according to their authorial and aesthetic interests.[4] In light of their birth narratives and genealogies, the baptism scene now functions almost redundantly since Jesus has already been identified as the son of a deity in each account. Matthew precedes the baptism story by John the Baptist's condemnation of Pharisees and Sadducees who wish to be baptized by him. After relenting to baptize them with water, he foretells that another will come with the power to baptize with divine pneuma and fire. In the next verse, Jesus arrives to be baptized by John, who does not see himself worthy of baptizing Jesus. After again relenting, Matthew writes, "Just as he came up from the water, behold, the

---

2. Unless otherwise noted, all translations are my own.

3. In his commentary on Matthew, John Nolland refers to the dove/voice/pneuma as "coordinated efforts." See John Nolland, *The Gospel of Matthew: A Commentary on the Greek Text* (Grand Rapids, MI: Eerdmans, 2005), 155.

4. For a word-by-word account of how Matthew and Luke edit this passage in Mark, see W. D. Davies and Dale Allison, eds. *A Critical and Exegetical Commentary on the Gospel According to Saint Matthew. Volume I: Introduction and Commentary on Matthew I-VII* (Edinburgh: T&T Clark, 1988), 330–31.

heavens were opened to him and he saw the *pneuma* of god descending like a dove (ὡσεὶ περιστερὰν) and come to him (ἐρχόμενον ἐπ' αὐτόν). And a voice from the heavens said, 'This is my son, the beloved, with whom I am well pleased'" (Mt. 3.16-17). Like Mark 1.12, Matthew 4.1 claims that this divine *pneuma* then led Jesus into the wilderness for forty days, where he was tempted by the devil.[5] Matthew copies Mark closely, but frames Jesus' baptism within John's condemnation of the Pharisees and Sadducees.

Luke's elongated and elaborated connection between John the Baptist and Jesus places the baptism scene farther into the gospel narrative. Like Matthew, Luke leads the reader to the baptism pericope by an additional, larger story regarding tax collectors, soldiers and their wages, and a crowd whom he addresses as a "brood of vipers!" (in Matthew, the Pharisees and Sadducees are the brood of vipers, not the general crowd). This leads the reader to the baptism scene, during which, "the heaven was opened and the divine *pneuma* (τὸ πνεῦμα τὸ ἅγιον) in bodily form of a dove (σωματικῷ εἴδει ὡς περιστερὰν) descended to him, and a voice came from heaven, 'You are my son, the beloved; with you I am well pleased'" (Lk. 3.21-22). Lest there be any confusion over metaphor, Luke is clear to add that the actual body of a dove, not a figurative dove, descended. Luke clarifies the vagueness of Mark's account.[6]

Although the Gospel of John lacks even an echo of many synoptic stories, there is a kind of baptism scene which is primarily recounted by the Baptist himself: "'I did not know him; but I came baptizing with water so that he might be made known to Israel through this.' And John testified, saying, 'I saw the *pneuma* descending from heaven like a dove (τὸ πνεῦμα καταβαῖνον ὡς περιστερὰν), and it rested on him (καὶ ἔμεινεν ἐπ' αὐτόν). I did not know him, but the one who sent me to baptize in water said to me, 'The one on whom you see the *pneuma* descend and rest—he is the one who baptizes with the divine *pneuma*.' And I have seen and have testified that this is the son of God'" (Jn 1.31-34).

Exegetes of these passages have tended to look for explanations of the symbolism or literary precedents of the dove within Jewish literature exclusively, or as the vestige of earliest Christian community in Palestine (especially in the case of Mark 1.10-11). For example, Francois Bovon's commentary on Luke argues that Luke's ὡς περιστερὰν, "pertains to the

---

5. In Mark, this figure is τοῦ Σατανᾶ, whereas in Mathew, Jesus is tempted by τοῦ διαβόλου.

6. As John Nolland observes, at least three early MSS of Matthew also attempt to resolve Mark's vagueness by writing: "*katabonta ek tou ouranou hōs…*" (Nolland, *The Gospel of Matthew*, 150).

style of an apocalyptic vision."[7] Bovon views the dove as a riddle, and while borrowed from Mark, he puzzles that "no one has yet found a direct parallel in Jewish literature."[8] Leander Keck's detailed analysis concludes that the baptism scene could not have arisen among Hellenistic Christians outside Palestine" and instead he locates the dove's presence with the "old Palestinian Jewish Aramaic Christian tradition," in which Mark is not describing the appearance of a dove, but rather, the descent of the *pneuma* is dove-like.[9] Keck argues that once the Hellenistic Christians (i.e., Luke) get ahold of the story, the adverbial sense of the image (the *pneuma* descended dove-like) was taken to be literal. Grammatically, Keck's interpretation, especially as it concerns translating various phrases from Hebrew or Aramaic into Greek, is certainly a possibility (he compares, for example, Exod. 15.5 and Hos. 12.2 in Hebrew and Greek). Yet, Keck's interpretation depends on quite early dating of Mark and the author's direct connection to the earliest Palestinian followers of Jesus. Such a view of Mark is increasingly scrutinized, based on a growing sophistication in our understanding of ancient writing practices and the development of early Christian literature.[10] In their commentary on Matthew, W.D. Davies and Dale Allison marshall sixteen possible explanations for the presence of the dove; like other commentators, they look exclusively at Jewish and Christian parallels, disregarding any larger Greek or Roman influence. They are unconvinced by most explanations and conclude that the passage is most likely an allusion to Gen. 1.2, when the spirit of God hovered over the face of the waters.[11] Stephen Gero has argued that Mark is assembling two "pre-Markan traditions," namely, the role of the dove in the 24th Ode of Solomon, and the baptism scene in

---

7. François Bovon. *Luke 1: A Commentary on the Gospel of Luke 1:1–9:50* (Minneapolis, MN: Fortress, 2002), 129.

8. Bovon, *Luke 1*, 130.

9. Leander E. Keck, "The Spirit and the Dove." *New Testament Studies* 17 (1970–71), 41–67. Keck, "The Spirit and the Dove," 62. He writes, "…in the pre-Markan story too the coming of the Spirit was probably compared to the action of a descending dove, not to the dove-like Spirit that is descending" (Keck, "The Spirit and the Dove," 64).

10. See Robyn Faith Walsh, "The *Satyrica* and the Gospels in the Second Century," *TCQ* 70.1 (2020): 1–12, esp. 2–5; For critique of the "community" and "oral transmission" theories of gospel origins, see also Robyn Faith Walsh, *The Origins of Early Christian Literature: Contextualizing the New Testament within Greco-Roman Literary Culture* (Cambridge: Cambridge University Press, 2021).

11. Davies and Allison, *A Critical and Exegetical Commentary*, 331–6. Alison reasserts this conclusion in his own work: Dale C. Allison, "The Baptism of Jesus and a New Dead Sea Scroll," *BAR* 18.2 (1992): 58.

the Gospel of the Hebrews (a fragment of which is preserved in Latin by Jerome).[12]

Edward Dixon's analysis reminds us that even the topic of the dove has been shaped by the Judaism/Hellenism divide common, until very recently, in New Testament scholarship.[13] He notes that while there are literary allusions to OT texts in the baptism scene, there is no explicit literary precursor in Jewish sources for a bird descending from a heavenly realm as the messenger of a god, or even the god in him/herself.[14] This has stumped NT scholars, and Dixon helpfully suggests that Jewish texts are not the only place scholars should be looking. Instead, he argues that the simile of a descending bird finds an easy home in a range of Greek stories about gods.

Pigeon or Dove?

The Greek word περιστερὰ refers simultaneously to the pigeon and the dove. Thus, it is impossible to determine whether a pigeon or dove descended during the gospel scenes. This ambiguity is commonly overlooked by scholars, but the ambiguity is significant insofar as the *peristera* has a few associations in Greek that are more explicitly affiliated with pigeons than with turtledoves, rock doves, or other subspecies. Within three centuries, Christian art will assume a white dove but this is not what the gospels say. As Aristotle observes in *Historia Animalium*, "peristera" is the larger generic class of pigeon and dove birds, of which there are numerous subtypes:

> There are many different kinds in the pigeon family (περιστεροειδῶν): thus the pigeon (περιστερὰ) and the peleias (πελειάς) are different birds. The peleias is smaller (whereas the other is easily domesticated), and it is black and small, and its feet are red and rough, so no one bothers to keep it. The largest of this family is the ring-dove (ἡ φάττα); next largest is the oinas (ἡ οἰνάς), which is a little larger than the common pigeon (τῆς περιστερᾶς). The smallest of them all is the turtle-dove (ἡ τρυγών). Pigeons breed and hatch at all

---

12. The Ode of Solomon is complicated insofar as it cannot be dated and it reflects very closely the events of Jesus' baptism. Either the Ode is later and modeled on a by-then widespread gospel baptism story, or the Ode is earlier and Mark incorporates it into his narrative. Jerome's version of the baptism scene in the Gospel of the Hebrews lacks a bird but does describe the *Spiritus* descending to Jesus. See Stephen Gero, "The Spirit as Dove at the Baptism of Jesus," *NovT* 18.1 (1976): 17–35, esp 18–19.

13. Dixon also provides a helpful synopsis of the history of interpretation of the Markan passage. See Edward P. Dixon, "Descending Spirit and Descending Gods: A 'Greek' Interpretation of the Spirit's 'Descent as a Dove' in Mark 1:10," *JBL* 128.4 (2009): 759–80.

14. Indeed, he observes, "…no ancient Jewish text depicts a 'descent' of any heavenly being in the form of a bird" (764).

seasons if they can get a warm sunny place and everything they need: otherwise in summer only. The spring and autumn broods are the best; the summer brood and those hatched in the hot periods are the worst. (544b)[15]

Philo provides a physical description of the *peristera* that matches what we know of common pigeons more than the white dove of Christian iconography: "Again, have you never perceived the neck of the dove (τῆς περιστερᾶς) changing colour to assume a countless variety of hues in the rays of the sun? Is it not by turns red, and purple and fiery coloured, and cinereous, and again pale, and ruddy, and every other variety of colour, the very names of which it is not easy to enumerate?" (*On Drunkenness* 173.1).[16] Given the available and widely known names for the various types of doves, it is curious that the gospel authors refer to the common pigeon but subsequent Christianity assumes the presence of a dove. At best, we cannot be sure that the authors were referring to a dove since none of the many types of doves is mentioned, but the word for the generic, domesticated pigeon clearly is.

Among Greek speaking authors the *peristera* is generally associated with domesticity, sacrificial offerings, docility, and gregariousness. Such birds, when domesticated, were commonly kept in large aviaries and their dung collected and sold as an additive for fertilizer or as kindling for fires.[17] Varro indicates that some pigeon houses (*peristerotrophia*) held up to five thousand birds (Varro, 3.75). If not in aviaries, dovecotes (*peristeriones* or *columbaria*) were also widespread from Italy and Greece to Palestine, Egypt, and ancient Iran, where pigeons and doves roosted and their dung collected. Archaeologists have discovered ancient dove houses and inscriptions regarding pigeon tending by the dozens. A dedicatory inscription near the temple to Zeus near Sahab (modern Jordan), for example, affiliated with a columbarium nearby, indicates that the dove dung contributed to the fertilization of local fields, while keeping the temple to Zeus clean.[18] This is

---

15. Aristotle. *History of Animals, Volume I: Books 1-3.* Translated by A. L. Peck. Loeb Classical Library 437. Cambridge, MA: Harvard University Press, 1965. There is disagreement among ancient authors regarding which type of bird is which. See for example, Athenaeus quote Aristotle's five types (pigeon/*peristera*; rock dove, ring dove, stock dove, and turtle dove), but indicates that Dorians use *peleias* (wild pigeon) for *peristera* (domesticated pigeon). He indicates dispute over which word referred to which bird (9.50).

16. C. D. Yonge, trans. *The Works of Philo* (Peabody, MA: Hendrickson Publishers, 1993).

17. Sian Lewis and Lloyd Llewellyn-Jones, eds., *The Culture of Animals in Antiquity* (New York: Routledge, 2018), 261–2.

18. H. W. Pleket, R. S. Stroud, and Strubbe, J. H. M., "SEG 42-1789. Pigeons and Pigeonries," in *SEG*, A. Chaniotis, T. Corsten, N. Papazarkadas, and R.A. Tybout. By

to say that the *peristera* was no anomaly or rare bird; on the contrary, its utterly common presence contributed to the landscape of daily life, and its interactions with humans were widespread and regular. As Pliny observes, "many people are insane with love for these [birds]" (*Nat Hist.* 10.53).

Biblical Greek narratives, like non-biblical Greek narratives, reflect the *peristera* as part of the landscape of daily life, used as literary symbols, and offered in ritual sacrifices.[19] Such references occur thirty-six times throughout the Septuagint. In Genesis, Noah sends a pigeon-dove out to test whether the water had subsided (Gen. 8.8-12).[20] The bird also figures early in the Abraham cycle, when God instructs Abraham to make a sacrificial offering that includes a turtledove and pigeon (τρυγόνα καὶ περιστεράν) (Gen. 15.9). *Peristera* appears nine times in Leviticus, typically in the context of ritual sacrifice offering (e.g. Lev. 1.14—should an Israelite priest make an offering of a bird, it must be either a turtledove or pigeon).[21] Such birds rank halfway in the list of ideal offerings, between a female sheep or goat and flour (5.11). In every instance of sacrificial offerings, the turtledoves and pigeons are interchangeable—they are usually suggested in the form of "two turtledoves or two young pigeons" (δύο τρυγόνας ἢ δύο νεοσσοὺς περιστερῶν) (e.g., Lev. 15.29 or Num. 6.10). Such birds are not associated with predatory behavior, violence, or consuming carrion. Nevertheless, Greek biblical uses of the *peristera* shed little light on Mark's choices of the bird.[22]

---

housing the birds in the columbarium, the birds stayed out of the rafters of the temple. This facilitated the collection of their dung and kept the temple relatively dung-free.

19. In biblical Hebrew, the dove, the turtle dove, and the pigeon are often interchangeable and also distinguished by specific terms. The dove and pigeon are typically called *yonah*, while turtle-dove is *tor* (as in Song of Songs 2.11). See Shlomo P. Toperoff, "The Dove, Turtle-Dove, and Pigeon in Bible and Midrash," *Dor-le-dor* 15.3 (1987): 181–5. As the gospel writers are writing in Greek, this essay focuses on the Greek terminology; it is unlikely that gospel authors are learned in Hebrew, and thus, if they are consciously crafting biblical allusions to the dove, it would be to the biblical Greek *peristera* and not the Hebrew *yonah* (Jonah).

20. Cf. the Deucalion myth recounted in Apollonius of Rhodes' *Argonautica*, Ovid's *Metam.*, Ps.Apollodorus' *Library*, and the so-called Parian Chronicle.

21. See also Lev. 12.6-8; 14.21-31.

22. Doves show up poetically in the Septuagint. For example, in Canticles/Song of Songs 1.15, "behold, you are beautiful; your eyes are doves (περιστεραί)." Throughout this collection of love poetry the pigeon-dove appears in the context of intimate adoration and longing: "His eyes are like doves beside teeming pools of water…" (Cant. 5.12). Hosea is familiar with the Assyrian veneration of doves, since we see at Hos 11.11 that the Lord's roar will frighten so terribly that everyone will be amazed like a bird from Egypt, and a "*peristera* from the land of the Asssyrians" (Hos. 11.11). In Isaiah, doves are associated with mourning (Isa. 38.14) and a docile temperament (Isa. 59.11).

The Precedent of Divine Pigeon-Dove Associations

Regardless of its commonness, at times the *peristera* was associated with a range of deities including Aphrodite/Venus, Zeus, Dione, and the Assyrian Astarte. According to Aelian (*VH* 1.15) and Athenaeus (395a), Zeus transformed himself into a pigeon-dove after falling in love with Phthia of Aegium.[23] Silius Italicus claims that the bird was sacred to Dione (4.106), and according both to Aelian (*AN* 10.33) and Ovid (*Fasti* 1.451.52), the bird was sacred to Aphrodite and Venus. Indeed, in Apuleius' *Metamorphoses*, Venus' chariot is pulled by four white doves (*quattuor candidae columbae*), followed by a train of sparrows and other songbirds (6.6). Aelian (*VH* 1.15) and Athenaeus (*Deip.* 9.51) recount the same story regarding pigeon-doves at the temple of Aphrodite in Eryx, Sicily: At the annual *Anagōgia* (or, Departure) festival the goddess is understood to depart for Libya, and all the dove-pigeons birds fly away with her. Athenaeus adds that nine days later the *Katagōgia* (or, Return), of the goddess is celebrated as soon as the first *peristera* returns like a messenger, followed by the entire fleet of birds.

That Jesus is identified as the progeny of a god through the intervention or apparatus of a dove (especially through the god's co-mingling with a mortal, in the cases of Matthew and Luke) has precedent. Diodorus Siculus tells the story of the legendary Neo-Assyrian queen, Semiramis (likely a reference to the historical Sammu-rmat, who reigned as queen-regent in the final years of the ninth century BCE). According to Diodorus, Semiramis's very name is an adaptation of the archaic Syrian dialect for "doves" because she herself was protected and nourished by doves in her infancy, having been cast out by her divine mother, Derecto, for being the shameful result of the goddess' union with a mortal man. After a lengthy description of the staggeringly vast military and architectural undertakings during her reign, Diodorus (citing Ctesias of Cnidus) closes her biography just as it opened: with doves. He claims that, aware of a prophecy of Ammon that her son would conspire against her, she turned power over to him and disappeared, possibly by turning into a dove and being translated to the gods. To his day, he claims, the Assyrians worship the dove as a god—a deified Semiramis (Diodorus 2.1-20). This last detail—that doves are worshipped by Syrians as gods—is corroborated by Xenophon (*Anab* 1.4.9).[24]

---

23. Zeus is more often associated with the eagle. For example, Ovid and Vergil both point to the eagle as the bird who abducts Ganymede to be the cupbearer of the gods. Ovid claims that the eagle is actually Zeus in disguise (*Aeneid* 5.253; *Metamorphoses* 10.155).

24. Herodotus (1.105) equates the Assyrian goddess with Aphrodite, as do Pausanias (1.14.7) and Lucian (*Syrian Goddess* 33).

Divine Descent and Bird Divination

Edward Dixon has argued that to understand the presence of the descending dove in these baptism scenes, we must look less at the dove and more at the descending: "By placing emphasis on the bird simile, rather than on the dove, one discerns that the Spirit's 'descent as a dove' has no clear antecedent in Jewish literature precisely because the bird simile is a literary device that finds a natural home in Greek mythology—where such similes are used to describe arrivals and departures of gods."[25] Without denying the possible OT allusions (Noah; Gen. 1.2), Dixon emphasizes that by the first century, any person educated well enough to write Greek would have received such an education through some contact with the Homeric epics. He is not wrong.[26] And indeed, as early as the Homeric epics (as well as later epics modeled on Homer such as Vergil's *Aeneid*) the descent and departure of gods is repeatedly likened to the flight of birds.

In Book 15 of the *Iliad,* Apollo is described as descending like a "like a fleet falcon, the slayer of doves, that is the swiftest of winged things" (*Il.* 15.237-38).[27] When Thetis descends to Achilles, the poet sings, "like a falcon she sprang down from snowy Olympus..." (*Il.* 18.616-17). When Zeus later sends Athena down to aid Achilles, the goddess, "like a falcon, wide of wing and shrill of voice, leapt down upon him from out of heaven through the air" (*Il.*19.349-50). The flight of a bird is regularly used as a simile to describe the fleetness of divine descent to the human realm. Such similes are so widespread that anyone in antiquity familiar with Greek epic poets would be likewise familiar with the notion that divine powers descend as birds descend. If Dixon is correct, this would include the author of Mark and all other canonical gospels.

Not only did gods swoop down and alight upon the earth as birds, birds themselves bore divine messages. "Divination" refers to the practices of identifying, interpreting, and translating information from a divine realm.[28] Such practices come in innumerable ways, and one of the most common in antiquity was the interpretation of birds—their flight direction, colors,

---

25. Dixon, "Descending Spirit and Descending Gods," 760.

26. See, for example, Margalit Finkelberg, "Homer as a Foundation Text," in *Homer, the Bible, and Beyond*, edited by Margalit Finkelberg and Guy Stroumsa (Leiden: Brill, 2003), 75–96.

27. Homer. *The Iliad*, trans. A.T. Murray (Cambridge: Harvard University Press, 1924).

28. See Ann Jeffers, *Magic and Divination in Ancient Palestine and Syria* (New York: Brill, 1996); Sarah Iles Johnston, *Ancient Greek Divination* (Malden, MA: Blackwell, 2008); Patrick Curry, ed. *Divination: Perspectives for a New Millennium* (New York: Routledge, 2010).

nests, squawks and squabbles, and their songs.[29] Regardless of the gods that one venerated (Zeus, Venus, Yahweh), birds were widely viewed as "signs" sent from the god(s).[30] The observation of birds was such a staple in ascertaining divine will that the two common Greek words for "bird" (ὄρνις and οἰωνός) double in meaning as "sign" or "omen" (cf. Josephus *Ant.* 2.234; 18.201)

The divinatory significance of birds was nearly universally shared in antiquity. As Steven Green points out, the interpretation of bird behavior as indicating divine will assumed "a sense of harmony between gods and birds, whereby benevolent gods send true signs by means of compliant messenger birds."[31] In Aeschylus' *Prometheus Bound*, the god describes a range of ways that he creates for humans to discern divine will, including, "the flight of crook-taloned birds I distinguished clearly—which by nature are auspicious, which sinister—their various modes of life, their mutual feuds and loves, and their consortings…" (484-95).[32] In Aristophanes *Birds*, the eponymous chorus declares that birds are the very gods of prophecy—Delphi, Dodona, and Apollo—and that people undertake no significant business without first consulting the divine messengers (*Birds* 716-24). Among some people, bird divination was a specialized and discrete skill such as the professional Roman *augures* who read the birds daily (Livy 1.36.2-6). Even lacking such official positions, however, evidence suggests that people nearly everywhere assumed that God or gods could utilize a bird to gesture toward something important that humans ought to know. Dio Cassius and Plutarch both recount Cleopatra's concern for the outcome of the battle of Actium when a group of swallows landed and built a nest on her flagship, the *Antonias*. Plutarch called this a "terrible sign" (*sēmeion deinon*) when the nest was attacked by other swallows.[33] As Xenophon explains in the *Memorabilia*, rather than assume that divine will is stumbled upon by

---

29. Jeremy Mynott, *Birds in the Ancient World* (Oxford: Oxford University Press, 2018), 249–66.

30. Jennifer Eyl, *Signs, Wonders, and Gifts: Divination in the Letters of Paul* (New York: Oxford University Press, 2019), 60–2. Abundant evidence demonstrates that Israelites and, later, Judeans engaged in a range of divinatory practices despite prohibitions in Exodus, Leviticus, and Deuteronomy. For more on this, see Eyl, *Signs, Wonders, and Gifts*, 81–5.

31. Steven Green, "Malevolent Gods and Promethean Birds: Contesting Augury in Augustus' Rome," *TAPA* 139 (2009): 165.

32. Aeschylus, *Prometheus Bound*, trans. Herbert Weir Smyth (Cambridge: Harvard University Press, 1926).

33. Dio Cassius 50.15.1-2; Plutarch *Antony* 60.7.

chance, gods make their will known through birds (lit. *they signal these things through them* [birds]).[34]

Gospel descriptions of the pigeon-dove descent find their home among ancient literary images of divine beings (or powers) descending as birds, as well as the common understanding that birds bear divine information. This does not explain Mark's choice of *peristera* in that role. Why the pigeon/dove? Why not the eagle, hawk, or owl, whose associations would link Jesus to divine power, as so often described in Homer? It is possible that Mark did not want to link Jesus to a bird already intractably associated with a powerful god whom the Judeans did not venerate. There would be difficulty, for example, in insisting that the owl alighted on Jesus, when the owl was so historically tied to Athena. Yet, the passive avoidance of certain birds does not explain the active choosing of the *peristera*. An allusion to Gen. 1.2 also fails to account for the choice of bird. I suggest that two associations with the *peristera* emerge strongly enough to explain why Mark chose this bird and other gospel authors chose to repeat it: the *peristera*'s role as the most effective and reliable messenger of all birds, and the moral/ethical qualities associated with the bird.

Carrier Pigeons of the Gospel

As part of daily life in antiquity, the *peristera* was famous for its ability to deliver messages. Numerous ancient authors comment in passing on the bird's innate homing mechanism, which renders it ideal for flying to a designated location with important news. Such practices predate Greek culture by centuries, as archaeological and epigraphic evidence indicate Egyptians were using carrier pigeons as early as 2000 BCE. The oldest reference to its use by Greeks is found in Athenaeus 9.395, which preserves a fragment of Pherecrates' *Graes* ("Old Women"). In the tiny surviving portion of this fifth century BCE comedy a character comments, "Send the pigeon to tell the news."[35] Aelian tells us that upon victory at the Olympics, Taurosthenes notified his father on the very day of the victory by sending a *peristera*, decorated in purple, back to his hometown of Aegina (*Varia Hist.* 9.1; a version of this is also recounted by Pausanias 2.9). The author of Ecclesiastes is aware of the power of birds to deliver private information: one ought not

---

34. "…ἀλλὰ τοὺς θεοὺς διὰ τούτων αὐτὰ σημαίνειν…" Xenophon, *Memorabilia*, 1.1.3.
35. Albert C. Leighton, "Secret Communication Among the Greeks and Romans," *Technology and Culture* 10.2 (1969): 139–54.

think ill of the king or speak badly of the rich, lest, "a bird in the sky may carry your voice, and a winged omen may report your words" (Eccl. 10.20).

In his examination of ancient technologies for relaying secret messages (cryptography, smoke signals, etc), Albert Leighton points to birds: "The swiftest and the least liable to interception of such means was the use of birds as couriers. The pigeon was the usual choice as the most efficient and dependable bird for message carrying."[36] As message bearers, letters were fastened under the birds' wings, to their feet, or around their necks by a fine thread. Varro comments on this courier ability (3.76), and according to Frontinus (*Stratagems* 3.13.7-8), Julius Caesar used pigeons (a domesticated form of the rock dove) to deliver secret military information to and from various locations. In his *Natural History*, Pliny writes, "Moreover they have acted as go-betweens in important affairs, when at the siege of Modena[37] Decimus Brutus sent to the consuls' camp despatches tied to their feet; what use to Antony were his rampart and watchful besieging force, and even the barriers of nets that he stretched in the river, when the message went by air?"[38] While the sparrow was also occasionally used to deliver messages, the *peristera* was the messenger bird par excellence in antiquity. Comments made in passing by so many ancient authors indicate that such use of the *peristera* was nearly universal in the ancient Mediterranean and Near East, and entirely commonplace.

Gospel authors double-dip, so to speak, when they link the divinatory uses of birds with the message-bearing renown of the pigeon-dove. Yet, gospel accounts are hardly the first to do so; the arrival of a dove accompanied by a voice that announces divine will has literary precursors. Indeed, if this bird operated as the premium messenger bird for mortals, it was doubly so for the gods. Herodotus recounts the occasion when two black doves flew from Thebes in Egypt—one to Ammon in Libya and the other to Dodona. At Dodona the dove spoke aloud in a human voice, informing listeners that this must be the site for the oracles of Zeus. Obeying the divine message delivered by the dove, locals established the oracular shrine at Dodona and Ammon, respectively (Hdt. 2.55):

> That, then, I heard from the Theban priests; and what follows, is told by the prophetesses of Dodona: to wit, that two black doves (δύο πελειάδας μελαίνας)[39] had come flying from Thebes in Egypt, one to Libya and one to Dodona this last settled on an oak tree, and uttered there human speech,

---

36. Lieghton, "Secret Communication,"141.
37. 44–43 BCE.
38. Pliny, *Nat Hist* 10.53. LCL 353, trans. H. Rackham (Cambridge, MA: Harvard University Press, 1940).
39. Recalling Aristotle, the *peleias* is a smaller subspecies of *peristera*.

declaring that there must be there a place of divination from Zeus; the people of Dodona understood that the message was divine, and therefore they established the oracular shrine. The dove which came to Libya bade the Libyans (so they say) to make an oracle of Amnion; this also is sacred to Zeus. Such was the tale told by the Dodonaean priestesses, of whom the eldest was Promeneia and the next in age Timarete, and the youngest Nicandra; and the rest of the servants of the temple at Dodona likewise held it true.[40]

The priestesses at Dodona were eventually called Peleiades ("Wild Doves"; Hdt. 2.57). This does not mean that the author of Mark was reading Herodotus, of course, but that there was already precedent for strategies of authorizing a person, place, or practice through the means of a pigeon-dove sent by the god(s).

Moral Qualities of the Peristera

Dixon is correct that the descent of the *peristera* in Mark finds its most obvious home in stories about the descent of divine powers as birds. Yet, the bird in Mark and subsequent gospels is no fierce falcon or eagle, as in Homer; it is the docile, gregarious pigeon-dove—widely adored and bearing no harm. Thus, again, we ask, why the *peristera*? In addition to the significance of birds in divination and the *peristera* in delivering messages for mortals and gods, Mark's use of the pigeon-dove makes sense when we consider how Judean figures interpret the symbolism of this species of bird—its behavior in relation to other creatures and its connection to moral character. Long associated with gregariousness, sociability, and pacific/non-predatory behavior, Judean authors also link the *peristera* to wisdom and moral perfection.

In the *Special Laws*, Philo claims that God chose the turtledove and pigeon for the fact that the pigeon is by nature the most gentle and gregarious of domesticated birds, and the turtledove the gentlest of the birds that love solitude (*Special Laws* 1.162). Later, he claims that Moses allowed that, because these birds are not carnivorous, plotting, venomous, or predatory, the "doves, pigeons, and turtle-doves: are to be domesticated, edible, and tamed (φάττας δὲ καὶ περιστερὰς καὶ τρυγόνας) (4.117). According to Philo, Noah sends the raven and dove out from the ark in Genesis because the dove is a clean, civilized, tame animal associated with humanity. While the raven is a symbol of wickedness, the dove is a symbol of virtue.

Ever the allegorist, Philo likens the turtledove and pigeon (*peristera*) to divine and human wisdom, respectively, in *Who is the Heir of Divine*

---

40. Herodotus. *The Persian Wars, Volume I: Books 1-2*. Translated by A. D. Godley. LCL 117 (Cambridge, MA: Harvard University Press, 1920).

Things. Unlike divine wisdom, which seeks solitude, human wisdom seeks the company of humanity:

> Besides all these things, "a turtle dove and a pigeon," (τρυγόνα καὶ περιστεράν) that is to say, divine and human wisdom, both of them being winged, and being animals accustomed to soar on high, still different from one another, as much as genus differs from species or a copy from the model; for divine wisdom is fond of lonely places, loving solitude, on account of the only God, whose possession she is; and this is called a turtledove, symbolically; but the other is quiet and tame, and gregarious, haunting the cities of men, and rejoicing in its abode among mortals, and so they liken her to a pigeon (περιστερᾷ) (126-27).[41]

Later in same treatise, Philo suggests that human and divine wisdom are inextricable aspects of a similar thing, of which humans are a part:

> For our own mind is here compared to a dove, since that is a creature which is tame and domesticated among us; and the turtle dove is compared to the model presented by the other, that is to say, by the mind of the world, the heaven; for the word [λόγος] of God is fond of retirement, and solitude, and privacy; not mixing itself up with the crowd of things which have been created and will be destroyed, but being at all times accustomed to roam on high, and being anxious to be an attendant only on the one supreme Being. Therefore, the two natures are indivisible; the nature, I mean, of the reasoning power in us, and of the divine Word [τοῦ θείου λόγου] above us; but though they are indivisible themselves, they divide an innumerable multitude of other things (234).[42]

For Philo, the *peristera* partakes of a wisdom from the divine realm but is particularly a kind of ideal human reasoning. Such an interpretation would make sense if the pneuma-dove, descending from the creator God, was imparted in the human being (Jesus) at the moment of adoption. Recall that Mark lacks the birth narratives added by Matthew and Luke; in Mark, the *pneuma*-dove delivers Jesus' divine adoption, bringing with it divine materiality and perfected reasoning and moral character.

Prior to Philo, however, we find another clue regarding the moral relevance of the *peristera*. The author of the *Letter of Aristeas* explains why Moses set out rules regarding which animals Israelites could consume. The rules are not arbitrary; they link the behavior of certain animals to moral qualities which the Israelites are expected to cultivate. The lengthy passage warrants full citation:

> For the sake of illustration, I will run over one or two points and explain them to you. For you must not fall into the degrading idea that it was out of regard to

---

41. Yonge, *The Works of Philo*.
42. Yonge, *The Works of Philo*.

mice and weasels and other such things that Moses drew up his laws with such exceeding care. All these ordinances were made for the sake of righteousness (δικαιοσύνης) to aid the quest for virtue and the perfecting of character. For all the birds that we use are tame and distinguished by their cleanliness, feeding on various kinds of grain and pulse, such as for instance pigeons, turtle-doves (οἶον περιστεραὶ τρυγόνες), locusts, partridges, geese also, and all other birds of this class. But the birds which are forbidden you will find to be wild and carnivorous, tyrannizing over the others by the strength which they possess, and cruelly obtaining food by preying on the tame birds enumerated above and not only so, but they seize lambs and kids, and injure human beings too, whether dead or alive, and so by naming them unclean, he gave a sign by means of them that those, for whom the legislation was ordained, must practice righteousness (δικαιοσύνη) in their hearts and not tyrannize (καταδυναστεύειν) over any one in reliance upon their own strength nor rob them of anything, but steer their course of life in accordance with justice (ἐκ δικαίου τὰ τοῦ βίου κυβερνᾶν), just as the tame birds, already mentioned, consume the different kinds of pulse that grow upon the earth and do not tyrannize to the destruction of their own kindred. Our legislator taught us therefore that it is by such methods as these that indications are given to the wise (τοῖς συνετοῖς), that they must be just and effect nothing by violence, and refrain from tyrannizing over others in reliance upon their own strength. For since it is considered unseemly even to touch such unclean animals, as have been mentioned, on account of their particular habits, ought we not to take every precaution lest our own characters should be destroyed to the same extent? Wherefore all the rules which he has laid down with regard to what is permitted in the case of these birds and other animals, he has enacted with the object of teaching us a moral lesson. For the division of the hoof and the separation of the claws are intended (lit. σημεῖόν, a *sign*) to teach us that we must discriminate between our individual actions with a view to the practice of virtue (τῶν πράξεων ἐπὶ τὸ καλῶς ἔχον).[43]

The *Letter* divides the behavior of birds into a binary of good and bad qualities: on the one hand is righteousness, the quest for virtue, tameness, cleanliness, perfecting one's character, wisdom, and steering one's life according to justice. The birds who embody these ideals are the dove-pigeon (*peristera*), turtledove, goose, and partridge. Opposite these virtues lie the carnivorous birds who embody wildness, tyranny, cruelty, force, violence, uncleanliness, predation, and injury to others. The letter does not enumerate the birds from this category, but we know this to include vultures, hawks, the other birds who hunt other birds or feast on carrion. In characteristic apologetic mode, the author intimates that by the time of the *Letter*, the national-ethnic character of Judeans has already been forged by centuries of such rules and practices whose object was to "teach a moral lesson."

---

43. *Letter of Aristeas*, 144–50, trans. R.H. Charles (Oxford: Clarendon Press, 1913).

Conclusion

Mark's Jesus is validated by the alighting of this bird and the accompanying divine voice. Choosing the *peristera* for this role is no accident, nor did subsequent gospel authors copy the bird haphazardly. Given that Matthew and Luke edit and alter Mark at will, it can be assumed that the *peristera* also functioned intentionally for them. The descent of the pigeon-dove makes a great deal of sense in light of shared views of birds in general, and of the pigeon-dove in particular. The behavior of a bird could confer divine authority upon a mortal figure. Birds were widely thought to signal divine will. More specifically, the pigeon-dove was the ideal bird for delivering messages and for symbolizing higher moral character and ideal reasoning. Nevertheless, this chapter raises two questions whose answers extend beyond its scope:

1. While it is true that people frequently viewed birds as delivering divine messages or conferring divine authority, the birds associated with such tasks typically included the owl, raven, sparrow, eagle, falcon, crow, woodpecker, and chicken. Rarely is the *peristera* on this divinatory bird list. What might it tell us about the gospel authors that they use this commonplace bird who is so uncommonly used as a divining rod? Are they signaling a critique of imperial power or even an outstripping of it (tyranny vs. righteousness as seen in the *Letter of Aristeas*)? Are they likening Jesus to a docile sacrificial offering?

2. Judean sources tend to treat the reading of bird behavior as a foreign form of divination (e.g., Josephus *Ant.* 18.201), although they are highly aware of the ubiquity the practice. It is naïve to trust proscriptive texts, insofar as actual practices often contradict the leanings of orthodox and/or authorized writers. If Judeans did not generally view birds as sent from God, but the gospel authors use the *peristera* in this manner, what does that tell us about the social location of gospel authors and their target audience? Is Mark to be viewed as evidence that Judeans did, indeed, portray birds as divinatory messengers, or are we to conclude that the author of Mark is no Judean?

My hope is that the potential direction of these questions pushes against what Willi Braun has identified as, "the restriction of curiosity" in the academic study of religion (481).[44] Instead of assuming that Judeans rejected divination, refrained from bird augury, and that gospel authors wrote silos of ethnic separateness, scholars of early Christianity may achieve greater

---

44. Willi Braun, "Introducing Religion," In *Introducing Religion: Essays in Honor of J.Z. Smith,* edited by Willi Braun and Russell T. McCutcheon (London: Equinox, 2008), 480–98.

understanding of their subject matter by approaching ancient people as though they were actual people—with overlapping interests, intersecting social locations, and who borrowed the symbols of and innovated on the practices of neighbors. The intellectual curiosity which Willi has so consistently encouraged (a throwing off of intellectual self-restriction) might allow us to see that one of Christianity's most enduring visual symbols—the white dove—arises as a product of the Mediterranean world of bird divination, courier pigeons, and an allegory of moral perfection.

Author biography

Jennifer Eyl is an Associate Professor of Religion at Tufts University. Her work focuses on religions of the ancient Mediterranean and theory of religion.

Bibliography

Aeschylus. *Prometheus Bound*. Herbert Weir Smyth, trans. Cambridge: Harvard University Press, 1926.
Allison, Dale C. "The Baptism of Jesus and a New Dead Sea Scroll," *BAR* 18.2 (1992): 58–60.
Aristotle. *History of Animals*, Volume I: Books 1-3. A. L. Peck, trans. LCL 437. Cambridge, MA: Harvard University Press, 1965.
Bovon, François. *Luke 1: A Commentary on the Gospel of Luke 1:1-9:50*. Minneapolis, MN: Fortress, 2002.
Braun, Willi. "Introducing Religion," 480–98 in *Introducing Religion: Essays in Honor of J.Z. Smith*, Willi Braun and Russell T. McCutcheon, eds. London: Equinox, 2008.
Curry, Patrick, ed. *Divination: Perspectives for a New Millennium*. New York: Routledge, 2010.
Davies, W.D. and Dale Allison, eds. *A Critical and Exegetical Commentary on the Gospel According to Saint Matthew. Volume I: Introduction and Commentary on Matthew I-VII*. Edinburgh: T&T Clark, 1988.
Dixon, Edward P. "Descending Spirit and Descending Gods: A 'Greek' Interpretation of the Spirit's 'Descent as a Dove' in Mark 1:10," *JBL* 128.4 (2009): 759–80. https://doi.org/10.2307/25610218
Eyl, Jennifer. *Signs, Wonders, and Gifts: Divination in the Letters of Paul*. New York: Oxford University Press, 2019. https://doi.org/10.1093/oso/9780190924652.001.0001
Finkelberg, Margalit. "Homer as a Foundation Text," 75–96 in *Homer, the Bible, and Beyond*, eds. Margalit Finkelberg and Guy Stroumsa. Leiden: Brill, 2003. https://doi.org/10.1163/9789004496385_007
Finney, Paul Corby, ed. *Eerdman's Encyclopedia of Early Christian Art and Archaeology*. Grand Rapids, MI: Eerdmans, 2017.
Gero, Stephen. "The Spirit as Dove at the Baptism of Jesus," *NovT* 18.1 (1976): 17–35. https://doi.org/10.1163/156853676X00021

Green, Steven. "Malevolent Gods and Promethean Birds: Contesting Augury in Augustus' Rome," *TAPA* 139 (2009): 147–67. https://doi.org/10.1353/apa.0.0019

Herodotus. *The Persian Wars*, Volume I: Books 1-2. A. D. Godley, trans. LCL 117. Cambridge: Harvard University Press, 1920. https://doi.org/10.4159/DLCL.herodotus-persian_wars.1920

Homer. *The Iliad*. A.T. Murray, trans. Cambridge: Harvard University Press, 1924. https://doi.org/10.4159/DLCL.homer-iliad.1924

Johnston, Sarah Iles. *Ancient Greek Divination*. Malden, MA: Blackwell, 2008. https://doi.org/10.1002/9781444302998

Jeffers, Ann. *Magic and Divination in Ancient Palestine and Syria*. New York: Brill, 1996.

Keck, Leander E. "The Spirit and the Dove," *New Testament Studies* 17 (1970-71): 41–67.2. https://doi.org/10.1017/S0028688500014909

Leighton, Albert C. "Secret Communication Among the Greeks and Romans," *Technology and Culture* 10.2 (1969): 139–54. https://doi.org/10.2307/3101474

Lewis, Sian and Lloyd Llewellyn-Jones, eds. *The Culture of Animals in Antiquity.* New York: Routledge, 2018. https://doi.org/10.4324/9781315201603

Mynott, Jeremy. *Birds in the Ancient World*. Oxford: Oxford University Press, 2018.

Nolland, John. *The Gospel of Matthew: A Commentary on the Greek Text*. Grand Rapids: Eerdmans, 2005.

Philo. *The Works of Philo*. C.D. Yonge, trans. Peabody, MA Hendrickson Publishers, 1993.

Pleket, H.W., Stroud, R.S. and J.H.M. Strubbe, eds. *SEG*, 42–1789. Amsterdam 1995. http://dx.doi.org.ezproxy.library.tufts.edu/10.1163/1874-6772_seg_a42_1789

Pliny. *Natural History*. LCL 353. H. Rackham, trans. Cambridge: Harvard University Press, 1940.

Toperoff, Shlomo P. "The Dove, Turtle-Dove, and Pigeon in Bible and Midrash," *Dor-le-dor* 15.3 (1987): 181–5.

Walsh, Robyn Faith. "The *Satyrica* and the Gospels in the Second Century," *TCQ* 70.1 (2020): 1–12. https://doi.org/10.1017/S0009838820000488

—*The Origins of Early Christian Literature: Contextualizing the New Testament within Greco-Roman Literary Culture*. Cambridge: Cambridge University Press, 2021. https://doi.org/10.1017/9781108883573

Chapter Eight

Syriac Dialogue Hymns and New Comedy

Robyn Faith Walsh

Willi Braun: Dinosaur Hunter. Or, at least, that's what pops into my head whenever I encounter his name. Ever since reading his 2005 "Rhetoric, Rhetoricality, and Discourse Performances," this moniker has stuck with me. In that piece he charmingly describes the study of the ancient Mediterranean as more or less an examination of an "ancient word record, fossilized in textual form."[1] Meditating on the logocentrism and "logographic reasoning" of modernity, he persuasively argues that the "human 'voice'" has been "colonized" by the text.[2] In the course of this argument, he notes that "Graeco-Roman cultures generally preferred 'live' performances and visual representations to written texts" and suggests that the field has been seduced by the rhetoric and syntax of the static and bounded word.[3]

With Braun's cautions in mind, this essay reconsiders the compositional, stylistic, and conceptual construction of Syriac dialogue hymns, with concern for how the use of stock characters, story lines, and dialogue within New Comedy—and related forms of "live" entertainment from late antiquity (e.g., miming and declamation)—acted as potentially useful comparanda for the authors of the dialogue hymns. Much like performances set in the theater, the dynamic established by the dialogue hymn offered a space for the retelling of well-known myths with familiar characters and plots. Coupled with the popularity of comedic theater as a local, civic amusement, I suggest that the dialogue hymn embodies what amounted to an open competition between the church and the theater. And it is arguably a relic of speech-in-action— a live experience preserved in the amber of a fixed text.

***

---

1. Willi Braun, "Rhetoric, Rhetoricality, and Discourse Performances," in *Rhetoric and Reality in Early Christianities*, ed. Willi Braun (Waterloo, ON: Wilfrid Laurier University Press, 2005), 1–26, cit. 1.
2. Braun, "Rhetoric, Rhetoricality, and Discourse Performances," 2.
3. Braun, "Rhetoric, Rhetoricality, and Discourse Performances," 2.

Traditionally Syrian dialogue hymns[4] are described as inheriting their particular form from ancient Mesopotamian contest literature.[5] Characterized by two opposing figures debating the merits of their respective positions, evidence for this popular genre spans some four millennia and is first attested in cuneiform Sumerian in the early second millennium BCE.[6] Often a dialogue between personified non-human entities (e.g., Summer versus Winter; the Hoe versus the Plough;),[7] it boasts a relatively stable compositional structure: a brief introduction of the core adversarial situation and its players; each rival makes their case in turn (occasionally in verse)[8]; concluding with a declared victor.[9]

Reflecting on its remarkable resilience, some scholars maintain that the genre has traversed myriad cultural and temporal divides "virtually unchanged."[10] In other words, this contest literature is not demonstrative of a certain conservatism of thought or formulae but, rather, is defined by a simple persistent structure. Given the broad contours which define this genre and the more specific compositional features that dialogue hymns share in kind with other so-called dispute poems, there is little doubt that this thesis is fundamentally correct. It is the case, for instance, that these hymns are

---

4. Robert Murray, "Aramaic and Syriac Dispute-Poems and their Connections" in *Studia Aramaica: New Sources and New Approaches*, ed. M. J. Geller et al. (Oxford: Oxford University Press, 1995), 157.

5. For instance, Sebastian Brock, "Syriac Poetry on Biblical Themes: The Prophet Elijah and the Widow of Sarepta," *The Harp* 3 (1990): 75–86, esp. 76; Sebastian Brock, "Syriac Dispute Poems: The Various Types," in *Dispute Poems and Dialogues in the Ancient and Mediaeval Near East*, ed. G. J. Reinink and H. L. J. Vanstiphout (Leuven: Department Oriëntalistiek, 1991), 109–19; Sebastian Brock, "Mary and the Angel, and Other Syriac Dialogue Poems," *Marianum* 68 (2006): 117–51; Kristi Upson-Saia, "Caught in a Compromising Position: The Biblical Exegesis and Characterization of Biblical Protagonist in the Syriac Dialogue Hymns," *Hugoye* 9.2 (2006): 194 (§4). Averil Cameron, "Disputations, Polemical Literature and the Formation of Opinion in the Early Byzantine Period," in Reinink and Vanstiphout, *Dispute Poems and Dialogues*, 91–108.

6. Brock, "Mary and the Angel," 118.

7. See Herman L. J. Vanstiphout, "Lore Learning and Levity in the Sumerian Disputations: A Matter of Form, or Substance?," in Reinink and Vanstiphout, *Dispute Poems and Dialogues*, 23–46.

8. See Brock, "Mary and the Angel," 118 and Reinink and Vanstiphout, *Dispute Poems and Dialogues*, 1.

9. Reinink and Vanstiphout, *Dispute Poems and Dialogues*, 2.

10. That is, save slight local variations such as human or divine adversaries, more than two speaking figures, or the use of particular rhetorical devices. Reinink and Vanstiphout, *Dispute Poems and Dialogues*, 1. Also see Vanstiphout, "Lore Learning and Levity in the Sumerian Disputations," 31 in which he discusses the use of lists as evidence of "trainee scribe" material.

dialogical in nature with alternating stanzas in verse, usually addressing a particular point of contention or theological issue.[11] The oft-cited dispute between Death and Satan is a useful example: each character argues for their superiority over humanity, using a variety of rhetorical techniques to prove their case; yet, in the end, they learn that Christ's death and descent into Sheol has rendered them powerless.[12] A contentious repartee between two like figures concludes with the declaration of a victor (albeit in this case the victor is a third party) or, at least, a resolution. Kristi Upson-Saia argues that the roughly fifty ancient Syriac poems which survive[13] represent a clear amalgamation of this genre with both narrative *aggadah* and what she deems "freeze-frame exegesis"—that is, a focused view on a particular biblical/apocryphal passage or problem, expanded through dialogue.[14] The dialogue or dispute genre, therefore, was employed strategically as an exegetical tool; through dialogue "authors did not simply comment on the biblical narratives but rather placed their... interpretations into the voices of the original biblical characters."[15] As a result, biblical figures were fashioned to sanction and legitimize the moral psychological position(s) of their author. The dispute poem offered a unique opportunity to the poet or hymnist for open position-taking through the authority of biblical characters in an otherwise relatively static literary field.

Yet character development, "plot" advancement, and the performance of these works remain undertheorized. When considering the contemporaneous literary and performative landscape of the hymn writers, the theater and Greek and Roman tragedy and comedy present many striking parallels to the Christian dispute poem. Both are primarily driven by dialogue, with disagreement or dispute often the motivating force behind the storyline. Arguments become fodder for the explication of a character's thoughts, motivations, or beliefs[16] and, in many cases, dialogue is metered and set to music.[17] The presentation of stock characters and plots, particularly in New Comedy, mirrors elements in the hymns as well: themes of unexpected

11. Brock, "Syriac Dispute Poems," 109.
12. Cf. Brock, "Mary and the Angel," 118.
13. Brock, "Syriac Dispute Poems," 109; Brock, "Mary and the Angel," 3; Sebastian Brock, "Dialogue and other *Sughyotho*," in *Mélanges offerts au Prof. P. Louis Hage*, ed. A. Ayoub Chahwan (Kaslik: PUSEK, 2009), 363–84.
14. Upson-Saia, "Caught in a Compromising Position," 192–5 (§5–7).
15. Upson-Saia, "Caught in a Compromising Position,"198–9 (§13).
16. Ariana Traill, *Women and the Comic Plot in Menander* (Cambridge: Cambridge University Press, 2008), 15.
17. R. L. Hunter, *The New Comedy of Greece and Rome* (Cambridge: Cambridge University Press, 1985), 42; Erich Segal, *The Death of Comedy* (Cambridge, MA: Harvard University Press, 2001), 192.

pregnancy, mistaken identity, the reification or establishment of familial structures, skeptical husbands, jealous lovers, and both chaste and sinful women are all shared by these chronicles. To my knowledge these associations have not been considered. Despite rhetoric that has pitted the so-called secular "Church of Satan"[18] (the theater) against Christian congregations, a closer consideration of the relationship that Christians had with urban theaters reveals a far more complex story.[19] As Jacob of Sarug once quipped: "I do not go [to the theater] that I may believe, but I go that I may laugh. It is a game; it is not paganism."[20] As such, it is not unimaginable that the hymnists in question referred to the form and structure of the popular works of Menander, Plautus, or Terence for inspiration when building upon the dispute genre by composing more complex characters, character dialogues, and central controversies in their hymns.

Dispute Poems and Dialogues: A Brief History

The dispute poem genre can be traced back as far as Sumerian literature by means of Akkadian sources.[21] These early protagonistic exchanges largely feature charming but prosaic personifications—Cattle and Grain, Pickaxe and Plough, the Ox and the Horse—and over time found popularity throughout the Mediterranean.[22] A fifth-century BCE Aramaic dispute between the Thorn-bush and the Pomegranate exemplifies the genre:

> The Thorn-bush to the Pomegranate: "What is the use
> of your many thorns for him who would touch your fruit?"
>
> The Pomegranate replied to the Thorn-bush and said:
> "You are nothing but thorns for anyone who touches you"[23]

The earliest examples of Christian dispute poems appear in the fourth century in the Nisibene cycle of Ephrem with a hymn detailing Christ's descent into Sheol and a subsequent contest of words between Death and Satan.[24] The majority of the remaining corpus of these *sughyotho* is anonymous.

---

18. John of Ephesus, *Ecclesiastical History* 5.17; cf. Peter Brown, *The Rise of Western Christendom: Triumph and Diversity, A.D. 200–1000*, 2nd ed. (Oxford: Blackwell, 2003), 171.

19. Brown, *Rise of Western Christendom*, 170ff.

20. Jacob of Sarug, *On the Spectacles of the Theater* 30; cf. Brown, *Rise of Western Christendom*, 170.

21. Sebastian P. Brock, "The Dispute Poem: From Sumer to Syriac," *Journal of the Canadian Society for Syriac Studies* 1 (2001): 3.

22. Brock, "Dispute Poem," 3.

23. Cited from Brock, "Dispute Poem," 3.

24. Hymn no. 52; Brock "Dispute Poem," 4.

The *sughyotho* were a subset of *mimre*, "verse homilies chanted in a simple meter"[25] and were characterized not only by the fact that they had abandoned prose for verse,[26] but also by their dramatic overtones and the use of biblical figures or personified Christian imagery (e.g., Body and Soul). Although these particular dispute hymns—like the dispute dialogues which predated them—often continued to feature two-character debates over precedence through an impassioned listing of their respective merits, the Christian Syrian dispute genre also incorporated "theological arguments"[27] or deliberation over certain virtues and vices, usually expressed by biblical figures. Framed by short, contextualizing introductions and summarizing conclusions, these hymns generally followed an isosyllabic pattern (7 + 7), often featuring alternating alphabetic acrostics. Another common structural feature was for each speaker to adopt the (accusatory) words of their interlocutor from the previous stanza to begin their response, while transposing their meaning.[28] This approach is illustrated well in *The sinful woman and Satan (I)*:

> Satan: "You are brazen and impudent
> and only debauched men love you;
> you are an unclean corpse,
> so why are you off to this holy man?"
> Woman: "Yes, I am brazen and impudent
> and debauched men love me,
> but Christ the Bridegroom has betrothed me
> and he has made me holy, to be with himself."[29]

Likely sung antiphonally by choirs of women (with occasional interjections from community responses),[30] these charged exchanges marked a clear shift in the Syriac hymn tradition from melodic musings on the nature of divinity or biblical figures to a more dramatized— or, indeed, theatrical— rendering and subject matter. And because the structure and form of the genre was built, in part, on the back of dispute literature, it lent itself to subject matter already laced with themes of conflict, controversy, misrecognition, and suspense— as well as expansions on biblical scenes in which the stakes were

---

25. Susan Ashbrook Harvey, "2000 NAPS Presidential Address Spoken Words, Voiced Silence: Biblical Women in Syriac Tradition," *JECS* 9. 1 (2001): 107–108.

26. There are very few exceptions to this rule. In fact, Brock only identifies one prose dispute hymn in the corpus of Syriac literature. Brock "Dispute Poem," 5.

27. Brock, "Syriac Dispute Poems," 109.

28. Brock, "Syriac Dispute Poems," 110.

29. §§34–37; Cited from Sebastian P. Brock, "The Sinful Woman and Satan: Two Syriac Dialogue Poems," *Oriens Christianus* 72 (1988): 48–49.

30. Harvey, "2000 NAPS Presidential Address," 108.

high for the characters involved. Popular pairings such as Cain and Abel, Christ and the Pharisees, Church and Synagogue, and even Nero and Peter were well suited to this model. Furthermore, this kind of perpetual and, often, overtly combative literary tête à tête offered numerous possibilities for incorporating rhetorical strategies, literary tropes, or political stances into the arguments of the interlocutors, making it a convenient option for the hymnist.

Turning to New Comedy, the similarities between the stock characters and themes rife in the works of Menander and the scenarios featured in a number of the Syrian dialogue hymns are striking, suggesting that perhaps the dramatic interplays found on the stage may have influenced the Christian hymnist when composing the exchanges taking place between their own characters.

The (New) Comic Model

The notion that New Comedy was somehow in fact "new" is itself somewhat amusing given that it is essentially a creative reworking of the Euripidean formula of Aristotelian ἀναγνώρισις (lat. *cognitio*) and μηχάνημα (lat. *frustratio*)—that is, recognition "followed by intrigue."[31] New Comedy flips this formula on its head by withholding the resolution of conflict until the very end of the play. Instead of kings and queens and highly politicized *tragic* episodes, New Comedy featured characters and situations of a humbler nature, *res publica* verses *res privata*.[32] In this respect New Comedy is almost maddeningly formulaic, particularly in the case of the highly regarded Menander. Virtually without exception, it is concerned with the pursuit and fulfillment of love, and the confusions, complications, and hijinks that ensue from its initial *frustratio* are the well from which the playwright draws humor.

In his *Moralia*, Plutarch proclaimed that Menander, like Homer, possessed an unparalleled and sophisticated style and asked plainly "what other reason would a cultivated man have to go to the theater?"[33] Plutarch also claimed that Menander "of all Greek authors, was the one most read and

---

31. For instance, Hunter, *New Comedy of Greece and Rome*, 1–23; W. D. Howarth, ed., *Comic Drama: The European Heritage* (London: Methuen, 1978), 32; Segal, *Death of Comedy*, 152; Netta Zagagi, *The Comedy of Menander: Convention, Variation, and Originality* (Bloomington: Indiana University Press, 1995), 15; *Vita Euripidis*, P. Oxy. 1176, fr. 39.

32. Gilbert Murray, *Aristophanes: A Study* (Oxford: Clarendon, 1933), 251; cf. Segal, *Death of Comedy*, 154.

33. Plutarch, *Moralia*, 853–54.

discussed at banquets, in the classroom, and at competitions."³⁴ Evidence from progymnasmata as well as the practiced *sententiae* of declamations bears this out as school γνῶμαι—the so-called "wisdom sayings" excerpted, practiced, and commented upon by students at all levels of rhetorical training—were often cited from Menander and students were asked to comment on maxims like "A bride without a dowry has no frankness of speech" or "A prudent woman is a storehouse of virtue."³⁵ Aelius Theon, author of preliminary school exercises, advised "What would be a better example of *prosopopoeia* [speech-in-character] than in the poetry of Homer and the dialogues of Plato and other Socratics and the dramas of Menander?"³⁶ Similarly, Quintilian advised looking to Menander as a superior model for the composition and development of character in declamation:³⁷

> And a careful reading of Menander alone would, in my judgment, be sufficient to develop all the qualities I am recommending [for declamation]: so complete is his representation of life, so rich his invention and so fluent his style, so perfectly does he adapt himself to every circumstance, character and emotion...³⁸

Without doubt Menander was the most celebrated and imitated of the New Comics with his formulaic, yet artful, presentation of character being one of the reasons for his acclaim.

The quintessential Menander plot was largely based on what has been termed "rape and recognition" with only "cosmetic changes."³⁹ The storyline begins with an unexpected pregnancy, with the status of the mother and child at the center of the subsequent *frustratio* and series of misrecognitions. The conclusion features resolution of the turmoil, generally through an appropriate marriage or restoration of a birthright, intended to represent a certain renewal of society—an "almost subliminal leitmotif of resurrection."⁴⁰ Or, as Erich Segal summarizes, the plot resolution assures that a "line of Athenian upper-class twits is perpetuated."⁴¹

---

34. Segal, *Death of Comedy*, 155.
35. Heather Irene Waddell Gruber, "The Women of Greek Declamation and the Reception of Comic Stereotypes," (PhD diss., University of Iowa, 2009), 33–34.
36. Gruber, "Women of Greek Declamation," 4.
37. Richard Hawley, "Female Characterization in Greek Declamation," in *Ethics and Rhetoric: Classical Essays for Donald Russell on His Seventy-Fifth Birthday*, eds. Doreen Innes, Harry M. Hine, and C. B. R. Pelling (Oxford: Clarendon, 1995), 255.
38. *Inst.* 10.1.69; 1.11.12-13. Also see Hermogenes *Id.* 2.3 = Sp. 305-6.
39. Segal, *Death of Comedy*, 155.
40. Segal, *Death of Comedy*, 161.
41. Segal, *Death of Comedy*. See Menander's *Dysc* (842), *Mis* (444), *Periceir* (1013); *Samia* (727).

Along the way, of course, a cast of familiar or stock characters engages in dispute and misrecognition to elicit humor. The love-struck youths, the disagreeable father, the nagging wife, the virtuous maiden, the boastful solider, the clever slave, the harlot with the heart of gold[42] were all staples of New Comedy.[43] Women in particular were often portrayed as either "suitable for partying [or] parturition"[44]—that is, either as concerned mothers, wives, or tarted-up prostitutes. The stock nature of these characters allowed Menander a great deal of latitude to develop a sufficiently nuanced portrayal of familiar faces through dialogue.

The misrecognition or misperception which was so pervasive in the Menandrian plot also acted as a tool by which one could display the central concerns, motivations, virtues, and vices of a character. As Henri Bergson explains: "Menander is by no means concerned with *ethos* [character] by itself, but rather with the way his characters think, the way they make assessments and deductions, the way that *ethos* is sometimes a function of *dianoia* [intelligence, intellectual capacity]."[45] Skillful use of rhetorical technique offered a measure of distinctiveness in an otherwise formulaic stock framework. That said, familiar characters in familiar situations continued to think along broadly familiar lines, which is to say that the character types that made frequent appearances in routine scripts found themselves making choices on similar grounds. Indeed, ancient audiences were trained to anticipate particular responses from various characters depending on factors such as age, sex, or status.[46] Audiences who had been trained in rhetoric—or those who had simply been exposed to public declaimers, mimes, or even the law courts—would have readily recognized these same tropes "in the mouth of comic characters."[47] Ariana Traill suggests that "It is not surprising that orators found common ground with playwrights. Both needed to appeal to common beliefs and opinions (what Aristotle called ἔνδοξα) in order to write effective speeches."[48] It was Menander's convincing mastery of this technique that led to praise for the "realism" of his portrayals and

---

42. Katharine Haynes, *Fashioning the Feminine in the Greek Novel* (London: Routledge, 2003), 113.

43. Segal, *Death of Comedy*, 158; Haynes, *Fashioning the Feminine*, 113–14.

44. Haynes, *Fashioning the Feminine*, 154.

45. Adele Scafuro, "When a Gesture Was Misinterpreted: Didonai Titthion in Menander's Samia," in *Gestures: Essays in Ancient History, Literature, and Philosophy Presented to Alan L. Boegehold: On the Occasion of His Retirement and His Seventy-Fifth Birthday*, eds. Geoffrey W. Bakewell and James P. Sickinger (Oxford: Oxbow, 2003), 115; Traill, *Women and the Comic Plot*, 15.

46. Traill, *Women and the Comic Plot*, 84.

47. Traill, *Women and the Comic Plot*, 85.

48. Traill, *Women and the Comic Plot*, 84.

made him a model for those seeking to add "flesh to the bones" of their own literary characters.

One common pairing of the comedic type described above was the genteel man, besotted or engaged to a maiden curiously bearing what Menander routinely deems, tongue-in-cheek, a "child of the gods."[49] With that in mind, let us turn to the dialogue hymns.

The Dialogue Hymn of Mary and Joseph

Based on a short passage in the Gospel of Matthew 1.18–25, the dialogue hymn of Mary and Joseph imagines an exchange between the couple upon Joseph's realization that his fiancée is with child. Notably, there is no mention of such a conversation in the gospel itself; thus, this hymn (as with many others) is directed at a narrative lacuna. Before Joseph is able to carry out a relationship exit strategy, an angel appears to him and explains that the child was divinely conceived and he need not hesitate in accepting Mary as his wife (cf. Matt 1.20).

Given the social, legal, and ethical issues connected with a child being born out of wedlock, the subject of Joseph's reaction to Mary's premarital condition lends itself quite nicely to the dispute genre. Not only is the circumstance a subject of controversy, but the question of Joseph's ultimate acceptance of the situation is pedagogically useful as a meditation on the limits of faith. In the hymn, Mary explains to Joseph that she has been impregnated by the Holy Spirit; Joseph is initially incredulous and proceeds to "chide and reproach" the "young girl":[50]

> Joseph: "Reveal to me the secret of what has happened to you;
>   it is most shocking, what you speak of:
>   who led you astray, virgin,
>   and snatched your wealth, chaste girl?"
>
> Mary: "I will reveal to you how it happened,"
>   says Mary, "So listen, Joseph.
>   A man of fire came down to me,
>   he gave me a greeting and this took place."
>
> Joseph: "That I should believe this is hard:
>   it is not nice, so do not repeat it.
>   If you are willing, speak to me
>   about what took place: who led you astray?"[51]

---

49. Cf. n. 41 above.
50. §4; Brock, "Mary and the Angel," 132.
51. §§ 5–7; Brock, "Mary and the Angel," 132.

The dialogue continues along these lines until Mary's persistence begins to crack Joseph's accusatory veneer. He begins to abandon what reason tells him is the only possibility (Mary's unfaithfulness) and considers the implications should Mary be telling the truth,[52] all while continuing to offer forensic evidence on the situation before him:

> Joseph: "There are two possibilities, and both disturb me:
> if what you say is true, it is most frightening for me,
> but if it is untrue, that is a great grief.
> How I wish I could escape from the two."[53]

Joseph remains skeptical until the final verse of the dialogue in which the angel appears and informs him that "Mary… had not lied." The next morning Joseph returns to Mary and kneels "in worship" before her "full of wonder."[54] Overall, this hymn offers a number of creative additions to the meager version of the tale told in Matthew, fashioning Joseph in the mold of the cuckolded husband or spurned lover.

The subject of unexpectedly pregnant women and their disbelieving fiancés or husbands was an exceedingly common trope in New Comedy. A useful example of this trope is Menander's *Samia*: a man named Demeas has taken into his household a low status woman (possibly an ἑταίρα) named Chrysis who assumes the role of his wife—although their union is never formalized. During a long period in which Demeas is unable to be at home, his son, Moschion, rapes the daughter of a neighbor and, after a child is born as a result, Chrysis accepts the illegitimate baby as her own. Demeas returns and, through a series of misunderstandings, learns that the child is Moschion's, but imagines an affair between Moschion and Chrysis in his absence. The ensuing argument between Demeas and Chrysis results in Demeas breaking their union on account of her perceived adultery and ingratitude. Demeas' suspicions are false, but he is unable to cleave himself from what he judges to be the truth about Chrysis and her baby. Only third parties are able to assuage his ire.

Similar to strategies found in forensic speeches, Demeas tries and judges Chrysis on the basis of probability (τὰ εἰκότα)—that is, what he assumes is characteristic of women in her (perceived) situation—an approach commonly advised in rhetorical handbooks for those attempting to convince an audience

---

52. Joseph: "I am astounded at what you say: how can I listen to your words? Virgins simply do not get pregnant unless they have intercourse or get married"; Sebastian P. Brock, *The Bible in the Syriac Tradition*, 2nd ed. (Piscataway, NJ: Gorgias, 2006). 83.
53. Brock, *Bible in the Syriac Tradition*, 83.
54. Brock, *Bible in the Syriac Tradition*, 83.

that an individual's actions are consummate with their character.⁵⁵ Rhetorical handbooks like the *Rhetorica ad Alexandrum*, for instance, advise speakers to consider what is characteristic of certain persons in various circumstances and "infer what is normally the case from people resembling them (ἀπό τῶν ὁμοίων) ... for example ... say that [a young man] has acted as persons of that age usually do act, for the allegations will be believed against him too on the ground of similarity."⁵⁶ Drawing on negative female stereotypes from Helen to prostitutes, Demeas engages in precisely this brand of rhetorical acrobatics until he has thoroughly convinced himself of Chrysis' infidelity; she was a low-class woman and acted in a manner consistent with that status. As Traill notes, "accusations of greed, promiscuity, shamelessness and deceit all belong to this stock type," as does the interpretation of ambiguous evidence "to realize [the husband or lover's] worst fears."⁵⁷

Joseph engages in similar discernment in the dialogue hymn. Whereas in the gospel account we are presented with a man who seemingly dispassionately assesses Mary's situation and desires to resolve the matter quietly, the Joseph of our hymn is distressed and "dumbfounded" at Mary's infidelity.⁵⁸ He "chides and reproach[es]"⁵⁹ her, as does Demeas of Chrysis, disbelieving her tale of a "man of fire" and deeming that her youth ("Listen, young girl"), rape or seduction ("who led you astray, virgin"⁶⁰) are far more likely scenarios. The tension between the characters builds through Joseph as he experiences twofold distress both over the fact that his intended is pregnant before marriage and that her defense is contrary to what he is apt to believe. As with Demeas and Chrysis, this tension can only be resolved through a third party— the angel— who calms his fears. Before the angel intercedes, however, the audience is encouraged to sympathize with the accused woman who has, in truth, acted virtuously and is therefore a sympathetic figure, despite the use of common rhetorical arguments against the stock type of deceitful and cunning women.

Although things do not work out as well for Demeas and Chrysis as they do for Joseph and Mary (Chrysis finally runs off with the baby to avoid further wrongful persecution), both the comedy and hymn play on a common comic trope: "what happens when people observe and judge those they care

---

55. *Rhetorica ad Alexandrum* 1428a27-32; cf. Aristotle, *On Rhetoric*, 1392b19-21; cited from Traill, *Women and the Comic Plot*, 104, n. 76.
56. *Rhetorica ad Alexandrum* 1428b25-9; cited from Traill, *Women and the Comic Plot*, 105.
57. Traill, *Women and the Comic Plot*, 97; 92.
58. §4; Brock, "Mary and the Angel," 132.
59. Brock, "Mary and the Angel," 132.
60. §5; Brock, "Mary and the Angel," 132.

about most."⁶¹ Men leaping to conclusions about their mates without sufficient evidence is ubiquitous in these plots. Traill explains:

> It is more important to cast the women as outsiders, blaming them for the misdeeds of φίλοι, than to salvage anything of the romantic relationship. The dramatic purpose of detailing the men's mistaken reasoning is to reveal their fears and anxieties, as well as their emotional and moral priorities, not to characterize the women…⁶²

Given Joseph's apparent grief over Mary's condition, it is clear that he is wrestling between feelings of affection for her and condemnation of her moral character. He suspects she is a deceiver, an adulteress and—with her story of a miraculous conception—a liar, and his dialogue with her bears this out. He is not won easily as assumptions about feminine immorality lead him to reason that the worst conclusion is in fact the truth. Joseph, therefore, plays to type: he misunderstands the circumstances of his beloved, he jumps to conclusions, and his dialogues with other characters are characterized by misperception and appeals to reason on the merits of probability over and against the protests of his partner.⁶³ These thematic similarities between the New Comic dialogues and this hymn—that is, of misrecognition, assumption, and failed attempts at persuasion as they relate to the stock character of the "cuckolded husband"—are striking in that they suggest more than a passing awareness on the behalf of the hymnographer of the rhetorical, theatrical, and agonistic tradition—whether it be from paideia, handbooks, declaimers, the theater, or mimes. More than simply understanding how to portray the betrayed spouse convincingly, the composer of *Mary and Joseph* amplifies a brief mention in Matthew of Joseph's intention to divorce the pregnant Mary into a dispute between the two figures centered on issues of status, fidelity, and reason through the same strategies found in comedic dialogue. While this is not to suggest that the author of *Mary and Joseph* had *Samia*—or any other Menandrian New Comedy for that matter—directly in mind, a comparison of the common threads in each offers a much more thoroughgoing understanding of the characters of Mary and, especially, Joseph than is provided by a comparison with the dispute genre alone.

---

61. Traill, *Women and the Comic Plot*, 110.
62. Traill, *Women and the Comic Plot*, 110.
63. His continued skepticism has the additional purchase of creating space for Mary to wax doctrinal on her pregnancy, insisting that the child himself will inform Joseph of the truth and define the nature of their future relationship. Mary: "Now I shall pour out my words and address my Son hidden within my womb; he will reveal to you that I shall have no other children, and that I shall not be deprived of your company" (Brock, *Bible in the Syriac Tradition*, 83).

The Dialogue Hymn of the Sinful Woman and Satan

Closely inter-related with the stock character of the cuckolded husband was the spurned lover. Both aching as a result of a perceived betrayal of their loyalties or affections, these characters often shared similar expressions of disappointment and remorse, although with some very particular distinctions. Unlike the cuckolded husband who is loathe to take back his spouse, the spurned lover is frequently found not only desiring a reunion with their beloved but also contemplating ways to win them back despite their dalliances. There is a certain theme of loyalty in the face of betrayal for this figure that eludes other stock characters of a similar ilk.

In *The Sinful Woman and Satan (II)*, the character of Satan wears the guise of the spurned lover, making appeals to the sinful woman to rekindle their relationship. Primarily based on the so-called sinful woman character in Luke 7, the dialogue plays on a wholly imaginary discourse between the woman who washes Jesus' feet and Satan—a character with whom the woman never directly interacts in the gospel account.[64] In Luke 7.47-50 the woman is forgiven of her sins by Jesus on the merit of her faith and, presumably, proceeds with a reformed life. The scene of the dialogue hymn is set in the moments before the sinful woman departs to make her appeal to Jesus at the home of Simon the Pharisee when "The Evil One became aware that the sinner wished to become a penitent."[65] He approaches the sinful woman and bemoans their lost love and questions why she has been "[led] astray"[66]:

> Woman: "(Take) your gold with you to perdition
>   and your silver with you to burn (in hell).
>   I do not want you to give me (anything),
>   or that I should give you (in return)."
>
> Evil One: "With all this hostility
>   and such great enmity
>   why is it that you hate and abhor me,
>   seeing that I love you?"[67]

As the dialogue proceeds, Satan refuses to relent in his pursuit of the woman's affections, even as she reveals that her love is now firmly with Jesus and that *he* is her only desire:

---

64. Harvey, "2000 NAPS Presidential Address," 121.
65. §5; Brock, "The Sinful Woman," 59.
66. §7; Brock, "The Sinful Woman," 59.
67. §8–9; Brock, "The Sinful Woman," 60.

Woman: "My eyes have not beheld the like of you.
    how brazen is your impudence!
How many words will you make me listen to?
    I have no desire for you."

Evil One: "Turn back from following this man:
    he is a man who was not conceived in wedlock with man;
if he sees you, I will feel sorry,
    for he will destroy you with the twinkling of an eye."

Woman: "It is to this man that I run,
    and I will not turn back from him.
Even if he actually kills me,
    I do not want anything apart from him."[68]

The highly charged language between the characters recalls the plight of the jilted lover whose beloved has left him for another man. Despite his best appeals to the worst possible scenario, she is unwavering to the point that his insistence tries her temper.[69] As Satan is repeatedly rebuked, he shifts his argumentative strategies to New Comic tropes. Appeals to remembrances of past gifts and other niceties are coupled with harsh accusations focused on her status as a prostitute and, as was the case with Demeas in *Samia*, a fundamental (and, in the case of Satan, willful) misrecognition of her personal morality in favor of what her character represents socially and legally.

In Menander's *Perikeiromene*, for instance, a solider named Polemon is led to believe (mistakenly) that his betrothed, Glykera, has begun a liaison with another man. Polemon proceeds to wallow, his friends chiding him that he is no more to Glykera than a "lover in a sorry state."[70] He determines that she must have "left" (ἀπελήλυθεν) him because he has treated her "inappropriately" (οὐ κατὰ τρόπον) and he endeavors to win her back by changing his ways, valuing her more, and reforming his attitude.[71] In the course of this soul searching, Polemon begins to recall bitterly to his friend Pataikos his past generosity to Glykera and, particularly, the finery (κόσμος) he has bestowed upon her:

---

68. §20–22; Brock, "The Sinful Woman," 61.
69. §20; "The Sinful Woman," 61.
70. Traill, *Women and the Comic Plot*, 42.
71. See Traill, *Women and the Comic Plot*, 43–4.

Polemon: "If I don't go on striving in every way—if you could just see her clothing!"
Pataikos: "That's okay."
Polemon: "Take a look, Pataikos, for god's sake. You'll pity me more."
Pataikos: "Oh, Poseidon!"[72]

Implicit in Polemon's lament is the realization that his past generosity has imposed "an obligation which has not been met"—namely, the reciprocation of love.[73] He implores Pataikos to go speak to Glykera on his behalf, ostensibly to remind her of the very gifts he has mentioned and the fond memories they shared. Satan evokes a similar lament in his dialogue with the sinful woman, listing all of the material gifts he has given her, distressed that they no longer hold sway:

Evil One: "The scarlet of brides
    and the purple of queens
have I spread beneath your feet,
    and do you thus revile me?"

Woman: "Dust and ashes are preferable to me,
    A sackclothe [sic] garment is what I desire;
your clothing and purple are hateful to me
    for they come with every kind of disadvantage."

Evil One: "All of Syria's luxuries,
    Cyprus' finest wine
have I got ready for you, but now you hate me
    (using) that deceitful tongue of yours."

Woman: "Fie upon your luxuries, how evil they are;
    fie on your wines, how they unsettle one.
Your luxuries I consider a calamity,
    your wine a fountain of filth."[74]

Like Polemon, Satan conjures memories of his gifts to his beloved and bemoans that she no longer feels obligated to return his favors.[75] This tactic is coupled with reference to her social status and perceived character, despite displaying no intention of continuing her sinful ways. He references her "deceitful tongue,"[76] despite her sincerity. He even threatens that Jesus and his disciples might kill her because of her past.[77] Satan's insistence that

---

72. *Perik.* 515–22; cited from Traill, *Women and the Comic Plot*, 44.
73. Traill, *Women and the Comic Plot*, 44.
74. §§ 11–15; Brock, "The Sinful Woman," 60–1.
75. §§15; 18; Brock, "The Sinful Woman," 61.
76. §13; Brock, "The Sinful Woman," 60.
77. §23; Brock, "The Sinful Woman," 61.

the woman's moral character remains unchanged is consistent with both stereotypes of women in general and prostitutes in particular.[78] The stock character of the prostitute was (and remains) a pervasive cult image, a "stock social problem"[79] as well as an "adaptable villain." In New Comedy, she was "a cultural stereotype, alluded to time and again… even if she does not appear *in propria persona* in any of the preserved plays."[80] She is also a useful foil for any author interested in exploring the parameters of virtue and vice, a fact to which Luke's account alone testifies—that is, if we are to understand that her "sins" (ἁμαρτίαι) in Luke are based on sexual immorality. Traill explains:

> A kind of all-purpose malefactor, she represents one side of a pervasive cultural image. That she comes readily to mind when characters think about female misconduct is consistent with what anthropologists have identified as the paradox of the prostitute in general, a figure who is often "socially marginal" but "culturally central" because she is so useful, conceptually, as a negative example for groups that *are* socially central to use in their own self-definition.[81]

In Luke's account, as well as in the dialogue hymn, misperceptions about the sinful woman abound as judgments on her character are framed by stock expectations. Yet, despite the pervasiveness of this motif, there are a number of aspects to the character of the sinful woman/prostitute in the dialogue hymn that distinguish her from the figure in Luke and align her more closely with New Comedy.

The first is that she is explicitly given a voice in the dialogue, something of which she is deprived in Luke.[82] Furthermore, her imagined interlocutor is a character absent from the gospel account and one that is clearly presented as her abandoned lover, a common comedic trope. Through her dialogue she emerges as a significantly more complex character than the wanton ἑταίρα in that she is a *reformed* or penitent prostitute. While it is the case that she is also reformed in Luke, the way in which she rhetorically embodies the character in the hymn is wholly consistent with the treatment of this stock character in New Comedy, as well as among declaimers and rhetoricians who drew from the New Comic precedent. The fourth-century CE rhetor Libanius, for example, writes explicitly on "good *hetaera*" with the exercise: "*What speech would a prostitute who has been chaste (πόρνη σωφρονήσασα) utter?*"[83] A paradoxical quandary based in, as Richard Hawley describes, "just another

---

78. Traill, *Women and the Comic Plot*, 79.
79. Harvey, "2000 NAPS Presidential Address," 125.
80. Traill, *Women and the Comic Plot*, 79.
81. Traill, *Women and the Comic Plot*, 79–80.
82. See Harvey, "2000 NAPS Presidential Address," 105.
83. Cited from Hawley, "Female Characterization," 265.

stereotype from New Comedy,"[84] Libanius begins by cataloging the presumed qualities of the πόρνη, followed by instructions on how the prostitute can convincingly reject Aphrodite in favor of Athena and ἐπιείκεια (decency) by means of "future noble actions."[85] Vowing to erect an inscription encouraging other women to avoid wantonness and promising to destroy the brothel (ἐργαστήριον) from whence she came, she attempts to persuade her audience of her newfound chastity.[86] Similarly, the sinful woman meets each of Satan's references to her decadent past with a counterclaim that embraces antithetical qualities. When Satan speaks of "the scarlet of brides and the purple of queens," the sinful woman asserts that "dust and ashes are preferable to me" and that a "sackcloth garment is what I desire."[87] Gold crowns and silk garments are rejected with cries of resentment and invective.[88] Fine wine and other luxuries are countered with the proclamation that such riches are "a calamity" and "filth."[89] As is also the case with Libanius' "good *hetaera*," the sinful woman has turned against her previous life "with such vehemence that she wants to destroy its very physical manifestation"[90]—an observation which rings true as the sinful woman repeatedly demands that Satan take his trifles and trinkets with him back "to perdition."[91] The sinful woman of the dialogue hymn, therefore, uses a rhetorical strategy of rejection and profession in a manner adhering strongly with the New Comic chaste prostitute, vowing to reject all aspects of her former existence in an attempt to persuade her audience that her moral character is reformed.

Interestingly, the sinful woman of the dialogue hymn also mirrors another character popular in New Comedy: the loyal wife. Having rejected Satan, she makes it clear that her affections and allegiances are now with Jesus, to the point that she is willing to die at his hands, if that is his wish, as she does not "want anything apart from him."[92] Her final words in the dialogue illustrate the depth of her desire without any ambiguity:

Woman: "I do not want your friendship,
    you are my enemy, that I know.
  Jesus is mine, and he will belong to me:
    he will be mine, and I will be his.

---

84. Hawley, "Female Characterization," 266.
85. Hawley, "Female Characterization," 265.
86. Hawley, "Female Characterization," 266.
87. §11; 12; Brock, "The Sinful Woman," 60.
88. §15; 16; Brock, "The Sinful Woman," 61.
89. §13; 14; Brock, "The Sinful Woman," 60.
90. Hawley, "Female Characterization," 266.
91. See §8 and 16; Brock, "The Sinful Woman," 60, 61.
92. §22; Brock, "The Sinful Woman," 61.

> Praise to him—how beautiful he is,
> > radiant above all light,
>
> He turned me back, for I had sinned;
> > he called me (and rescued me) from Satan's fall.
>
> Thanksgiving to his great name,
> > how glorious he is in all that is good!
>
> He desired me and said to me,
> > 'Come, find your delight in the bridal chamber.'"[93]

The use of such strong romantic language makes her fidelity to her new beloved clear. The conviction of her love is also what appears to give her the gumption necessary to spar successfully with Satan as her interlocutor, despite her low status.

The trope of the faithful lover is the centerpiece of New Comedy, and in Menander's *Epitrepontes*, the young woman who maintains her fidelity to her husband at all costs must do so in the face of a number of challenges, the least of which is the disapproval of her father. The play opens with two newlyweds, Charisios and his wife Pamphile, who begin their lives together quite happily until Pamphile delivers a baby only five months after their wedding. Devastated by what he believes is his wife's infidelity, Charisios leaves the home and essentially goes on an extended bender full of liquor and women; making only half-hearted attempts to decide how to proceed with his marriage. During one of his drunken stupors, Charisios unwittingly rapes his wife, resulting in another pregnancy, and his debaucheries continue unabated to the point that he is suspected of using bad behavior to drive Pamphile to divorce him, so he need not initiate the deed himself. As Charisios' actions become increasingly outrageous, Pamphile's father, Smikrines, continually debates with his daughter over her willingness to remain Charisios' wife. Fearful that her dowry is being wasted on "harp girls" and other amusements, Smikrines insists she seek a divorce; however, she refuses to abandon her marriage vows. She meets her father's protests head-to-head, insisting that her marriage is for better or worse,[94] even directly challenging his authority over her ("Dad, what is this? Are you always to be [my] *kyrios*?").[95] Smikrines appeals to her sense of jealousy, presenting a series of imaginative circumstances:

---

93. §§24–26; Brock, "The Sinful Woman," 62.
94. Menander, *Epitrepontes*, 817–20; 824–5; cited from Traill, *Women and the Comic Plot*, 180.
95. Menander, *Epitrepontes*, 820; Traill, *Women and the Comic Plot*, 180.

Smikrines: "He'll say he has to walk over to Piraeus.
When he gets there he'll settle in…
You'll wait all night, without dinner.
… he'll be drinking with *her*…"[96]

His attempts at persuasion are reminiscent of Satan's admonitions to the sinful woman that, should she attempt to approach Jesus and his disciples, they will strike her dead.[97] But much like the sinful woman, Pamphile remains loyal to her spouse. Both women rebuke those who question their resolve and are not afraid to challenge their interlocutors. Their conviction is a testament to their moral character.

Drawing from these New Comedic tropes, the hymn writer gives a strong voice to biblical characters whose actions were previously the sole means of communicating a change in moral status. By portraying Satan as the jilted lover, the sinful woman is given further opportunity to reject his advances—along with the other vestiges of her previous life—in an illustrative, rhetorically compelling, and dramatic manner. Each of the agonistic strategies employed in this hymn have ties to New Comedy characters and stock plots and are utilized to advance the dialogue in ways that are significant for understanding the moral psychology of these figures. They function as a didactic tool for the audience on everything from faith to the trappings of the material world.

***

Whether it was through direct knowledge of the plays of Menander and other notable New Comics; school exercises and the rhetorical handbooks that were based, in part, on the works of the New Comics; declaimers and lawyers with intimate knowledge of persuasive characterizations and speeches drawn from these same rhetorical handbooks; or mimes and other public entertainers who imitated the characters of New Comedy in their performances, it is my contention that the hymns writers were at the very least aware of these stock characters and how to use them to great effect in their dialogues. By applying the known characteristics and stereotypes of the jilted husband, the spurned lover, or penitent harlot, to certain biblical figures, the hymnist was able to give new life to their subjects. Audiences were trained to expect as much from any modality engaged in the exploration of the human psyche, emotion, ethics, and reason through persuasive argumentation. Composed in a cultural climate of competition and repetition,

---

96. Menander, *Epitrepontes,* 752–55; Traill, *Women and the Comic Plot,* 183.
97. §21; 23; Brock, "The Sinful Woman," 61.

that the literary genres of tragedy and comedy, hymns and liturgy would meet should not come as a surprise.

Author biography

Robyn Faith Walsh is Associate Professor of Religious Studies at University of Miami. She is the author of *The Origins of Early Christian Literature: Contextualizing the New Testament within Greco-Roman Literary Culture* (CUP).

Bibliography

Braun, Willi. "Rhetoric, Rhetoricality, and Discourse Performances," 1–26 in *Rhetoric and Reality in Early Christianities*. Edited by Willi Braun. Waterloo, ON: Wilfrid Laurier University Press, 2005.

Brock, Sebastian P. *The Bible in the Syriac Tradition*. 2nd ed. Piscataway, N.J: Gorgias, 2006. https://doi.org/10.31826/9781463211127

Brock, Sebastian P. "The Dispute Poem: From Sumer to Syriac." *Journal of the Canadian Society for Syriac Studies* 1 (2001): 3–20. https://doi.org/10.31826/9781463216214-002

Brock, Sebastian P. "Dialogue and Other Sughyotho," 363–84 in *Mélanges Offerts Au Prof. P. Louis Hage*. Edited by Ayoub Chahwan. Kaslik: PUSEK, 2009.

Brock, Sebastian P. "Mary and the Angel, and Other Syriac Dialogue Poems," *Marianum* 68 (2006): 117–51.

Brock, Sebastian P. "The Sinful Woman and Satan: Two Syriac Dialogue Poems," *Oriens Christianus* 72 (1988): 21–62.

Brock, Sebastian P. "Syriac Dispute Poems: The Various Types," 109–19 in *Dispute Poems and Dialogues in the Ancient and Medieval Near East: Forms and Types of Literary Debates in Semitic and Related Literatures*. Edited by G. J. Reinink and H. L. J. Vanstiphout. Leuven: Departement Oriëntalistiek, 1991.

Brock, Sebastian P. "Syriac Poetry on Biblical Themes: The Prophet Elijah and the Widow of Sarepta," *The Harp* 3 (1990): 75–86.

Brown, Peter. *The Rise of Western Christendom: Triumph and Diversity, A.D. 200-1000*. 2nd ed. Oxford: Blackwell, 2003.

Cameron, Averil. "Disputations, Polemical Literature and the Formation of Opinion in the Early Byzantine Period," 91–108 in *Dispute Poems and Dialogues in the Ancient and Medieval Near East: Forms and Types of Literary Debates in Semitic and Related Literatures*. Edited by G. J. Reinink and H. L. J. Vanstiphout. Leuven: Departement Oriëntalistiek, 1991.

Gruber, Heather Irene Waddell. "The Women of Greek Declamation and the Reception of Comic Stereotypes," PhD diss., University of Iowa, 2009.

Harvey, Susan Ashbrook, "2000 NAPS Presidential Address Spoken Words, Voiced Silence: Biblical Women in Syriac Tradition," *JECS* 9.1 (2001): 105–31. https://doi.org/10.1353/earl.2001.0007

Hawley, Richard. "Female Characterization in Greek Declamation," 255–68 in *Ethics and Rhetoric: Classical Essays for Donald Russell on His Seventy-Fifth Birthday*.

Edited by Doreen Innes, Harry M. Hine, and C. B. R. Pelling. Oxford: Clarendon, 1995.

Haynes, Katharine. *Fashioning the Feminine in the Greek Novel*. London: Routledge, 2003. https://doi.org/10.4324/9780203167212

Howarth, W. D., ed. *Comic Drama: The European Heritage*. London: Methuen, 1978.

Hunter, R. L. *The New Comedy of Greece and Rome*. Cambridge: Cambridge University Press, 1985. https://doi.org/10.1017/CBO9780511627361

Meredith, George. *Comedy: An Essay on Comedy*. Baltimore: Johns Hopkins University Press, 1980.

Murray, Gilbert. *Aristophanes: A Study*. Oxford: Clarendon, 1933.

Murray, Robert. "Aramaic and Syriac Dispute-Poems and Their Connections," 157–87 in *Studia Aramaica: New Sources and New Approaches: Papers Delivered at the London Conference of the Institute of Jewish Studies University College London 26th-28th June 1991*. Edited by Markham J. Geller, Jonas C. Greenfield, and M. P. Weitzman. Oxford: Oxford University Press, 1995.

Reinink, G. J., and H. L. J. Vanstiphout. "Introduction," 1–6 in *Dispute Poems and Dialogues in the Ancient and Medieval Near East: Forms and Types of Literary Debates in Semitic and Related Literatures*. Edited by G. J. Reinink and H. L. J. Vanstiphout. Leuven: Departement Oriëntalistiek, 1991.

Scafuro, Adele. "When a Gesture Was Misinterpreted: Didonai Titthion in Menander's Samia," 113–35 in *Gestures: Essays in Ancient History, Literature, and Philosophy Presented to Alan L. Boegehold: On the Occasion of His Retirement and His Seventy-Fifth Birthday*. Edited by Geoffrey W. Bakewell and James P. Sickinger. Oxford: Oxbow, 2003. https://doi.org/10.2307/j.ctv13nb8zd.14

Segal, Erich. *The Death of Comedy*. Cambridge, MA: Harvard University Press, 2001. https://doi.org/10.4159/9780674043411

Segal, Erich, ed. *Oxford Readings in Menander, Plautus, and Terence*. Oxford: Oxford University Press, 2001.

Traill, Ariana. *Women and the Comic Plot in Menander*. Cambridge: Cambridge University Press, 2008. https://doi.org/10.1017/CBO9780511482410

Upson-Saia, Kristi. "Caught in a Compromising Position: The Biblical Exegesis and Characterization of Biblical Protagonists in the Syriac Dialogue Hymns," *Hugoye* 9. 2 (2006): 189–211.

Vanstiphout, H. L. J. "Lore Learning and Levity in the Sumerian Disputations: A Matter of Form, or Substance?" 23–46 in *Dispute Poems and Dialogues in the Ancient and Medieval Near East: Forms and Types of Literary Debates in Semitic and Related Literatures*. Edited by G. J. Reinink and H. L. J. Vanstiphout. Leuven: Departement Oriëntalistiek, 1991.

Zagagi, Netta. *The Comedy of Menander: Convention, Variation, and Originality*. Bloomington: Indiana University Press, 1995.

Chapter Nine

Diamonds and Rust:
Q, Mythic Marcion, and the (De)Contextualization of Divine Wisdom

Glen J. Fairen

In the last paragraph of *The Lost Gospel: The Book of Q and Christian Origins*, Burton Mack writes:

> So goodbye Q. You might be taken up by many different hands. Do take care. You are no longer as strong and illustrious a text as once you were. Christians may think you embarrassing, and critics may find you trite. So much has changed since first you were read. But my, what a difference you could make if read anew and seriously questioned. Who knows? The story of things lost and found may never sound the same.[1]

While this was written close to 30 years ago, this sentiment nicely articulates the importance of Q[2] for reconstructing the social histories of so-called early Christianities. When Q has been taken seriously—as both a coherent document and as a full-fledged expression of the early Jesus Movement[3]—scholars have at their disposal a methodological wedge that has

---

1. Burton L. Mack, *The Lost Gospel: The Book of Q & Christian Origins* (New York: Harper Collins, 1993), 258.
2. While the SBL convention is that "abbreviations for the Hebrew Bible / Old Testament, New Testament, Apocrypha, and Septuagint titles *do not* require a period and *are not* italicized" (Alexander, P. H. The SBL Handbook of Style: For Ancient Near Eastern, Biblical, and Early Christian Studies. [Peabody, MA: Hendrickson, 1999], 73 emphasis original), this is not the case with many non-canonical counterparts; either in title (i.e., compare [Gospel of] John with *Gospel of Thomas*) or abbreviation (John with *Gos. Thom.*). This intentionally or not parses off some texts in antiquity over and above other equally significant texts based on what appears to be modern theological preference. Therefore, since one of the implications of the following is that *theological* preference should have no bearing on *historical* reconstructions, this project will italicize the titles of all ancient texts and while the conventional abbreviations will be employed none will be rendered in italics.
3. John S. Kloppenborg Verbin, *Excavating Q: The History and Setting of the Sayings Gospel* (Minneapolis: Fortress Press, 2000), 332.

helped revise many of the traditional power-cords of what scholarship has assumed *should* have been Christian in antiquity.[4]

But while *Q*'s utility has been used to "reclaim" texts from caricatures of "Gnosticism"[5] and provided analogies for early Jesus movements that do not rely on "biblical" or stereotypical "Jewish" paradigms,[6] the utility of *Q* has certainly not been exhausted, particularly in examining the "story of things lost and found."

So when one considers that both texts are "hypothetical" and that both have been primarily mined out of *Luke*, it is surprising that the critical and methodological insights provided by *Q* have very rarely been applied to Marcion's *Gospel* or the *Euangelion*.[7]

---

4. According to James Robinson ("Jesus as Logos and Sophia: Wisdom Tradition and the Gospels," in *The Sayings Gospel Q: Collected Essays by James M. Robinson*, ed. Christopher Heil and Joseph Verheyden [Dudley, MA: Leuven University Press, 2005], 129) *Q* has provided a means for conceiving of a Christianity outside of the *a priori* assumption that all Christians attributed salvific meaning to the death and resurrection of Jesus. This conclusion has been given credence by the archaeological evidence which, according to Graydon Snyder, shows that "[m]any of the scenes [of Jesus of the pre-Constantine era] portray him as a deliverer, the heroic Jesus, who conquers disease ... Later Jesus appears as a boy wonder-worker who miraculously multiplies the loaves and the fishes or changes the water into wine ... This all fits well with the observations made here. Jesus did not suffer or die in pre-Constantine art. There is no cross symbol, nor any equivalent ... [Christian] faith in Jesus Christ centres on his delivering power. More, their Christology fits more the heroic figure of Mark (without the cross) than the self-giving Christ of the Apostle Paul" (*Ante Pacem: Archaeological Evidence of Church Life before Constantine*, Macon, GA: Mercer University Press, 2003, 109–10). In summary, Snyder claims that "from 180 to 400 [CE] artistic analogies of self-giving, suffering sacrifice, or incarnation are totally missing. The suffering Christ on a cross first appeared in the fifth century, and then not very convincingly" (Snyder, *Ante Pacem*, 298).

5. Stevan L. Davies, *The Gospel of Thomas and Christian Wisdom* (New York: Seabury, 1983), 10–15.

6. Burton L. Mack, *Myth of Innocence: Mark and Christian Origins* (Philadelphia, PA: Fortress Press, 1988); Leif E. Vaage, *Galilean Upstarts: Jesus' First Followers According to Q* (Valley Forge, PA: Trinity Press International), 1994.

7. Matthias Klinghardt, in an attempt to address the synoptic problem has claimed that the Gospel of Marcion could be a way to "dispense" with *Q*. "The inclusion of [Marcion] avoids the methodological weakness of the 2DH with regard to the minor agreements and hypothetical character of *Q*. Compared to 'Q', [Marcion] is clearly less 'hypothetical', even though its text must be critically reconstructed ... On the other hand, the basic observation that lead to the hypothesis of 'Q' in the first place ... [is] equally confirmed ... by Marcion [as the text] easily explains the ambiguity of the material" ("The Marcionite Gospel and the Synoptic Problem: A New Suggestion," *NovT* 50 [2008]: 1–27). See also Jason D. BeDuhn who states that if the *Euangelion*, "rather than Luke, is taken as the point of comparison with Matthew to establish the text of Q, all of [the problems of the 2DH] evaporate with one stroke." (*The First New Testament:*

While this lack may be due in part to the scholarly incorporation of the heresiological claims that the *Euangelion* as a theological hack-job, it is more likely to be a product of the default assumptions used by scholars. For instance where *Q* is generally understood to be an early first-century example of the Jesus movement that appeals to the wisdom traditions of mythic Israel, the *Euangelion* is a writing of the second century "heretic" Marcion who is thought to have performed a literary epispasm on *Luke* and "rejected" the Hebrew Bible due to what is assumed to be some kind of animus towards Judaism or all things Jewish.[8] On the surface, this is not a comparison of similar types—such as apples and oranges—but of radically different discourses (more akin to apples and dragons).

This view of Marcion editing *Luke*, however, while common in scholarship is not universal. While the relationship between *Luke* and Marcion has been addressed from a variety of perspectives,[9] is perhaps most clearly challenged by Joseph Tyson who, by building on the work of John Knox[10], has argued that instead of the traditional understanding that large portions of *Luke* were later excised from Marcion's *Euangelion*, that the reverse is more plausible, with the author of *Luke* adding to an earlier source to counter the growing threat of Marcionism.[11]

Marcion's Scriptural Canon, Santa Rosa, CA: Polebridge Press, 2013, 95). See also David Trobisch, "The Gospel According to John in the Light of Marcion's Gospelbook," in Jan Heilmann, Matthias Klinghardt, eds., *Das Neue Testament und sein Text im 2. Jahrhundert*, TANZ 61 (Tübingen: Francke, 2018), 171–81.

8. See Susannah Heschel, *The Aryan Jesus: Christian Theologians and the Bible in Nazi Germany*. (Princeton, NJ: Princeton University Press, 2008); Doris L. Bergen, "Nazism and Christianity: Partners and Rivals? A Response to Richard Steigmann-Gall, the Holy Reich. Nazi Conceptions of Christianity, 1919-1945." *JCH* 42.1 (2007): 25–33; Bart D. Ehrman, *Lost Christianities: The Battle for Scripture and the Faiths We Never Knew* (New York: Oxford University Press, 2003); Judith M. Lieu, *Image and Reality: The Jews in the World of the Christians in the Second Century* (Edinburgh: T&T Clark, 1996), 267; Alan T. Davies, "Aryan Christ: A Motif in Christian Anti-Semitism," *JES* 12.4 (1975): 569–79.

9. Trobisch, "Gospelbook," 2018.

10. John Knox, *Marcion and the New Testament: An Essay in the Early History of the Canon* (Chicago: University of Chicago Press, 1942).

11. "The relation between [the *Euangelion*] and canonical Luke is not accurately described either by the simple statement that Marcion abridged Luke or by the simple statement that Luke enlarged Marcion. The position would rather be that a primitive gospel, containing approximately the Markan and Matthean elements which our Luke contains and some of its peculiar materials, was somewhat shortened by Marcion or some predecessors and later enlarged by the writer of our Gospel, who was also the maker of Luke-Acts" (Knox, *Marcion and the New Testament*, 110; see also Dieter T. Roth, "Marcion's Gospel and Luke: The History of Research in Current Debate," *JBL* 127 (2008): 513–27). If Marcion is extracted from the perspective of *Luke*'s anti-Jewish redactor and

And while this relationship proposed by Tyson between *Luke* and the *Euangelion* is perhaps too black and white,[12] what is intriguing about the proposal is that it suggests that a comparison between the *Euangelion* and Q[13] would be a fruitful area of inquiry; especially considering the amount of overlap that appears to exist between both texts. For example, in a comparison of Q with a relatively conservative reconstruction of the *Euangelion*[14] some interesting parallels come to light.

a) Approximately half of the *Euangelion* is made up of Q.
b) Out of the 62 sections or units of Q, 46 have a parallel in the *Euangelion*.
c) Out of the approximately 250 verses in Q, only 52 are not found or do not have parallels in the *Euangelion*.

But before a comparison can take place, we need to consider the issue of whether or not a reasonable or "accurate" reconstruction of the *Euangelion* is even possible. For while the *Euangelion* is (like Q) "hypothetical" in that no ancient copy of it exists and (again, like Q) is thought to be recoverable out of *Luke*, there is simply no methodological equivalent of the Two Document Hypothesis for Marcion's *Euangelion*.

Even more problematic, the only site for the *Euangelion* recovery is—unlike anonymous Q which was "discovered" in, and excavated out of, *Luke* and *Matthew*—within the hostile commentaries of heresiologists who went

---

compared with Q, certain methodological and textual problems noted by both Knox and Tyson are addressed. "It is doubtful that we will ever know just what was in this source gospel, but it is not imprudent to suggest that the text bears substantial similarities to what we now have in Luke 3-23. Having said this, it is most important to stress our fundamental conclusion: *Whatever text lies behind* [the *Euangelion*] *and canonical Luke, it almost certainly did not contain the birth narratives or the preface, and it probably had only a trace of the resurrection account that now appears in canonical Luke*" (Joseph B. Tyson, *Marcion and Luke-Acts: A Defining Struggle* [Columbia, SC: University of South Carolina Press, 2006], 119 emphasis original). Considering that Q predates Marcion, contains no birth narrative, no resurrection account and roughly parallels *Luke* 3-23, it not only seems prudent to examine the overlaps between what we can reconstruct of the *Euangelion* with Q, but is something that is sorely in need of investigation.

12. BeDuhn, *New Testament*, 29. See also 93–4.

13 The units or sections of Q referred to above are the divisions found in John S. Kloppenborg, et al., eds., *Q-Thomas Reader* (Sonoma, CA: Polebridge Press, 1990), 35–74.

14. The "sources" for this conservative estimate are Tertullian *Adversus Marcionem, Books IV&V*. Ernest Evans ed. (Oxford: Oxford University Press, 1972); Adolph von Harnack, *Marcion: Das Evangelium vom fremden Gott* (Leipzig: Buchhandlung 1924); and BeDuhn, *New Testament*.

to great pains to represent Marcion, his text and his theological ideas as the antithesis of "true" belief. In other words, if *Q*'s discovery was like finding a new high-quality diamond in the rough, the *Euangelion* has always been preserved as a cheap cubic zirconia in a rusty setting.

This does not mean, however, that a "fuzzy" (re)construction or approximation of the *Euangelion* is impossible or undesirable. But it should be stressed that a reconstruction of Marcion's "original" or "authentic" text (however that is conceptualized) *is* an impossibility given the nature of our sources. Unlike those scholars who have winnowed a text out of a variety of hostile polemics,[15] we must be very cautious in assuming the accuracy of the heresiologists in recording what Marcion "really wrote" or what he "really believed."[16]

At best all we can recover is how the *Euangelion*, and by extension Marcion, was *represented* in these sources, and what rhetorical and theological purposes they might have served for the heresiologists who deployed them. For instance, BeDuhn points out that:

> [b]ecause it is evident that Tertullian had an actual copy of Marcion's New Testament in front of him as he worked, modern researchers universally rate his evidence very highly...This has proven problematic, however. Research since Harnack has pointed out that Tertullian, in all his writings, quotes the Bible loosely, sometimes from memory, sometimes paraphrased. Although Tertullian is being careful to argue against Marcion on the basis of the content of passages actually included in the Marcionite Bible, there is no reason to think that he reliably quotes these passages verbatim.[17]

While BeDuhn is correct in that we should be cautious regarding the reliability of Tertullian, his caution unfortunately does not go far enough. Indeed, when one considers how even Tertullian's opening paragraphs of "*Adversus Marcionem*"[18] is so loaded with hyperbole, falsehoods, and name-call-

---

15. See Harnack, *Das Evangelium*; BeDuhn, *New Testament*; Dieter T. Roth, *The Text of Marcion's Gospel* (Boston, MA: Brill, 2015).

16. This point was made abundantly clear to me when, during a presentation at the graduate seminar at the University of Alberta, Dr. Braun challenged me on my—as it turns out, naïve—claim to understand Marcion's "religion" or "theology" as if this too could be accurately mined from the hostile accounts of the heresiologists. Indeed, Dr. Braun gently pointed out that, while I was willing to be critical of the textual reconstructions of Marcion's Gospel by other scholars based on these hostile accounts, I was assuming I could find a historical Marcion in the same sources when in fact all we could find was the "mythic Marcion." This is just one of the many "wisdom tidbits" I gleaned due to the privilege of being a student of Dr. Braun's and for that I will always be grateful.

17. BeDuhn, *New Testament*, 34–5.

18. According to Tertullian, Pontus is a place where "only the fiercest nations inhabit

ing, it is a bit of a surprise that scholars assume *any* accuracy on the part of Tertullian, let alone that Tertullian would faithfully record what Marcion may have actually written even if we can say he had Marcion's text in front of him. Tertullian's agenda is not about preserving the words of a "fellow" Christian, or recording the "truth," but of utterly debunking and de-legitimating what he thought was the worst kind of "heresy." Therefore, it seems that the need and the ability to "find" the "historically" reliable nuggets of what Marcion actually wrote or thought within these polemical accounts is perhaps more about modern desires for accuracy than a reflection of what can actually be winnowed from the data.[19]

So in much the same way that we need to be suspicious of claims of finding so-called evidence of a real "historical" Jesus out of purely mythical accounts of the gospels,[20] the same kind of caution must be applied

---

it, if indeed it can be called habitation, when life is passed in wagons ... their life has no germ of civilization; they indulge their libidinous desires without restraint, and for the most part naked ... The dead bodies of their parents they cut up with their sheep, and devour at their feasts ... Their women are not by their sex softened to modesty. They uncover the breast, from which they suspend their battle-axes, and prefer warfare to marriage. In their climate, too, there is the same rude nature. The day-time is never clear, the sun never cheerful; the sky is uniformly cloudy; the whole year is wintry; the only wind that blows is the angry North. Waters melt only by fires; their rivers flow not by reason of the ice; their mountains are covered with heaps of snow. All things are torpid, all stiff with cold... Nothing, however, in Pontus is so barbarous and sad as the fact that Marcion was born there... (Marc. I.1,1). Of course, beyond assuming that ancient Pontus was in fact as hostile, "uncivilized," (and apparently as confusing) as the above indicates, it is perhaps safe to say that this description is less than honest. Indeed, considering that the whole point of this description is in the service of an epic bit of name calling, it is safe to say that Tertullian is lying to his readers to make a larger rhetorical point; that no matter how bad Pontus is, it is not as bad as Marcion. Unfortunately, because these kinds of rhetorical exaggerations or flat out lies are imbedded in our only sources for reconstructing the figure of Marcion, winnowing the historical wheat from the rhetorical chaff is all but impossible especially considering that the heresiologists were not concerned with what we moderns would consider "unbiased" history. They had no interest in discussing "Marcion the theologian," "Marcion the Christian," or even "Marcion the human." Their agenda is primarily about establishing his mythic status: Marcion as the "Arch-heretic" or "the first born of Satan" (Mart. Pol. 22.2; Ign. Phld 7.3). As such, it is surprising that scholars have any accuracy on the part of Tertullian or the other heresiologists in regards to any element of their reconstruction of Marcion.

19. "What one holds dear and wants to preserve is normative, intramurally and extramurally, in a given socio-religious formations...[and] may be authorized by means of inscribing current interests on the past as what has always been the case, thus a given" (Willi Braun, "Foreword" to *The Commerce of the Sacred: Mediation of the Divine among Jews in the Greco-Roman World* by Jack N. Lightstone [New York: Columbia University Press, 2006], x).

20. According to William Arnal the so-called historical Jesus "keeps transforming

to Marcion, his apparent theology and in particular the gospel attributed to him. In other words, we do not have access to a "true" or "authentic" *Euangelion* or Marcion any more than we do for a true or authentic Jesus; we only have, in the Bruce Lincoln sense the "myth"[21] and as such any reconstruction must be seasoned with more than just a few grains of skeptical salt.

However, while a rendering of a precise text of the *Euangelion* is impossible, a way to account for a representation like that found in the heresiological sources is certainly conceivable, particularly if we look past the assumption that the *Euangelion* was a heretical or "anti-Jewish" redaction of *Luke*. So in much the same way that *Q* needed to be divorced from the canonical "norm" of what constituted a full gospel in order for it to be taken seriously as a complete expression of the Jesus movement,[22] so too does the *Euangelion* need a similar separation in order to help account for it as a potentially viable "Christian" configuration in its own right, beyond an epispasm of *Luke*. And *Q* offers this kind of methodological wedge.

But to exploit this utility of *Q* in looking at the representation of the *Euangelion*, the presence of textual overlaps is simply not enough. Indeed, considering the traditional view that Marcion simply redacted *Luke*, any overlap between *Q* and the *Euangelion* would be hardly surprising. But to reasonably deploy Marcion outside of the paradigm of *Luke*'s redactor, generic or thematic similarities between the *Euangelion* and *Q* would have to be present. Or to put it another way: if we can think of the *Euangelion* as *not* simply an edit of *Luke*, what could it have been about *Q* or a source that

---

into a theological entity in front of our very eyes [because] the main sources on which we base our reconstructions present him in a theological entity in the first place. Whether Jesus himself existed as a historical figure or not, the gospels that tell of him are unquestionably mythic texts" (*The Symbolic Jesus: Historical Scholarship, Judaism and the Construction of Contemporary Identity* [Oakville, CT: Equinox, 2005], 75).

21. Bruce Lincoln, *Discourse and the Construction of Society: Comparative Studies of Myth, Ritual, and Classification* (Oxford: Oxford University Press, 1989). See also, Judith M. Lieu, *Marcion and the Making of a Heretic: God and Scripture In the Second Century* (Cambridge: Cambridge University Press, 2015).

22. James M. Robinson, "ΛΟΓΟΙ ΣΟΦΩΝ: On the Gattung of Q" in *The Sayings Gospel Q: Collected Essays by James M. Robinson*, eds. Christopher Heil and Joseph Verheyden. Dudley, MA: Leuven University Press, 2005), 37–74. As Kloppenborg Verbin so cogently stated, "[i]n a single stroke, Robinson had offered an explanation both for the generic peculiarities of Q—its lack of narrative framework and its concentration upon sayings—and for its theological distinctiveness—its association of Jesus with Heavenly Sophia and the absence of any interest in developing any a salvific understanding of Jesus' death" (Kloppenborg Verbin, *Excavating Q*, 348).

heavily incorporated *Q*, that made it amenable to the *Euangelion* of our representations, or similar enough that we can help explain its agenda?

While there are many points of overlap and divergence between the two, it seems that *Q*'s understanding of Divine Wisdom and its relationship to Jesus might offer an important insight in accounting for an expression like that represented in the *Euangelion*.

In *Q*, for instance, the idea of Wisdom is not only rooted within the mythic history of Israel, but also fits with the overall ancient Near and Middle Eastern construction of Wisdom figures, who sat within a heavenly court, who helped create through the use of divine law according to a divine, written plan, and who helped relate the desires of heaven to the earthly realm below.[23]

And while anthropomorphized Wisdom's desire is for humanity to be guided and protected by her is a common wisdom trope,[24] what is most striking about these traditions, is the idea that Wisdom will ultimately be rejected by the people she was sent to teach. According to John Kloppenborg, this rejection of Wisdom is best understood as part of a mythical narrative that depicts the "Deuteronomic history" of Israel as

> a repetitive cycle of sinfulness, prophetic calls to repentance (which are ignored), punishment by God, and renewed calls to repentance with threats of judgement. Common in this schema is the motif of the rejection of the prophets and even of their murder, in spite the fact that the Tanak itself records no instance of the murder of a named prophet.[25]

We find this, of course, in *Q* where the figure of Divine Wisdom states:

> I will send them prophets and apostles, some of whom they will kill and persecute and that the blood of all the prophets that has been shed from the foundation of the cosmos will be required of this generation, from the blood of Abel to the blood of Zechariah who was killed between the altar and the inner temple; Yes I tell you, it will be required of this generation.[26]

---

23. Johnathan Z. Smith, *Imagining Religion: From Babylon to Jonestown* (Chicago, IL: University of Chicago Press, 1982), 103.

24. "Wisdom cries out in the street; in the squares she raises her voice. At the busiest corner she cries out; at the entrance of the city gates she speaks: 'How long, O simple ones, will you love being simple? How long will scoffers delight in their scoffing and fools hate knowledge? Give heed to my reproof; I will pour out my thoughts to you; I will make my words known to you. Because I have called and you refused ... Because they hated knowledge and did not choose the fear of the Lord, would have none of my counsel, and despised all my reproof, therefore they shall eat the fruit of their way and be sated with their own devices. For waywardness kills the simple, and the complacency of fools destroys them; but those who listen to me will be secure and will live at ease, without dread of disaster'" (Prov. 1.24-33; see also Prov. 8.4-5, Sir. 24.1-11, Bar. 4.1-12).

25. Kloppenborg Verbin, *Excavating Q*, 121.

26. Q 11.49-51.

In line with this "Deuteronomic history" of Israel, *Q* is invested in claiming that both Jesus and John are part of this continuum of (rejected) emissaries of Wisdom.

> To what then shall I compare this people of this generation, and what are they like? They are like children seated in the agora and addressing one another, 'We piped to you, and you did not dance; we sang a dirge and you did not mourn.' For John came neither eating bread nor drinking wine and they say, 'He is a demon.' The Son of man came eating and drinking; and they say, 'Behold a glutton and a drunk, a friend of tax collectors and sinner!' Yet Wisdom is vindicated by her children.[27]

However, while John and Jesus are *both* emissaries of Wisdom, in *Q* there is a hierarchy between them, granting Jesus a place of greater significance than John.

> The queen of the South will arise at the judgement with this generation and condemn them; for she comes from the ends of the earth to hear the Wisdom of Solomon, and behold, something greater than Solomon is here. The Ninevite men will arise at the judgment with this generation and condemn it: for they repented at the preaching of John, and behold, something greater than John is here.[28]

By deploying Jesus as "greater than John," *Q* is displaying in its wisdom sections a tendency "to relativize the uniqueness of Jesus by embedding his pre-eminent message within a long chain of wisdom's spokesmen thought the Old Testament and, though culminating in John and Jesus, continuing in the community."[29] *Q* doesn't just describe Jesus as the best mediator of Wisdom in the history of Israel, but "describes [Jesus] as the sole mediator of divine knowledge"[30]

---

27. Q 7.31-35. According to Arland Dean Jacobson the "integration of the figure of Wisdom into the Deuteronomistic sketch of history served to draw John and Jesus into Israel's *Heilsgeschichte* as the last in a series of Wisdom's envoys" ("The Literary Unity of Q." *JBL* 101.3 [1982]: 365–89).

28. Q 11.31-32.

29. Robinson, "Jesus as Logos," 123.

30. "Jesus has shared the role as Sophia's spokesman with John the Baptist, but also with the prophets of the Old Testament and the community… Jesus, rather than being identified with the exclusive Sophia, has been identified as the *primus inter pares*, the most important, of her many spokesmen. But at least in the last stage of the Q tradition this no longer prevails. The exclusivity of Sophia is attributed to the Son, who is identified with Jesus. Although one may concede the inappropriateness of speaking of Sophia Christ logically in Q by and large, if by that one would mean Jesus is identified as the pre-existent Sophia incarnate (in analogy to the Johannine prologue) it seems appropriate that one acknowledge at least at the last stage of Q that the shift to a Sophia Christology has been made" (Robinson, "Jesus as Logos," 126).

> I praise you Father, Lord of heaven and earth, that you have hidden these things from the sages and the learned and revealed them to babes. Yes, Father, for such was your gracious will. All things have been handed over to me by my Father; and no one knows the son except the Father, or the Father except the Son and any one to who the Son wishes to reveal him.[31]

Now when it comes to the various representations of the *Euangelion,* there is, as noted, above broad textual overlap between it and *Q.* One thing to consider, however, is that of all the passages from *Q* involving the personification of Wisdom, it is only *Q* 10.21-22 that is paralleled in the *Euangelion.* The implications of this, particularly in regards to the methodological utility of *Q* to re-examine and account for how the *Euangelion* is represented beyond a truncated *Luke,* is telling.

Like other Christian expressions of antiquity, such as *Q* but also *Matthew* and *James*, the *Euangelion* is represented to have thought of Jesus as sitting in a unique position in regards to the divine.[32] However, unlike *Q, Matthew* or *James* which portray Jesus as functioning as either the "first among equals" of Wisdom's emissaries of the Hebrew God[33] or as personified Wisdom of mythic Israel, the *Euangelion*—while maintaining Jesus' unique position in regards to the divine—is represented as having gone through great lengths to *separate* him from any affiliation with the traditions of not just mythic Israel, but any other ancient cultural genealogy.

But while the *Euangelion* is represented as separating Jesus from any previous revelation, it nonetheless casts him in terms that are still utterly recognizable as a Wisdom-like figure from the ancient Near and Middle East. The *Euangelion*'s Jesus *is* Wisdom, but a Wisdom who is not specifically "Jewish", "Israelite" or any other cultural configuration. The *Euangelion*'s Jesus is a novel Wisdom. He is Wisdom decontextualized.

So as opposed to *Luke* or *Matthew* which went to great lengths to cast Jesus in continuity with the myths of Israel via convoluted "Jewish" genealogies, or as in *John* and *Q* that place Jesus in continuity with mythic history of Israel, the representation of the *Euangelion* abruptly begins

> [i]n the fifteenth year of Tiberius Caesar, Pontius Pilate being governor of Judea, Jesus descended [out of heaven] into Capernaum, a city in Galilee, and was teaching [in the synagogue] on the Sabbath days.[34]

---

31. Q 10.21-22; see also Q 10.16.
32. Marc I.11.8. See also R. J. Hoffmann, *Marcion on the Restitution of Christianity. An Essay on the Development of Radical Paulinist Theology in the Second Century* (Chico, CA: Scholars Press, 1984), 222–3.
33. Robinson, "Jesus as Logos," 122.
34. Euan. 3:1a / Luke 4:7.

The *Euangelion*'s Jesus is represented as utterly unanticipated and unpredicted by any cultural expression from antiquity.[35] Hence, while *Q* 10.21-22 deploys Jesus as the best representation of mythic Israel's emissaries of Wisdom, the *Euangelion*'s parallel of *Q* 10.21-22—while maintaining Jesus' Wisdom-like status—renders his uniqueness as decontextualized from the myths of Israel: a reflection of Jesus' "new" and unprecedented revelation of the "new" and alien god, in which "and no one knows the son except the Father, or the Father except the Son and any one to who the Son wishes to reveal him."[36]

While the representations of Marcion's understanding of Christianity has been assumed to be fundamentally anti-Jewish because of this decontextualization, this kind of evaluation is in a large part based upon the assumption that Marcion purged from *Luke* any reference of Jesus' "Jewish" genealogy and his affiliation with the Hebrew God due to anti-Jewish bias. However, without denying that if Marcion (as a representation or otherwise) used *Q* he would have consciously omitted any links between Jesus and mythic Israel, as this very brief comparison with *Q* shows, the thematic links between the *Euangelion* and *Q* such as their similar concepts of Wisdom, offer a better accounting of Marcion's apparent text, than it is simply an anti-Jewish hack-job truncated from *Luke*.[37]

Indeed, even though Marcion seems to have understood that the pedigree of nostalgic Israel was ultimately irrelevant to Christianity in terms of its value as "revelation" or as a method of authenticating its truth claims, he is represented by our heresiological sources as seeing the myths of Israel as nonetheless an accurate account of human history.[38] If Marcion was as anti-Judaic

---

35. Marc 1.19, 4.25. See also Harnack, *Das Evangelium*, 67; Hoffman, *Marcion*, 155–208; Tyson, *Struggle*, 44.

36. Euan 10:21-22 / Marc. 4.25.

37. According to Tyson (*Struggle*, 88–9) the uniquely Lukan sections—such as the infancy narrative, genealogy, post resurrection account and the story of the prodigal son—were not excised by Marcion from *Luke* in the service of his "anti-Judaic" purge as has been a staple of scholarly representations, but were later Lukan additions in the service of a "anti-Marcionite" agenda to a pre-Lukan source and as such not available to Marcion (See also BeDuhn, *New Testament*, 29; 93–4).

38. "In this sense [Marcion saw the Hebrew Bible as] trustworthy Scripture, accurately describing the Creator-God, giving a truthful account of history. ... But Marcion was pointed in his criticism of this God. A Creator-God was no more acceptable to Marcion as to the Gnostics, although he was not interested in describing the creative activity in those terms. For him, neither the creation stories of Genesis nor the Torah as a whole was to be challenged on the grounds of their accuracy but rather in terms of the god portrayed in them" (Tyson, *Struggle*, 33; See also Sebastian Moll, *The Arch-Heretic Marcion* [Tübingen: Mohr Siebeck, 2010], 78).

as he has been assumed by virtue of his supposed editorial work of *Luke*, it is somewhat surprising then that our heresiologists claim that Marcion left "Judaism" (however defined) relatively intact: he does not appropriate the Messiah, the "Old Testament" or the covenant with the Creator.[39] Indeed, it is this apparent refusal on the part of Marcion that leads Tertullian to accuse him a century or so after his death, of essentially being a Judaizer:[40] one who "borrow[ed] poison from the Jew—the asp, as the adage runs, from the viper."[41]

Like other "Christians" before and after him, Marcion (the representation or otherwise) must have grappled with reconciling the relationship between so-called "Judaism(s)" or what could have been "Jewish," the myths of Israel, and what gets to be "Christianity." But unlike some, such as Justin Martyr, who required a series of mental contortions to interpret the Hebrew Bible in such a way as to appropriate the salvation history of nostalgic Israel *from* the Jews for Christianity,[42] the representations of Marcion that we have left "Judaism" relatively intact and deployed his Christ as new and *sui generis*. With this in mind, and considering the overlaps between the *Euangelion* and *Q*, any assumption of Marcion's anti-Judaism should be seen as academically naïve at best. As noted, a more plausible accounting of how the *Euangelion* was deployed is that of a Jesus who is a novel and decontextualized Wisdom-like figure.

Hence, considering that Marcion's own words are lost to us and can only be mediated by hostile commentaries, the value of *Q* in deconstructing the theological / academic assumptions about Marcion is hardly overstated. Indeed, as Burton Mack has told us: Q has the potential to tell us "[t]he story of things lost and found," and when it comes to Marcion or the *Euangelion*, they "may never sound the same."[43]

Author biography

Glen J. Fairen is a Visiting Assistant Professor in the Religious Studies Program at Oklahoma State University and a Lecturer at the University of

---

39. Marcion's second "[Jewish] Christology is historical ... The Christ of the Jews will be known as Emmanuel (*Adv. Marc* 3.12.1; Isa 7.14); he will be a warrior and delivered (*Adv. Marc* 3.13.1), 'born of a young woman' (*Adv. Marc* 3.13.5); he will take up the strength of Damascus and the spoils of Samara against the king of Assyrians (Isa 8.4; *Adv. Marc* 3.13.1). In nature his is 'the son and the spirit and the substance of the Creator' (*Adv. Marc* 3.6.8). But it is not prophesied in Scripture that he will suffer and die on a cross" (Hoffman, *Marcion*, 228).
40. Marc. 1, 20.1 2, 21.2; 3, 5.4.
41. Marc. 3.8.1.
42. *Dialogue with Trypho* 29, 40.
43. Mack, *Lost*, 258.

Texas, El Paso. His publications include *As Below, So Above: Apocalypticism, Gnosticism, and the Scribes of Qumran and Nag Hammadi* (Gorgias) and his research focuses on ancient Gnosticism, Marcion, Magic, and Witchcraft.

Bibliography

Ancient Sources

The Apostolic Fathers: Greek Texts and English Translations. Edited by Michael W. Holmes. Grand Rapids: Baker Books, 1999.

The New Oxford Annotated Bible: NRSV with the Apocrypha. Edited by Michael D. Coogan. Oxford: Oxford University Press, 2001.

The Old Testament Pseudepigrapha: Vol. 1& 2. Edited by James H. Charlesworth. Garden City, NY: Doubleday, 1983.

Tertullian *Adversus Marcionem, Books IV&V*. Edited by Ernest Evans. Oxford: Oxford University Press, 1972.

Modern Sources

Arnal, William. *The Symbolic Jesus: Historical Scholarship, Judaism and the Construction of Contemporary Identity*. London; Oakville, CT: Equinox, 2005.

Alexander, P. H. *The SBL Handbook of Style: For Ancient Near Eastern, Biblical, and Early Christian Studies*. Peabody, MA: Hendrickson, 1999.

BeDuhn, Jason D. *The First New Testament: Marcion's Scriptural Canon.* Santa Rosa, CA: Polebridge Press, 2013.

Bergen, Doris L. "Nazism and Christianity: Partners and Rivals? A Response to Richard Steigmann-Gall, the Holy Reich. Nazi Conceptions of Christianity, 1919-1945." *JCH* 42.1 (2007): 25–33. https://doi.org/10.1177/0022009407071629

Braun, Willi. Foreword to *The Commerce of the Sacred: Mediation of the Divine among Jews in the Greco-Roman World* by Jack N Lightstone. New York: Columbia University Press, 2006.

Davies, Alan T. "Aryan Christ: A Motif in Christian Anti-Semitism,"*JES* 12.4 (1975): 569–79.

Davies, Stevan L. *The Gospel of Thomas and Christian Wisdom*. New York: Seabury, 1983.

Ehrman, Bart D. *Lost Christianities: The Battle for Scripture and the Faiths we Never Knew*. New York: Oxford University Press, 2003.

von Harnack, Adolph. *Marcion: Das Evangelium vom fremden Gott*. Leipzig: Buchhandlung 1924.

Heschel, Susannah. *The Aryan Jesus: Christian Theologians and the Bible in Nazi Germany*. Princeton: Princeton University Press, 2008. https://doi.org/10.1515/9781400851737

Hoffmann, R. J. *Marcion on the Restitution of Christianity. An Essay on the Development of Radical Paulinist Theology in the Second Century.* Chico, CA: Scholars Press, 1984.

Jacobson, Arland Dean. "The Literary Unity of Q," *JBL* 101.3 (1982): 365–89. https://doi.org/10.2307/3260350

Klinghardt, Matthias. "The Marcionite Gospel and the Synoptic Problem: A New Suggestion," *NovT* 50 (2008): 1–27. https://doi.org/10.1163/156853608X257527

Kloppenborg Verbin, John S. *Excavating Q: The History and Setting of the Sayings Gospel.* Minneapolis: Fortress Press, 2000.

Knox, John. *Marcion and the New Testament: An Essay in the Early History of the Canon.* Chicago: University of Chicago Press, 1942.

Lieu, Judith M. *Marcion and the Making of a Heretic: God and Scripture In the Second Century.* Cambridge: Cambridge University Press, 2015.

—*Image and Reality: The Jews in the World of the Christians in the Second Century.* Edinburgh: T&T Clark, 1996.

Lincoln, Bruce. *Discourse and the Construction of Society: Comparative Studies of Myth, Ritual, and Classification.* Oxford University Press, 1989.

Mack, Burton L. *The Lost Gospel: The Book of Q & Christian Origins.* New York: Harper Collins, 1993.

—*Myth of Innocence: Mark and Christian Origins.* Philadelphia: Fortress Press, 1988.

Moll, Sebastian. *The Arch-Heretic Marcion.* Tübingen: Mohr Siebeck, 2010. https://doi.org/10.1628/978-3-16-151539-2

Robinson, James. "Jesus as Logos and Sophia: Wisdom Tradition and the Gospels," 119–30 in *The Sayings Gospel Q: Collected Essays by James M. Robinson.* Edited by Christopher Heil and Joseph Verheyden. Dudley, MA: Leuven University Press, 2005 [1975].

—"ΛΟΓΟΙ ΣΟΦΩΝ. On the Gattung of Q," 37–74 in The Sayings Gospel Q: Collected Essays by James M. Robinson. Edited by Christopher Heil and Joseph Verheyden. Dudley, MA: Leuven University Press, 2005 [1964].

Roth, Dieter T. "Marcion's Gospel and Luke: The History of Research in Current Debate," *JBL* 127 (2008): 513–27. https://doi.org/10.2307/25610137

—*The Text of Marcion's Gospel.* Boston: Brill, 2015.

Smith, Johnathan Z. *Imagining Religion: From Babylon to Jonestown.* Chicago: University of Chicago Press, 1982.

Snyder, Graydon F. *Ante Pacem: Archaeological Evidence of Church Life before Constantine.* Macon, GA: Mercer University Press, 2003.

Trobisch, David. "The Gospel According to John in the Light of Marcion's Gospelbook," *Das Neue Testament und sein Text im 2. Jahrhundert.* Editor(s): Jan Heilmann, Matthias Klinghardt, TANZ 61 (Tübingen: Francke, 2018), 171–81.

Tyson, Joseph B. *Marcion and Luke-Acts: A Defining Struggle.* Columbia: University of South Carolina Press, 2006.

Vaage, Leif E. *Galilean Upstarts: Jesus' First Followers According to Q.* Valley Forge, PA: Trinity Press International, 1994.

Chapter Ten

The Past as Simulacrum:
Shifting Our Focus in Studying "Religion" in the Ancient World

Vaia Touna

Willi Braun's work has been very important to the way that I approach the ancient Greek world. His work, among a group of like-minded scholars (Jonathan Z. Smith, Bruce Lincoln, Russell McCutcheon, to name just a few), made me rethink not only the concept of "religion" (and its derivatives) as a self-evident concept in the scholarly works of the ancient Greek world but also to rethink the way I was approaching the ancient material in general. For, in my reading, I saw in his work an invitation to a shift of approach in how we describe and use "the past," understanding that, as Braun once phrased it, any "history and its repertoire of symbols" is "an instance of ordinary human history-making."[1]

For example, in that same 2001 article, "The Past as Simulacrum in the Canonical Narratives of Christian Origins," Braun uses as his exemplum the way Jesus was represented in the canonical narratives of Christian origins in order to discuss the concept of "history" and the role it played in Christian thought. He proposes that Christian origins be understood as a simulacrum, that is a representation of the past, made by scholars and ordinary people alike, a process that ends up revealing more about the present than the past. Braun concludes that article by proposing a shift of approach in the way we read the early Christian literature, that is:

> [A]n extraordinary interesting and worthwhile thing to do [is] to read the early Christian literature as exemplars, cases in point, of a theory of historical production that begins with real, intentional 'human doings' in the past and ends with the creation of the simulacrum of the canonical historical narrative in the present. Observing the processes at work in this sort of elongated chronology of production puts us in a good position to think deeply about the question why we invest so much in the past and why it is so important that the past looks just so, rather than just any old way, and why it is apparently necessary to forget as

---

1. Willi Braun, "The Past as Simulacrum in the Canonical Narratives of Christian Origins," *RTheol.* 8.3-4 (2001): 213–24.

much as we remember, and why what and how we remember is not so much a matter of 'the past' as it is a matter of *our* present.[2]

This is a shift that, in my experience, most scholars who study the ancient world are yet to make, despite the seeming progress in the field as it pertains to acknowledging the anachronism contained in the concept of "religion." In the next few pages I would like to discuss four recent books where this is particularly evident, in an effort not only to support Braun's call but to demonstrate the gains that we can make in no longer assuming so easily that our claims about the past are in a one-to-one relationship to what might have actually taken place.

To begin, we should note that a long tradition in the study of the ancient Greek world has assumed that there is a way to accurately describe the past by paying attention to the ancient people themselves, and by trying to understand the meaning of their texts and of their material artifacts, often times by looking at the context in which they appear. Given the limited space I have to present the various scholarly works, consider as an example of this approach the work of Jon Mikalson, a very well-known classicist and scholar of the ancient Greek world; in the preface of his 2010 second edition book, *Ancient Greek Religion*, he writes the following:

> [T]his book is largely descriptive, based on the ancient evidence that survives, and it limits discussion of modern theoretical interpretations of these complex subjects. Over the last hundred and fifty years a number of theoretical systems to explain major elements of Greek religion have come and sometimes gone. These theoretical approaches hold great interest in themselves, but one needs to know what the Greeks themselves did and said about their religion before one can adequately apply or evaluate the various theoretical systems to explain it all.[3]

With Braun's work in mind, there are two things that are of interest in Mikalson's statement. First, Mikalson is making the distinction between description as a neutral way to present information about the ancient world, on the one hand, and, on the other, modern theoretical interpretations of that information. Second, building on this distinction (and despite recognizing the importance of theoretical approaches), he argues that one should pay attention to the origins, to the people themselves and to their "religion." As suggested above, this is a common scholarly move that often takes the form of studying people or texts "on their own terms." Mikalson therefore explicitly suggests that, before we move to any meta-analyses, we should be paying

---

2. Braun, "The Past as Simulacrum," 223.
3. Jon Mikalson, *Ancient Greek Religion* (2nd ed.; Oxford and Chichester: Wiley-Blackwell, 2010), xv.

attention to ancient religion itself and to the ancient people's own voices. In the rest of the book, despite the fact that Mikalson doesn't provide an actual definition of religion, he is able to tune into the people of the ancient world, "see" their religion the way they did, and thus describe it for his readers.

Mikalson's book is a perfect example of what Brent Nongbri nicely critiques in *Before Religion*—that is, the common "I know it when I see it" approach to the study of ancient religion.[4] This approach is often justified by the claim that if a culture has "beliefs" (a word that has been critiqued by many scholars[5] but which, in the classical literature, is, generally speaking, still regularly used uncritically) in gods and rituals related to them, then that's a sufficient indication that there was religion or that the people were religious—whether they used the term or not in their own self-representations. Many scholars have found this sort of approach problematic and tried to offer ways by which scholars could move forward in the study of the ancient Greco-Roman world.

Among such scholars Brent Nongbri, in his already mentioned 2015 book, *Before Religion: A History of a Modern Concept*, takes a rather different approach from that advanced by Mikalson, attempting instead to historicize the term "religion," by arguing that it is solely a modern category. In doing so, he contributes to an on-going and by now field-wide discussion regarding its usefulness or not, especially in relation to how we study ancient people who lacked that very category.

The points that Nongbri makes in the book regarding the history of the emergence of the word "religion," and its significant changes in different periods, nicely illustrates that, despite Mikalson's approach, modern categories are *not* neutral descriptors of apparently stable things that are just out there in the past but, instead, are driven by scholarly interests, a point that nicely places him along with Braun's call to a shift of approach. Yet, despite Nongbri critiquing the ease with which scholars, especially those who study antiquity, project this modern term "religion," thereby identifying its anachronistic usage, at the end of his book he suggests that this problematic approach may "distort" how ancient people themselves might have described their own worlds or how they might have understood their own, local words that we commonly translated into "religion."

Intent to correct this distortion, Nongbri argues that, although "informed and strategic deployment of anachronism" on the level of description doesn't

---

4. Brent Nongbri, *Before Religion: A History of a Modern Concept* (New Haven, CT and London: Yale University Press, 2013), 15.
5. See for example, Donald S. Lopez, Jr. "Belief." In *Critical Terms for Religious Studies* (ed. Mark C. Taylor; Chicago, IL: The University of Chicago Press, 1998), 21–35.

necessarily exclude "religion," when talking about ancient people, alternative vocabulary such as "tradition," "ethnicity," "heresy," etc.,[6] may prove to be more appropriate in describing the ancient world, concluding that:

> The different type of descriptive accounts that I have in mind would allow what we have been calling "ancient religions" (that is, the contents of all those books called *Mesopotamian Religion, Religions in Rome, Ancient Greek Religions*, etc.) to be disaggregated and rearranged in ways that correspond better to ancient people's own organizational schemes.[7]

Although far closer to answering Braun's challenge than was Mikalson's more traditional approach, Nongbri's effort to acknowledge our anachronisms, thereby signaling our recognition of the gap between the modern "us" and the ancient "them" (generalizations that we should also be mindful of), still results in an effort to bridge that historical gap, by devising a way to get behind or beyond representation. However he fails to see that the alternative vocabulary he proposes, though it may seem to be solving somehow the problem of "religion," may insert new problems given that, not unlike "religion," these words *also come with their own modern baggage*. It seems, then, that the problem is not "religion" per se; instead, I would argue, the problem is our effort to bridge the gulf between ourselves and the ancients, for it is impossible to un-see particular data as our objects of study, that is, the data that the concept "religion" allowed us to pull together from the archive of the past (what Braun's refers to as the process of *artificiality* which I will discuss later on) and study in the first place still remains despite recognizing the anachronism of our terms. For studying the same artifacts but under a different name (e.g. calling the same thing tradition or ethnicity instead of religious) may tell us nothing really about the actual, ancient people and the way that they divided up and understood their world; recalling Braun's focus on our representation of the past, it inevitably speaks instead of the way that *we* divide, organize, and therefore impose system in *our* world (imposed upon, in this case, material understood by us *as* ancient, *as* Greek, *as* Roman, etc.).

Similarly to Nongbri, Carlin Barton and Daniel Boyarin in their 2016 book *Imagine No Religion: How Modern Abstractions Hide Ancient Realities*, also identified the modern problems with the word "religion," and then, having gotten rid of it, they claim to be able to "see [in the ancient material] what it was possible to see when we ceased to look for what was not there [that is, religion]";[8] and so, by lifting the distorting veil of religion from the data, they

---

6. Nongbri, *Before Religion*, 159.
7. Nongbri, *Before Religion*, 159.
8. Carlin A. Barton and Daniel Boyarin, *Imagine No Religion: How Modern Abstractions Hide Ancient Realities* (New York: Fordham University Press, 2016), 1.

conclude that they, not unlike Mikalson, are now able to see what is actually out there—the ancient realities of which their book's subtitle speaks. But, as discussed just above, arriving at this conclusion requires such authors either to forget or to overlook that simply getting rid of one map, i.e., "religion," by which previous scholars organized their artifacts, and substituting another, one that is equally theirs and thus equally modern, *doesn't unveil anything*; instead, it simply makes possible a new form of modern organization, allowing new interpretations to be made of these new representations—none of which are necessarily in synch with some actual, ancient reality. Simply put, the ancient world that Barton and Boyarin claim to describe is no less posited *by them* than the one made possible by means of others using the term "religion"—in both cases there is no ancient standard by which we might judge which of these readings was closer to the truth.

I place these first three books alongside each other to demonstrate that, while Mikalson's highly traditional but nonetheless problematic assumptions about the ease with which we can describe past realities, prior to ever using modern theories to understand them better, might be painfully evident to someone inclined to support Braun's focus on representation, Nongbri as well as Barton and Boyarin's much celebrated critical studies *fall into the very same trap*. Despite how these latter books have been received, I therefore find their methodological approach to the past (i.e., substituting terms, to unveil the actual past) not particularly progressive; for it is as if our only option is going on an origins quest to describe better the ancient world as it was experienced or lived by the ancients themselves, as if by using some imaginative device we can overcome the historical gulf. So, in fact, despite the supposed methodological progress promised by the latter two works, we are still at point zero; we've gotten nowhere since the same flaws and issues that we critique in the situated and invested nature of previous, traditional scholarship all remain.[9] So, whether armed with the category "religion" or having thrown it out in favor of some other (and no less modern) conceptual tool, scholars fail to see that they inevitably go to the data with preset criteria that will determine which of the material artifacts from the almost limitless archive of the past will satisfy *their* curiosities and therefore be useful *to their study*; simply put, the data don't determine the scholarly choices

---

9. Failing also to see that, as Russell McCutcheon wrote in a response to Professor Robert Campany's attempt to find ancient Chinese analogies to our modern concept religion, "[E]xamining, [...] which taxonomy better fits the facts on the ground, so to speak, is an unhelpful way to advance our studies, for the positivist facts on the ground can be argued to be products of the classification systems themselves." Russell T. McCutcheon, *Entanglements: Marking Place in the Field of Religion* (Sheffield: Equinox Publishing, 2014), 169.

but, instead, those choices and the concepts will determine what will be constituted by them *as particular sorts of data*. For, as Braun wrote: "concepts are products of scholar's cognitive operations to be put to work in the service of scholar's theoretical interest in the objects of their research. Concepts are not given off by the objects of our interest. They neither descend from the sky nor sprout out of the ground for our plucking."[10] The implication of this is that a different choice of categories does not give us any better (i.e., closer to the original) insight into the ancient world itself, since we cannot think outside of our own classifications, outside of our own linguistic schemata; rather, opting for different ways of seeing the past (such as calling what we study culture instead, for example) is a way of answering different theoretical questions in the present.

The whole idea of letting the ancient voices be heard on their own terms, something that is especially prominent in Barton and Boyarin's new book no less than Mikalson's more traditional approach—when the questions asked of the sources surely are necessarily products of the scholars themselves—is therefore where, to me, the issue lies. For not only do we risk by "uncritically reproducing—instead of studying!—local classification systems will lead to us, as scholars, normalizing participant distinctions and the interests that drive them";[11] but, even worse: we will mistakenly think that our concepts, organizations, and the knowledge that derives from them, all used in how we live in this modern world, are necessarily universal or, better, that they somehow transcend time and space.

In fact, even the ancient contexts into which we work so hard to read our artifacts, to better understand them, are also *ours*—which means that, although we may acknowledge that artifacts can be distorted by our modern and therefore anachronistic concepts, we mistakenly think that the context in which the artifact (whether a text, statue, body, etc.) is placed and consequently understood by us is not equally of our own doing as well. Take, for example the ancient author Euhemerus. It is widely known that, sometime in the 3rd or 4th century BCE, an author named Euhemerus wrote a text called Ιερά Αναγραφή or what scholars translate as "Sacred Inscription," a text, we must note, that has not survived but exists only in fragmentary form in translations and interpretations of yet other authors who wrote between 300 and 600 years *after Euhemerus's time*. For example, in the 1st century CE (300 or 400 years after Euhemerus is thought to have lived), an author named Diodorus Siculus references Euhemerus's ideas, but the chapter of his

---

10. Willi Braun, "Religion," in *Guide to The Study of Religion* (ed. Willi Braun and Russell McCutcheon; London and New York: 2000), 9.
11. McCutcheon, *Entanglements*, 171.

book that scholars suggest most deals with Euhemerus *is itself lost*—which prompts an important correction in my account: Diodorus did not reference Euhemerus but, rather, *was later said to have referenced him.* Then, in the 2nd century CE, an author named Ennius translates the "Sacred Inscription"—but his translation, we learn, *is also lost*—so, yes, he is in fact said by even later writers to have translated it. By now, it should begin to be apparent the difference between mere description of the past and representations of the past.

Now, fragments of Diodorus' reference to Euhemerus appear in the work of another author named Eusebius, who wrote in the 3rd century CE (200 years after Diodorus and thus *600 years after* Euhemerus). While fragments of Ennius' translation appear in the work of yet another author, named Lactantius, who also wrote around the 3rd century CE. This extremely suspect transmission history—one that strikes me as remarkably similar to the untrustworthy transmission history of the speeches on Eros found in the prologue to Plato's *Symposium*[12]—I think, paints a rather bleak picture of any possible way to bridge the gaps and reach the original lost text and therefore its meaning (if that is ever possible). Scholars though have written numerous books on Euhemerus and "his book." Recently, Nickolas Roubekas wrote just a book in order to "rectify," as he writes, "one of the most ancient theories of religion."[13] In a way, the book is an archaeological effort to extract from the tertiary "primary" sources (i.e., Eusebius and Lactantius) that which constitutes Euhemerus's *actual* euhemerism, which is described in detail in Roubekas's first chapter. From then on Roubekas doesn't simply juxtapose *his* interpretation or construction of Euhemerus's euhemerism as being yet another, and possibly more persuasive, interpretation, a move that would allow him to speak about similarities and differences in the authors who he is reading, but, rather, almost all of the other interpreters, we learn, "misinterpret and occasionally misuse Euhemerus's theory from antiquity

---

12. In the prologue of Plato's *Symposium*, Apollodorous encounters a friend who wants to learn about a banquet that took place in a playwright's house named Agathon and who asked those attending (among which Socrates, Aristophanes, and other notable men of Athens) to give speeches in praise of Eros. Apollodorous tells his friend that he was not present at the banquet himself, since it took place when he was only a child but that he heard about it from another man, who was there: "'tell me when this gathering took place.' And I told him: 'When we were only children; when Agathon won with his first tragedy, right after the day he and his actors celebrated by offering sacrifices.' 'Ah, quite a long while ago, then,' he said; 'but who narrated you about it? Socrates himself?' 'No, in the name of Zeus!' I answered. 'It was the person who told Phoenix—Aristodemus of Cydathenaeum' (Plato's *Symposium* 173a—my translation).

13. Nickolas P. Roubekas, *An Ancient Theory of Religion: Euhemerism from Antiquity to the Present* (New York and London: Routledge, 2017), 11.

onwards—and even more so today."[14] This is a position that we surely see in many scholarly works on the ancient world (such as the three books already cited), that is, the common idea that previous scholarship (or scholarship with which we disagree) distorts, misappropriates, mutilates, and misunderstands the past—as Roubekas frequently writes. It is as if there exists some original and thus authoritative standard to which such authors somehow have access, despite that faulty (to say the least) transmission history that I've already described. One of the ways that scholars try to bridge the fragmented knowledge about past material, such as for example a text, is by looking at that already mentioned term: context.

In the second chapter Roubekas tries to contextualize both Euhemerus and his theory, in his effort to correctly interpret the ancient work, concluding: "it was within such an intellectual context that Euhemerus of Messene introduced his own approach to religion."[15] So the problem here is that, despite scholars identifying the existence of gaps in the historical archive, they fail to see that they are also actively engaging in producing historical narratives by means of *selecting* so-called primary sources and secondary sources; for by piecing together *their* descriptions of those sources scholars hope to arrive at the bigger picture, what is known as the actual context of the text. But they fail to see, as Braun wrote about historical narratives, that such contexts are "made largely in retrospect and thus subject to the inventive, occluding, refractive ramifications of retrospections."[16] If we take this seriously, it seems that no matter how many texts we have carefully read, we never really are in, say, Euhemerus's time nor the setting in which a text was composed; to put it another way, we never have an unhindered glimpse into the world, let alone the minds and intentions of authors long dead. As Russell McCutcheon argued on another occasion:

> [W]hen anyone of us picks up a text, there is no time-travel happening; the text is not old for it is always—inasmuch as one can see and touch it—contemporaneous with the reader. If a text is always in the present, then it is never old but, instead "old"; its antiquity (and thus the status of authenticity that comes from its apparent age) is always an item of discourse only."[17]

---

14. Roubekas, *An Ancient Theory of Religion*, 10.
15. Roubekas, *An Ancient Theory of Religion*, 44.
16. Braun, *The Past as Simulacrum*, 220. On this point see also Hayden White, *Tropics of Discourse: Essays in Cultural Criticism* (Baltimore, MD: Johns Hopkins University Press, 1986), 89.
17. Russell T. McCutcheon, "Filling in the Cracks with Resin: A Response to John Burris' 'Text and Context in the Study of Religion,'" *Method & Theory in the Study of Religion* 15 (2003): 294.

Keeping in mind Braun's call for more serious consideration of the implications of representation in work on antiquity, it is important to recall that on several occasions throughout the book, Roubekas wisely cautions his readers to ask "whose euhemerism"[18] scholars employ when they use Euhemerus's theory. Again, this cautionary remark, and his rather sincere and helpful question, is effective because, either implicitly or explicitly, it presupposes an original standard, something that lies outside of later scholarly discourses (and thus representations), against which we can measure the later abuses. For in looking, in chapter 3, at the differences between Ennius, Diodorus, Eusebius, and Lactantius, Roubekas rightly concludes: "the question here is not who conveys the original text—this is *probably* lost forever—but what one can discern from the different versions and contexts within which the theory is presented"[19] (emphasis added); although the probability here is intriguing, it seems that we do indeed have various representations. But in the opening of the next chapter we read the following: "Euhemerus's view of the heavenly or celestial gods radiates a sense of acceptance of their divinity *regardless of the lack of sources that would clarify this issue beyond any doubt*"[20] (emphasis added); and so here it seems that we are back to the original—Euhemerus's *own* view and not Roubekas's version of it. Despite the suspect transmission history itemized above, the original apparently is not really lost since Roubekas seems, at places in his book, to function as a mediator of sorts, like Eros in Plato's *Symposium*, moving between the two realms, that of distortions (what we instead might also call discourses or representations) and originals.

I would not argue that the four examples that I've discussed so far are the same. Certainly, as implied above, I consider Nongbri's book, as well as Barton and Boyarin's, to be significant contributions in the on-going discussions regarding the problem of using "religion" as a descriptive word for studying the ancient world. However, all four of them are nonetheless examples of a persistent problem in classics: a longing to return to the origins, whether that is a period or a text, in order to retrieve what actually happened, doing so by means of modern concepts that, they maintain, correspond better to past worlds that scholars happen to have interest in studying, failing to see that "our dealing in past is itself a moment of historical production that is rife with special interests that do not belong in the past at all."[21] This sort of approach seems to me as erroneously reproducing the

---

18. Roubekas, *An Ancient Theory of Religion*, 173; 182.
19. Roubekas, *An Ancient Theory of Religion*, 66.
20. Roubekas, *An Ancient Theory of Religion*, 73.
21. Braun, "The Past as Simulacrum," 223.

problem some see in how we use the parable of the blind men and the elephant, since popular readings of this tale fail to recognize that, unlike the men in the tale, we, the tellers and the listeners, *already know that there is an elephant*, a reality out there that our modern language is incapable of describing. This approach (i.e., saying we are bound by history but occasionally breaking free of it) allows scholars to perform an interesting trick right before our eyes; having found a scapegoat in the word "religion," thereby seeing it as the problem that distorts the data (that is, the elephant, the ancient reality), scholars are able to naturalize and authorize alternative words, words no less of their own making, that are now claimed to more closely correspond to ancient people and their self-understandings.

Obviously, perhaps, I'm no proponent of working to identify some original point in time, against which everything can be measured; the original *is* lost (if there is ever *an* original) and it is not merely "probably lost." What we are left, then, are layers of readings, descriptions, and interpretations of texts, what Braun (borrowing from Jean Baudrillard) calls "simulacra," each one of which reflects the time when those were produced, thereby serving different (possibly contradictory) interests. Consequently, then, I'm not against offering our own descriptions and interpretations of the data we each study—as scholars this is what we do—but we should take seriously that they are always situational, stemming from a specific present context that we need to take seriously in the narratives, interpretations, and descriptions that *we* produce, making them no more authoritative than other interpretations, given that they can never be any closer to any kind of stable exterior or pre-representational reality.

So, if going back to the past in an effort to retrieve what actually happened proves to be a lot messier than we think, and lacking the power of Eros to fly between the gods and mortals, ensuring the correct message is conveyed despite the gaps and inevitably faulty transmission, I would therefore argue that scholars ought to be a little more modest in their claims about the past—a past that forever springs from our narratives rather than from the head of Zeus. But this also raises a pressing question: How do we then study the ancient world? Or how do we move forward in our studies without moving backward?

Relying on Braun's work, at least in my reading of it, I would like to offer a few ways by which we can move forward and how such a shift of approach to the ancient world can occur.

1. *Self-awareness.* I would argue (contrary to Mikalson) that any encounter with material sources begins with contemporary interests and theoretical questions that not only precede that encounter with the artifact but also

inform the choice of concepts by which we in the present transform past material into particular data to be studied. We therefore can't possibly start any study regarding the ancient world without first acknowledging that all the categories by which we will organize, classify, and then interpret/talk about that ancient world, and the meanings we will later ascribe to its actors, *are ours*.[22] So we are not just dealing with problems associated with the word religion, let alone the many terms that we routinely relate to that word (such as myth, ritual, cults, sacred, gods, beliefs, etc.), not to mention all of the ancient words that we want to use instead to name much the same items in the past (such as "ιερό," "ευσεβές," "θρησκεία"), because sooner or later we will have to translate those ancient words in a way that makes sense to us. Rather, we also have to be self-aware of the various terms that we sometimes substitute for "religion," yet often don't bother to think much about, such as "nation-states," "gender," "ethnicity," "economics," "power," "culture," "identity," etc. Our first task, then, is to be self-aware that the concepts we use to describe other people's worlds are *ours* and therefore the descriptions of a world so remote to our own comes already with certain interests, that are located in the present. Failing to do so means that we risk falling into the very thing we critique.

2. *Positionality.* On many occasions Braun argues that dealings with the past have more to do with interests in the present. Therefore, as just argued, substituting the category religion with some other words that are no less situated in the present and therefore equally modern does not really solve any problem. Doing so simply perpetuates the problem of failing to see that our descriptions are situational, and thereby constitute the objects that we think we are only passively witnessing.[23] A situation similar to this would be the modern criteria and debates that determine what gets to be displayed in a museum's exhibit case. For the inattentive museum visitor fails to see the choices that led to this and not that being put behind the glass and displayed, thereby rendering invisible the absent curator who actively constituted the past through which visitors stroll. In fact, simply getting rid of the word "religion" and substituting another word or a cluster of words (as Barton and Boyarin suggest) that "better correspond" to ancient people's organizational schemes, implicitly supposes that ancient material artifacts have fixed and hidden meanings and relationships that, should we be using

---

22. Braun, "Religion," 9.
23. See also, Vaia Touna, "Scholars and the Framing of Objects," in *Constructing "Data" in Religious Studies: Examining the Architecture of the Academy*, ed. Leslie Dorrough Smith (Sheffield: Equinox Publishing, 2019).

the wrong tools, we are just unable to fully grasp or access. In other words, self-awareness can help us to recognize *our own* positionality in the process of historical production and representation, meaning that, again to rely on Braun: "there is no place to hide form the imperative to take responsibility for history, both in terms of our lived doings in the present and in terms of how we describe and use 'the past' to rationalise our doings, worldviews, social arrangements, and the multitudinous instrumentalities, material and symbolic, by which we contrive powerful tangible worlds in accordance with our imagined worlds."[24]

3. *Exposure.* Our efforts, then, ought to be directed not so much toward a return to origins and how ancient people themselves might have organized their worlds but instead, our research should "expose the complexities of history-making,"[25] that is, the various ways by which the past is fabricated in the present, the way it is represented via different discursive techniques. Our efforts should therefore be toward exposing the often-unnoticed elements of the discursive practice itself—the discourse on "religion" being but one among many. Seeing "the past" not as a stable entity that we need to discover and access with better vocabulary and having little interest in trying to imaginatively bridge the historical gap, we should instead try to identify and expose those gaps and discontinuities that gave rise to the emergence of specific discursive narratives that constitute a certain sort of past by means of this or that type of representation. Making this shift means, then, that the discourses on "religion," "ethnicity," "gender," "tradition," etc., are always seen to be our very object of study, and not our re-descriptive, analytical tools by which we will eventually see what is (or, better, was) actually there to see. While this shift is usually confused with an effort to correct the misunderstandings and misinterpretations of previous scholarship, I propose, instead, that contemporary claims of so-called distortions or misunderstandings be understood themselves as curious representations that should attract our attention, seeing them as but more parts of the process of history-making (that is, ways by which authorized artifacts are made). In making this shift, then, there is no substantial distinction between so-called primary and secondary sources since the later are part of the on-going process of making the former into a particular kind of *simulacrum*. In fact, I would go so far as to say that without so-called secondary sources there are no primary sources.

---

24. Braun, "The Past as Simulacrum," 224.
25. Braun, "The Past as Simulacrum," 224.

4. *Artificiality*. Artificiality, as Braun argues, can take many forms, but one that he discusses is: amnesia. Following Michel-Rolph Trouillot, he argues that loss happens in at least four stages of historical production: a) making the facts, b) assembling the facts, c) retrieving the facts, d) signifying the facts.[26] Understanding artifacts as part of *our* making should force us to re-consider the very process of why and how certain items of the ancient world have been classified, organized, and explained under the term "religion" and its derivatives. This means that historical narratives should be viewed as processes by which a particular item from the past becomes a particular type of *simulacrum* in the present, ensuring that artificiality and thus representation are present at every step of the historical production.

5. *Cases in Point*. Most importantly, I'm not suggesting that going back to the sources is in vain, but it should not be done in an effort to find what "really" happened, since any return to the source, to the origins if you will, is always anchored in present interests and discourses. Instead, our informed and methodologically sound (re)interpretations of the sources, our (re)descriptions of them, should always be viewed as operating on the level of theory; they should serve as *examples of*[27] broader issues such as power structures, social formation, acts of identification etc. Such a re-description on the level of theory will allow us perhaps not to just think about but to answer "why we invest so much in the past and why it is so important that the past looks just so, rather than just any old way."[28]

In other words, considering these five propositions, the focus of our study—not only the study of the ancient Greco-Roman world—should not be any more on discovering what really happened, and therefore in moving forward by moving backward; instead, our focus should be on

> [T]he theoretical imagination that can translate the merely curious or puzzling data of "religion" or the self-evidently significant but spectral objects of religious discourses into categories that can help us as scholars of religion—and the various publics who value (or merely tolerate) our labors—to understand the human interests and social arrangements in which religious discourses play their various generative and representational roles.[29]

---

26. Braun, "The Past as Simulacrum," 221–3.
27. What Jonathan Z. Smith calls "exempli gratia" in *Drudgery Divine: On the Comparison of Early Christianities and the Religions of Late Antiquity* (Chicago: University of Chicago Press, 1990). See also Willi Braun and Russell T. McCutcheon, *Reading Smith: Interviews and Essays* (Oxford: Oxford University Press, 2018), viii.
28. Braun, "The Past as Simulacrum," 223.
29. Braun, "Religion," 15.

The gains from such a shift of approach can be multiple since it positions the scholar of religion in such a way so as to contribute to the advancement of knowledge not only among like-minded colleagues, but more importantly the applicability of methods and theories will prove to be of relevance beyond one's own field of expertise, while also gaining from the knowledge as it is advanced in other areas and fields within the academy—making interdisciplinary and inter-area collaborations a natural outcome. In fact, it is this shift of approach that, I think, encapsulates Braun's *mentalité* and work, for despite being a scholar of early Christianity, he supervised my own work in ancient and modern Greece,[30] while I was pursuing a Ph.D. at the University of Alberta; he thereby helped me to understand that "the study of religion is more like an organized, specific-purpose field-trip into the general region of social and cultural processes than it is a fenced-in disciplinary or departmental acre with its own, non-shared, special-to-religion methods."[31]

Author biography

Vaia Touna is Associate Professor in the Department of Religious Studies at the University of Alabama, Tuscaloosa. She is author of *Fabrications of the Greek Past: Religion, Tradition, and the Making of Modern Identities* (Brill) and editor of *Strategic Acts in the Study of Identity: Towards a Dynamic Theory of People and Place* (Equinox). Her research focuses on the sociology of religion, acts of identification and social formation, as well as methodological issues concerning the study of religion in the ancient Graeco-Roman world and of the past in general.

Bibliography

Barton, Carlin A. and Daniel Boyarin. *Imagine No Religion: How Modern Abstractions Hide Ancient Realities*. New York: Fordham University Press, 2016. https://doi.org/10.1515/9780823271221

Braun, Willi. "The Past as Simulacrum in the Canonical Narratives of Christian Origins." *RTheol* 8.3 (2001): 213–28. https://doi.org/10.1163/157430101X00107

—"Religion," 3-18 in *Guide to The Study of Religion*. Edited by Will Braun and Russell McCutcheon. London and New York, 2000.

Braun, Willi and Russell T. McCutcheon, *Reading Smith: Interviews and Essays*. Oxford: Oxford University Press, 2018.

---

30. Which resulted in my dissertation that later became my book, *Fabrications of the Greek Past: Religion, Tradition, and the Making of Modern Identities* (Netherlands, Leiden Brill, 2017).

31. Braun, "Religion," 15.

Lopez, Donald S., Jr. "Belief," 21–35 in *Critical Terms for Religious Studies*. Edited by Mark C. Taylor. Chicago, IL: The University of Chicago Press, 1998.

McCutcheon, Russell T. "Filling in the Cracks with Resin: A Response to John Burris' 'Text and Context in the Study of Religion.'" *Method & Theory in the Study of Religion* 15 (2003): 284–303. https://doi.org/10.1163/157006803322393404

—*Entanglements: Marking Place in the Field of Religion*. Sheffield: Equinox Publishing, 2014.

Mikalson, Jon D. *Ancient Greek Religion*. 2nd ed., Oxford and Chichester: Wiley-Blackwell, 2010.

Nongbri, Brent. *Before Religion: A History of a Modern Concept*. New Haven, CT and London: Yale University Press, 2013. https://doi.org/10.12987/yale/9780300154160.001.0001

Roubekas, Nickolas P. *An Ancient Theory of Religion: Euhemerism from Antiquity to the Present*. New York and London: Routledge, 2017.

Smith, Jonathan Z. *Drudgery Divine: On the Comparison of Early Christianities and the Religions of Late Antiquity*. Chicago, IL: University of Chicago Press, 1990.

Touna, Vaia. "Scholars and the Framing of Objects," 175–82 in *Constructing "Data" in Religious Studies: Examining the Architecture of the Academy*. Edited by Leslie Dorrough Smith. Sheffield: Equinox Publishing, 2019.

—*Fabrications of the Greek Past: Religion, Tradition, and the Making of Modern Identities*. Netherlands: Leiden Brill, 2017.

White, Hayden. *Tropics of Discourse: Essays in Cultural Criticism*. Baltimore, MD: Johns Hopkins University Press, 1986.

Chapter Eleven

The Corinthian Funerary Cultural Context and Baptism on behalf of the Dead Ritual

Mark Wheller

1 Corinthians has funerary language.[1] The cultural context of Corinth had a distinctive chthonic element in its institutions and sanctuaries. To analyze the ritual, "Baptism on behalf of the Dead," i.e. οἱ βαπτιζόμενοι ὑπὲρ τῶν

---

1. 1 Corinthians has references to funerary rites, ancestry claims, and mortuary concerns. 1 Corinthians 5.1-5 describes a ceremony of ritual execration, a type of magical curse involving a "dynamistic ceremony," (David Aune, *Apocalypticism, Prophecy, and Magic in Early Christianity: Collected Essays* [Grand Rapids: Baker Academic, 2006], 416–17) where a person in the community is handed "over to Satan for the destruction of his flesh.") Hans Conzelmann, *1 Corinthians: A Commentary on the First Epistle to the Corinthians,* trans. James W. Leitch, Ed. George W. MacRae (Philadelphia, PA: Fortress Press, 1975), 97. This curse is the same type of formula used in Greek magical papyri curses and is connected to spirits, supernatural beings, and graves. (Adela Yarbro Collins, "The Function of 'Excommunication' in Paul," *HTR* 73 [1980]: 255–6; Adolf Deissmann, *Light from the Ancient East: The New Testament Illustrated by Recently Discovered Texts of the Greco-Roman World,* trans. Lionel Strachan [Toronto: Hodder and Stoughton, 1911], 304). The expulsion formula and ceremony may have involved funerary rites (Richard DeMaris, "Funerals and Baptisms, Ordinary and Otherwise: Ritual Criticism and Corinthian Rites" *BTB* 29 [1999]: 31) and some scholars associate this magical ritual ceremony with baptism for the dead in 1 Cor. 15.29 (Conzelmann, *1 Corinthians*, 276). Funerary meals or memorial meals for the dead, explained in 1 Cor. 8–10, provide another funerary reference. The Christ-association would gather for meals in tomb dining rooms (Charles Kennedy, "The Cult of the Dead in Corinth," *Love and Death in the Ancient Near East: Essays in Honor of Marvin H. Pope* [Connecticut: Four Quarters Publishing Company, 1987], 229). These meals would be in connection to the Lord's Supper and are associated with the phrase "do this in remembrance of me" (1 Cor. 11.24) (Stanley K. Stowers, "Kinds of Myth, Meals, and Power: Paul and the Corinthians," *Redescribing: Paul and the Corinthians*. Ed. Ron Cameron and Merrill P. Miller [Society of Biblical Literature Series 5, Atlanta: SBL], 136). Ancestry is closely connected to mortuary practices to legally legitimize citizenship and because there was a family obligation to care for the dead ancestor's spirits. First Cor. 10.1-13 makes reference to ancestors being baptized into Moses in relation to the Exodus and Numbers stories. Paul's references to speaking in tongues (1 Cor. 12–13) can be understood in relation the dead as Plutarch makes the same type of association between spirits of the dead and oracles (John Parrish, "Speaking in Tongues, Dancing with Ghosts:

νεκρῶν (1 Cor. 15.29), this study will focus on the Corinthian cultural context of funerals.

As Corinth was re-founded in 44 BCE as a Caesarian colony (*Colonia Laus Iulia Corinthiensis*), Corinthian funerary practices with a Roman influence will be the focus in this paper. Finally, the application of the funerary evidence to the Christ-hero association will highlight the ancestry aspects of the cult.

Corinthian Funerary Evidence

DeMaris' cultural context analysis reveals that there was a common attitude in the Roman and Greek world with respect to death.[2] That common attitude included a concern with mourning and burial rites so much so that funeral clubs starting to develop in order to ensure proper burials were undertaken.[3] Tombs were elaborate and people paid a great deal of attention to the

---

Redescription, Translation, and the Language of Resurrection," *SR/SR* 39 [2010]: 41). Plutarch argues that "disembodied souls have the gift of prophecy just as embodied souls possess the faculty of memory" (Parrish, "Speaking in Tongues," 41). Lastly, Paul's reference to baptism for the dead in 1 Cor 15.29 describes a ritual that the Corinthian Christ Association practiced (Richard DeMaris, "Corinthian Religion and Baptism for the Dead [1 Corinthians 15.29]: Insights from Archaeology and Anthropology," *JBL* 114.4 [1995]: 672).

2. DeMaris, "Corinthian Religion and Baptism," 663.

3. DeMaris, "Corinthian Religion and Baptism," 664. This study focuses on the practices associated with Roman funerals, as Corinth was a Roman Colony with a dominant Roman culture. Corinth was based around the Roman "town-planning grid" called *centuriation* (Bruce Winter, *After Paul Left Corinth: The Influence of Secular Ethics and Social Change* [Grand Rapids, MI: William B. Eerdman's Publishing Company, 2001], 8). The cults represented in Corinth (i.e., of Asklepios, Zeus, Demeter and Kore, Aphrodite, and Apollo) were "recognized by the Romans and incorporated into their own worship at a time already in the past" (Bookidis, "Religion in Corinth," 161). Winter states that, "Corinth, therefore, was not a Greek city with a Roman facade. It was conceived of, and deliberately laid out, as a thoroughly Roman colony" (Winter, *After Paul Left Corinth*, 11). However, it is extremely important to understand that separating Greek, Jewish and Roman funerary data is messy, and although Roman data is used in the study as a way to understand elite funerary process, similar if not the same process was occurring amongst the Greeks and Jews.

Smith in "Fences and Neighbours: Some Contours of Early Judaism," writes, "In both theory and practice, taxonomies are determined by *monothetic* procedures and presuppositions, the quest for a single item of discrimination, the *sine qua non*—the *that without which* a taxon would not be itself but some other" (Jonathan Z. Smith, "Fences and Neighbours: Some Contours of Early Judaism," in *Imagining Religion: From Babylon to Jonestown* [Chicago, IL: The University of Chicago Press, 1982], 2). Smith explains a theory which replaces the monothetic one is a "polythetic mode of classification which

details of their tombs, placing offerings to ensure that the dead had "adequate goods," having places for lamps, wall paintings, and a water well shaft

surrendered the idea of perfect, unique, single differentia—a taxonomy which retained the notion of necessary but abandoned the notion of sufficient criteria for admission to a class" (Smith, "Fences and Neighbours," 4). This classification method essentially explains that "no one characteristic is definitive" (Smith, "Fences and Neighbours," 5). As this applies to this study, Smith uses funerary data to make his argument. Smith uses inscriptions from Rome, Beth She'arim, and Egypt (Smith, "Fences and Neighbours," 15). The majority (three-quarters) are Greek with "the most fundamental form of self-identification, are of Greek or Latin derivation" (Smith, "Fences and Neighbours," 15). Based upon basic taxonomic features ascribed to Judaism, Smith attempts to sort the data to collect the Jewish samples. Smith concludes that his "picture is not neat, and there remain specific problems of interpretation. Nevertheless, it has been possible to rough out a preliminary map, a set of characteristics centered largely on the synagogue which may be used as one cluster toward the eventual polythetic classification of Judaism. What has animated these reflections and explorations is the conviction that students of religion need to abandon the notion of "essence," of a unique differentium for early Judaism as well as the socially impossible correlative of a community constituted by a systematic set of beliefs. The cartography appears far messier. We need to map the variety of Judaisms, each of which appears as a shifting cluster of characteristics which vary over time" (Smith, "Fences and Neighbours," 18). In fact, recent classification theory has tended to reject Smith's approach for a more inclusive one: there will always be some features which are regarded as more or less prototypical of a type, and others which are more peripheral. For example, with Jews there were some very strong differentiating markers which everyone knew e.g., abstention from pork, Sabbath observance, and others which were much fuzzier e.g. the status of "God fearers."

Rutgers in "Archaeological evidence for the interaction of Jews and non-Jews in Late Antiquity" concludes that for Roman Judaism there is no evidence for a distinct Jewish community with regards to burial practices. Rutgers states that the "most striking feature of the approximately 40 Jewish sarcophagi from Rome is the dominance of pagan or at least religiously neutral imagery, in some cases to such an extent that it is impossible today to determine if these sarcophagi were used for Jewish or for non-Jewish burials" (Leonard Rutgers, "Archaeological evidence for the interaction of Jews and non-Jews in Late Antiquity," *AJA* 96 [1992]: 104). In some cases, like the menorah, which seems distinctly Jewish, Rutgers explains that it is impossible to tell if they were used in tombs of Jews, Samaritans, Christians, or pagans (Rutger, "Archaeological evidence for the interaction of Jews and non-Jews in Late Antiquity," 105). As Roman workshops were often used to create the sarcophagi, Jewish tombs employed Roman motifs. It seems that Rutgers would even question that idea of clusters that Smith mentions above, because the practices were so interrelated that it is too difficult to specifically sort into Roman, Greek, Jewish, and even later on into Christian tombs. I think interrelated practices builds to Green's point which explains what several scholars have concluded, that "the rabbis to be just as Hellenized and influenced by Roman culture as other local and Diasporic Jews," (Deborah Green, "Sweet Spices in the Tomb: An Initial Study on the use of Perfume in Jewish Burials," in *Commemorating the Dead: Texts and Artifacts in Context. Studies of Roman, Jewish, and Christian Burials* [Berlin: Walter de Gruyter, 2008], 153) and that (as found in one Corinthian tomb).[4] Expression for the world of the dead was also found in the Isthmia games (Panhellenic games) with the dead hero Palaimon-Melikertes, who had funerary rites associated with his cult.[5] Numismatic and architectural data provide evidence for the chthonic focus during the Roman period.[6]

For DeMaris, "the emergence during the middle of the first century CE of a religious outlook focused intensely on the dead and the world of the dead."[7] Because both inhumation and cremation happened simultaneously, DeMaris explains that this "emphasis on the dead" may have resulted from the conflicting or different burial practices in Roman Corinth in the first century CE.[8] Furthermore, the Corinthians were using jars, tile graves, and sarcophagi to bury their dead. For DeMaris, this signaled that the Roman Corinthians used mixed practices.[9]

Ancient Greco-Roman society "devoted considerable resources to the dead, in part for fear of them."[10] This fear can be seen in Corinth where Mary Walbank explains a scene in a tomb:

they did not "have the power they asserted in their texts" to maintain their own customs rather they "adopted Hellenistic mores" (Green, "Sweet Spices in the Tomb," 153–4). See, however, Rutgers (107), who shows how Roman Jews would make their tombstones "Jewish."

In Corinth, attempting to identify distinct groups (Roman, Greek, and Jew) is not a task that this study will undertake. Instead, I will argue that there was a funerary process which the Corinthians followed. Smith, Rutgers, and Green also assist this study by highlighting that out of funerary practice we do not find a monothetic Jew, possibly phrased as a "common Jew." Accepting the premise that there is no distinctive Jewish practice in Corinth assists this study in two ways, (1) critics of this model may state no Jewish member would ever understand Christ like that and (2) the polythetic nature of classification allows for the argument that Corinth was distinct and so was the group that followed the Christ-hero—they do not fall in line with the template Christian that we read about in Acts 18.

4. DeMaris, "Corinthian Religion and Baptism," 664.
5. DeMaris, "Corinthian Religion and Baptism," 665.
6. DeMaris, "Corinthian Religion and Baptism," 665–70.
7. DeMaris, "Corinthian Religion and Baptism," 670.
8. DeMaris, "Corinthian Religion and Baptism," 665–70.
9. DeMaris, "Corinthian Religion and Baptism," 676–7. When analyzing baptism for the dead in the "Corinthian Religious Environment," DeMaris uses Van Gennep's theory in the *Rites of Passage* to explain how baptism on behalf of the dead fits as a liminal stage of transitioning the dead into the afterlife, and explains the Christ-Association's practices as focused on transitioning recently deceased Christians into the "world of the dead."
10. Richard DeMaris, *The New Testament in its Ritual World* (New York: Routledge, 2008), 65.

> One particular scene, ... a pygmy is standing in a boat with two crossed sticks held in each hand. ... sticks can ward off the Evil Eye. If this interpretation is correct, it is worth noting that the pygmy is facing inwards, which is a reminder not only that the burial place should remain undisturbed, but also that the dead were considered to be a source of supernatural, and often malign, influences from which the living had to be protected.[11]

Outside of this fear the "living were obliged to help the deceased become integrated into the realm of the dead."[12] A scene from the painted tomb in Corinth portrays an attractive Nilotic scenes, "divided by stylized lotus flowers and reeds, show small figures going about daily tasks, such as hauling nets and catching fish. ... The dead may have been laid out temporary on the platform above the frescos, and the placing of the Nilotic scenes below would imply a journey across the water to life beyond the grave."[13] Walbank explains "such help was crucial, for the moment of physical death was thought to mark only the beginning of a long and sometimes difficult transition to the next world."[14]

Shear describes a tomb with painted walls constructed in the latter part of the first century CE and used sporadically in the second and third centuries up until the end of the fourth century where bodies where simply dumped.[15] The painted walls of the tomb were constructed in the first century.[16] In the tomb a well shaft "where water is encountered,"[17] that the presence of a well within the tomb may be because of the soul's need to drink once it reaches Hades, as "Orphic fragments record ... and a fragment of Aristophanes."[18] Shear further relates that the soul's need for water is usually provided with a jug of water or a cup placed close to the deceased mouth.[19] The well was used "for many interments and it is probable that the presence of the well here is in some way connected with the rites of the dead."[20] Shear also describes the murals found in the tomb where tritons, dolphins, a vase, and wands[21] which he interprets as being associated with a Dionysiac ritual.[22]

---

11. Walbank, "Unquiet Graves," 265.
12. Walbank, "Unquiet Graves," 265.
13. Walbank, "Unquiet Graves," 263.
14. Walbank, "Unquiet Graves," 263.
15. T. L. Shear, "The Excavations of Roman Chamber Tombs at Corinth 1931," *AJA* 35 (1931): 436.
16. Shear, "The Excavations of Roman Chamber Tombs," 436.
17. Shear, "The Excavations of Roman Chamber Tombs," 429.
18. Shear, "The Excavations of Roman Chamber Tombs," 430.
19. Shear, "The Excavations of Roman Chamber Tombs," 430.
20. Shear, "The Excavations of Roman Chamber Tombs," 430.
21. Shear, "The Excavations of Roman Chamber Tombs," 431.
22. Shear, "The Excavations of Roman Chamber Tombs," 431.

The community between the living and the dead extended to family obligations as well, where:

> Remembering the dead also involved visiting the grave, a visit that might include sacrifices and feasts held for them. A few Greek graves even had feeding tubes so that blood offerings and libations could be communicated directly to the deceased. Many of these practices appear to reflect a belief that the dead could benefit directly from the actions performed on their behalf, particularly at the grave.[23]

An epitaph expresses this expectation, "Aurelius Primitivus, who will tend my grave with piety and will preserve my resting-place."[24] In Corinth, there is evidence of holes in top of graves for libations to be poured:

> In the cover slab on the west grave, directly over the place where the skull would have been placed on the pillow, there was a hole for libations. Pouring food and drink onto the bones of the dead in the expectation of nourishing the spirit was common, albeit illogical, practice in the ancient world, but this is the only example of a hole for such libations found so far at Corinth.[25]

Furthermore, evidence is found in the painted tomb in Corinth:

> Interments in single graves and in the chamber tombs were almost always accompanied by, at least, a dish and drinking cup; providing sustenance for the dead was part of the burial ritual. In two of the Painted Tomb graves, round-mouth pitchers that would have held liquids were buried above the body, which suggests that they were used at the time of the burial, probably for libations, and then interred with the bodies. There is additional evidence for funeral meals. This is most apparent in the Painted Tomb, where vessels suitable for both cooking and serving a meal had been stored. The chamber tombs also preserve evidence for a commemorative cult of the dead.[26]

Blegen, et al. found in the North Cemetery a particular vase, unguentarium, which had been specifically made for funeral use[27] which was presumably "of foreign origin."[28] Blegen also mentions deep bowls, lamps, terracotta figurines, coins, eggs, and sea shells.[29] Some lamps also seem to be imported but the bowls and cinerary urns are Corinthian made.[30] Furthermore, the local Corinthian lamps dated mid first century CE had an "Apollo

---

23. Walbank, "Unquiet Graves," 257–8.
24. CIL VI 17985a; Vidman, Sylloge, 451.
25. Walbank, "Unquiet Graves," 257.
26. Walbank, "Unquiet Graves," 272.
27. C. Blegen, H. Palmer, and R. Young, *Corinth: Volume 13, The North Cemetery* (Princeton, NJ: American School of Classical Studies at Athens, 1964), 82.
28. Blegen, *Corinth*, 167.
29. Blegen, *Corinth*, 82.
30. Blegen, *Corinth*, 167.

head in profile; a crudely modeled lion; and a Dionysos with attendant and dog."[31] The graves that Blegen uncovers begin in 44 BCE and do not extend past the first century CE.[32] Roman coins were found close to the head "and it may be assumed that they had been placed in the mouth of the dead."[33]

Walbank also explains that the Painted Tomb in Corinth was not for a single family, but was probably for a "group of individuals," and so collective tombs (i.e., tombs owned by a club or association) are located in Corinth as well.[34] Furthermore, there were different types of burials ranging from (roof) tile graves, sarcophagi, to cremation. Some other features of tombs in Corinth are that there were a number of grave offerings found which mostly consisted of small glass bottles, jugs and lamps.[35] One grave had a figure of "Aphrodite wrapped in a cloak and seated on a billy goat."[36] Walbank explains that "It is not surprising to find Aphrodite, who was immensely popular in both Greek and Roman Corinth as a civic goddess, but she also had a chthonic role."[37]

Grave space was a commodity, due in part because of Roman laws that prescribed specific burial areas. Lack of grave space meant that sometimes people would bury their dead in already-occupied spaces or would reuse graves.[38] If a sarcophagus was reused, but the newer body was too long, then the "foot of the grave was cut out and the legs extended through the aperture."[39] The older pots were either removed or left and new pots simply placed in with the new dead.[40] This particular kind of re-use was common in the Roman period.[41] Tile graves were used in the Roman period with both flat and curved tiles being used.[42] In addition to tile graves, cremation urns were also found.[43] In Corinth, "within the sarcophagi, earlier bones were either pushed aside to make room for the latest burial or else the corpse was laid on top. Some of the skulls were repositioned to make more space."[44] Walbank explains that there was "Only one sarcophagus [that] did not hold

---

31. Blegen, *Corinth*, 168.
32. Blegen, *Corinth*, 167.
33. Blegen, *Corinth*, 84.
34. Walbank, "Unquiet Graves," 268.
35. Walbank, "Unquiet Graves," 258.
36. Walbank, "Unquiet Graves," 258.
37. Walbank, "Unquiet Graves," 258.
38. Blegen, *Corinth*, 71, 78.
39. Blegen, *Corinth*, 76.
40. Blegen, *Corinth*, 76.
41. Blegen, *Corinth*, 76.
42. Blegen, *Corinth*, 75.
43. Blegen, *Corinth*, 71.
44. Walbank, "Unquiet Graves," 271.

multiple burials, but simply the fragmentary bones of an adolescent (age unknown) and fragments of a small child's skull."[45] She attributes the grave being left alone to "Two curse tablets were found with the bones, and this may account for the fact that the sarcophagus was not reused."[46] Walbank also finds "bronze coins often found in mouth or hand for Charon's fee"[47]; talismans (gold foil coins with impression of dove)—late Roman[48]; a bronze bell, and an iron nail—both second century; as well as curse tablets—date unknown. All of these were found in Corinthian tombs and were used to ward off evil and for protection against supernatural forces.[49]

Use of *defixiones* (lead curse tablets) is mentioned in several of the findings.[50] *Defixiones* were inscribed on lead, papyrus, or wax[51] and were used to communicate the curse to "the powers of the underworld."[52] *Defixiones* were usually buried in graves, wells, or sacred waters.[53] Walbank finds curse tablets in connection to graves,[54] and Winter also mentions that "three tombs excavated near the National Highway north of Corinth" held curse tablets.[55]

The mortuary physical evidence provides part of the picture of Corinthian funerary practices and needs to be combined with evidence from Roman funerary rites before "baptism on behalf the dead" can be fully analyzed.[56] It should be stressed that Roman funerary rites can be understood as 'redemptive hegemony' where the different class structures of Roman funerals (i.e., elite, freedman, slave) display the different levels of power in society. In this way, the elite funerals renew elite hegemony, by reminding

45. Walbank, "Unquiet Graves," 271.
46. Walbank, "Unquiet Graves," 271.
47. Walbank, "Unquiet Graves," 274.
48. Walbank, "Unquiet Graves," 276–7.
49. Walbank, "Unquiet Graves," 277.
50. Walbank, "Unquiet Graves," 277.
51. Johnston, "Corinthian Medea," 367.
52. Johnston, "Corinthian Medea," 367.
53. Johnston "Corinthian Medea," 367.
54. Walbank, "Unquiet Graves," 277–8.
55. Winter, *After Paul Left Corinth*, 164.
56. Bell would agree, as she proposes that ritualization as a practice "should not be analyzed by being lifted out of the context formed by other ways of acting in a cultural situation," (Catherine Bell, *Ritual Theory, Ritual Practice* [New York: Oxford University Press, 2009], 90.) Thus, the Corinthian Christ-hero Association as a "social body" interacting in a funerary context that is the "symbolically constituted spatial and temporal environment" (Bell, *Ritual Theory*, 92). So, funerary rites shape "in a circular production" the Christ-hero Association as a "ritualized body" thus producing "ritualized practices" (like baptism for the dead) within a funerary "spatial and temporary environment" which is a "symbolically structured environment" (Bell, *Ritual Theory*, 92).

citizens of the importance of who just died through funeral processions. Thus, Roman funerals create and recreate hegemony in Corinth.[57]

The practices of the freedmen, slaves and the Corinthian Christ-hero association can be understood within a frame of consent and resistance when they borrow from elite funeral practices that they are not allowed to use, so as to recreate them into schemes for themselves. Adapting elite funerary practices provides social empowerment to nonelite groups and provides a means to control their environment through ritual. I will use these aspects of power and empowerment through remaking schemes, strategically transforming their rituals into a seemingly privileged experience, in my analysis of Roman funerary practices detailing vicariousness and ancestor pedigree.[58]

Classification of Roman Funerary Practices

Roman funeral practices differed depending on class. Commonly, Roman aristocratic funerals took place during the day.[59] During the initial mourning rite people would pay their respects to the dead for up to seven days.[60] The dead bodies were most likely prepared the same for aristocrats and freemen. That is, they would have a last kiss, their name called out, they would be placed on the ground and wrapped in cloth strips, washed, a coin would be placed in their mouth and the jaw bound and their body wrapped in a shroud.[61] With respects to slaves, Beryl Rawson explains that despite the tenuous relationship between members of a slave family there was "the

---

57. This paragraph is applying Bell's framework to Roman funerals (see Bell, *Ritual Theory*, 83).

58. Bell argues that power is a part of ritualization. Ritual is understood not as a means for control, but social empowerment (Bell, *Ritual Theory*, 181) within a frame of "consent and resistance" (Bell, *Ritual Theory*, 217). As well, Bell argues that "ritual mastery" which "...is the ability—not equally shared, desired, or recognized—to (1) take and remake schemes from the shared culture that can strategically nuance, privilege, or transform, (2) deploy them in the formulation of a privileged ritual experience, which in turn (3) impresses them in a new form upon agents able to deploy them in a variety of circumstances beyond the circumference of the rite itself" (Bell, *Ritual Theory*, 116).

59. Harriet Flower, *Ancestor Masks and Aristocratic Power in Roman Culture* (Oxford: Oxford University Press, 2000), 96.

60. Jocelyn Toynbee, *Death and Burial in the Roman World* (Baltimore, MD: John Hopkins University Press, 1996), 45.

61. Valerie Hope, *Roman Death: The Dying and the Dead in Ancient Rome* (London: Continuum, 2009), 71; Emma-Jayne Graham, "Memory and Materiality: Re-Embodying the Roman Funeral," in *Memory and Mourning: Studies on Roman Death*, eds. Valerie Hope and Janet Huskinson (Oxford: Oxbow Books, 2011), 29–30.

belief that it was a family's duty to come together to commemorate the death of one of its members."[62] Rawson thinks that this is a "Roman characteristic" which was "adopted readily by many people of foreign birth or foreign extraction."[63] This was especially so during the Augustan period, because there was a dramatic rise of "family groups represented on funerary reliefs" including "small children" probably due to Augustus' "emphasis on the family, in his legislation and in the publicity given to his own family."[64]

For aristocratic families the final stage for preparing the body for the funeral was to have a death mask, *imagine*, made.[65] The deceased was laid in front of cupboards that held the *imagine*[66] while people prepared for the procession.[67] Music and professional female mourners accompanied the procession.[68] The dead were carried to the forum with actors and sometimes family members preceding the body wearing *imagines* and acting like the ancestors and the deceased with the family following behind.[69] The actors wearing the masks of ancestors and the deceased were brought "to life by an actor or relative wearing his mask."[70] Polybius explains in *Histories VI* the effect of actors wearing *imagines* on the audience:

> Next after the interment and the performance of the usual ceremonies, they place the image of the departed in the most conspicuous position in the house, enclosed in a wooden shrine. This image is a mask reproducing him with remarkable fidelity both in its modeling and complexion of the deceased. On the occasion of public sacrifices they display these images, and decorate them with much care, and when any distinguished member of the family dies they take them to the funeral, putting them on men who seem to them to bear the closest resemblance to the original in stature and carriage. These representatives wear togas, with a purple border if the deceased was a consul or praetor, whole purple if he was a censor, and embroidered with gold if he had celebrated a triumph or achieved anything similar. They all ride in chariots preceded by the fasces, axes, and other insignia by which the different magistrates are wont to be accompanied according to the respective dignity of the honors held by each during his life; and when they arrive at the rostra they all seat themselves in a row on ivory chairs. There could not easily be a more ennobling spectacle for a young man who aspires to fame and virtue.

---

62. Beryl Rawson, *The Family in Ancient Rome: New Perspectives* (Ithaca, NY: Cornell University Press, 1987), 37.
 63. Rawson, *The Family in Ancient Rome*, 96.
 64. Rawson, *The Family in Ancient Rome*, 171.
 65. Hope, *Roman Death*, 71.
 66. Flower, *Ancestor Masks*, 95.
 67. Flower, *Ancestor Masks*, 95.
 68. Toynbee, *Death and Burial in Roman World*, 45; Flower, *Ancestor Masks*, 94.
 69. Flower, *Ancestor Masks*, 98–9.
 70. Hope, *Roman Death*, 74.

> For who would not be inspired by the sight of the images of men renowned for their excellence, all together and as if alive and breathing? What spectacle could be more glorious than this?[71]

The procession arrived at the forum and the eulogy praising the deceased and describing their careers was read aloud to all who attended.[72] Thus, the funeral procession was a mix of mourning and a "carnival parade."[73] As *imago*s "were denied to the freedmen,"[74] it is also probable that a death mask was not created for that class. John Pollini explains that in the first century BCE images of freedmen on grave stelae may be an example where non-elite Romans wanted to copy the concept of the *imagines* and funeral masks but could not directly do so.[75]

Freedmen, not allowed to use funeral masks, copied the idea of ancestral representation through portrait sculpture to represent the dead actively engaging in and being a part of the funerary rites.

"Roman portrait sculpture appears to have been ultimately inspired by the ancestral wax masks of the Roman nobility. This ancient cultural tradition was thereby perpetuated in an altered form in more enduring media [for the non-elite]."[76] The sculptures or reliefs represent the recent dead participating in their funeral coincides with the belief that the dead were present at the funeral and at the grave (Figure 1).[77] As the dead are vicariously portrayed through actors in funeral masks at elite funerals, sculptures of dead family members vicariously share the funerary meal with living family members at the burial site (Figure 2).[78]

---

71. Polybius, *The Histories*. Books 5–8, trans. W. R. Paton, F. W. Walbank, and Christian Habicht (Cambridge, MA: Harvard University Press, 2011), 431–2.
72. Flower, *Ancestor Masks*, 98.
73. Hope, *Roman Death*, 74.
74. John Pollini, "Ritualizing Death in Republican Rome: Memory, Religion, Class Struggle, and the Wax Ancestral Mask Tradition's Origin and Influence on Veristic Portraiture," in *Performing Death: Social Analyses of Funerary Traditions in the Ancient Near East and Mediterranean*, ed., Nicola Laneri; Oriental Institute Seminars 3 (Chicago, IL: University of Chicago, 2007), 261.
75. Pollini, "Ritualizing Death in Republican Rome," 261–2. Further, David Jackson argues that sculpture verism is connected to funeral masks in "Versim and the Ancestral Portrait," *Greece & Rome* 34 (1987): 32–47.
76. Pollini, "Ritualizing Death in Republican Rome," 262.
77. Figure 1 permission to use image from the British Museum. Pryce, F.N.; Smith, A.H., *Catalogue of Greek Sculpture in the British Museum, I-III* (London, BMP, 1892).
78. Figure 2 permission to use image from the British Museum. Pryce, F N; Smith, A H, *Catalogue of Greek Sculpture in the British Museum, I-III* (London, BMP, 1892).

192 *Worth More than Many Sparrows*

Figure 1: *Marble stele of Alexander, a Bithynian. His family is shown at the funerary meal. 200–300 CE (Roman Period). Location: Smyrna*

Figure 2: *Marble stele showing a funerary meal with tree and snake. A man reclines on a couch and a woman is seated on a stool. 2nd century BCE–1st century BCE (Hellenistic Period). Location: Smyrna.*

The burial itself was private and only the family and close friends would proceed to the grave.[79] Pollini explains that it was "likely that the mask-wearing actors accompanied corpse to the grave and stood by as sacrifices were offered to the *Di Manes,* or *Di Parentes,* whom the ancestral wax *imagines* represented."[80] Burying grave goods with the dead was a practice common for the majority of Romans.[81] Common types of items included "jewelry, and other personal adornments, arms and pieces of armor and other military equipment, toilet boxes and toilet articles, some in precious metals, eating and drinking vessels occasionally of gold and silver, more often of bronze, glass, and pottery, lamps, cooking vessels and implements, dice and gaming-counters."[82] For freemen most bodies were probably taken by the family or club members to the burial site.[83] For funeral clubs, they probably had the basic equipment needed to conduct a funeral "such as a bier, cloth and incense burners."[84] Sometimes a *sandapila* was used which was a stretcher for carrying the body and a coffin for burying the body.[85] For slaves sometimes the body would be buried in one location and then if the family felt the need they would commemorate the deceased as well at another location, "[presumably] they also staged a 'funeral' for him, since it was possible to 'bury' an absent body in an imaginary funeral, a *funus imaginarium*."[86] Staging an imaginary funeral is one of the provisions made in the regulations of the burial society at Lanuvium.[87] Furthermore, the club could pay for bodies to return home "and to hold a funeral for an image of the deceased if the body was unavailable."[88] Funding transport was especially important if a master of the slave did not release a body.[89] For slaves, a cenotaph was set up to commemorate the deceased with an inscription.[90] Maureen Carroll mentions that memory is a significant factor in funerals from eulogies, portraits and statues, inscriptions, and funerary monuments

---

79. Flower, *Ancestor Masks*, 93.
80. Pollini, "Ritualizing Death in Republican Rome," 243.
81. Toynbee, *Death and Burial in the Roman World*, 52.
82. Toynbee, *Death and Burial in the Roman World*, 52.
83. Hope, *Roman Death*, 74.
84. Hope, *Roman Death*, 76.
85. Hope, *Roman Death*, 77.
86. Maureen Carroll, *Spirits of the Dead: Roman Funerary Commemoration in Western Europe* (Oxford: Oxford University Press, 2006), 166.
87. Carroll, *Spirits of the Dead*, 166.
88. Hope, *Roman Death*, 68.
89. Hope, *Roman Death*, 68; Keith Hopkins, *Death and Renewal*, Sociological Studies in Roman History Series 2 (Cambridge: Cambridge University Press: 1983), 215.
90. Carroll, *Spirits of the Dead*, 166.

in public spaces.[91] Furthermore, libations and meals in honor of the dead would have sustained memory.[92]

For aristocrats a private meal was held at the burial[93] outside of the city[94] and full mourning would commence for nine days when the family had another meal at the grave site.[95] "Dinners were regularly held to mark the occasion of a funeral, with offerings of food made to the deceased themselves."[96] The funeral meal "in which the deceased was thought to partake, was also eaten at the site of burial."[97] Tombs contained kitchens to prepare meals and the sharing of the meal brought together "the living and the dead."[98] Commemoration rites of the deceased would be repeated on public festivals, anniversaries, and at the deceased's birthday.[99] Elaborate funerals may have a public banquet or games and theatrical performances held on a separate day.[100] These games took place in the Roman Forum, until Augustus constructed a permanent amphitheater.[101] For freemen a meal would have occurred with mourners and family bringing bread and wine for the feast at the grave site.[102] A eulogy spoken by a club member or family member during the ceremony would likely be included. Mourning would continue for nine days when another meal would have taken place at the grave, thus ending the mourning period.[103]

For all three groups, aristocratic, freedmen and slaves, elements of vicariousness are evident during funerals rituals. During aristocrat funerals the images or death masks were used with actors to portray the ancestors of the deceased and to participate at the funeral. Freedmen burials incorporated statues that depicted accurate representations of the deceased that represented the deceased as partaking in the funerary meal. For funerals without a body, as would be the case often with slaves, an image or cenotaph was used to represent the dead at the *funus imaginarium*.

91. Carroll, *Spirits of the Dead*, 279.
92. Carroll, *Spirits of the Dead*, 280.
93. Flower, *Ancestor Masks*, 93.
94. Toynbee, *Death and Burial*, 48.
95. Flower, *Ancestor Masks*, 93; Daniel Harmon, "The Family Festivals of Rome," *ANRW* 2, 2.16.2 (1978): 1601.
96. Catherine Edwards, *Death in Ancient Rome* (New Haven, CT: Yale University Press, 2007), 164.
97. Harmon, "Family Festivals," 1602.
98. Edwards, *Death in Ancient Rome*, 164.
99. Flower, *Ancestor Masks*, 93.
100. Flower, *Ancestor Masks*, 92.
101. Edwards *Death in Ancient Rome*, 48.
102. Carroll, *Spirits of the Dead*, 72.
103. Flower, *Ancestor Masks*, 93.

Application of Funerary Evidence to the Christ-Hero Association

The Corinthian Christ-hero association as a ritualized body practicing within a mortuary environment would have had Corinthian Roman funerary structures impressed upon them. The Corinthian association found meaning in the Corinthian Roman practices and mobilized funerary references into their practices. As with all Roman Corinthians, the Christ-hero association would have gathered for meals in tombs.[104] These meals would be in connection to the Lord's Meal and would be associated with the phrase "do this in remembrance of me" (1 Cor 11.24).[105]

As Bell stresses that power is part of ritualization, the power relations in Corinthian society are most obvious in funerary rites where the Roman elite would use funeral masks to vicariously represent their ancestors who legitimized their status in society. Freedmen, not allowed to use funeral masks, copied the idea of ancestral representation through portrait sculpture verism[106] to represent the dead actively engaging in and being a part of the funerary rites. The Corinthian Christ-hero association utilized the practice of vicariousness, not through funeral masks which were illegal for them to use, or through sculptural verism (as the costs would be too high), but through vicariously representing their dead, or themselves, in their rites. In this way, they differentiate their practices from other funerary practices in Roman Corinth. People within the Corinthian Christ-hero association had the ability to take Corinthian Roman funerary schemes and nuance their rites enough to transform them into a differentiated practice. They deployed the funerary rites within their group providing a sense of "privileged ritual experience"[107] which in turn caused them to form a separate association with separate rites that they were able to deploy in a "variety of circumstances beyond the circumference"[108] of the baptism on behalf of the dead rite and bringing their ancestors and deceased into a broader Jewish context where they understood their "… ancestors were all under the cloud, and all passed through the sea, and all were baptized into Moses (καὶ πάντες εἰς τὸν Μωϋσῆν ἐβαπτίσθησαν[109]) in the cloud and in the sea" (1 Cor. 10.1-2).[110] By

---

104. Kennedy, "The Cult of the Dead in Corinth," 229.
105. Stowers, "Kinds of Myth, Meals, and Power: Paul and the Corinthians," 136.
106. Pollini, "Ritualizing Death in Republican Rome," 262.
107. Bell, *Ritual Theory*, 116.
108. Bell, *Ritual Theory*, 116.
109. *The Greek New Testament*, 588.
110. *The New Oxford Annotated Bible with the Apocryphal/Deuterocanonical Books NRSV*, eds. Bruce M. Metzger and Roland E. Murphy (New York: Oxford University Press, 1991), 239.

baptizing their dead, the Christ Association was able to align their ancestors to Christ, thus establishing a pedigree through Christ to Moses.

The Corinthian Christ-hero association baptized their dead ancestors vicariously on their behalf, thus allowing them to be part of the voluntary association. Christ was the ancestor that they were aligning themselves and their ancestral dead to within a regional Corinthian context and then to Moses within a broader trans-local[111] Jewish context. So, as Stowers states:

> baptism for the dead would incorporate those dead into the distinguished lineage and ancestry. Without baptism for the dead, their own baptisms might cut them off from their extended families of the significant dead. This scenario makes sense, if the Corinthians or some of them were people concerned about their own ambiguous and ignoble ancestry.[112]

The Christ-hero association used vicarious means to represent their dead because they were not high enough in status to create funeral masks, nor did they have the financial resources to commission a statue, relief or stele. Analyzing ancestry in the context of their mortuary concerns shows ancestor pedigree tracing through Christ to Moses. The Corinthian Christ Association, working within their funerary cultural and ritual context, devised a rite, baptism on behalf of the dead, that addressed both their mortuary and ancestral concerns.

Author biography

Mark Wheller completed his PhD at the University of Alberta in Religious Studies, where he also received a Graduate Student Teaching Award. He currently serves as a Team Lead for the Learning Centre's Learning and Development programs at Edmonton.

Bibliography

Ascough, Richard, Philip Harland, and John Kloppenborg. *Associations in the Greco-Roman World: A Sourcebook.* Waco, TX: Baylor University Press, 2012.

Ascough, Richard. "Paul's 'Apocalypticism' and the Jesus Associations at Thessalonica and Corinth," in *Redescribing Paul and the Corinthians*. Edited by Ron Cameron and Merrill P. Miller. Atlanta, GA: Society of Biblical Literature, 2011, 151–86.

—"Translocal Relationships among Voluntary Associations and Early Christianity," *JECS* 5.2 (1997): 223–41. https://doi.org/10.1353/earl.1997.0054

---

111. Richard Ascough, "Translocal Relationships among Voluntary Associations and Early Christianity," *JECS* 5.2 (1997): 223–41.

112. Stowers, "Kinds of Myth, Meals, and Power: Paul and the Corinthians," 125.

Aune, David. *Apocalypticism, Prophecy, and Magic in Early Christianity: Collected Essays.* Grand Rapids, MI: Baker Academic, 2006.

Blegen, C., H. Palmer, and R. Young, *Corinth: Volume 13, The North Cemetery.* Princeton, NJ: American School of Classical Studies at Athens, 1964. https://doi.org/10.2307/4390687

Bell, Catherine. *Ritual Theory, Ritual Practice.* New York: Oxford University Press, 2009.

Bell, Catherine. *Ritual: Perspectives and Dimensions.* New York: Oxford University Press, 1997.

Bookidis, Nancy, and J. Fisher. "The Sanctuary of Demeter and Kore on Acrocorinth, Preliminary Report IV: 1969-1970," *Hesperia* 41 (1972): 283–331. https://doi.org/10.2307/147436

Bookidis, Nancy, and Ronald Stroud. *Demeter and Persephone in Ancient Corinth Notes 2.* Princeton, NJ: American School of Classical Studies at Athens, 1987.

Bookidis, Nancy. "Religion in Corinth: 146 BCE. to 100 CE," *Urban Religion in Roman Corinth: Interdisciplinary Approaches.* Edited by Daniel N. Schowalter and Steven J. Friesen. Cambridge, MA: HTS, 2005: 141–64.

Bultmann, Rudolf. *Theology of the New Testament.* 2 Volumes. Translated by Kendrick Grobel. Waco, TX: Baylor University Press, 2007.

Carroll, Maureen. *Spirits of the Dead: Roman Funerary Commemoration in Western Europe.* New York: Oxford University Press, 2006.

Collins, Adela Yarbro. "The Function of 'Excommunication' in Paul," *HTR* 73 (1980): 255–6. https://doi.org/10.1017/S0017816000002145

Conzelmann, Hans. *1 Corinthians: A Commentary on the First Epistle to the Corinthians,* Translated by James W. Leitch. Philadelphia, PA: Fortress Press, 1975.

Deissmann, Adolf. *Light from the Ancient East: The New Testament Illustrated by Recently Discovered Texts of the Greco-Roman World,* Translated by Lionel Strachan. Toronto: Hodder and Stoughton, 1911.

DeMaris, Richard. "Corinthian Religion and Baptism for the Dead (1 Corinthians 15:29): Insights from Archaeology and Anthropology," *JBL* 114.4 (1995): 661–82. https://doi.org/10.2307/3266480

—"Funerals and Baptisms, Ordinary and Otherwise: Ritual Criticism and Corinthian Rites," *BTB* 29 (1999): 23–34. https://doi.org/10.1177/014610799902900103

—"Demeter in Roman Corinth: Local Development in a Mediterranean Religion," *Numen* 42 (1995): 105-17. https://doi.org/10.1163/1568527952598701

—*The Colossian Controversy: Wisdom in Dispute at Colossae.* Sheffield: Sheffield Academic Press, 1994.

—*The New Testament in its Ritual World.* New York: Routledge, 2008. https://doi.org/10.4324/9780203930793

Edwards, Catharine. *Death in Ancient Rome.* New Haven, CT: Yale University Press, 2007.

Flower, Harriet. *Ancestor Masks and Aristocratic Power in Roman Culture.* Oxford: Oxford University Press, 2000.

Graham, Emma-Jayne. "Memory and Materiality: Re-Embodying the Roman Funeral," in *Memory and Mourning: Studies on Roman Death.* Edited by Valerie Hope and Janet Huskinson. Oxford: Oxbow Books: 2011.

Greek New Testament: The SBL Edition Edited by Michael W. Holmes. SBL, 2010.

Green, Deborah. "Sweet Spices in the Tomb: An Initial Study on the use of Perfume in Jewish Burials." *Commemorating the Dead: Texts and Artifacts in Context. Studies* of Roman, Jewish, and Christian Burials. Berlin: Walter de Gruyter, 2008, 145–73. https://doi.org/10.1515/9783110211573.2.145

Harmon, Daniel. "The Family Festivals of Rome," *ANRW* 2, 2.16.2 (1978): 1592–1603.

Holmes, Michael. *The Greek New Testament: SBL Edition* 2014. http://sblgnt.com/

Hope, Valerie. *Death in Ancient Rome: A Sourcebook.* Cardiff: Routledge, 2007. https://doi.org/10.4324/9780203392485

Hope, Valerie. "Remembering Rome: Memory, Funerary Monuments and the Roman Soldier," in *Archaeologies of Remembrance. Death and Memory in Past Societies.* Edited by H. Williams. London: Kluwer Academic/Plenum Publishers, 2003: 113–40. https://doi.org/10.1007/978-1-4419-9222-2_6

Hope, Valerie. *Roman Death: The Dying and the Dead in Ancient Rome*. London: Continuum: 2009.

Hopkins, Keith. *Death and Renewal* in *Sociological Studies in Roman History Series 2*. Cambridge: Cambridge University Press: 1983. https://doi.org/10.1017/CBO9780511552663

Johnston, Sarah Iles. "Corinthian Medea and the Cult of Hera Akraia," in *Medea: Essays on Medea in Myth, Literature, Philosophy and Art* (Princeton, NJ: Princeton University Press, 1997. https://doi.org/10.1515/9780691215082-005

—*Religions of the Ancient World: A Guide.* Cambridge, MA: Belknap Press, 2004. https://doi.org/10.4159/9780674264823

—*Restless Dead: Encounters Between the Living and The Dead in Ancient Greece.* Berkeley, CA: University of California Press, 1999.

Kennedy, Charles. "The Cult of the Dead in Corinth," *Love and Death in the Ancient Near East: Essays in Honor of Marvin H. Pope.* GIVE CITY, CT: Four Quarters Publishing Company, 1987: 227–36.

New Oxford Annotated Bible with the Apocrypha. Edited by Bruce M. Metzger and Roland E. Murphy. New York: Oxford University Press, 1991.

Ohio History Central. http://www.ohiohistorycentral.org/w/Grave-robbing?rec=2701

Parrish, John W. "Speaking in Tongues, Dancing with Ghosts: Redescription, Translation, and the Language of Resurrection," *SR/SR* 39 (2010): 25–45. https://doi.org/10.1177/0008429809355750

Plutarch. *Lives*, Volume XI: Aratus. Artaxerxes. Galba. Otho. General Index. Translated by Bernadotte Perrin. Loeb Classical Library 103. Cambridge, MA: Harvard University Press, 1926. https://doi.org/10.4159/DLCL.plutarch-lives_artaxerxes.1926

—*Moralia*. Translated by Gregorius N. Bernardakis. Leipzig: Teubner, 1892.

—*Moralia, Volume IV: Roman Questions. Greek Questions. Greek and Roman Parallel Stories. On the Fortune of the Romans. On the Fortune or the Virtue of Alexander. Were the Athenians More Famous in War or in Wisdom?* Translated by Frank Cole Babbitt. Loeb Classical Library 305. Cambridge, MA: Harvard University Press, 1936. https://doi.org/10.4159/DLCL.plutarch-lives_artaxerxes.1926

—*Moralia, Volume V: Isis and Osiris. The E at Delphi. The Oracles at Delphi No Longer Given in Verse. The Obsolescence of Oracles.* Translated by Frank Cole Babbitt. Loeb Classical Library 306. Cambridge, MA: Harvard University Press, 1936. https://doi.org/10.4159/DLCL.plutarch-moralia_oracles_delphi_no_longer_given_verse.1936

Pollini, John. "Ritualizing Death in Republican Rome: Memory, Religion, Class Struggle, and the Wax Ancestral Mask Tradition's Origin and Influence on Veristic Portraiture," in *Performing Death: Social Analyses of Funerary Traditions in the Ancient Near East and Mediterranean.* Edited by Nicola Laneri; Oriental Institute Seminars 3. Chicago, IL: University of Chicago, 2007.

Polybius. *The Histories.* Books 5-8, Trans. W. R. Paton, F. W. Walbank, and Christian Habicht. Cambridge, MA: Harvard University Press, 2011. https://doi.org/10.4159/DLCL.polybius-histories.2010

Pryce, F.N. and Smith, A.H., *Catalogue of Greek Sculpture in the British Museum, I-III*, London, BMP, 1892.

Rawson, Beryl. "The Roman Family," *The Family in Ancient Rome: New Perspectives.* Edited by Beryl Rawson. Cornell University Press: New York, 1986.

Rutgers, Leonard Victor. "Archaeological Evidence for the Interaction of Jews and Non-Jews in Late Antiquity," *AJA* 96 (1992): 101–18. https://doi.org/10.2307/505760

Shear, T.L. "The Excavations of Roman Chamber Tombs at Corinth 1931," *AJA* 35 (1931): 394–423. https://doi.org/10.2307/498099

Smith, Jonathan Z. "Fences and Neighbours: Some Contours of Early Judaism," in *Imagining Religion: From Babylon to Jonestown.* Chicago, IL: The University of Chicago Press, 1982.

Smith, Jonathan Z. "Here, There, and Anywhere," in *Relating Religion: Essays in the Study of Religion.* Chicago, IL: Chicago University Press, 2004.

Smith, Jonathan Z. "Re The Corinthians," in *Relating Religion: Essays in the Study of Religion.* Chicago, IL: University of Chicago Press, 2004.

Stowers, Stanley K. "Kinds of Myth, Meals, and Power: Paul and the Corinthians," *Redescribing: Paul and the Corinthians*. Edited by Ron Cameron and Merrill P. Miller. SBLS 5. Atlanta, GA: SBL: 105–50.

Toynbee, Jocelyn. *Death and Burial in the Roman World,* Baltimore, MD: John Hopkins University Press, 1996.

Walbank, Mary. "Unquiet Graves: Burial Practices of the Roman Corinthians," in *Urban Religion in Roman Corinth: Interdisciplinary Approaches.* Edited by Daniel N. Schowalter. Cambridge: Harvard Theological Studies, 2005.

Winter, Bruce. *After Paul Left Corinth: The Influence of Secular Ethics and Social Change.* Grand Rapids, MI: William B. Eerdman's Publishing Company, 2001.

Chapter Twelve

Reconstructing Socio-Cultural Institutions in the Gospel of Mark

Allan Wright

It is often noted that the Gospel of Mark is a text of social lamentations.[1] Indeed, Mark does display disillusionment with his new post-war realities, consisting of the losses of socio-ethnic identification, the symbolic (physical and discursive) representations of such identities, and communal association. However, these arguments generally omit a critical element of Mark's Gospel, namely reconciliation. While indeed displaying personal alienation and social disenchantment, Mark also engages in the restitution of these social incongruities. In other words, Mark's Gospel is *not* merely a document of lamentations; it also attempts to reconcile his current social-political struggles. The very beginning of Mark's text (1.1) displays his intention of providing "good news" to the reader: "The beginning of the good news."[2] By immersing himself in a reconcilable discourse, Mark proposes various solutions for his tenacious communal struggles.

Jonathan Z. Smith's theory of situational incongruity applies to Mark. The social incongruity of displacement, his alienation, and loss of socio-ethnic identification all provided an intellectual opportunity, or a pressing need, to reformulate his personal and communal identity. Mark's text is his "relentless human activity of thinking through a[n incongruent] situation."[3] As Smith states, "the incongruity of myth is not an error, it is the very source of its power. Or ... a myth is a 'strategy for dealing with a situation.'"[4]

---

1. Maia Kotrosits and Hal Taussig, *Re-Reading the Gospel of Mark Amidst Loss and Trauma* (New York: Palgrave Macmillan, 2013). Kotrosits and Taussig state, "Mark describes what it means and feels like to be in pain, but importantly, even while it tries to understand the significances and effects of pain and loss, it does so without resolving, redeeming, or justifying much ... Mark importantly does not evoke this common ancient understanding of universal citizenship to try to solve or override the problems of fracture. Mark finds hope neither in national institutions or structures themselves" (42, 72).
2. I am interpreting "τοῦ εὐαγγελίου" here as "good news."
3. Jonathan Z. Smith, "When the Chips are Down." In *Relating Religion: Essays in the Study of Religion* (Chicago, IL and London: University of Chicago Press, 2004), 1–60, 32.
4. Jonathan Z. Smith, "Map is Not Territory." In *Map Is Not Territory* (Chicago, IL, and London: University of Chicago Press, 1978), 299.

Therefore, myth is "a limited collection of elements with a fixed range of cultural meanings which are applied, thought with, worked with, experimented with in particular situations."[5]

Through his intellectual activity, Mark offers specific discourses that rectify his chaotic world. In other words, the natural and social world is messy, but Jesus can calm the storm. William F. McInerny argues that Mark 4.35-41 should be seen in relation to 1.1.[6] Although I concur with McInerny's overall assessment, his argument relates to the issue of Jesus' identity, which is convincing with regard to Mark's context. However, 1.1 and 4.35-41 also depict Jesus as representing hope and calm among the chaos. Mark 4.35-41 is essential to highlight. While Jesus and the disciples' boat was in peril, the disciples display sentiments of fear and loss: "Master, do you not care that we are perishing?" Jesus' response is one of assurance: "And he said to them, 'why are you scared? How do you not have belief?'" The overall message can be interpreted as Jesus dispelling the chaotic social circumstances. Mark's chaotic sea illustration would resonate with readers experiencing social upheaval. However, Jesus calms the tumultuous storm upon the chaotic sea and provides a composed transition "into the other side." Elizabeth Struthers Malbon argues that Mark's sea voyages "elaborate and dramatize both teaching and healing."[7] Through this narrative, Mark sketches "the healing nature of that power in the lives Jesus touches."[8]

The Destroyed Temple Reconciliation

Questions revolving around Jerusalem's temple (and temples in antiquity in general) are largely related to spatial concerns. James H. Charlesworth declares, "For many early Jews, the Jerusalem Temple was the *axis mundi*; that is, the Temple was the center of the world, and the specific spot where heaven meets earth was Zion."[9] Karen J. Wenell rightly states, "In order for land to be sacred, it must be interpreted and communicated as such."[10] Exodus 40.34-38, 1 Kings 8.10-13, and Psalms 132.13-14 definitively

---

5. Smith, *Map Is Not Territory*, 308.

6. See William F. McInerny, "An Unresolved Question in the Gospel Called Mark: 'Who is This Whom Even Wind and Sea Obey' (4:41)," *PRS* (January 1, 1996): 255–68.

7. Elizabeth Struthers Malbon, "The Jesus of Mark and the Sea of Galilee," *JBL* 103.3 (1984): 363–77, 364.

8. Malbon, "Jesus of Mark," 365.

9. James H. Charlesworth, "Jesus and Temple," in *Jesus and Temple: Textual and Archaeological Explorations*, ed. James H. Charlesworth (Minneapolis, MN: Fortress Press, 2014), 145–81, 148.

10. Karen J. Wenell, *Jesus and Land: Sacred and Social Space in Second Temple Judaism* (London and New York: T & T Clark, 2007), 3.

link God's abode with Jerusalem. This is significant because God himself declares where he will reside. Each instance presents a spatial argument, one in which "God's presence is uniquely connected with Jerusalem and more specifically with the temple."[11] Therefore, it is not a controversial statement that the destruction of Jerusalem's second temple caused a serious identification crisis for many in the post-70 CE Jewish population. Francis D. Alvarez states, "The temple, in Jewish belief, is the center of the universe. Its destruction is a sign of cosmic [social and political] upheaval."[12] Although temple sentiments were not universal and static, its symbolic importance was respected. While various individuals or communities contested various aspects of the temple (i.e., corruptness), they still recognized "its symbolic power as a sacred place."[13]

To overcome this situational incongruity, Mark reinterprets the notion of "sacred space" and constructs a reimagining of temple sacrality. Throughout the text, in hindsight, he reflects upon and showcases how the temple has become corrupted (11.15-17; 12.1-12; 12.38-44). Despite the lost temple causing an identity crisis, Mark suggests that temple activities and hierarchies had become too concerned with "earthly" matters or "human tradition" (7.8-9; 12.38-40), resulting in its divinely ordained destruction (13.1-2). H. N. Roskam summarizes this argument nicely: "Jesus' cleansing of the temple ... indicates his rejection of the Jerusalem temple cult and those responsible for it, the Jewish religious leaders, i.e., the chief priests and scribes."[14] Burton Mack also places Mark's temple condemnation in a post-70 CE timeframe. He describes Mark 11.12-14 as a symbolic metaphor directed toward the temple, "Not of cleansing, but of condemnation and destruction."[15] Echoing Mack, William Arnal describes the cursing of the fig tree "as a sort of commentary on the 'temple tantrum' episode that it encloses (11.15-19), presumably in order to evoke the typically Markan motif of Israel's failures and to serve as an *ex eventu* foreshadowing of the destruction of the temple."[16] Roskam also employs the fig tree episode as an

---

11. Jonathon Lookadoo, *The High Priest and the Temple* (Tubingen: Mohr Siebeck, 2018), 206.

12. Francis D. Alvarez, "The Temple Controversy in Mark," *Landas* 28.1 (2014): 115–52, 149.

13. See Wenell, *Jesus and Land*, 30–31.

14. H. N. Roskam, *The Purpose of the Gospel of Mark in its Historical and Social Context* (Leiden and Boston: Brill, 2004), 163.

15. Burton L. Mack, *A Myth of Innocence: Mark and Christian Origins* (Philadelphia, PA: Fortress Press, 1998), 243.

16. William A. Arnal, "Mark, War, and Creative Imagination," in *Redescribing the Gospel of Mark*, eds. Barry S. Crawford and Merrill P. Miller (Atlanta, GA: Society of Biblical Literature, 2017), 401–82, 406.

example of Mark's temple condemnation: "Jesus' cleansing of the temple ... indicates his rejection of the Jerusalem temple cult and those responsible for it, the Jewish religious leaders, i.e., the chief priests and scribes ... He regards the Jerusalem temple cult, therefore, as fruitless."[17] Additionally, Donald Juel interprets this episode as being direct condemnation against the temple's leadership. He states, "The cleansing of the temple must in some sense imply the rejection of the official representatives of Israel, the leaders of the temple establishment ... the cleansing, interpreted by the cursing of the fig tree, points to the rejection of a particular group within Israel. Those in charge of the temple have borne no fruit."[18] Employing Jeremiah 7 as a sort of template, Mark reflectively (post factum) outlines why the Temple was and had to be, destroyed. The Temple was no longer a house of prayer, but a den of robbers (11.17). Overall, the Temple system was seen to be socially and financially corrupt and so required destruction. In other words, the Jerusalem temple cult was fruitless.[19] Thus we get an attack on the economic sector, those buying and selling.[20]

One method Mark could utilize to rectify the temple's destruction is by illustrating Jesus as an authorized "replacement" for the temple. Indeed, this view is held by some scholars to some degree.[21] Through mythic narratives, Mark constructs Jesus as a national mediator. His lost "here" and "there" identity and institutions are universalized and merged into a new "anywhere"[22] social institution through the narrative figure of Jesus. Eric Stewart argues that, in Mark, people travel from numerous surrounding

---

17. Roskam, *The Purpose of the Gospel of Mark*, 163.
18. Donald Juel, *Messiah and Temple* (Missoula, MT: Scholars Press, 1977), 131.
19. Also see Roskam, *The Purpose of the Gospel of Mark*, 163.
20. James G. Crossley, "Mark's Christology and the Scholarly Creation of a Non-Jewish Christ of Faith," in *Judaism, Jewish Identities and the Gospel Tradition: Essays in Honour of Maurice Casey*, ed. James G. Crossley (London and Oakville: Equinox Publishing, 2010), 118–51, 129.
21. For example, see Nicholas Perrin, *Jesus the Temple* (Grand Rapids, MI: Baker Academic, 2010); Harold W. Attridge, "The Temple and Jesus the High Priest in the New Testament," in *Jesus and Temple: Textual and Archaeological Explorations,* ed. James H. Charlesworth (Minneapolis, MN: Fortress Press, 2014), 213–37. Especially see 222–3, where Attridge argues that Jesus is presented as "a new Torah ... [which] moves beyond general evocation of the dwelling of God among God's people to a symbolic equation of the body of Jesus with the Temple." It should be noted, however, that Attridge is primarily relying on the Gospel of John for his argument. Also see Charlesworth, "Jesus and Temple," 186. Here Charlesworth declares that "Christian theologians, for most of two millennia, have understandably argued that Jesus eventually becomes the cornerstone of the 'New Temple.' [Since] Jesus is the *axis mundi*, then the Temple is redundant." Charlesworth, however, does not provide any examples for his assertion.
22. For clarification, see Jonathan Z. Smith, "Here, There, and Anywhere," in

areas to hear Jesus speak, heal, teach, or to become a part of his congregation; therefore, Mark is indicating that the temple and the synagogues are no longer the fixed "sacred" centers of socio-ethnic identification.[23] Jesus becomes an itinerant "anywhere" center or the new socio-ethnic institution. Stewart sums this point up nicely:

> Jesus is a traveller and a centripetal force in the Gospel of Mark. People are drawn to him from every quarter of Mark's [geographical] world. As a "travelling" center, the space of Jesus' company represents fluid sacred space. It is no longer the temple, which is in any event about to be destroyed or the synagogues ... in which Jesus' followers will "gather." Rather they "gather" around Jesus.[24]

Following this line of thought, if Jesus is considered to be the "anywhere" center, does physical location(s) have any bearing? Willi Marxsen boldly claims that the temple is not relevant and is no longer a concern for Mark; instead, Galilee is Mark's focal point. Marxsen states, "Galilee establishes the identity of the now Risen Lord with the earthly Jesus, just as the awaited Parousia, likewise in Galilee, secures his identity with the one who is to return."[25] Christopher Zeichmann argues that Mark's Gospel is an effort to authorize Galilee as a focal point for refugees fleeing from the Judean War and reconfiguring their cultic practices with the loss of the Jerusalem temple. Employing the examples of tax practices, the Temple's replacement, and Capernaum as the preeminent focal point for post-Judean War Jewish activity, Zeichmann states, "Mark is less interested in navigating so-called 'Christian' or 'theological' matters relegated to the realm of belief, than it is querying what practices would constitute a post-War, post-temple, Galilean Judaism and retroactively authorizing them by locating them in the life of Jesus."[26] Concentrating on his latter two points, Zeichmann argues that Mark resituates the "temple's cultic functions onto Jesus' person, Mark's implicit links between synagogues and the temple, and various other elements indicate a recurrent interest in *replacing* the temple."[27] The impetus for this restitution is a deep underlying concern for the destruction of the temple and renegotiating

---

Jonathan Z. Smith, *Relating Religion: Essays in the Study of Religion* (Chicago, IL, and London: University of Chicago Press, 2004), 323–39.

23. Eric Stewart, *Gathered Around Jesus: An Alternative Spatial Practice in the Gospel of Mark* (Cambridge: James Clark & Co., 2009), 172–3.

24. Stewart, *Gathered Around Jesus*, 211.

25. Willi Marxsen, *Mark the Evangelist*, trans. James Boyce et al. (Nashville, TN: Abingdon, 1969), 215.

26. Christopher Zeichmann, "Mark's Jesus as Post-War Subject in Pre-War Galilee," *Conference Paper*, 3.

27. Zeichmann, "Mark's Jesus as Post-War Subject," 9–10 (original emphasis).

temple practices and discourses. An example of this restitution can be seen in Mark 14.57-58. These verses imply that the temple "made with hands," is the lost "there" institution after its destruction; however, a suitable replacement is Jesus' universal "anywhere" institution "not made with hands." The renegotiation of temple practices and discourses is also prevalent throughout the text.[28] Zeichmann's third point, Capernaum being the preeminent focal point for post-Judean War Jewish activity, is also significant. Indeed the underlying motivation for Mark resituating the temple's cultic activities onto Jesus is the temple's destruction, but the fact that Mark is an exile is equally important. Mark not only lost his "there" institution, but he also lost his "here" identity. To overcome this gap, he places a large emphasis on Jesus' activities in Galilee, thereby identifying Galilee, and especially Capernaum, as a new gathering point for displaced peoples. In other words, Mark is attempting to turn his location of exile into a new "home."[29] This explanation is important to note because through the continuing exile, Mark creates a new national "anywhere" institution away from the previous locus of the temple, Jerusalem, and synagogues. Thus, he transitions the "sacred" focal point, he seeks to "… encompass a 'transformation.' The outsider was transformed into the powerful insider; the peripheral became central, displacing the previous center to the periphery."[30] Mark's transition of the sacred space is convincing as he does appear to engage in spatial redefinition. Elizabeth Struthers Malbon states, "Galilee—not Jerusalem—is the sphere of culminating action … and Galilee—not Jerusalem—bears the positive connotations within the pair of spatial terms. In these two ways, the traditional (Jewish) valuation of Galilee and Jerusalem is reversed in the Markan narrative."[31] Arnal parallels Malbon: "*Mark is engaged in redefining Jewish space.* More than this, the distinctive or surprising feature of this redefinition is *the inversion of the expected valences of Judea versus Galilee as instances of Jewish territory.*"[32]

At first glance, the argument of Jesus directly replacing the Temple is fairly convincing and holds certain sway. However, it does have problems. First, nowhere in the text does Mark claim that Jesus proclaimed himself to

---

28. See Stewart, *Gathered Around Jesus*, 195–200. Stewart outlines the renegotiation of Jesus' idea of purity contrasted against temple purity laws.

29. William A. Arnal, "The Gospel of Mark as Reflection on Exile and Identity," in *Introducing Religion: Essays in Honor of Jonathan Z. Smith*, eds. Willi Braun and Russell T. McCutcheon (London and Oakville: Equinox, 2008), 57–67, 66.

30. Jonathan Z. Smith, "Conjectures on Conjunctures and Other Matters: Three Essays," in *Redescribing the Gospel of Mark*, eds. Barry S. Crawford and Merrill P. Miller (Atlanta, GA: Society of Biblical Literature, 2017), 17–98, 38.

31. Elizabeth Struthers Malbon, *In the Company of Jesus: Characters in Mark's Gospel* (Louisville, KY: Westminster John Knox Press, 2000), 153.

32. Arnal, "Mark, War, and Creative Imagination", 476.

be the "new Temple." Crossley bluntly states, "There is no indication that the Markan Jesus intended his death as replacement of the Temple."[33] Second, such an assertion is not consistent with previous Jewish scriptures where king or messiah figures are described more in terms of rebuilders (2 Sam 7.13; Zech 6.12). Both passages refer to a future king who will build the temple. Although certain texts mention that a "messiah" figure will rebuild a temple (2 Sam 7.13; Zech 6.12), *they do not proclaim that the character will themselves become the temple.* Mark follows a rebuilding pattern, albeit in a slightly altered manner. He does not proclaim that Jesus himself will build another physical temple. What Mark does accomplish is a portrayal of Jesus as a (re)builder, or mediator, of another "anywhere" socio-ethnic institution by shaping and constructing "anywhere" self-identifications, usually referred to as the "kingdom of God."

Instead of Jesus himself directly replacing the Temple, others have argued that Mark establishes his, or the overall "Christian," community as the new Temple. Timothy Grey suggests that the previous temple is withering away, and a new place, composed of prayer and forgiveness will succeed it. This new "place" is the Christian community, as Grey states, "The supplanting of the temple by the community, begun in [Mark 11.12-25]."[34] In other words, the community itself is, or replaces, the destroyed Temple. Juel proclaims that "Mark seems to view the Christian community as a replacement for the temple."[35] Charlesworth argues that "Mark seems to propose that the true purpose of the Temple as the house of prayer calls for fulfillment not in a building, but in a community ... Mark may allude to the fulfillment of true Temple worship by the replacement of the Temple with Jesus' disciples."[36] Ernest Best relays a similar argument: "In 14:58 this anti-temple polemic is balanced by a promise about the new community expressed in terms of a new temple ... Within v. 17 we note the contrast between 'my house' and 'den of robbers' and the reference to 'my house' as 'a house of prayer for all nations.'"[37] Scholars who hold this view rely on and cite 1 Cor 3.16, 1 Cor 6.19, 2 Cor 6.16, various Qumran texts,[38] Hebrews, and even the epis-

---

33. Crossley, "Mark's Christology and the Scholarly Creation," 129.

34. Timothy C. Grey, *The Temple in the Gospel of Mark: A Study in Its Narrative Role* (Grand Rapids, MI: BakerAcademic, 2008), 53–5.

35. Juel, *Messiah*, 167.

36. Charlesworth, "Jesus and Temple," 184–5.

37. Ernest Best, *Following Jesus: Discipleship in the Gospel of Mark* (Sheffield: Journal for the Study of the New Testament Supplement Series 4, 1981): 216, 218.

38. For example, see Juel, *Messiah*, 159–68, where he states, "The [Qumran] Scrolls provide evidence of pre-Christian use of community-as-temple" (159). Also see George J. Brooke, "Eschatological Wisdom and the Kingship of God: Light from some of the Dead Sea Scrolls on the Teaching of Jesus?" in *Judaism, Jewish Identities and the*

tles of Ignatius.³⁹ For example, Georg Klinzing examines different temple imagery in the Qumran texts and concludes that early Christians adopted the community as temple imagery from Qumran literature.⁴⁰ In regard to Pauline literature, Jonathon Lookadoo argues that although the Corinthians are referred to in the plural, jointly they encompass God's particular temple. God resides in the Corinthian community, establishing "them as God's people and temple."⁴¹ Paul's interest lies primarily in communal unity. One method for developing unity is through symbolic metaphor. Lookadoo continues, "The connection between a unique God and the importance of single representative elements remains and binds the people together in unity … one of these objects is the temple."⁴² Paul, therefore, "employs the temple metaphor to portray unity in the congregation."⁴³ In a similar assertion, Charlesworth states, "Paul takes cultic language out of the cult and moves sacred space from Temple to the individual."⁴⁴ Finally, W. D. David proclaims, according to Paul, "The whole community constitutes the shrine or temple of God … [Paul] is anxious to emphasize that God no longer dwells *with* his people in a tent or temple, but actually dwells *in* them."⁴⁵

Although considering early "Christian" communities to be the new Temple is intriguing, in Mark's actual text, evidence of such a correlation is lacking. First, as others have convincingly argued, Mark's adherence to a specific community is problematic.⁴⁶ Arnal points out that Mark's emphasis "is on Jesus as a transformative epic character, a focus that directly and necessarily dictated his own generic innovations. *Mark does not appear to be deeply rooted in any identifiable 'Christian community' formation at all.*"⁴⁷ Additional, Robyn Faith Walsh astutely argues,

---

Gospel Tradition: Essays in Honour of Maurice Casey, ed. James G. Crossley (London and Oakville: Equinox, 2010), 45–61, especially 53.

39. For example, see Lookadoo, *The High Priest*, especially 100–262.

40. See Georg Klinzing, *Die Umdeutung des Kultus in der Qumrangemeinde und im Neuen Testament* (Gottingen: Vandenhoeck and Ruprecht, 1971).

41. Lookadoo, *The High Priest*, 207.

42. Lookadoo, *The High Priest*, 247.

43. Lookadoo, *The High Priest*, 247.

44. Charlesworth, "Jesus and Temple," 192. Charlesworth's main argument here is that despite Paul's rhetoric of a communal temple, the temple itself and "the sacred cult" were still important for Paul.

45. W.D. Davies, *The Gospel and the Land: Early Christianity and Jewish Territorial Doctrine* (Berkley, CA: University of California Press, 1974), 186–7 (original emphasis).

46. Especially see Stanley K. Stowers, "The Concept of 'Community' and the History of Early Christianity," *MTSR* 23 (2011): 238–56.

47. Arnal, "Mark, War, and Creative Imagination", 463 (emphasis added).

The notion that the practices, interpretive innovations, teachings, and literature of what comes to be known as Christianity emanated from an identifiable, powerful genesis is central to the idea of the early Christian big bang. Implicit to this theory is the premise that Christianity as a social phenomenon materialized in a manner otherwise unprecedented for a new religious movement. Certainly, in order for there to have been thousands converted or "turned" in a single day, as claimed by Acts 21.20, the projected rate of growth of the movement would have to have been nothing short of miraculous. In terms of the texts that document this big bang, it is a standard claim among scholars of early Christianity that a "community" is the proper social context for imagining their composition. Usually, the writer is described as belonging to a discrete community of Christians that possesses its own particular theological outlook. As such, the author, the proverbial voice of this group, has developed his thinking within a very specific environment and, therefore, writes his gospel (or other Jesus material) reflecting—either indirectly or, as is more regularly thought, directly—the interests and holdings of that community. The result is an approach that accepts communities as a fundamental and axiomatic element of the compositional fabric of early Christian literature. Moreover, these writings are understood to reflect not only the collective perspectives of these communities, but also to document strands of Jesus tradition that have been faithfully passed on by generation after generation of early Christians.[48]

Instead of focusing on Mark's "Big Bang" community, emphasis should be directed toward Mark's endeavors to solve his situational incongruities. As Arnal rightly indicates, "Mark provides so little information about his audience that we cannot even be sure that he has *any* discrete group in mind."[49] The second problem is, unlike Paul and the author of Hebrews, Mark makes no mention, explicit or implicit, of Jesus' followers or community becoming the new Temple.

Whether intentional or not, Mark's "kingdom of God" rhetoric appears to rely on an institutional belonging—more akin to an "anywhere" Temple.[50] The title itself, "The Kingdom of God," speaks volumes. God resides within his kingdom, similar to his previous residence with the temple. As George J. Brooke states, "The temple is described as the 'Temple of the Kingdom' not least because as in the *Songs of the Sabbath Sacrifice* that is where God's kingship, his sovereignty, most clearly resides."[51] "Kingdom"

---

48. Robyn Faith Walsh, "Q and the 'Big Bang' Theory of Christian Origins," in *Redescribing the Gospel of Mark*, eds. Barry S. Crawford, Merrill P. Miller (Atlanta, GA: Society of Biblical Literature, 2017), 483–533, 489–90.

49. Arnal, "Mark, War, and Creative Imagination", 473.

50. For clarification, it should be noted that I am not suggesting that the kingdom of God directly *replaces* the temple. Rather, I suggest it is more a *reimagining* of the lost temple.

51. George J. Brooke, "Eschatological Wisdom and the Kingship of God: Light from

denotes a sizable socio-ethnic institution, though Mark transforms its spatial arrangement and the entrance criteria from a nationalist perspective to "righteousness."[52] Mark makes this point clear in 12.28-34, where entrance into the kingdom of God relies on the "greatest commandments"—to love God and your neighbor. This practice and mentality is more vital than "burnt offerings and sacrifices." Therefore, God's residence does not have a physical barrier, guarded by priestly authorities, "but was available simply through right [thought and] worship."[53] Christopher R. Matthews provides a critical point to Mark's compositional timeframe: "It would be remarkable if the political history of the Levant and its surroundings did not assure an ever-present unconscious fatigue with respect to this 'long history of hegemonies.' In such a context a mythic appeal to a kingdom of god would be a most 'attractive' counterpoint to the incongruity presented by reality."[54] Again, Mark's incongruous reality is the loss of the "there" temple. If the temple's destruction was one of Mark's primary situational incongruities, which I suggest it is, he puts forth his reconciliation right at the beginning of his text, namely, in the form of "the kingdom of God." Mark 1.14 states, "Jesus [went] into Galilee proclaiming the message of the kingdom of God." Additionally, Mark 10.13-16 and 10.23-27 both employ rhetoric akin to entering an "anywhere" institution; i.e., "entering into her." Bruce Chilton argues that for certain Jews in antiquity, God's "kingdom is transcendent in space."[55] Employing various Psalms as intellectual background for such views, Chilton states,

---

Some of the Dead Sea Scrolls on the Teaching of Jesus?" in *Judaism, Jewish Identities and the Gospel Tradition: Essays in Honour of Maurice Casey*, ed. James G. Crossley (London and Oakville: Equinox, 2010), 45–61, 54.

52. Although it should be noted that various scholars primarily view the kingdom of God as a political mechanism. For example, see Halvor Moxnes, *Putting Jesus in His Place: A Radical Vision of Household and Kingdom* (Louisville, KY: Westminster John Knox Press, 2003); William Herzog II, *Jesus, Justice, and the Reign of God: A Ministry of Liberation* (Louisville, KY: Westminster John Knox Press, 2000); and David R. Kaylor, *Jesus the Prophet: His Vision of the Kingdom on Earth* (Louisville, KY: Westminster John Knox Press, 1994). Overall, these scholars argue that Jesus, or in this case Mark, "preached and taught a message that was thoroughly political" (Kaylor, 3).

53. Brooke, 54.

54. Christopher R. Matthews, "Markan Grapplings," in *Redescribing the Gospel of Mark* (eds. Barry S. Crawford, Merrill P. Miller; Atlanta: Society of Biblical Literature, 2017), 169–80, 177–8.

55. Bruce Chilton, "The Aramaic Lord's Prayer," in *Judaism, Jewish Identities and the Gospel Tradition: Essays in Honour of Maurice Casey*, ed. James G. Crossley (London and Oakville: Equinox, 2010), 62–82, 75.

> Ps 145 anticipates a universal acknowledgement of the kingdom because, in its conception, the divine rule even now extends to every place and creature ... [The] final image of the Psalm (145.21), that all flesh should bless the holy name of the LORD, is an ideal that is realized for the moment only within the place of his holiness. But the coordinate of transcendence makes the locality of the Temple a model for what the entire creation is to be. What is local, in Zion, is the pattern for what is to be universal, throughout creation ... Mark has Jesus specify the extent of God's establishment of the kingdom (Mk 11.17).[56]

There have been many arguments revolving around the notion that Jesus' kingdom of God rhetoric was eschatological.[57] Christian eschatology has usually been interpreted as an "end of the world" scenario. However, within Mark's timeframe, this reading can be seen as anachronistic, a later Christian interpretation incorporated into the text. At first glance, Mark 13.29-37 appears to resemble later Christian eschatology. Indeed, one can see how easy this representation can be made. A (mis)reading of Alvarez seems to confirm this argument. He states, "Eschatology refers to a time in the future when the course of history will be changed—no one knows exactly when or precisely how—to such an extent that there is an entirely new state of reality about which the only thing certain is that it is new ... The whole of Mark therefore can be seen as a process of inauguration, the establishment of a new period."[58] Alvarez provides a good counter-argument, "Jewish eschatology is not about the end of the world ... Jewish eschatology is centred on the faithfulness of God to his covenant with Israel ... and seemingly restored upon the return of God's people to Jerusalem ... Jewish eschatology looks to the future."[59] Alvarez's argument is more in line with Mark's concerns and compositional timeframe. As a result, Mark 13.29-37, does not need to rely on the notion of a future apocalyptic eschatology.

---

56. Chilton, "The Aramaic Lord's Prayer," 76, 78.

57. For example, see George R. Beasley-Murray, *Jesus and the Kingdom of God* (Grand Rapids, MI: Eerdmans, 1986); Grey, *The Temple in the Gospel of Mark*, 94–155. Overall, Grey argues, "The temple theme in Mark is deeply eschatological" (Grey, *The Temple in the Gospel of Mark*, 196). Also see John A. McEvoy, "Realized Eschatology and the Kingdom Parables," *CBQ* 9.3 (1947): 329–57. McEvoy is responding to Charles H. Dodd's argument, that the kingdom of God is already present in the material world. See Charles H. Dodd, "The Thesis of Realized Eschatology," *Catholic Biblical Quarterly* V (1943): 396–440. Concluding, McEvoy states, "A kingdom of God which would be inaugurated only after [Jesus'] death and at the end of the world which He expected soon to come. Christ's ministry would be, then but a preparation for this purely eschatological kingdom of God" (McEvoy, "Realized Eschatology," 356).

58. Alvarez, "The Temple Controversy," 128–9. Alvarez, however, is not advocating a Christian eschatology.

59. Alvarez, "The Temple Controversy," 125–6.

Throughout his text, Mark speaks about the kingdom of God primarily through parables and abstract aphorisms. Mark 4.1-32 is a primary example. First, Mark declares that people who are "sown" on "good soil" bear fruit and have been given the secret of the kingdom of God. He contrasts the people who know the kingdom of God with others who have no roots. They desire wealth and earth desires and could potentially lead to a "socio-cultural system which undermines Israel's quest for Torah obedience,"[60] a condemnation (against the previous temple authorities) that he repeats throughout the text. Nicholas Perrin argues that the people "sown on shallow soil refers to those who after a promising start eventually cave to external political pressures."[61] Immediately after, Mark likens the kingdom God to a sprouting seed that should be harvested, or attended. Then the parable of the mustard seed also equates the kingdom of God to a seed that grows to become the most magnificent shrub where birds can take refuge and build their home. The seed metaphor, especially in regard to the mustard seed, resembles the rhetoric of an "anywhere" temple, an allegorical institution where people can build their new homes and take sanctuary. The symbolic seed "can be seen as initiating a redemptive-historical ... setting the stage for the [anywhere] temple."[62] Robert Bach argues that Jeremiah's use of "plants" and "building" metaphors is derived from salvation rhetoric, resulting in a restoration prophecy, especially in terms of the community.[63] Shozo Fujita, through his intertestamental examination, makes a similar argument, stating that "the metaphor of God's people as his plants are further detected in Jewish literature of the intertestamental period."[64] Examining the Psalms of Solomon 14.3-5, Fujita concludes that "renegade Jews, do not flourish by being cut off from the source of living water, the Law, and will wither and be plucked up. By contrast, the righteous plants are privileged to share a portion in God's paradise forever ... The Law like water nourishes them as thriving plants. The metaphor of plant thus carries various ideological assertion."[65] Mark 12 (the parable of the tenants) also utilizes agricultural allegory. However, the ending of this parable is

60. Nicholas Perrin, *Jesus the Priest* (London: SPCK, 2018), 107.
61. Perrin, *Jesus the Priest*, 105. Perrin states that the "external political pressures" primarily consist of persecution.
62. Perrin, *Jesus the Priest*, 108.
63. See Robert Bach, "Bauen und Pflanzen," in *Studien zur Theologie der alttestamentlichen Überlieferungen*, eds. Rolf Rendtorff and Klaus Koch (Neukirchen: Neukirchener Verlag der Buchhandlung des Erziehungsvereins 1961), 7–32.
64. Shozo Fujita, "The Metaphor of Plant in Jewish Literature of the Intertestamental Period," *JSJ* 7.1 (1976): 30–45, 30.
65. Fujita, "The Metaphor of Plant in Jewish Literature," 30, 33. Although Fujita eventually arrives at seeing the community-as-temple.

vital—namely, Mark's change of symbolism. As Alvarez notes, "But Jesus suddenly switches metaphors at the end of the parable. He shifts from agricultural to temple imagery."[66] Overall, the "plant" metaphor resembles a community. Mark appears to continue this metaphor—a perceived community is cultivated by "water" (becoming or remaining "righteous") and is, therefore, able to enter into the kingdom of God. By employing temple language and imagery, Mark is able to reimagine place and construct a new locative reality, namely, an institutional "anywhere" kingdom.

Jesus the Social Healer

Many scholars have examined the concept or notion of Jesus as a healer. For example, Geza Vermes claims that Jesus was a popular healer and exorcist for "the sick and possessed."[67] Shailer Mathews also proclaims, "There was another appeal which Jesus made to the crowds that gathered about him, his power to cure the sick."[68] Therefore, "As a healer, Jesus belongs within a category of charismatic or shamanistic figures found in the ancient world."[69] Continuing this trajectory, certain scholars discuss the particular reasons why Jesus performed healings. Gerald O'Collins, utilizing Mark 2.1-12 as a reference, argues "This story from Mark sets what is visible over against what is invisible: the visible power exercised by Jesus in curing the paralytic as evidence for his invisible power to forgive sins."[70] O'Collins see this line of thought as the overall motif for healing narratives. In regard to afflicted people, he states, "His visible handicapped condition reflected and symbolized something invisibly wrong with him in his relationship with God. Jesus dealt with the visible and the invisible handicap."[71] O'Collins' argument, however, relies purely on individual experience, physically

---

66. Alvarez, "The Temple Controversy," 146.

67. Geza Vermes, *The Changing Faces of Jesus* (Toronto: Penguin Press, 2000), 163.

68. Shailer Mathews, *Jesus on Social Institutions* (Philadelphia, PA: Fortress Press, 1971), 47.

69. Jan-Olav Henriksen and Karl Olav Sandnes, *Jesus as Healer: A Gospel for the Body* (Grand Rapids, MI: Eerdmans Publishing Company, 2016), 21. However, Henriksen and Sandnes later argue that Jesus was portrayed, and thus should be seen, as "unique" (Henriksen and Sandnes, *Jesus as Healer*, 23).

70. Gerald O'Collins, *Jesus: A Portrait* (Maryknoll, NY: Orbis Books, 2008), 53. O'Collins states that a person who was healed received forgiveness for their sins: "This story from Mark sets what is visible against what is invisible: the visible power exercised by Jesus in curing the paralytic as evidence for his invisible power to forgive sins" (O'Collins, *Jesus*, 53).

71. O'Collins, *Jesus*, 67.

and spiritually. He briefly states that Jesus' healing of the leper resulted in a restored life.[72] Again, this is centered on individual restoration. Don Capps instead opts for a psychosomatic interpretation to Jesus' healings.[73] Capps thinks that the healing participants had a mental illness that manifested into physical ailments, possibly due to Hellenistic cities and policies. Capps' concern, however, runs into the same problem as O'Collins' interpretation, namely, a complete emphasis on the individual. Another scholar who places prominence on the "healed" individuals is Gerd Theissen.[74] Theissen argues that the healing narratives are not creative endeavors from the Gospel authors but are somehow based upon historicity—"they are no invention."[75] He argues that Jesus employed faith as a type of "placebo effect" in combination with ritual. This placebo improves "the general conditions of health and thereby makes it easier to live with an illness."[76] Overall, the problem with these arguments is that they entirely disregard social "illness," which mainly stems from dislocation and alienation. Additionally, all assume these healing stories are based upon a dependable foundation. Their entire arguments revolve around the postulation of "why" the individuals were healed to "why" Jesus felt inclined to treat them. This argument disregards the actual author of the gospels. Mark's ideology, purpose, and discourse would not completely resemble past concerns. Furthermore, Mark produced a narrative, one that displays his dispositions and proclivities and therefore does not fit with assumptions and conjectures regarding the "Historical Jesus" and his patients.

Regardless of a hypothetical "why" Jesus performed healings, scholarly debate revolves around a perceived dichotomy of "curing disease" and "healing illness."[77] This polemic stems from recent scholarship employing a medical anthropological method for studying healings in antiquity and other scholars who see the method as helpful but ultimately inadequate.[78]

---

72. See O'Collins, *Jesus*, 51.

73. Don Capps, *Jesus the Village Psychiatrist* (Louisville, KY: Westminster John Knox Press, 2008).

74. See Gerd Theissen, "Jesus and His Followers as Healers: Symbolic Healing in Early Christianity," in *The Problem of Ritual Efficacy*, eds. William S. Sax, Johannes Quack, and Jan Weinhold (Oxford: Oxford University Press, 2010), 45–65; Gerd Theissen, *Miracle Stories of the Early Christian Tradition*, trans. Francis Mcdonagh (Edinburgh: T & T Clark, 1983).

75. Theissen, *"Jesus and His Followers as Healers,"* 50.

76. Theissen, *"Jesus and His Followers as Healers,"* 55.

77. See John J. Pilch, *Healing in the New Testament: Insights from Medical and Mediterranean Anthropology* (Minneapolis, MN: Fortress Press, 2000) for a categorical review and observation.

78. For example, see Pieter F. Craffert, "Medical Anthropology as an Antidote for

Medical anthropology attempts to examine the cultural representations of sickness and health, overcoming ethnocentric notions of medicine, especially in regard to modern Western biomedicine as the definitive, and seemingly axiomatic, reality. Perhaps the influential medical anthropological study was John J. Pilch's *Healing in the New Testament: Insights from Medical and Mediterranean Anthropology*.[79] Pilch states, "What a Western reader might interpret as a loss of function, namely lameness, an ancient reader would see as a disvalued state of being."[80] The sense of devaluing derives from one's reception, or lack thereof, within their community. Mediterranean culture highly depended on social cooperation and the reciprocation, especially under the social umbrella, of kinship. Pilch states,

> Emphasis on collateral relationships or cooperation with others (rather than competition) is also revealed in passages that reflect aspects of dyadic contract as well as patron-client relationships. ... Jesus himself advises the seventy of an alternative, acceptable form of reciprocity in terms of collateral relationships. ... Healing, then, can be an integral part of collateral relationships ... The people who appear in Mark's gospel are collectivistic or dyadic personalities, that is, individuals who depend heavily on the opinions and evaluations of others; they are socialized to intense group orientation rather than individualism. ... The person's focus is on social relations or kinship.[81]

Since kinship was a major formal social institution in antiquity, one's removal from the institution resulted in a form of social illness. Jesus

---

Ethnocentrism in Jesus Research? Putting the Illness-Disease Distinction into Perspective," *HTS* 61.1 (2011). Craffert argues that Jesus should be perceived as a type of shamanic healer. Also see John Dominic Crossan, *The Historical Jesus: The Life of a Mediterranean Jewish Peasant* (San Francisco, CA: HarperSanFrancisco, 1991); John Dominic Crossan, *Jesus: A Revolutionary Biography* (San Francisco, CA: HarperSanFrancisco, 1994); John Dominic Crossan, "Jesus and the Challenge of Collaborative Eschatology," in *The Historical Jesus: Five Views*, eds. James K. Beilby and Paul Rhodes Eddy (Downers Grove, Illinois: IVP Academic Press, 2009), 127–9. For counter views, see Henriksen and Sandnes, *Jesus as Healer,* 32. They suggest that illness and disease should not be seen as separate categories. Rather, "[t]he two are not necessarily separate realities"; Frederick J. Gaiser, *Healing in the Bible: Theological Insight for Christian Ministry* (Grand Rapids, MI: Baker Academic Press, 2010); Wendy J. Cotter, *The Christ of the Miracle Stories: Portrait through Encounter* (Grand Rapids, MI: Baker Academic Press, 2010). However, Henriksen and Sandnes, Gaiser, and Cotter's oppositional views fall into the trap of historical assumption and conflating numerous independent texts to provide an all-encompassing interpretation. Additionally, some arguments rely on the anachronism of "Christology" for explanation (see Henriksen and Sandnes, *Jesus as Healer*, 39, in particular).

79. John J. Pilch, *Healing in the New Testament: Insights from Medical and Mediterranean Anthropology* (Minneapolis, MN: Fortress Press, 2000).
80. Pilch, *Healing in the New Testament*, 13.
81. Pilch, *Healing in the New Testament*, 9, 65.

accounts for this exclusion (sickness), and his healings result in social reintegration. Pilch employs Jesus' healing of the leper as an example. Traditionally, leprosy could result in removal from the community; however, through Jesus' healing, the former leper was allowed back into his social institution. Pilch states, "Jesus' willingness to associate with lepers ... reduces the social and cultural oppressiveness of exclusion from the community ... Jesus reduces and removes the experiential oppressiveness associated with such afflictions. In all instances of healing, meaning is restored to life and the sufferer is returned to purposeful living."[82] Another example is Mark 1.30-31. The narrative describes Peter's mother-in-law being confined to bed with a fever, a sickness that secludes her from her kinship relations, duties, and status. However, after Jesus lifts her fever, "she began to serve them" or "waited upon them." Upon being healed, Peter's mother-in-law immediately returned to her previous duties and status; therefore, she is once again a part of her kinship community. Overall, Pilch's argument is that,

> Healers mediate culture ... [Therefore,] human sickness, or illness, can thus be conceived as a coherent syndrome of meaning and experience that is linked to society's deep semantic and value structures. ... System can be viewed at a macro-level (whole societies or regions) or at a micro-level (localities: communities, neighbourhoods, groups of families) ... [Jesus] provides social meaning for the life problems resulting from the sickness ... [and] highlights the importance of key cultural factors in the text, such as kinship, social networks, power/authority, and the like.[83]

Despite Pilch's important arguments of healings as social reinstatement, he could, I think, push the point further, namely, into Mark's social narrative layer. In other words, Jesus presented as a social healer within a socio-ethnic restorative text. After Jerusalem's takeover, the temple's destruction, and the resulting exile, a social curative was essential. In every healing narrative (Mark 1.23-31, 40-45; 2.1-12; 3.1-6; 5.1-34; 6.54-56; 7.24-37; 8.22-26; 9.14-27; 10.46-52), the sick show symptomatic conditions (such as leprosy) that would somehow exclude them from their kinship and community, or they are encumbered with an ailment (for example, a withered hand) that would prevent them from participating and working in their community, thereby establishing, determining, and labeling them a social hindrance or liability. Additionally, Mark laments and even condemns previous attempts at social healing from other "professional" physicians. For example, Mark 5.26 states, "And much suffering under many healers and spent all she had, and nothing benefited but rather became worse." Mark, again, is

---

82. Pilch, *Healing in the New Testament*, 14.
83. Pilch, *Healing in the New Testament*, 15, 42, 61, 72–3.

chiding a previous social institution, one that can be presumed lost, as being inadequate. His reflective consideration and ultimate judgment are clearly on display; indeed, all the previous afflictions separated and segregated the sufferers from their social identities.

Overall, even though his social organizations are in chaos, Mark's narrative myth-making attempts to reconcile and conflate these lost institutions. Despite the organizational disarray, lost social institutions can be reconciled, reconfigured and reimagined. Mark's narrative can be seen as a type of institutional bricolage reconciliation. Though this bricolage, one can still connect to their lost national institutions, albeit in a different manner. Mark's exilic circumstance, stemming from the Judean War, provided a situation that forced him to rethink his nationhood and identity. The narrative surrounding the bricolage institutional replacements is Mark's attempt to reconsider his identity and nationhood within his new social surroundings. Overall, Mark is faced with various situation incongruities and is forced to rethink how his socio-ethnic identity utilizes, and reflects upon, previous socio-ethnic institutions. Jonathan Z. Smith splendidly summarizes Mark's circumstances and response:

> Each society has moments of ritualized disjunction, moments of "descent into chaos," or ritual reversal, of liminality, of collective anomie. But these are part of a highly structured scenario in which these moments will be overcome through the creation of a new world, the raising of an individual to a new status, or the strengthening of community. ... When the world is perceived to be chaotic, reversed, liminal, filled with anomie. Then man finds himself in a world which he does not recognize; and perhaps even more terrible, man finds himself to have a self he does not recognize. Then he will need to create a new world, to express his sense of a new place.[84]

Author biography

Allan Wright is an Assistant Lecturer at the University of Alberta. His research focuses on the Gospel of Mark, the New Testament, and Monsters.

Bibliography

Alvarez, Francis D. "The Temple Controversy in Mark," *Landas* 28.1 (2014): 115–52. https://doi.org/10.13185/LA2014.28107

Arnal, William. "The Gospel of Mark as Reflection on Exile and Identity," 57–67 in

---

84. Jonathan Z. Smith, "The Influence of Symbols Upon Social Change," in *Map is not Territory: Studies in the History of Religions* (Chicago and London: University of Chicago Press, 1978), 129–46, 145–6.

Introducing Religion: Essays in Honour of Jonathan Z. Smith. Edited by Willi Braun and Russell T. McCutcheon. London and Oakville: Equinox, 2008.
—"Mark, War, and the Creative Imagination," 401–82 in *Redescribing the Gospel of Mark*. Edited by Barry S. Crawford and Merrill P. Miller. Atlanta, GA: Society of Biblical Literature Press, 2017.
Attridge, Harold W. "The Temple and Jesus the High Priest in the New Testament," 213–37 in *Jesus and Temple: Textual and Archaeological Explorations*. Edited by James H. Charlesworth. Minneapolis, MN: Fortress Press, 2014. https://doi.org/10.2307/j.ctt22h6s4f.13
Bach, Robert. "Bauen und Pflanzen," 7–32 in *Studien zur Theologie der alttestamentlichen Uberlieferungen*. Edited by Rolf Rendtorff and Klaus Koch. Neukirchen: Neukirchener Verlag der Buchhandlung des Erziehungsvereins 1961.
Beasley-Murray, George R. *Jesus and the Kingdom of God*. Grand Rapids, MI: Eerdmans, 1986.
Best, Ernest. *Following Jesus: Discipleship in the Gospel of Mark*. Sheffield: JSNTS 4, 1981.
Brooke, George J. "Eschatological Wisdom and the Kingship of God: Light from some of the Dead Sea Scrolls on the Teaching of Jesus?" 45–61 in *Judaism, Jewish Identities and the Gospel Tradition: Essays in Honour of Maurice Casey*. Edited by James G. Crossley. London and Oakville: Equinox, 2010.
Capps, Don. *Jesus the Village Psychiatrist*. Louisville, KY: Westminster John Knox Press, 2008.
Charlesworth, James H. *Jesus and the Temple: Textual and Archaeological Explorations*. Minneapolis, MN: Fortress Press, 2014. https://doi.org/10.2307/j.ctt22h6s4f
Chilton, Bruce. "The Aramaic Lord's Prayer," 62–82 in *Judaism, Jewish Identities and the Gospel Tradition: Essays in Honour of Maurice Casey*. Edited by James G. Crossley. London and Oakville: Equinox, 2010.
Cotter, Wendy J. *The Christ of the Miracle Stories: Portrait through Encounter*. Grand Rapids, MI, Baker Academic Press, 2010.
Craffert, Pieter F. "Medical Anthropology as an Antidote for Ethnocentrism in Jesus Research? Putting the Illness-Disease Distinct into Perspective," *HTS* 61.1 (2011). https://doi.org/10.4102/hts.v67i1.970
Crossan, John Dominic. *The Historical Jesus: The Life of a Mediterranean Jewish Peasant*. New York: HarperOne, 1991.
—*Jesus: A Revolutionary Biography*. New York: HarperOne, 1994.
—"Jesus and the Challenge of Collaborative Eschatology," in *The Historical Jesus: Five Views*. Edited by James K. Beilby and Paul Rhodes Eddy. Downers Grove, IL: IVP Academic Press, 2009.
Crossley, James G. "Mark's Christology and the Scholarly Creation of a Non-Jewish Christ of Faith," 118–51 in *Judaism, Jewish Identities and the Gospel Tradition: Essays in Honour of Maurice Casey*. Edited by James G. Crossley. London and Oakville: Equinox, 2010.
Davies, W.D. *The Gospel and the Land: Early Christianity and Jewish Territorial Doctrine*. Berkley, CA: University of California Press, 1974.
Dodd, Charles H. "The Thesis of Realized Eschatology," 396–440 *CBQ* V (1943).
Fujita, Shozo. "The Metaphor of Plant in Jewish Literature of the Intertestamental Period," *JSJ* 7.1 (1976): 30–45. https://doi.org/10.1163/157006376X00032
Gaiser, Frederick J. *Healing in the Bible: Theological Insight for Christian Ministry*. Grand Rapids, MI: Baker Academic Press, 2010.

Grey, Timothy C. *The Temple in the Gospel of Mark: A Study in Its Narrative Role.* Grand Rapids, MI: BakerAcademic, 2008. https://doi.org/10.1628/978-3-16-151585-9

Henriksen, Jan-Olav and Karl Olav Sandnes. *Jesus as Healer: A Gospel for the Body.* Grand Rapids, MI: Eerdmans Publishing, 2016.

Herzog II, William R. *Jesus, Justice, and the Reign of God: A Ministry of Liberation.* Louisville, KY: Westminster John Knox Press, 2000.

Juel, Donald. *Messiah and Temple.* Missoula, MT: Scholars Press, 1977.

Kaylor, David R. *Jesus the Prophet: His Vision of the Kingdom on Earth.* Louisville, KY: Westminster/John Knox Press, 1994.

Klinzing, Georg. *Die Umdeutung des Kultus in der Qumrangemeinde und im Neuen Testament.* Gottingen: Vandenhoeck and Ruprecht, 1971.

Kotrosits, Maia and Hal Taussig. *Re-Reading the Gospel of Mark Amidst Loss and Trauma.* New York: Palgrave Macmillan, 2013. https://doi.org/10.1057/9781137342645

Lookadoo, Jonathon. *The High Priest and the Temple.* Tubingen: Mohr Siebeck, 2018. https://doi.org/10.1628/978-3-16-156072-9

Mack, Burton L. *A Myth of Innocence: Mark and Christian Origins.* Philadelphia, PA: Fortress Press, 1989.

Malbon, Elizabeth Struthers. *In the Company of Jesus: Characters in Mark's Gospel.* Louisville, KY: Westminster John Knox Press, 2000.

—"The Jesus of Mark and the Sea of Galilee," *JBL* 103.3 (1984): 363–77. https://doi.org/10.2307/3260778

Marxsen, Willi. *Mark the Evangelist.* Translated by James Boyce et al. Nashville, TN: Abingdon, 1969.

Mathews, Shailer. *Jesus on Social Institutions.* Philadelphia, PA: Fortress Press, 1971.

Matthews, Christopher R. "Markan Grapplings," 169–80 in *Redescribing the Gospel of Mark.* Edited by Barry S. Crawford, Merrill P. Miller. Atlanta, GA: SBL, 2017. https://doi.org/10.2307/j.ctt1qd8zmm.10

McEvoy, John A. "Realized Eschatology and the Kingdom Parables," *Catholic Biblical Quarterly* 9.3 (1947): 329–57.

McInerny, William F. "An Unresolved Question in the Gospel Called Mark: 'Who is This Whom Even Wind and Sea Obey' (4:41)," *PRS* 1 (1996): 255–8.

Moxnes, Halvor. *Putting Jesus in His Place: A Radical Vision of Household and Kingdom.* Louisville, KY: Westminster john Knox Press, 2003.

O'Collins, Gerald. *Jesus: A Portrait.* Maryknoll, NY: Orbis Books, 2008.

Perrin, Nicholas. *Jesus the Priest.* London: SPCK, 2018.

—*Jesus and the Temple.* Grand Rapids, MI: Baker Academic, 2010.

Pilch, John J. *Healing in the New Testament: Insights from Medical and Mediterranean Anthropology.* Minneapolis, MN: Fortress Press, 2000.

Roskam, Hendrika N. *The Purpose of the Gospel of Mark in its Historical and Social Context.* Leiden and Boston: Brill, 2004. https://doi.org/10.1163/9789047413943

Smith, Jonathan Z. "Conjectures on Conjunctures and Other Matters: Three Essays," 17–98 in *Redescribing the Gospel of Mark.* Edited by Barry S. Crawford, Merrill P. Miller. Atlanta, GA: SBL, 2017. https://doi.org/10.2307/j.ctt1qd8zmm.6

—*Map Is Not Territory.* Chicago, IL., and London: University of Chicago Press, 1978.

—*Relating Religion: Essays in the Study of Religion.* Chicago, IL., and London: University of Chicago Press, 2004.

—*To Take Place: Toward Theory in Ritual.* Chicago, IL., and London: The University of Chicago Press, 1987.

Stewart, Eric. *Gathered Around Jesus: An Alternative Spatial Practice in the Gospel of Mark.* Cambridge: James Clark & Co., 2009. https://doi.org/10.2307/j.ctt1cgf70f

Stowers, Stanley K. "The Concept of 'Community' and the History of Early Christianity," *MTSR* 23 (2011): 238–56. https://doi.org/10.1163/157006811X608377

Theissen, Gerd. "Jesus and His Followers as Healers: Symbolic Healing in Early Christianity," 45–65 in *The Problem of Ritual Efficacy.* Edited by William S. Sax, Johannes Quack, and Jan Weinhold. Oxford: Oxford University Press, 2010. https://doi.org/10.1093/acprof:oso/9780195394405.003.0003

—*Miracle Stories of the Early Christian Tradition.* Translated by Francis Mcdonagh. Edinburgh: T & T Clark, 1983.

Vermes, Geza. *The Changing Faces of Jesus.* Toronto: Allen Lane: The Penguin Press, 2000.

Walsh, Robyn Faith. "Q and the 'Big Bang' Theory of Christian Origins," 483–533 in *Redescribing the Gospel of Mark.* Edited by Barry S. Crawford and Merrill P. Miller. Atlanta, GA: SBL, 2017. https://doi.org/10.2307/j.ctt1qd8zmm.14

Wenell, Karen J. *Jesus and Land: Sacred and Social Space in Second Temple Judaism.* London and New York: T & T Clark, 2007.

Zeichmann, Christopher B. "Mark's Jesus as Post-War Subject in Pre-War Galilee," *Conference Paper.*

Chapter Thirteen

"After This, Nothing Happened":
Historical Vulnerability and the End of (Cultural) Time in the Gospel of Mark

John W. Parrish[1]

> The past is not dead; it's not even past.
> —William Faulkner, *Requiem for a Nun*

> Certain ways of behavior, certain reactions against fate, throw mutual light on one another.
> — Edouard Perroy, *The Hundred Years War*

In the powerful opening essay that introduces the *Guide to the Study of Religion*,[2] Willi Braun states that "[c]oncept formation, which is never a once-for-all-time process, in the service of a successful research strategy, is not just the prerogative of the scholar, but it is indeed her or his primary obligation as a scholar."[3] While recognizing the tremendous importance of the more "technical" skills of scholarly work,[4] Braun also insists that

> [t]he *sine qua non* of the religion scholar's contribution to a general science of culture and society lies less in disciplined deployment of this or that *technē*, though this is not unimportant by any means, than in the theoretical imagination that can translate the merely curious or puzzling data of "religion" or the self-evidently significant but spectral objects of religious discourses into categories that can help us as scholars of religion…to understand the human interests and social arrangements in which religious discourses play their various generative and representational roles.[5]

One need not delve very deeply into Braun's published work to see that he has indeed made the theoretical imagination of concepts for the study of

---

1. I thank William Arnal, Scott Elliott, Stephen Moore, and especially Sarah Rollens for very helpful comments on an earlier version of this paper.
2. Willi Braun, "Religion," in Willi Braun and Russell T. McCutcheon (eds), *Guide to the Study of Religion* (London: Cassell, 2000), 3–18.
3. Braun, "Religion," 10.
4. Braun ("Religion," 14) specifically lists archeology, art history, demography, linguistics, and philology amongst such skills, recognizing that none of these skills are "learnt or taught overnight."
5. Braun, "Religion," 14–15.

religion his "primary obligation." His undoubted mastery of his specialized data domain—namely, Christian Origins—allows him to draw upon these data to provide "e.g.'s" illustrating the concepts and fleshing out the categories that his rigorous and insightful theoretical work calls forth. Those of us lucky enough to be his students can also attest that this aspect of his written work carries over exponentially into his pedagogical practice. It is, therefore, in deep gratitude that I dedicate this exercise in comparative concept formation to my teacher, Willi Braun.

Toward a New Concept of "Apocalypticism"

In this essay, I want to attempt a redescription of the concept of "apocalypticism," so prevalent in scholarly discourse on Christian origins, by reflecting upon the way cultures and histories exist together in colonial situations, and upon the possibility of cultural erasure and historical exhaustion. It has long been noted that social groups facing these threats often seem to experiment with "apocalyptic" or "millenarian" ideologies, variously described as "nativistic" or "revitalization" movements, "sects," or even "crisis cults." It can be argued that a pattern is perceptible here: a socio-cultural formation on the brink of expiration, whose constituents, facing physical annihilation or cultural assimilation, draw upon their native tools of intellectual and ritual (read: "religious") practices of cultural maintenance in an effort to avoid becoming their own "other," and maintain their traditional ways of being "selves." When described in this way, rather than by reference to (primarily Judeo-Christian) notions of "apocalypticism" or "millenarianism," these movements become anthropologically intelligible, recognizable based upon culturally specific "logics," rather than "exotic" or incomprehensible phenomena.

In what follows, I will reflect upon the possibility of developing the concepts of historical erasure and cultural expiration as possible tools for rethinking what we mean when we describe a textual production or social formation as "apocalyptic." I will rely heavily upon close readings of sources—both primary and secondary—which have proved especially useful to me in thinking through this matter. Once I have developed an optic through which to view "apocalyptic" texts without reference to traditional notions of apocalyptic*ism*, I will turn to an alleged example of an apocalyptic text which has been especially privileged in the academic study of religion, and attempt to situate it socially and historically, before providing a (tentative) re-reading of the text through that optic. The text in question is the Gospel of Mark, and the main source through which I will develop my reflection will be Jonathan Lear's philosophical investigation of the historical devastation of Crow Indian culture that occurred once the Crow had been relocated to a reservation by the American government.

Cultural Collapse and the Vulnerability of History

Drawing upon the ethnographic work of Frank Linderman,[6] Lear has explored the cultural and historical implications of the story of Plenty Coups, a Crow chieftain who served as Linderman's informant, and who eventually came to call Linderman his friend. Plenty Coups told the story of his life, the history of his people, and the complex process of American colonization and Indian relocation that left these people confined to a reservation and—among other things—unable to hunt buffalo. This all happened when Plenty Coups was rather young, but he stopped relating his story at the point where the Crow moved onto the reservation. It was as if he considered his story, and even his life, to have ended at that point. Linderman explains:

> Plenty Coups refused to speak of his life after the passing of the buffalo, so that his story seems to have been broken off, leaving many years unaccounted for. "I have not told you half of what happened when I was young," he said, when urged to go on. "I can think back and tell you much more of war and horse-stealing. But when the buffalo went away the hearts of my people fell to the ground, and they could not lift them up again. After this nothing happened. There was little singing anywhere. Besides," he added sorrowfully, "you know that part of my life as well as I do. You saw what happened to us when the buffalo went away."[7]

"After this, nothing happened." What could that mean? Is it just a careless phrase, a slip of the tongue, or is Plenty Coups providing us with a major insight into the nature of human existence? "If we take him at his word," Lear explains, "he seems to be saying that there was an event or a happening—the buffalo's going away—something Plenty Coups can refer to as a 'this,' such that after *this*, there are no more happenings...It would seem to be the retrospective declaration of a moment when history came to an end. But what could it mean for history to exhaust itself?"[8]

Avoiding, for the moment, the question of how such cultural apocalypses could occur, Lear notes an interesting tension in Plenty Coups' odd phrase. Plenty Coups actually told Linderman that "you know that part of my life as well as I do." This is quite an astonishing claim. Generally, "we take ourselves to have authority when it comes to the narratives of our own lives," and while we may be open to the insights we gather from other peoples' perspectives, we would not likely claim that they know us just as well as we

---

6. Frank B. Linderman, *Plenty-Coups, Chief of the Crows* (Lincoln, NE: University of Nebraska Press, 2002).
7. Quoted in Jonathan Lear, *Radical Hope: Ethics in the Face of Cultural Devastation* (Cambridge, MA: Harvard University Press, 2006), 2.
8. Lear, *Radical Hope*, 2–3.

know ourselves.⁹ However, Plenty Coups "seems to suggest that *anyone*—not just [Linderman]—who saw what happened when the Buffalo went away would be competent to tell that part of his life as well as he could. That is, any competent third-person observer would know all there was to know. This suggests that, according to Plenty Coups, there is no importantly first-person narrative to tell of this period. It is as though there is no longer an I there".¹⁰ But Plenty Coups is not just disavowing his own agency and subjectivity here. He seems to go one step further, and actually deny that he lives *in history* at all. Why?

Although I, like Lear, will not "pretend to say with confidence what Plenty Coups really meant," I do believe that his remark points to something deeper than a simple brush-off or an expression of sadness and despair. I follow Lear in treating this statement as though, in speaking, Plenty Coups "gave expression to an insight into the structure of temporality: that at a certain point things stopped happening".¹¹ Lear takes this as his starting point for a brilliant exercise in philosophical anthropology. Granted that we are, by nature, cultural animals, it follows that "we necessarily inhabit a way of life that is expressed in a culture. But our way of life—whatever it is—is vulnerable in various ways. And we, as participants in that way of life, thereby inherit a vulnerability".¹² What Plenty Coups' statement suggests is that, "if our way of life collapsed, things would cease to happen. What could this mean?" Further, "[w]hat would it mean to be a witness to this breakdown?" ¹³

Lear describes his meditations on the possibility of historical mortality as a work of "philosophical anthropology," rather than an historical ethnography.¹⁴ He admits that he is "not primarily concerned with what actually happened to the Crow tribe or to any other group," but rather, "with the field of possibilities in which all human endeavors gain meaning".¹⁵ In a sense, Lear's work is also a contribution to social ontology, for, although it does deal with the actual experience of the Crow, who had endured a cultural catastrophe, Lear notes that "the possibility that concerns [him] is not the special province of this or any other culture: it is a vulnerability that we all share simply in virtue of being human".¹⁶

9. Lear, *Radical Hope*, 3.
10. Lear, *Radical Hope*, 3.
11. Lear, *Radical Hope*, 5.
12. Lear, *Radical Hope*, 6.
13. Lear, *Radical Hope*, 6.
14. Lear, *Radical Hope*, 7.
15. Lear, *Radical Hope*, 7.
16. Lear, *Radical Hope*, 7.

Marshall Sahlins has written that "an event becomes such as it is interpreted. Only as it is appropriated in and through a cultural scheme does it acquire historical *significance*." This is because "history is culturally ordered, differently so in different societies, according to meaningful schemes of things"[17] Thus, if we want to understand how Crow history could exhaust itself, we need to know something of the cultural schemata by which they ordered their historical experience.

The Crow, known to themselves as Absarokee, were a nomadic hunting tribe which emerged out of its ancestral tribe, the Hidatsa, as a distinct group which migrated from the edge of the Mississippi River up to North Dakota around the beginning of the sixteenth century.[18] A Crow chieftain named No Vitals "had a vision in which he received sacred tobacco seeds from the Great Spirit, who told him to go west to high mountains to plant them." After a brief stay among the Mandan along the Missouri River, the Crow headed west to find the mountains. As the Crow historian, Joseph Medicine Crow, has explained it:

> When No Vitals left, he started out afresh as a brand-new tribe without a name; he literally and symbolically decided to travel light, for he left all heavy impedimenta behind him for good. His band became an instant tribe capable of existing as a separate and distinct entity, and one motivated with desire and dream of someday receiving the blessings of the Great Spirit when it reached the promised land![19]

By 1700, it seems that the Crow had "settled in what is now Montana and Wyoming. To survive as a nomadic tribe, they had to be good hunters, but they also had to be good at protecting themselves against rival tribes—notably the Sioux, the Blackfeet, and the Cheyenne. Fighting battles, defending one's territory, preparing to go to war—all this permeated the Crow way of life".[20]

---

17. Marshall Sahlins, *Islands of History* (Chicago, IL: University of Chicago Press, 1985), xiv, quoted in Lear, *Radical Hope*, 9.
18. For what follows, I am entirely reliant upon Lear, *Radical Hope*, 10–52.
19. Quoted in Lear, *Radical Hope*, 11.
20. Lear, *Radical Hope*, 11. Robert Lowie, an anthropologist who visited the Crow during the early twentieth century, described the place of war in Crow life in this lengthy passage [*The Crow Indians* (Lincoln, NE: University of Nebraska Press, 1983), 215. Quoted in Lear, *Radical Hope*, 12]:

> War was not the concern of a class nor even of the male sex, but of the whole population, from cradle to grave. Girls as well as boys derived their names from a famous man's exploit. Women danced wearing scalps, derived honor from their husbands' deeds, publicly exhibited the men's shield or weapons; and a woman's lamentations over a slain son was the most effective goad to a punitive expedition…

But no two aspects of warfare were more constitutive of Crow culture—and thus, Crow history—than the planting of the coup-stick and the counting of coups.[21]

Planting a coup-stick was the paradigmatic act of establishing Crow space and marking Crow boundaries. Each time a war party entered battle against a non-Crow enemy, the party's leader would carry a coup-stick with them. In the Crow cultural scheme, the coup-stick was an object which defined Crow subjectivity, especially masculine subjectivity, and was attached to codes of honor and group definition. The "fundamental principle of warrior honor was this: if in battle a warrior stuck his stick in the ground, he must not retreat or leave the stick. A Crow warrior must hold his ground or die losing his coup-stick to the enemy".[22] This was "symbolic of the planting of a tree that could not be felled," thus marking "a boundary across which a non-Crow enemy must not pass. This was a paradigm of courage," and it was what men were trained to become ever since childhood, and how women were socialized to expect men to behave.[23] This type of warfare defined Crow identity and marked them apart from enemy tribes. Anthropologically speaking, it forms a perfectly intelligible, ordered cultural schematic. Yet also from an outsider's perspective, it seems rather a strange way to define a culture, around such a potentially wasteful form of warfare. "After all," Lear notes, "everyone who went into battle was risking his life; and there may well have been occasions when the best military strategy would have been to retreat. Why valorize this form of standing fast? Obviously, planting a coup-stick may

> Most characteristic was the intertwining of war and religion. The Sun Dance, being a prayer for revenge, was naturally saturated with military episodes; but these were almost as prominent in the Tobacco ritual, whose avowed purpose was merely the general welfare. More significant still, every single military undertaking was theoretically inspired by a revelation in dream or vision; and since success in life was so largely a matter of martial glory, war exploits became the chief content of prayer.
>
> Training for war began in childhood. Apart from athletic games, the boys counted coups on game animals, made the girls dance with the hair of a wolf or coyote in lieu of a scalp…On the subject of warfare the older generation, otherwise little inclined to interfere with youth turned didactic. "Old age is a thing of evil, it is well for a young man to die in battle," summed up the burden of their pedagogy.

21. Lear, *Radical Hope*, 159 n. 13, notes that the word "coup" (blow) derives from the French, and is thus a translation of the Crow words for "coup" (*alaxch-iia* and *da*akshe*), and "coup-stick" (*baláxxiihachke* and *kakeé*).
22. Lear, *Radical Hope*, 11.
23. Lear, *Radical Hope*, 11.

have been of psychological value in rallying the other warriors; it may have served to unnerve the enemy. And thus it did have military value. But there remains a symbolic element that needs to be explained. In planting the coup-stick the Crow warrior was not only risking his life; he was also in effect "saying": *Beyond this point, penetration by a non-Crow enemy is impossible*".[24] This statement of impossibility, and the Crow warriors' risking of all their existential possibilities on enforcing Crow boundaries, creates a ritual space that gives the Crow boundaries and the Crow way of life a phenomenological reality—or, to invoke the Foucauldian notion of "bio-power" here, we might say that the Crow are using their bodies as living, moving boundaries which "embody" the cultural codes of Crow life and give it a lived reality. This "existential declaration of impossibility" thus has the effect of "saying": "*There is a fate worse than death*"—namely, that "it is better for me to die (in a glorious battle) than for the Crow tribe to be threatened by the penetration of the boundary at this point".[25]

The recognition of how central this "culturally embedded form of insistence," was in establishing Crow reality as a specific, culturally ordered ontology makes it easier to understand the significance of "a derivative act of boundary-setting that was known as counting coups".[26] Plenty Coups gave the following description of what it meant to count coups:

> To count coup a warrior had to strike an armed and fighting enemy with his coup-stick, quirt, or bow before otherwise harming him, or take his weapons while he was yet alive, or strike the first enemy falling in battle, no matter who killed him, or strike the enemy's breastworks while under fire, or steal a horse tied to a lodge in an enemy's camp, etc. The first named was the most honorable, and to strike such a coup a warrior would often display great bravery.[27]

---

24. Lear, *Radical Hope*, 13–14.
25. Lear, *Radical Hope*, 14.
26. Lear, *Radical Hope*, 14–15.
27. Quoted in Lear, *Radical Hope*, 15. Lear further adds that the phrase "to count coup" was "used ambiguously to name any of these brave acts *and* to name a ritual ceremony, after the battle, in which each of the warriors sitting in a circle *re*counted his coups: he then planted a feather in front of himself, one for each of his coups. He was then allowed to wear those feathers, either in his hair or on a coup-stick or on his shield. If a young warrior counted coup he could immediately pick a wife and marry; otherwise he had to wait until he was twenty-five years old. The wife of a coup-counting warrior could ride proudly ahead of her husband in a procession, carrying his shield; the wife of a non-coup-carrying man had to ride behind her husband. In ceremonial processions, the men who counted coups, along with their wives, rode first" (Lear, *Radical Hope*, 15). Thus, it becomes clear just how constitutive the act of counting coups was to Crow social relations, structuring everything from marriage customs to gender hierarchies, to assignations of high- and low-status among Crow warriors.

Coup-counting valorized bravery in battle, which was necessary if the Crow were to survive amidst the competition for land and resources in the Montana and Wyoming regions. But, Lear notes, coup-counting cannot be explained away merely in terms of the necessity for the survival of the Crow. In fact, it is counter-intuitive when seen as a means of cultivating Crow survival. "If the survival of the Crow tribe as a social unit had been the primary good," and the point of the Crows' military ideology, then "one might expect that highest honor would go to the warrior who *killed* the first enemy in battle, or the warrior who *killed* the most. But to count coups it was crucial that, at least for a moment, one *avoided* killing the enemy. There is a certain symbolic excess in counting coups. One needed not only to destroy the enemy; it was crucial that the enemy recognize that he was about to be destroyed".[28] Thus, just as the planting of a coup-stick is an act in which the Crow warrior embodies the reality of a Crow boundary, thus affirming its ontology, it may be said that counting coups against a Crow enemy forces that enemy to realize, negatively, the reality of Crow space: if "the reality of a boundary is established when people on both sides recognize it as such," then it is essential that the "about-to-die Sioux warrior can see that he is about to die because he has threatened a Crow boundary. He sees that this is the end of his life—his possibilities have run out—and they have run out because he has come up against a reality he cannot alter: *Crow reality*... Crow meaning has become his necessity... And the Crow tribe, when they celebrate their victory later that night, can see that even their most deadly enemy had to acknowledge the reality of the boundary that the Crows themselves assert. Thus an act that looks gratuitous from the point of physical survival is on target when it comes to the maintenance of the boundaries of Crow life".[29] It is culturally intelligible, even if not—from our perspective—entirely practical.

There is an obvious element of risk in maintaining the lived reality of Crow boundaries in this way. Most obviously is the risk to the individual warrior's life, but also to the tribe as a whole, should the war party be overrun after planting a coup-stick. But there is also a subtler, more insidious risk, which could potentially threaten the Crows' ability to maintain the experience of space-time in which their way of life makes sense. The centrality of warfare to the Crow way of life was not entirely an arbitrary choice; although the cultural and ideological elaborations may not have been necessary, the decision to base Crow life around warfare was *entirely* necessary if the tribe was to defend itself against devastation and possible annihilation. As Richard White has argued, the Crow "wars were not

---

28. Lear, *Radical Hope*, 16 (emphasis original).
29. Lear, *Radical Hope*, 17–18 (emphasis original).

interminable contests with traditional enemies, but real struggles in which defeat was often catastrophic." It must be remembered that

> [t]he history of the northern and central American Great Plains in the eighteenth and nineteenth centuries is far more complicated than the tragic retreat of the Indians in the face of an inexorable white advance. From the perspective of most northern and central plains tribes the crucial invasion of the plains during this period was not necessarily that of the whites at all. These tribes had few illusions about American whites and the dangers they presented, but the Sioux remained their most feared enemy.[30]

The Sioux steadily advanced upon Crow lands, gaining control of the hunting grounds between the Yellowstone, Rosebud, and Big Horn Rivers, which the Crows had once dominated. Sioux military expansion was so successful that

> [b]y the 1840s…the once formidable Crows were a much weakened people. As late as the 1830s they had possessed more horses than any other tribe on the upper Missouri and estimates of their armed strength had ranged from 1,000 to 2,500 mounted men, but the years that followed brought them little but disaster. Smallpox and cholera reduced their numbers from 800 to 460 lodges, and rival groups pressed into their remaining hunting grounds.[31]

Plenty Coups grew up during this period, a period "in which, by his own account, things were still happening."[32] But it was also a period in which things were in very real danger of *ceasing* to happen, and not because of historical expiration, but of actual annihilation. The historical context, as outlined by White, makes clear that Plenty Coups and the other Crow warriors "not only knew what they were fighting for," but also "had a vivid sense of what they were fighting against." They risked "*utter devastation* at the hands of the Sioux. This was the prospect of a Crow holocaust: a weakened tribe being fatally overrun by the Sioux," with the very few Crow survivors being taken as slaves.[33] Plenty Coups lived with this possibility, and it was in this context, this dark hour, "that the Crow tribe decided to ally with the white man, in particular the U.S. government, in what became a common battle against the Sioux".[34]

At this point, the Crow seemed to be living in a world of possibilities that they could control or at least predict: either they would survive and flourish, regaining their lost land, or they would fight the Sioux off and maintain what land they controlled, or, finally, they would perish. But the nature of the destruction they predicted is of a very particular kind: even if a Crow

---

30. Quoted in Lear, *Radical Hope*, 21–2.
31. Quoted in Lear, *Radical Hope*, 22–3.
32. Lear, *Radical Hope*, 23.
33. Lear, *Radical Hope*, 23.
34. Lear, *Radical Hope*, 24.

holocaust occurred, and the few surviving Crow were taken into slavery, it is possible to imagine that, "however unrealistic, [they might have harbored] dreams of escape, revenge—of planting [their] coup-stick again!—[and these dreams] would make complete sense to [them]." Even without any chance of this revival actually happening, the possibility would still be culturally intelligible down to the last surviving Crow.[35]

Lear argues that this latent possibility demonstrates "that the type of devastation the Crow actually endured as they willingly moved onto the reservation in the 1880s was of a different order from anything they could thoughtfully plan".[36] It also differed from any kind of domination that American imperial policy could have formulated, because it was derived from within the field of Crow culture. This is because the field of future possibilities that were intelligible within the Crows' cultural order may be summed up as follows: "*Either our warriors will be able to plant their coup-sticks or they will fail.*" From a Crow perspective, "nothing is being left out [of this formulation]: these are all the possibilities there are".[37]

Although Lear emphasizes that his work is merely a "philosophical" anthropology, his analysis fits together well with insights from cultural and social anthropology. The work of Marshall Sahlins on the relation between cultural structures and historical "events" provides an important assist in making Lear's philosophical reflections amenable to theoretical generalization and cross-cultural comparison. The "event" that effectively ended Crow history and culture—and for Sahlins, the two are ultimately inseparable—was the treaty that moved the Crows onto an American reservation and required them to behave in accordance with American law. This rendered their way of life impossible, or at least, illegal. What marks the settlement of the Crows onto the reservation as an "event" is

> a dynamics of the incident that alter[ed] the larger relations figuring there—that is, in the persons of the social-historical actors and their social-historical doings. And what makes the alteration of larger relations is the fact that in this lower-order incident, all kinds of considerations apart from the larger forces these actors instantiate, other forces of which they may be unaware, motivate them. Other beings and objects, with their own projects or causes and their own modes of action, affect them. Thus the famous "contingencies" of the event.[38]

What this means is that the Crows' actions as agents delivered them into a setting in which they could not meaningfully move within their own cultural order. Their history *as Crows* was at an end. This is not, of course, to

---

35. Lear, *Radical Hope*, 24.
36. Lear, *Radical Hope*, 24.
37. Lear, *Radical Hope*, 25.
38. Sahlins, *Culture in Practice: Selected Essays* (New York: Zone Books, 2000), 343.

say that they ceased to exist, or that, from a realist perspective, things did not happen. Yet Plenty Coups' statement, "after this, nothing happened," suggests that something was fundamentally altered about the way in which things could be *perceived as happening within Crow history—historical "events" could not culturally obtain*. This is not the same as saying the Crow were nostalgic for the halcyon days of yesteryear, when things were better and the Sioux were not as powerful. Nor is it to say that the human beings who identified themselves as Crow Indians ceased to exist at that moment. But, in a certain sense, Plenty Coups' words seem to be expressing a feeling that it was no longer possible for him to exist *as Crow*. The culture that gave him his "nature" had passed away.

Such an experience is possible because human subjectivity is structured from the "outside in," through socialization. Human social formations create and exist within structures of meaning in which modes of cultural and social being are rendered possible and intelligible. Through socialization, we inherit traditional "modes of being" and come to "be" selves within historically and culturally specific structures. Thus, "by instantiation," the cultural and social totality within which we live "devolves upon the person, and in the denouement the destiny of the first [i.e., the totality] is submitted to the activity of the second [the agent], the society is [ultimately] decided by biography and—Durkheim and White forgive us—culture by psychology."[39] History becomes culture, and vice versa—and culture-as-history decides "human nature."[40]

With this in mind, we can see that the historical situation which Plenty Coups experienced could truly have led to the experience of a certain history—Crow history—coming to an end. For, the Crow assumption that either the warriors would continue to be able to plant their coup-sticks—and thus, could continue to exist *as Crow*—or they would fail—and thus cease to exist literally, because the Sioux would kill them—did not truly exhaust all the possibilities that could happen on the reservation. Noting, again, Sahlins' insight that every culture is "a gamble played with nature," Lear argues that the "Crow gambled on the continued availability of buffalo and other animals to hunt; they knew that their existence depended on their ability to fight off the Sioux. But there was a different kind of gamble that they didn't understand: *a gamble with necessity*. This is a gamble that the entire field of possibilities will remain stable; that one will continue to be able to judge

---

39. Sahlins, *Culture in Practice*, 343.
40. To support this claim, I have only to refer the reader to Marshall Sahlins' magisterial work, *Apologies to Thucydides: Understanding History as Culture and Vice Versa* (Chicago, IL: University of Chicago Press, 2004). A thorough engagement with Sahlins' thought in that volume and elsewhere would be essential if this paper were to be expanded into a larger project, but obviously cannot be presented here.

success or failure in its terms. This is what came under pressure".[41] Indeed, this is what ceased to exist: the United States government prohibited warfare between the tribes. Coup-sticks could not be planted, and coups could not be counted. Young men could not marry until 25, nor could assignations of status be determined. Traditional means of social advancement became means with no end. The ideal of bravery in battle, still highly valued, paradoxically brought shame to the whole tribe, who counted no coups that would cause them to be honored for such bravery. Eventually, the entire logic of Crow culture and the planting of a coup-stick—requiring that the enemy recognize that his possibilities are at an end before he dies—led to the death of Crow history: on the reservation, under American law and government, *Crow possibilities* were at an end. After this, nothing could happen.[42]

"Render unto Caesar...":
Mythic Revision and the Desire for Intelligibility

As a general rule, when scholars have discussed the "apocalypticism" found in the Gospel of Mark, much attention has been given to questions of the origins of Mark 13, or whether the Markan "apocalyptic" Jesus accurately represents the "historical" Jesus, but little or no attention has been paid to the function and significance of Mark's Gospel as apocalyptic discourse in a given social situation. Though historians and anthropologists of religion have long recognized that colonized peoples frequently adopt "apocalyptic" or "millenarian" discourses to help them resist or negotiate imperial encroachments upon their traditional ways of life, these insights have largely been ignored—or, at best, left un-pursued—by students of Mark's Gospel. In the final section of this essay, I want to apply Lear's concept of "historical vulnerability" and "historical exhaustion" as a way to rethink and redescribe Mark's "apocalypticism" as, precisely, an attempt to reflect upon and negotiate the cultural collapse occasioned by the fallout of the Jewish War with Rome and the destruction of the Jewish Temple during the sacking of Jerusalem.

Although a thoughtful and thorough re-reading of the text, with careful attention to Markan scholarship, would be necessary to argue the thesis fully, here I will only be able to indicate briefly a few of the more important features of the text which support this view. An important clue to Mark's conception of the course of history comes from the parable of the tenants (12.1-11). In Mark's narrative, Jesus tells this parable to the unresponsive priests and elders, warning them that God had sent many prophets, and

---

41. Lear, *Radical Hope*, 26.
42 Lear, *Radical Hope*, 26–52.

that they had all been killed. But now, God, as owner of the vineyard, had sent his "beloved son," and the consequences of killing him would be dire. This parable's place in Mark's narrative makes clear that he believes Jesus "conclude[s] the succession of servant-prophets sent by God to re-establish God's ownership" of the "vineyard" once and for all.[43] Jesus thus represents the fulfillment of Jewish history, the fulfillment, in bodily form, of the Promise made to Abraham.[44]

Another example of this function of Jesus in Mark comes from the scene of Jesus' transfiguration (9.2-8), where Jesus is seen speaking to Moses and Elijah, who symbolize the Law and the Prophets. Yet, a voice from heaven pronounces Jesus as the son of God. "Listen to him!" the voice commands, and the Law and the Prophets disappear. Only Jesus remains. In this way, it is revealed that Jesus fulfills Jewish scripture, and holds the authority to fulfill the history which God had promised.[45]

The manner in which Jesus will fulfill that promise is made clear by the episode in which Jesus encounters the Gerasene demoniac and drives "Legion," the unclean spirit, into the sea (Mk 5.1-13). Although earlier scholarship tended to reject the political implications of this passage, it is now a commonplace to accept that the most plausible meaning of this episode within a narrative composed in the wake of the Jewish War is also the most obvious: when he reaches Jerusalem, Jesus expects to drive the Roman legions into the sea like pigs.[46] However, when Jesus reaches Jerusalem, he finds that "it is not just the invaders who must be swept away, but [also] the comprador class who have made the invaders' continuing control of the land and its people possible."[47] Jesus goes to the temple, the seat of God's power on earth, and finds that the indigenous elite who are in charge of running the temple have become complicit in their own domination. They have become more interested in lining their pockets than in doing the work of God, and they will not accept him.

Much like the cleansing of the Gerasene demoniac drove out Legion, so the "'cleansing' of God's house...performed with such passion by Mark's

---

43. Tat-Tsiong Benny Liew, *Politics of Parousia: Reading Mark Inter(Con)Textually* (Leiden: Brill, 1999), 95.

44. The attempt to link Jesus to the promise made to Abraham was already attempted by Paul in the 50s, as evidenced by his letter to the Galatians.

45. Cf. Liew, *Politics of Parousia*, 102.

46. Stephen D. Moore, *Empire and Apocalypse: Postcolonialism and the New Testament* (Sheffield: Phoenix Press, 2006), 25. Cf. Moore, *Empire and Apocalypse*, 25 n. 2 for a lengthy bibliography of commentators who accept this view.

47. Stephen D. Moore, "Mark and Empire: 'Zealot' and 'Postcolonial' Readings" in Catherine Keller, Michael Nausner, and Mayra Rivera, eds., *Postcolonial Theologies: Divinity and Empire* (St. Louis, MO: Chalice Press, 2004), 134–48, here 138.

Messiah, and seen as so threatening by the Jerusalem elites...is a symbolic prelude to the 'cleansing' of the entire land that properly belongs to the owner of the house (cf. 12:1ff.)."[48] And although Jesus' own death will eventually be engineered by the local elite in retribution for this symbolic "cleansing" (11.18), they will also unwittingly engineer "the *actual* destruction of the temple, according to Mark, and...their own inevitable eradication."[49] But again, we must ask, why is this inevitable?[50]

Most scholars agree that the parable of the withering of the fig tree, which "frames" the cleansing of the temple (11.12-14, 20-22), explains why the temple's fate is linked to Jesus': because Jesus approached it expecting to find fruit, and did not, the tree was destroyed. The same will go for the "unproductive" temple.[51] However, I suggest another way of reading the link between Jesus' death and the temple's destruction. We have already seen that, in the Gospel of Mark, Jesus holds the authority to fulfill God's promise and re-establish Judea as a free land, the kingdom of God. He has the power to drive out the Romans. In fact, when Jesus enters the temple, it appears as though he is planning to establish Judean rule over *all the territory now controlled by Rome*. As he says, "Is it not written, 'My house shall be called a house of prayer *for all the nations*'?" (Mk 11.17). We have twice heard a voice from heaven say that Jesus is God's son (1.11; 9.7), and we know his authority. Yet, when the priests, scribes, and elders approach him in the temple, they question that authority (11.28). Jesus responds by speaking a parable against them (12.1-10), intended to illustrate the precise nature of his authority—to let them know that *he* is the beloved son discussed in the parable—and also to warn them of the consequences they will face if they have him killed (as he knows they are already plotting to do). Again they try to trap him to speak a word against Caesar, but he responds with what could be the gravest warning yet: "Give to Caesar what is Caesar's, and to God what is God's" (12.17). Still, this does not prevent the priests from giving up to Caesar what is God's most prized possession: Jesus himself, the beloved son, and the agent of the promise.

The crucifixion scene (15.36-39) has often been noted to mimic certain details of the baptismal scene (1.9-11).[52] Knowing, as we do, that Mark fre-

---

48. Moore, "Mark and Empire," 138.
49. Moore, "Mark and Empire," 138.
50. Apart from the fact that, for Mark, it already *had* happened, which meant that it *was* inevitable as well as irreparable.
51. For the standard work on this interpretation, see William Telford, *The Barren Temple and the Withered Tree* (Sheffield: JSOT Press, 1980).
52. David Ulansey ("The Heavenly Veil Torn: Mark's Cosmic *Inclusio*," *JBL* 110.1 [1991]: 123-5) has provided an analysis of these two passages and found many

quently "framed" stories together through a fairly sophisticated technique of ring composition, we can bet that this was intentional. This framing of the Markan narrative provides both the context and the message of the Markan text: with Jesus' death at the hands of the Romans, Jewish history—as Mark's Jesus movement understood it—expired. His execution is so closely linked to the destruction of the temple because it was the Roman destruction of the temple which occasioned the writing of Mark's gospel. This was a fatal blow to the Jesuanic ideologies that had so far been developed. No pre-Markan text which has survived bears any features which would suggest that the destruction of the Jerusalem temple would have been a positive occurrence. Paul would have been horrified. The Q scribes would not have known what to think.[53] The author of the *Gospel of Thomas*, though he might have coined a saying about an unproductive fig tree (logion 45), did not attempt to apply it to the temple. The pre-Markan texts that we now call "early Christian" would not have viewed this as a positive event because the authors of those texts were not "Christians," but Jews. The Jesus-centered ideologies and textual productions which were produced before Mark do not seem "Christian" in any contemporary sense of the term. Rather, it seems that they represent various forms of what I have been calling "Jesuanic Judaism." I do not think that the writers of any of these texts, Mark included, had abjured their Jewish identity. Instead, they had been experimenting with alternate ways of constructing and representing that identity in light of changed and changing social situations. If this is an acceptable proposal, then we can see why the Roman conquest of Jerusalem and the destruction of the temple would have been so traumatic to a consciousness steeped in Jesuanic ideology: while

---

parallelisms between them. In both stories there is a *voice* which proclaims Jesus to be the son of God; something is said to *descend* (the spirit-dove, the tear in the temple veil); *Elijah* is referenced (either as John the Baptist or as the figure who Jesus is mistakenly thought to be calling); and the *spirit* (*pneuma*) which Jesus receives at baptism is recalled as he "expires" (*ekpnew*, a cognate of *pneuma*). See Ulansey's brief article for the full discussion.

53. Although there is some evidence of an anti-Temple attitude to be found among the earliest bits of Q tradition, Kloppenborg has noted that "[a]t the final stage of [Q's] redaction there is evidence of a significant shift in the character of Q's rhetoric, and a striking elevation of the institutions of Torah and Temple in Q's symbolic universe" ("Literary History, Self-Evidence, and the Social History of the Q People" *Semeia* 55 [1991]: 101). This likely means that "during the course of the struggle with the southern scribes or Pharisees, the Q group either absorbed enough of its opponents' ethos to make the Torah and Temple an integral part of their system's architecture, or that in spite of Q's repeated statements about Israel's non-response, the group succeeded in attracting scholars...for whom the institutions of Temple and Torah had essential and positive meaning" (*Semeia* [1991]: 100). Thus, in either case, Q's ideology does not suggest that the destruction of the Temple would have been a positive thing to revel in.

Paul and possibly the author of Revelation[54] had entertained scenarios in which the Jewish god destroyed the Romans, no one had considered what would happen if Rome destroyed Jerusalem after performing an *evocatio deorum* ritual.[55] To social actors operating within the ideational context of Jesuanic Judaism, such an occurrence was quite literally unbelievable.

Until it *happened*.

Mark was composed in an effort to figure out how and why this occurred. The "epic revision" that was necessitated by this fatal blow to Jesuanic ideology as it had so far been developed resulted in an "apocalyptic" resolution which was essential to keep the self-understanding of this doubly-deracinated group of Judean refugees alive. The Romans had "bound the strong man" who promised to deliver the Jews from under their rule and had plundered his Father's house (Mk 3.27).[56] Jesus, who in Mark's narrative represents Jewish history, dies by Roman hands. The outer veil of the temple—which we know displayed a giant panorama of the heavens[57]—was rent asunder, indicating that Jewish space-time had been disrupted, even demolished. As with the Crow Indians who were moved to the reservation, Mark now perceived that there was no meaningful way to continue being "Jewish" in the same way as before. His gospel was composed as a reflection on this situation—and, in fact, his gospel is a reflection *of* this situation. There was obviously no chance of a military resolution of this invasion of space and destruction of time: Roman military might had crushed the Jewish rebellion, and destroyed their temple with the same callous indifference with which the centurion "recognized" Jesus' divine descent: "Yeah, right, this guy was the son of God" (Mk 15.39).[58] And, worst of all, in light of Kloppenborg's discussion of the implications of the *evocatio* with regard to the destruction of the temple, there would also be the horrible fear that—because the agent of

---

54. Assuming Revelation was penned during or in the wake of the Jewish War, as some scholars, such as John W. Marshall, have suggested.

55. John S. Kloppenborg, "*Evocatio deorum* and the Date of Mark," *JBL* 124.3 (2005): 419–50.

56. I am deliberately avoiding the claim that this is actually what Mark *intended* this saying to mean. However, in light of the reading I am proposing here, it seems appropriate to consider it as a possibility.

57. Josephus, *J.W.* 5.5.4: 212–4, says that the veil was some 80 feet high, and was a thick "Babylonian tapestry, with embroidery of blue and fine linen, of scarlet also and purple, wrought with marvellous skill. Nor was this mixture of materials without its mystic meaning: it typified the universe… Portrayed on this tapestry was a panorama of the entire heavens" (as quoted in Ulansey, "The Heavenly Veil Torn," 124–5).

58. Again, I propose this rendering only provisionally. The question of whether the centurion's utterance is mocking or reverent (or neither) is an open one. Both interpretations have been proposed.

the promise had been handed over to the Romans—perhaps *God had abandoned them in favor of the Romans*! In this fearful context, Mark composed his gospel in an attempt to bring some "good news" to a group of people who were experiencing a loss of identity from a position of exile.

In light of this, Burton Mack's assertion that "Mark tackled the problem of the right of the Jesus movement to exist independently of the synagogue" when he composed his gospel seems to miss the mark—no pun intended.[59] A more appropriate formulation might be that "Mark tackled the problem of how the Jesus movement could continue to exist *as a Jesus movement* in light of the social and political upheavals which had invalidated much of the symbolic order through with the group had so far defined itself." William Arnal's argument that Mark is attempting to turn Galilee into Jewish/ Judean space closely accords with this formulation, as it recognizes that the fundamental oppositions Mark seems concerned with overcoming are not between the synagogue and the Jesus movement, but, provisionally speaking, between Judea proper and Jewish space in general.[60] From this perspective, Mark is tackling the problem of finding the intellectual means to allow a sense of Jewish space to exist independently of Judea. Or, as Lear might put it: Mark is searching for the means to allow "being-Jewish" to regain its cultural intelligibility. Mark's Jesus exhorts "those who have ears" to endure until the end, when God, as the owner of the vineyard, would return and re-establish the field of intelligibility that has been lost.

With this in mind, it must be said that, if Mack is correct in saying "[t]he apocalyptic frame cannot be removed from Mark's Gospel without destroying its logic," it is *not* "because Mark gave up on the possibility of imagining a society fit for the real world."[61] If we have learned anything from our excursion to the Crow Indian reservations, and from the discussion and clarification of the concepts "historical exhaustion" and "cultural devastation" that I have tried to develop, then we must reformulate why the final, apocalyptic resolution that Mark's Jesus promises is necessary. If anything, we would have to say that "the world itself gave up on the possibility of imagining that Mark's social formation could continue to exist."

Mark's decision to write a Jesus-narrative was certainly an innovation in early "Christian" textual production. Yet this complicated piece of *bricolage* was necessary precisely because the conditions that had previously sustained

---

59. Burton L. Mack, *A Myth of Innocence: Mark and Christian Origins* (Philadelphia, PA: Fortress Press, 1988), 318.

60. William E. Arnal, "The Gospel of Mark as Reflection on Exile and Identity," in Willi Braun and Russell T. McCutcheon, eds., *Introducing Religion: Essays in Honor of Jonathan Z. Smith* (London: Equinox Press, 2008), 57–67.

61. Mack, *Myth of Innocence*, 349.

the Judean Jesus movements were now gone: "epic revision" or "mythmaking" was needed if the Jesus movement was to continue to exist in a way that maintained continuity—even the *illusion* of continuity—with its earlier way of life. With the fallout of the War, still reeling from the turbulence which had displaced so many people and disrupted, and even ended, the lives of so many others, traditional modes of life—and previous ways of believing and behaving in the Jesus movement—would have to change.

Until *that*, nothing could happen.

Author biography

John W. Parrish held an MA and a PhD from the University of Alberta. His research focused on Christian origins and contemporary theories and methods in the Study of Religion.

Bibliography

Arnal, William E. (2008) "The Gospel of Mark as Reflection on Exile and Identity," 57–67 in Willi Braun and Russell T. McCutcheon, eds., *Introducing Religion: Essays in Honor of Jonathan Z. Smith*. London: Equinox Press.

Braun, Willi. (2000) "Religion," 3–18 in Willi Braun and Russell T. McCutcheon, eds., *Guide to the Study of Religion*. London: Cassell.

Kloppenborg, John S. "Literary Convention, Self-Evidence, and the Social History of the Q People." *Semeia* 55 (1991): 77–102. https://doi.org/10.1016/S0031-9406(10)63600-0

—"*Evocatio deorum* and the Date of Mark," *JBL* 124.3 (2005): 419–50. https://doi.org/10.2307/30041033

Lear, Jonathan. (2006). *Radical Hope: Ethics in the Face of Cultural Devastation*. Cambridge, MA: Harvard University Press. https://doi.org/10.4159/9780674040021

Liew, Tat-siong Benny. (1999): *Politics of Parousia: Reading Mark Inter(con)textually*. Leiden: Brill. https://doi.org/10.1163/9789004493773

Mack, Burton L. (1988) *A Myth of Innocence: Mark and Christian Origins*. Philadelphia, PA: Fortress Press.

Moore, Stephen D. (2004) "Mark and Empire: 'Zealot' and "Postcolonial' Readings" in Catherine Keller, Michael Nausner, and Mayra Rivera, eds., *Postcolonial Theologies: Divinity and Empire* (St. Louis, MO: Chalice Press, 2004), 134–48.

—(2006) *Empire and Apocalypse: Postcolonialism and the New Testament*. Sheffield: Phoenix Press.

Sahlins, Marshall. (2000) *Culture in Practice: Selected Essays*. New York: Zone Books.

—(2004) *Apologies to Thucydides: Understanding History as Culture and Vice Versa*. Chicago, IL: University of Chicago Press.

Telford, William R. (1980) *The Barren Temple and the Withered Tree*. Sheffield: JSOT Press.

Ulansey, David. The Heavenly Veil Torn: Mark's Cosmic Inclusio. *JBL* 110.1 (1991): 123–5. https://doi.org/10.2307/3267155

Chapter Fourteen

Farm to (School)table: The Cultivation of *Paideia* in the *Gospel of Thomas*[1]

Ian Phillip Brown

In an excellent 1999 article, Willi Braun examined the Sayings Gospel Q alongside Graeco-Roman schools in order to posit a plausible social location for the text.[2] Braun was concerned with sharpening the categories of mythmaking and social formation and sought to provide a tangible and plausible location for the emergence of Q. In Braun's own words, the goal was to examine "the Graeco-Roman 'schools' as arenas of socio-mythic formation to see if we find there some help with the question of how Q was actively present at its own making and, presumably, how the focus on 'school' might help us to qualify the categories of mythmaking and social formation themselves."[3] Braun focused on a number of qualities in the text of Q that reflected textual practices and tendencies identifiable in Graeco-Roman schools: a focus on the composition of the text, the genre of the text, school technologies, erudition power and authorization within the text, and the social location of scribes (the presumed composers of the text).[4] Finally, he presented three possible analogies that also appeared "schoolish": Greek magical papyri as studied by Jonathan Z. Smith,[5] Epicurean

---

1. Versions of this paper were presented at the Italian Centre for Advanced Studies on Religions annual conference in Bertinoro, Italy, September 28, 2017, and the Canadian Society of Biblical Studies Annual Meeting, Regina, SK, May 26, 2018. I want to thank Pat Hart and Sarah Rollens for editing this Festschrift and inviting me to contribute, and Michelle Christian and William Arnal for their comments and suggestions on various stages of this project. This chapter is part of a larger research project on ancient agriculture and early Christianity funded by a SSHRC Postdoctoral Fellowship. I would like to thank SSHRC and my host Department of Gender, Religion, and Critical Studies at the University of Regina.
2. Willi Braun, "Socio-Mythic Invention, Graeco-Roman Schools, and the Sayings Gospel Q," *MTSR* 11 (1999): 210–35.
3. Braun, "Socio-Mythic Invention," 211.
4. Braun, "Socio-Mythic Invention," 215–21.
5. Jonathan Z. Smith, "The Temple and the Magician," in *Map Is Not Territory: Studies in the History of Religions* (Chicago, IL: University of Chicago Press, 1993), 172–89.

fraternities as studied by Bernard Frischer,[6] and the composition of the Mishnah as studied by Jack Lightstone.[7] Braun's argument that Graeco-Roman schools provide a social location with which to compare the emergence of Q is not only plausible but, I think, entirely convincing. Significantly, Braun invokes Graeco-Roman schools not to refer to an intellectual realm of ideas but, rather, to demonstrate how the comparison "brings into analytical focus the role of the intellectual in social formation."[8]

Comparing the *Gospel of Thomas* (*Gos. Thom.*) and what we know of Graeco-Roman schools is as productive as Braun's comparison of Q with the schools. That *Gos. Thom.* is an intellectual product is, at this point, an emerging if not established consensus. Evidence that *Gos. Thom.* is an intellectual product ranges from the text's emphasis on effort and interpretation,[9] familiarity with Platonic philosophy,[10] similarity with Philonic philosophy and

---

6. Bernard. Frischer, *The Sculpted Word: Epicureanism and Philosophical Recruitment in Ancient Greece* (Berkeley, CA: University of California Press, 1982).

7. Jack N. Lightstone, "Whence the Rabbis? From Coherent Description to Fragmented Reconstructions," *SR/SR* 26 (1997): 275–95; Braun, "Socio-Mythic Invention," 225–31.

8. Braun, "Socio-Mythic Invention," 212.

9. William E. Arnal, "The Rhetoric of Social Construction: Language and Society in the Gospel of Thomas," in *Rhetoric and Reality in Early Christianities*, ed. Willi Braun, Studies in Christianity and Judaism / Études Sur Le Christianisme et Le Judaïsme 16 (Waterloo, Ont: Wilfrid Laurier University Press, 2005), 27–48; William E. Arnal, "Blessed Are the Solitary: Textual Practices and the Mirage of a Thomas 'Community,'" in *"The One Who Sows Bountifully": Essays in Honor of Stanley K. Stowers*, ed. Caroline Johnson Hodge et al. (Providence, R.I.: Brown Judaic Studies, 2013), 271–81; William E. Arnal, "How the Gospel of Thomas Works," in *Scribal Practices and Social Structures among Jesus Adherents: Essays in Honour of John S. Kloppenborg*, ed. William E. Arnal et al. (Leuven; Paris; Bristol, CT: Peeters, 2016), 261–80; Ron Cameron, "Parable and Interpretation in the Gospel of Thomas," *Forum* 2 (1986): 3–39; Ron Cameron, "Ancient Myths and Modern Theories of the Gospel of Thomas and Christian Origins," *MTSR* 11 (1999): 236–57; Ron Cameron, "An Occasion for Thought," in *Introducing Religion: Essays in Honor of Jonathan Z. Smith*, ed. Willi Braun and Russell T. McCutcheon (Equinox, 2008), 100–12.

10. Elaine H. Pagels, "Exegesis of Genesis 1 in the Gospels of Thomas and John," *JBL* 118 (1999): 477–96; Stephen J. Patterson, "Jesus Meets Plato: The Theology of the Gospel of Thomas and Middle Platonism," in *Thomasevangelium: Entstehung, Rezeption, Theologie*, ed. Jörg Frey, Enno Edzard Popkes, and Jens Schröter, BZNW (New York: Walter de Gruyter, 2008), 181–205.

exegesis,[11] and general connections to moral philosophy.[12] I am in agreement that *Gos. Thom.* is an intellectual product, but "intellectual" as it has been applied to the text remains a vast and under-theorized category. So, while the majority of scholars writing on the social location of *Gos. Thom.* agree that the text is an intellectual product, few narrow down the intellectual world to a describable and plausible social location in the way that Braun has done with Q.[13] In my contribution to this Festschrift in honor of Willi's work, I will compare *Gos. Thom.* to Graeco-Roman schools on the basis of their shared use of agricultural metaphors for and about education (*paideia*). In doing so, my comparison is more genealogical than analogical, and I hope that by the end the reader will agree that there is indeed a genealogical relationship between *Gos. Thom.* and Graeco-Roman schools. Specifically, sayings about the agricultural practice of sowing seeds in *Gos. Thom.* show how the text makes extensive use of metaphors for education and virtue that were routine in Graeco-Roman schooling.

Agriculture in Ancient Writing

The ancient world was an agrarian world, survival depended on the harvest of cereal crops, and the harvest itself mobilized hundreds of thousands of itinerant workers every year.[14] But the sowing of seeds and reaping of crops were not merely material realities; they were also a significant trope in philosophical and educational thinking. As early as Plato, sowing seeds and reaping crops are used metaphorically to refer to human actions, primarily biological reproduction.[15] On the other end of the literary spectrum, fables frequently

---

11. Ian Phillip Brown, "Where Indeed Was the Gospel of Thomas Written? Thomas in Alexandria," *JBL* 138 (2019): 451–72; Anna Cwikla, "Become Male or Leave: Understanding the Gendered Language in the Gospel of Thomas Logion 114," unpublished paper presented to the Colloquium for Religions of Mediterranean Antiquity, University of Toronto, February 25, 2016, referenced with the permission of the author.

12. Karen King, "Kingdom in the Gospel of Thomas," *Forum, Foundations and Facets* 3 (1987): 48–97; Risto Uro, ed., *Thomas at the Crossroads: Essays on the Gospel of Thomas*, Studies of the New Testament and Its World (Edinburgh: T & T Clark, 1998), 54–79.

13. The notable exception is William Arnal who has argued that *Gos. Thom.* functions as a school text without a teacher, a text to be understood and interpreted by oneself. In classic fashion, he has hidden these arguments away in Festschriften, and my reference to them in another Festschrift is probably not helping matters. (Arnal, "Blessed Are the Solitary"; Arnal, "How the Gospel of Thomas Works.")

14. For discussion of agricultural life and work in the Roman world specifically, see Brent D. Shaw, *Bringing in the Sheaves: Economy and Metaphor in the Roman World*, Robson Classical Lectures (Toronto: University of Toronto Press, 2013), 11–24.

15. See for example, *Timaeus* 42d and 91d.

illustrate their morals through the figure of the wise farmer who possessed specialized knowledge of the land, the seasons, and sowing/reaping.[16] In the Hebrew Bible, the practices of sowing and reaping are used to discuss God's covenant with his people (Gen. 8.22) and to address apocalyptic judgment (2 Esdras 8.41-42, 4.23-32, 6.18-28, 8.6, 9.31-37; Isaiah 55.10-11; *Jubilees* 36.6; *1 Enoch* 10.19; *2 Baruch* 29.5; *Sibylline Oracles* 3.263-64).[17] In the first centuries of the Common Era, agricultural metaphors are used frequently in philosophical texts to discuss the nature of wisdom: Ben Sira uses the metaphor of ploughing and sowing to describe how one comes to wisdom (Sirach 6.19-21),[18] Philo talks about the importance of sowing instruction in virtue into students (Philo, *De agricultura*, 2.9-10), Epictetus compares teaching philosophy to growing a fig tree from seed with an emphasis on patience and the time commitment required to be a philosopher (Epictetus, *Diatribai* 1.15), and Musonius Rufus identifies the life of the farmer as the ideal life for the philosopher (Musonius Rufus, frag. 11). Agriculture is also discussed at length in agronomic texts that prescribe the proper management of estates (Cato, *De agricultura*; Varro, *De re rustica*). More than simple how-to manuals, agronomic writing of the early Roman period comment on morality, virtue, and the efficient management of one's household and property.[19] In a recent monograph, Leah Kronenberg has argued that the agronomic writings of Xenophon, Varro, and Virgil are all in one way or another commentaries on Greek and Roman conceptions of morality: discussions of farming became discussion about what it meant to be "cultured."[20]

All this is to say that writing about farming was extremely common in a wide variety of literary genres in antiquity. It should come as no surprise,

---

16. Farmers are frequent protagonists in Aesop's fables and stories of farmers appear in the fable collections of Babrius, Avianus, and Phaedrus.

17. See discussion in Cameron, "Parable and Interpretation in the Gospel of Thomas," 21.

18. See discussion in Frank Ueberschaer, "Jewish Education in Ben Sira," in *Second Temple Jewish "Paideia" in Context*, ed. Gabriele Boccaccinni and Jason M. Zurawski (Berlin; Boston: De Gruyter, 2017), 29–46.

19. Leah Kronenberg, *Allegories of Farming from Greece and Rome: Philosophical Satire in Xenophon, Varro and Virgil* (Cambridge; New York: Cambridge University Press, 2009); Aude Doody, "The Authority of Writing in Varro's *De Re Rustica*," in *Authority and Expertise in Ancient Scientific Culture*, ed. Jason König and Greg Woolf (Cambridge: Cambridge University Press, 2017), 182–202. Philip Thibodeau, *Playing the Farmer: Representations of Rural Life in Vergil's Georgics* (Berkeley, CA: University of California Press, 2011); Philip Thibodeau, "Ancient Agronomy as a Literature of Best Practices," in *Oxford Handbook of Science and Medicine in the Classical World*, ed. Paul T. Keyser and John Scarborough (New York: Oxford University Press, 2018), 463–80.

20. Kronenberg, *Allegories of Farming from Greece and Rome*, 94.

then, that early Christian writing generally, and *Gos. Thom.* specifically, are filled with stories of farmers and farming. Yet the presence of these stories does not indicate a rural setting (as some have argued) any more than they would suggest that Plato, Philo, or Epictetus were themselves a part of, or writing for, a rustic audience.[21] Rather, they indicate that early Christian writers were very much a part of the Greek, Roman, and Judean cultural traditions from which they emerged. But this is not all that a focus on agricultural writing in early Christianity can suggest. In addition to being a favoured metaphor for philosophers, agriculture, and sowing seeds in particular, were frequently used to discuss the instilling of *encyclia paideia* (education) in students. It is with this in mind that I turn to discussions of sowing seeds in educational writing and in *Gos. Thom.*

A Sower Sowing Seeds

> Just as in farming, first of all the soil must be good, secondly, the husbandman skilful, and thirdly, the seed sound, so, after the same manner, nature is like to the soil, the teacher to the farmer, and the verbal counsels and precepts like to the seed (Ps. Plutarch, *De liberis educandis* 4.11-15 [Babbitt, LCL]).

Without looking at the citation, one would be forgiven for thinking this passage from Ps. Plutarch came from the pen of someone trying to explain Jesus' Parable of the Sower (Mark 4.1-9, *Gos. Thom.* 9). And while the sower is, at present, best known from Jesus' parable, the figure of a farmer sowing seeds appears frequently in educational literature from the Hellenistic and Roman periods. Farming was a very popular metaphor for the educational process in antiquity. In addition to Ps. Plutarch *De liberis educandis* 4, Hippocrates *Lex* 3, Antiphon frag. 60, Seneca *Epistulae morales* 38.2, and Quintilian *Institutio oratoria* 5.11.24 all use the image of a sower sowing seeds to explain the nature of *paideia*:[22]

---

21. This may be setting up an artificial distinction between "urban" and "rural" cultures, but space does not permit the exploration of that question here. My point here is that because stories of farming and farmers appear in a variety of genres, we should not assume that the content of these stories has a simple relationship with the presumed composers or audiences. For recent discussions of the ways in which urban and rural spaces were intimately intertwined, see Ralph Mark Rosen and Ineke Sluiter, eds., *City, Countryside, and the Spatial Organization of Value in Classical Antiquity*, Mnemosyne, Bibliotheca Classica Batava 279 (Leiden; Boston: Brill, 2006) and David B. Hollander, *Farmers and Agriculture in the Roman Economy*, electronic resource (Abingdon, Oxon; New York: Routledge, 2019).

22. Both Ron Cameron and Burton Mack list these various sowers in their examinations of the Parable of the Sower in *Gos. Thom.* and the Gospel of Mark respectively. In spite of the clear parallels, however, I have not found any reference to their observations

Instruction in medicine is like the culture of the productions of the earth. For our natural disposition, is, as it were, the soil; the tenets of our teacher are, as it were, the seed; instruction in youth is like the planting of the seed in the ground at the proper season; the place where the instruction is communicated is like the food imparted to vegetables by the atmosphere; diligent study is like the cultivation of the fields; and it is time which imparts strength to all things and brings them to maturity (Hippocrates, *Lex* 3 [Jones, LCL]).

The most important thing in the world, I think, is education [παίδευσις]. For whenever you begin any matter whatsoever in the right way, the end too is likely to turn out right: whatever sort of seed you plant in the earth, this is the sort of crop you should expect. And whenever you plant in a young body an education [παίδευσιν] that is good, the end-product lives and blossoms through the whole of life, and neither rain nor drought can destroy it (Antiphon frag. 60).[23]

Words should be scattered like seed; no matter how small the seed may be, if it has once found favourable ground, it unfolds its strength and from an insignificant thing spreads to its greatest growth. Reason grows in the same way; it is not large to the outward view, but increases as it does its work. Few words are spoken; but if the mind has truly caught them, they come into their strength and spring up. Yes, precepts and seeds have the same quality; they produce much, and yet they are slight things. Only, as I said, let a favourable mind receive and assimilate them. Then of itself the mind also will produce bounteously in its turn, giving back more than it has received. Farewell (Seneca, *Epistulae morales* 38.2 [Gummere, LCL]).

For example, if you are talking about the cultivation of the mind, you can use the image of the earth, which produces thorns and thickets if it is neglected, and fruits if it is cultivated (Quintilian, *Institutio oratoria* 5.11.24 [Butler, LCL]).

While the wording changes slightly, there are several important points of similarity among these textual references to sowing. Hippocrates', the earliest version of the metaphor, is explicit that the cultivation of the study of medicine can be compared to the culture and production of the earth. As is the case with all versions of this metaphor, the soil is the mind and disposition of the student. Cultivation (diligent study) and time are required to ensure that the soil produces healthy plants. The seed is the instruction students receive in their youth, and while there is no explicitly mentioned

---

in subsequent studies. Burton L. Mack, *A Myth of Innocence: Mark and Christian Origins* (Minneapolis, MN: Fortress Press, 1988), 159–60; Cameron, "Parable and Interpretation in the Gospel of Thomas," 21–23.

23. Gerard J. Pendrick, *Antiphon the Sophist: The Fragments*, Cambridge Classical Texts and Commentaries 39 (New York: Cambridge University Press, 2002), 205.

sower, the teacher as sower is not only implied but assumed in Hippocrates' saying.[24]

Antiphon also situates the metaphor explicitly in a discussion of *paideia*. Antiphon stresses that, like all things, one's life must begin "the right way" with education. Like Hippocrates, the seed is education, and the earth is the student ("a young body"). Antiphon does not mention the role of the teacher, but again it can be safely assumed. Quintilian uses a single aspect of the metaphor: the mind is like the earth, it must be cultivated to produce fruit, and the uncultivated mind produces thorns and thickets. Ps. Plutarch's version is very similar to Hippocrates' in that the soil is the nature of the student and must be properly prepared, and the seed the teaching. Ps. Plutarch, however, introduces some new elements to the metaphor. First, this version explicitly identifies the teacher as the husbandman, adding that the husbandman must be "skillful" (ἐπιστήμονα). Second, while all versions comment on the requirement of the soil/student to be properly prepared, Ps. Plutarch is the only one to require a skillful teacher and also qualifies that the seed/teaching needs to be sound.

Seneca's letter is a particularly interesting deployment of metaphor, and the more casual setting in which we find the metaphor in Seneca suggests that its association with the processes of education was well enough known that it would be recognized without specific reference. Seneca paraphrases the metaphor to support his contention that conversation is preferable to written exchange for inculcating *paideia*: words "enter more easily, and stick in the memory; for we do not need many words, but, rather, effective words" (Seneca, *Epistulae morales* 38.1 [Gummere, LCL]). In support of the power of a few effective words, Seneca compares words to seeds that should be scattered to find favourable ground. In other words, size is not important for seeds or words. The important thing is that both have the possibility to produce much.

In similar fashion to Seneca's letter, Philo of Alexandria also appears to paraphrase the metaphor. Notably, Philo's treatise on education is called *On Agriculture* (*De agricultura*), and here Philo uses Noah's role as a farmer to speak to the proper education and rearing of children into adults. *De agricultura* is of particular interest as Philo describes the acquisition of education as a process of sowing and planting:

> But seeing that for babes milk is food, but for grown men wheaten bread, there must also be soul-nourishment, such as is milk-like suited to the

---

24. Hippocrates is distinct in containing an additional element: the place of instruction is compared to food fed to the plant to help it grow. The emphasis on the place of schooling is absent in other versions of this saying.

time of our childhood, in the shape of preliminary stages of school-learning (προπαιδεύματα) and such as is adapted to grown men in the shape of instructions leading the way through wisdom and temperance and all virtue. For these when sown (σπαρέντα) and planted in the mind will produce most beneficial fruits, namely fair and praiseworthy conduct (Philo, *De agricultura* 2.9-10, [Colson and Whitaker, LCL]).

From Hippocrates to Philo to Quintilian, Greek, Judean, and Roman intellectuals alike all used the agricultural practice of sowing seeds to illustrate the process and results of teaching *paideia*. It is in light of the tendency among ancient intellectuals to have agricultural production stand in for the process by which students receive education that *Gos. Thom.*'s agricultural sayings should be read.

The Cultivation of Paideia *in the* Gospel of Thomas

The *Gospel of Thomas* contains eleven sayings that make reference to agricultural activities and pursuits: *Gos. Thom.* 9 (parable of the sower), 20 (parable of the mustard seed), 21 (the kingdom is like children in a field/the arrival of the harvester), 40 (the grapevine planted apart from the father), 45 (grapes not harvested from thorns), 57 (parable of the good seed), 63 (parable of the rich farmer), 65 (parable of the vineyard), 73 (the crop is large but the workers are few), 107 (the parable of the shepherd), and 109 (the kingdom is like the treasure hidden in a field). While *Gos. Thom.*'s agricultural parables lack some of the secondary allegorization found in the synoptic versions (*Gos. Thom.* 20 does not claim that the mustard seed becomes a tree, and *Gos. Thom.* 65 has no allusion of Isaiah 5.1-7) and for that reason have been considered more realistic in their representation of agricultural activity,[25] the majority of these sayings betray little to no knowledge of actual farming techniques. Reasonable farmers would not sow seeds on a road; a farmer would know that one does not harvest grapes from thorns or figs from thistles; and a wise farmer would not abandon ninety-nine sheep in search of a single sheep, no matter how large. *Gos. Thom.*'s frequent references to agriculture, then, are not evidence of a rural background for its sayings. Rather, the agricultural sayings of *Gos. Thom.* show an awareness of how agriculture was a central metaphor within educational circles in antiquity.

---

25. For example, on the relative realism of *Gos. Thom.* 65, see John S. Kloppenborg, *Tenants in the Vineyard: Ideology, Economics, & Agrarian Conflict in Jewish Palestine* (Tübingen: Mohr Siebeck, 2006), 109–22, 326–30.

Gos. Thom. *9: Parable of the Sower*

> Jesus said, "Behold, the sower went out, filled his hands [with seed] and scattered [them]. Some fell upon the road and birds came and gathered them. And others fell upon rock and they did not put forth roots into the earth and they did not produce any heads of grain. And others fell upon thorns and they choked the seeds and worms ate them. And others fell upon good earth and it gave good fruit and it came up 60 per measure and 120 per measure."[26]

In a 1986 article Ron Cameron argues that *Gos. Thom.* 9 is best understood as a saying where,

> the employment of the stock metaphor of seed, soil, growth, and harvest; and the composition of these metaphors into illustrative similes identify their language and imagery as conventional, part of the established tradition of paideia. The Sower is to be located rhetorically within the same pedagogical context.[27]

In a footnote, Cameron thanks Burton Mack for bringing these parallels to his attention, and although Mack's *A Myth of Innocence* was not published until 1988,[28] Cameron credits Mack with having first raised this comparison. Cameron's and Mack's conclusions strike me as both correct and non-controversial. A parable that serves as a metaphor for teaching and learning fits perfectly within the context of the *Gospel of Thomas* (and Mark for Mack).[29]

However, more can be said on the Parable of the Sower in *Gos. Thom.*'s specific representation and context. The Parable of the Sower in the *Gos. Thom.* is similar but not identical to the parable in the Gospel of Mark, and both share features with sowing sayings (previously referenced) in ancient

---

26. All translations of *Gos. Thom.* are my own unless otherwise noted.
27. Cameron, "Parable and Interpretation in the Gospel of Thomas," 23.
28. Mack, *A Myth of Innocence*.
29. For whatever reason, and at least as far as I am aware, Cameron's and Mack's observations are rarely, if ever, taken up. With respect to Thomas 9, for example, April DeConick's 2006 commentary is the only work on Thomas that I have found that explicitly mentions Cameron's relation of *Gos. Thom.* 9 to *paideia*. And here she raises it only to dismiss it in her construction of an apocalyptic core of Thomas. Mark Goodacre cites the article as one example of an argument that does not interpret Thomas as apocalyptic; Mark Goodacre, *Thomas and the Gospels: The Case for Thomas's Familiarity with the Synoptics* (Cambridge: William B. Eerdmans Publishing Company, 2012). And while included in the bibliography of Simon Gathercole's 724-page commentary on Thomas, Cameron's article is not mentioned anywhere therein. Bernard Brandon Scott includes Seneca's formulation of the metaphor as an example of the ways in which Hellenistic wisdom elaborate on proverbs in the interest of *paideia*, but he does no pursue the parallel further, see Bernard Brandon Scott, *Hear Then the Parable: A Commentary on the Parables of Jesus* (Minneapolis, MN: Fortress Press, 1989), 358–9.

discussions of *paideia*. In spite of the parallels to ancient educational writing, modern readers have largely failed to notice the connection. Placing each saying of the sower side by side, however, will allow us to see the major points of similarity as well as difference.

	Hippocrates	Antiphon	Ps. Plutarch
Sower			Teacher, must be skilled
Seed	Tenets of teacher	Education that is good	Verbal counsel and precepts, must be sound
Soil	Natural disposition		Nature, must be good
Outcome	Strength and maturity	Living and blossoming through life	

	Seneca	Quintilian	Gos. Mark	Gos. Thom.
Sower			Jesus/teacher?	teacher?
Seed	words/precepts		The word	No comment
Soil	The mind, must be favourable	The mind	Receivers of the word, must be good	Must be good
Outcome	Producing bountifully and giving back more than received	Produces thorns and thickets if neglected, fruit if cultivated	Fails unless the seed falls in good soil, they accept it and bear fruit	Fails unless the seed falls in good soil, yields a good crop

Comparing the parable in *Gos. Thom.* with other similar sayings, there is one notable difference. The metaphors of the sower, seed, and soil are explained in the educational literature, and even in the Gospel of Mark has Jesus explain the parable to his students. *Gos. Thom.* is distinct in leaving the parable unexplained. This should not come as a surprise since *Gos. Thom.*'s overall hermeneutic is one that requires the reader to properly interpret the sayings.[30] In this case it is up to the reader to recognize that this parable is about teaching.

Gos. Thom. 9 names a sower, implies a handful of seeds, and lists several places where the seeds fell. Much like other authors, *Gos. Thom.* 9 makes no reference to the qualities of the sower (Ps. Plutarch is distinct in noting that the teacher should be "skillful"). *Gos. Thom.* 9 does not mention seeds explicitly, but it is clearly implied as the sower "took a handful" and "scattered" them, and the things scattered did or did not produce a crop based on where they landed. The emphasis in *Gos. Thom.* is on the places where

30. Cameron, "Ancient Myths and Modern Theories."

the seeds land. In the first three locations the seeds fail to take root due to birds, rocks, and thorns and worms. It is only when they land on "good earth" (ⲡⲕⲁϩ ⲉⲧⲛⲁⲛⲟⲩϥ) that the seeds take root and produce "good fruit." If we follow the educational writers, especially Seneca and Quintilian, then the good earth refers to the favourable minds of the student. This too makes sense in *Gos. Thom.*'s larger project of ensuring that the reader understands and is prepared for the secrets that Jesus will reveal to them. As the first of four seed-sayings that operate on the model of seed-teaching soil-student, *Gos. Thom.* 9 helps to clarify three other seed-sayings in *Gos. Thom.* 20, 40, and 57.

Gos. Thom. 20: *The Parable of the Mustard Seed*

As with the Parable of the Sower, the Parable of the Mustard seed is present in the synoptic tradition as well. Here, in three seemingly distinct versions, are *Gos. Thom.* 20, Mark 4.30-32, and Q 13.18-19.

Gos. Thom. 20	Mark 4.30-32	Q 13.18-19 (IQP)
The students said to Jesus, "Tell us what the kingdom of heaven is like." He said to them, "It is like a grain of mustard which is the smallest of all seeds. *When it falls on earth that was worked/prepared* [ϩⲟⲧⲁⲛ ⲇⲉ ⲉⲥϣⲁ ϩⲉ ⲉϫⲙ̅ⲡⲕⲁϩ ⲉⲧⲟⲩⲣϩⲱⲃ ⲉⲣⲟϥ], it produces a large branch and becomes a resting place for birds of the sky."	³⁰He also said, 'With what can we compare the kingdom of God, or what parable will we use for it? ³¹It is like a mustard seed, which, when sown upon the ground, is the smallest of all the seeds on earth; ³²yet when it is sown it grows up and becomes the greatest of all shrubs, and puts forth large branches, so that the birds of the air can make nests in its shade.'	¹⁸What is the kingdom of God like, and with what am I to compare it? ¹⁹It is like a seed of mustard, which a person took and threw into his garden. And it grew and developed into a tree, and the birds of the sky nested in its branches.

The version of the parable in Mark focuses on the difference between the tiny mustard seed and the large plant that grows from it: the *smallest* seed becomes the *greatest* shrub. Karen King argues that this is also the main point of the parable in *Gos. Thom.* 20 and identifies the parable as one of many that explains what the kingdom is like. King argues that to be a member of the Thomas community "means to have the capacity for transformation from smallness to greatness and nurturing strength."[31] *Gos. Thom.* 20 does indeed feature a small-to-large image—the mustard seed is

---

31. King, "Kingdom in the Gospel of Thomas," 55.

tiny but produces a large plant—but *Gos. Thom.*'s version is not as dramatic as Mark's. Yes, the mustard seed is named the *tiniest* seed, but it does not grow to become the *greatest* of all shrubs; it simply produces a large branch. The focus of the saying in *Gos. Thom.* 20 is not that the smallest thing becomes the largest thing, and a focus on the small-to-large theme misses the most interesting feature of *Gos. Thom.*'s version of the parable: the seed fell upon earth *that was worked/prepared*.

Both Simon Gathercole and Uwe-Karsten Plisch have commented on the fact that *Gos. Thom.* explicitly tells the reader that the seed fell on worked soil. Gathercole argues that this relates to the Gospel's general focus on labour,[32] and Plisch argues that it demonstrates the requirement for human participation in the growing of the kingdom.[33] Gathercole and Plisch both observe that the preparation of the soil requires labour, but neither recognizes this labour as *intellectual* labour, and interpreting the addition of "worked" earth as a reference to preparing for the kingdom is too vague. If, however, we turn back to the educational writings, we can get a clearer picture. If, for *Gos. Thom.*, the mustard seed is teaching (as seems to be implied even in more general interpretations of the parable), then the requirement of prepared earth harkens back to *Gos. Thom.* 9 where prepared earth is required for a seed to produce fruit. Put another way, a prepared hearer is required for the teaching to take hold. Recognizing that the seed-as-teaching and soil-as-student theme is at work here as elsewhere in *Gos. Thom.*, we can more accurately describe what is expected of whom in this parable.

Gos. Thom. *40: A Grapevine planted apart from the father*

> Jesus said, "A grapevine was planted away from the father. Because it was not strong it will be pulled up from its roots and perish."

At first glance, *Gos. Thom.* 40 does not seem to qualify as a seed saying. There is no reference to a sower, and the plant has already reached maturity. There is, however, an implied sower who has planted the grapevine apart from the father. And while there is no mention of the specific soil in which it was planted, the place of planting is identified as "away from the father." On its own, this saying might not catch our attention. But given the interpretive context provided by the parables of the Sower and Mustard Seed, it is possible to recognize the same metaphor being extended to the grape vine. Translated into our *paideic* language, the saying can be read as follows:

---

32. Simon Gathercole, *The Gospel of Thomas: Introduction and Commentary* (Leiden; Boston: Brill Academic Publishers, 2014), 297–8.
33. Uwe-Karsten Plisch, *The Gospel of Thomas: Original Text with Commentary* (Freiburg, Germany: Deutsche Bibelgesellschaft, 2008), 79.

> "A teaching was instilled in minds away from the father. Because the teaching is not strong, it will not last."

Such an understanding of the saying in *Gos. Thom.* is possible in light of the interpretation provided here for *Gos. Thom.* 9 and 20. The placement of saying 40 within *Gos. Thom.* provides a further clue. Immediately preceding saying 40 is *Gos. Thom.* 39, a saying stating that the Pharisees and scribes have taken the keys of knowledge and hidden them. The saying concludes by warning the hearer to be as shrewd as snakes and innocent as doves. April DeConick argues that saying 40 uses the image of the grapevine to refer directly to the Pharisees and scribes named in saying 39, "the Pharisees are like a grapevine that is not of the Father's planting, they will be yanked out by their roots."[34] Charles Hedrick also thinks this saying seeks to invalidate the other competitive plantings evoked in *Gos. Thom.* 39 (Hedrick interprets planting as God's planting of faith) and sees the saying in *Gos. Thom.* as a warning that competitors will be destroyed.[35] Gathercole agrees that *Gos. Thom.* 40 warns of the destruction of the Thomas-group's competitors, but he sees the competitors as "the Jews" as a whole and associates saying 40 with "similar condemnations" in sayings 43 and 102.[36]

I agree with DeConick that it is the Pharisees and scribes of saying 39 in view here, but I must disagree with Gathercole that the conflict is with "the Jews" as a competing religious group. The Pharisees and scribes are not a competing religious formation, but rather competing teachers with their own specialized knowledge. Saying 39 says as much, "the Pharisees and scribes have taken the keys of knowledge [ⲛ̄ϣⲁⲩⲧ ⲛ̄ⲧⲅⲛⲱⲥⲓⲥ] and hidden them." *Gos. Thom.* 40 comments on the failure of their teaching (it is away from the Father) and its ultimate fate: it will perish. On this reading, *Gos. Thom.* 40 both uses the seed/teaching soil/mind metaphor and employs another common feature of educational writing and ancient intellectual life, namely, criticizing other teachers and teachings.[37]

---

34. April D. DeConick, *The Original Gospel of Thomas in Translation: With a Commentary and New English Translation of the Complete Gospel* (London: T&T Clark, 2007), 161; April D. DeConick, *Recovering the Original Gospel of Thomas: A History of the Gospel and Its Growth*, Library of New Testament Studies (London: T&T Clark, 2006), 119.

35. Charles W Hedrick, *Unlocking the Secrets of the Gospel According to Thomas: A Radical Faith for a New Age* (Eugene, Or: Cascade Books, 2010), 85.

36. Gathercole, *The Gospel of Thomas*, 374–5.

37. On the importance of competition among ancient intellectuals, see Kendra Eshleman, *The Social World of Intellectuals in the Roman Empire: Sophists, Philosophers, and Christians* (Cambridge: Cambridge University Press, 2012), *passim*.

Gos. Thom. 57: Parable of The Good Seed

Jesus said, "the kingdom of the Father resembles a man who had a good seed, his enemy came in the night and he sowed darnel amongst the good seed. The man did not allow them to pluck the darnel, he said to them, 'so that you do not go plucking the darnel and you pluck the grain with it. For in the time of the harvest the darnel will become manifest, it is plucked and burned'."

Of the four seed sayings examined here, *Gos. Thom.* 57 has the least amount of consensus regarding its meaning. DeConick reads the parable eschatologically: the seeds are all people, and all will be held accountable on the day of judgement (the harvest).[38] Gathercole also interprets the seeds as people: the good seeds are the elect, the darnel is the non-elect, and people's true nature will be revealed at the harvest.[39] Both interpretations, however, give undue priority to Matthew 13.24-30.[40] In *Gos. Thom.* generally, and saying 57 specifically, there is no notion of apocalyptic judgment. Instead, we should follow King and Hedrick who read the figure of the reaper as a wise person who can recognize the times of harvest and differentiate wheat from weed.[41]

Both King and Hedrick understand the harvester in *Gos. Thom.* 21.9 as a wise figure who recognizes the time of the harvest. I argue that the man in saying 57 is more specifically a wise farmer who stands in for the wise (i.e., properly educated) person. Looking at *Gos. Thom.* 57, King argues that the parable describes the Thomas-community itself. For King, the focus of this parable is on the first man and his conflict with an enemy: "the point is the ineffectiveness of action against the wise man because he knows to

---

38. DeConick, *The Original Gospel of Thomas in Translation*, 193.
39. Gathercole, *The Gospel of Thomas*, 431. Gathercole's interpretation gives undue priority to Matthew 13.24-30. In *Gos. Thom.* generally, and saying 57 specifically, there is no notion of apocalyptic judgment. Instead, we should follow King and Hedrick
40. Matthew 13.24-30 (NRSV): He put before them another parable: "The kingdom of heaven may be compared to someone who sowed good seed in his field; but while everybody was asleep, an enemy came and sowed weeds among the wheat, and then went away. So when the plants came up and bore grain, then the weeds appeared as well. And the slaves of the householder came and said to him, 'Master, did you not sow good seed in your field? Where, then, did these weeds come from?' He answered, 'An enemy has done this.' The slaves said to him, 'Then do you want us to go and gather them?' But he replied, 'No; for in gathering the weeds you would uproot the wheat along with them. Let both of them grow together until the harvest; and at harvest time I will tell the reapers, Collect the weeds first and bind them in bundles to be burned, but gather the wheat into my barn.'"
41. King, "Kingdom in the Gospel of Thomas," 52; Hedrick, *Unlocking the Secrets of the Gospel According to Thomas*, 58.

overcome the strategies of his enemy."[42] King reads the parable as a lesson in morality "where good seeds are good deeds; the weeds are wicked deeds; and where the evil man's wickedness comes to naught,"[43] but given our recognition of how seeds often function metaphorically as teachings, once again we can sharpen our understanding of the parable.

> The kingdom of the Father is like the teacher (person) who had good teaching (seeds). The parable implies that those good teachings were shared with students.
> The enemy taught bad teachings (sowed darnel) to those students, so that the students knew both good and bad teachings.
> The teacher did not let other students speak against the bad teaching lest they accidently speak against the good teaching.
> When the students have matured, the bad teaching will be recognized and removed.

The passive construction of final part of the saying makes it impossible to determine who will pull up and burn the darnel, the saying notes only that the darnel will be pulled up and burned. This makes the conclusion to saying 57 slightly different than saying 21, where an unidentified "he" will come with "his sickle" and harvest. However, the point is the same: the wise person knows the time of the harvest, and the wise person knows how to distinguish between wheat and weeds.

Conclusion

If my argument that the four seed sayings in *Gos. Thom.* use the seed-as-teaching and soil-as-student metaphor is acceptable, then this leads us to conclude that the composers of *Gos. Thom.* were both aware of the meaning of the metaphor and expected at least some readers/hearers to recognize it as well. If the text is a teaching text, as Cameron and Arnal have argued, then the students should recognize themselves as the soil and endeavour to be prepared to receive teaching. Importantly, it is not apparent that every reader/hearer would recognize the metaphor, for unlike the Parable of the Sower in Mark, *Gos. Thom.* does not explain the meaning of the parable or make a connection between the sowers, seeds, soil, and *encyclia paideia*. It is up to the reader/hearer to correctly interpret the meaning of these sayings. Leaving these sayings unexplained rewards the people who recognize them, and those able to recognize them would likely have been able to do so due to their own familiarity with *encyclia paideia* and through their own training and socialization within it. In this way, *Gos. Thom.* rewards the reader/

---

42. King, "Kingdom in the Gospel of Thomas," 54.
43. King, "Kingdom in the Gospel of Thomas," 55.

hearer for their erudition: their possession of even a moderate level of education allows them to see what others cannot.

Author biography

Ian Phillip Brown is a postdoctoral fellow at the University of Regina. His research focuses on the *Gospel of Thomas* and educational practices in early Christianity.

Bibliography

Arnal, William E. "Blessed Are the Solitary: Textual Practices and the Mirage of a Thomas 'Community,'" 271–81 in *"The One Who Sows Bountifully": Essays in Honor of Stanley K. Stowers*. Edited by Caroline Johnson Hodge, Saul M. Olyan, Daniel Ullucci, and Emma Wasserman. Providence, R.I.: Brown Judaic Studies, 2013. https://doi.org/10.2307/j.ctt14bs6fv.27

—"How the Gospel of Thomas Works," 261–80 in *Scribal Practices and Social Structures among Jesus Adherents: Essays in Honour of John S. Kloppenborg*. Edited by William E. Arnal, Richard S. Ascough, Robert A. Derrenbacker, Jr., and Philip A. Harland. Leuven; Paris; Bristol, CT: Peeters, 2016.

—"The Rhetoric of Social Construction: Language and Society in the Gospel of Thomas." 27–48 in *Rhetoric and Reality in Early Christianities*. Edited by Willi Braun. Studies in Christianity and Judaism / Études Sur Le Christianisme et Le Judaïsme 16. Waterloo, Ont: Wilfrid Laurier University Press, 2005.

Braun, Willi. "Socio-Mythic Invention, Graeco-Roman Schools, and the Sayings Gospel Q." *MTSR* 11 (1999): 210–35. https://doi.org/10.1163/157006899X00032

Brown, Ian Phillip. "Where Indeed Was the Gospel of Thomas Written? Thomas in Alexandria." *JBL* 138 (2019): 451–72. https://doi.org/10.1353/jbl.2019.0024

Cameron, Ron. "An Occasion for Thought," 100–12 in *Introducing Religion: Essays in Honor of Jonathan Z. Smith*. Edited by Willi Braun and Russell T. McCutcheon. Equinox, 2008.

—"Ancient Myths and Modern Theories of the Gospel of Thomas and Christian Origins." *MTSR* 11 (1999): 236–57. https://doi.org/10.1163/157006899X00041

—"Parable and Interpretation in the Gospel of Thomas." *Forum* 2 (1986): 3–39.

Cwikla, Anna. "Become Male or Leave: Understanding the Gendered Language in the Gospel of Thomas Logion 114." Unpublished colloquium paper, 2016.

DeConick, April D. *Recovering the Original Gospel of Thomas: A History of the Gospel and Its Growth*. LNTS. London: T&T Clark, 2006.

—*The Original Gospel of Thomas in Translation: With a Commentary and New English Translation of the Complete Gospel*. London: T&T Clark, 2007.

Doody, Aude. "The Authority of Writing in Varro's De Re Rustica." 182–202 in *Authority and Expertise in Ancient Scientific Culture*. Edited by Jason König and Greg Woolf. Cambridge: Cambridge University Press, 2017. https://doi.org/10.1017/9781107446724.009

Eshleman, Kendra. *The Social World of Intellectuals in the Roman Empire: Sophists, Philosophers, and Christians*. Cambridge: Cambridge University Press, 2012. https://doi.org/10.1017/CBO9781139207300

Frischer, Bernard. *The Sculpted Word: Epicureanism and Philosophical Recruitment in Ancient Greece.* Berkeley, CA: University of California Press, 1982. https://doi.org/10.1525/9780520312135

Gathercole, Simon. *The Gospel of Thomas: Introduction and Commentary.* Leiden; Boston: Brill Academic Publishers, 2014. https://doi.org/10.1163/9789004273252

Goodacre, Mark. *Thomas and the Gospels: The Case for Thomas's Familiarity with the Synoptics.* Cambridge: William B. Eerdmans Publishing Company, 2012.

Hedrick, Charles W. *Unlocking the Secrets of the Gospel According to Thomas: A Radical Faith for a New Age.* Eugene, OR: Cascade Books, 2010.

Hollander, David B. *Farmers and Agriculture in the Roman Economy.* Electronic resource. Abingdon, Oxon; New York: Routledge, 2019.

King, Karen. "Kingdom in the Gospel of Thomas." *Forum* 3 Foundations and Facets (1987): 48–97.

Kloppenborg, John S. *Tenants in the Vineyard: Ideology, Economics, & Agrarian Conflict in Jewish Palestine.* Tübingen: Mohr Siebeck, 2006.

Kronenberg, Leah. *Allegories of Farming from Greece and Rome: Philosophical Satire in Xenophon, Varro and Virgil.* Cambridge; New York: Cambridge University Press, 2009. https://doi.org/10.1017/CBO9780511729973

Lightstone, Jack N. "Whence the Rabbis? From Coherent Description to Fragmented Reconstructions." *SR/SR* 26 (1997): 275–95. https://doi.org/10.1177/000842989702600301

Mack, Burton L. *A Myth of Innocence: Mark and Christian Origins.* Minneapolis, MN: Fortress Press, 1988.

Pagels, Elaine H. "Exegesis of Genesis 1 in the Gospels of Thomas and John." *JBL* 118 (1999): 477–96. https://doi.org/10.2307/3268185

Patterson, Stephen J. "Jesus Meets Plato: The Theology of the Gospel of Thomas and Middle Platonism." 181–205 in *Thomasevangelium: Entstehung, Rezeption, Theologie.* Edited by Jörg Frey, Enno Edzard Popkes, and Jens Schröter. BZNW. New York: Walter de Gruyter, 2008.

Pendrick, Gerard J. *Antiphon the Sophist: The Fragments.* Cambridge Classical Texts and Commentaries 39. New York: Cambridge University Press, 2002.

Plisch, Uwe-Karsten. *The Gospel of Thomas: Original Text with Commentary.* Freiburg, Germany: Deutsche Bibelgesellschaft, 2008.

Rosen, Ralph Mark, and Ineke Sluiter, eds. *City, Countryside, and the Spatial Organization of Value in Classical Antiquity.* Mnemosyne, Bibliotheca Classica Batava 279. Leiden; Boston: Brill, 2006. https://doi.org/10.1163/9789047409182

Scott, Bernard Brandon. *Hear Then the Parable: A Commentary on the Parables of Jesus.* Minneapolis, MN: Fortress Press, 1989.

Shaw, Brent D. *Bringing in the Sheaves: Economy and Metaphor in the Roman World.* Robson Classical Lectures. Toronto: University of Toronto Press, 2013. https://doi.org/10.3138/9781442661592

Smith, Jonathan Z. "The Temple and the Magician." 172–89 in *Map Is Not Territory: Studies in the History of Religions.* Chicago, IL: University of Chicago Press, 1993.

Thibodeau, Philip. "Ancient Agronomy as a Literature of Best Practices." 463–80 in *Oxford Handbook of Science and Medicine in the Classical World.* Edited by Paul T. Keyser and John Scarborough. New York: Oxford University Press, 2018. https://doi.org/10.1093/oxfordhb/9780199734146.013.28

—*Playing the Farmer: Representations of Rural Life in Vergil's Georgics.* Berkeley, CA: University of California Press, 2011.

Ueberschaer, Frank. "Jewish Education in Ben Sira." 29–46 in *Second Temple Jewish*

"Paideia" in Context. Edited by Gabriele Boccaccinni and Jason M. Zurawski. Berlin; Boston: De Gruyter, 2017. http://www.degruyter.com/view/title/529256 https://doi.org/10.1515/9783110546972-003

Uro, Risto, ed. *Thomas at the Crossroads: Essays on the Gospel of Thomas*. Studies of the New Testament and Its World. Edinburgh: T & T Clark, 1998.

Chapter Fifteen

Transgressing New Testament Classrooms with Thecla[1]

Anna Cwikla

In the introduction to his article "Body, Character and the Problem of Femaleness in Early Christian Discourse," Willi Braun reflects on the tension that emerges for him when studying women in ancient Christian literature:

> I am a feminist. If I nonetheless find, as I do, that early Christianity was almost without exception a world without women, it is by no means a finding that delights. *Au contraire!* Unfortunately history does not always present us with gifts that are beneficial and delightful.[2]

Braun's reflection encapsulates what I have experienced as a student and scholar of early Christianity. In my undergraduate classes, I enjoyed reading about Thecla, Mary, and other women who appeared to challenge the status quo in their narrative worlds. During my graduate school work, however, as I have kept reading and interrogating these texts, my questions and analyses have changed. Whereas years ago I might have delighted in the fact that a figure named Mary is mentioned twice in the *Gospel of Thomas*, I am now much more cynical and reserved about what actual purpose Mary serves in the text, especially in places where male figures (Peter and Jesus) might talk about her but do not grant her the space to speak for herself (*Gos. Thom.* 114).[3] The excitement I once felt about the appearance of women in early Christian literature has shifted to a cautious skepticism.

---

1. I thank the editors for the invitation to contribute to this volume to honor my MA advisor, Willi Braun, who has been tremendously influential in my thinking about ancient conceptions of gender and ancient Christian literature. Willi also helped build my confidence as a junior academic and hone my own research interests. I hope this essay serves as a worthy homage to his invaluable mentorship. I am deeply indebted to Ian Brown and Michelle Christian for their insightful discussions and feedback in all stages of developing and writing this paper, including suggestions for witty subsection titles. Many thanks are also due to Kelly Murphy, who allowed me to flood her Facebook Messenger inbox with half-baked, barely coherent paragraphs while I crafted this paper.

2. Willi Braun, "Body, Character and the Problem of Femaleness in Early Christian Discourse," *RTheol* 9.1 (2002): 109; italics original.

3. Anna Cwikla, "There's Nothing about Mary: The Insignificance of Mary in the Gospel of Thomas 114," *JIBS* 1.1 (2019): 95–112.

The tension that Braun expresses, being a feminist on the one hand, and not finding prominent women in the literature on the other, is heightened when it comes to teaching these figures and texts to students. One particular case is the *Acts of Paul and Thecla* (*APTh*). Feminist scholarship has produced no shortage of readings on Thecla, the text, and the woman.[4] The scholarship of the 1980s saw Thecla as a heroine figure and even posited that networks of women circulated the text.[5] There was a shift in the mid-1990s and early 2000s that was more critical of the prestige placed on Thecla as a type of proto-feminist, instead arguing that the text is more about the competition between men than it is about Thecla or women.[6] Others noted that Thecla must undergo changes to her appearance in order to make herself more manly to avoid being treated as a woman, which only reinforces androcentric structures.[7] Studies of Thecla from the 2010s are even more critical of seeing her story as a depiction of a woman challenging social norms. Rosie Ratcliffe, for instance, argues that "[n]owhere within the story can we find traces of the female protagonist's strategy to challenge dominant gender norms. Thecla remains a desirable, beautiful woman who pleasures the male gaze and her body is repeatedly flaunted for all to see."[8] In a study

---

4. An exhaustive literature review is beyond the scope of this essay. For an overview of issues in scholarship on Thecla, see, inter alia, Shelly Matthews, "Thinking of Thecla: Issues in Feminist Historiography," *Journal of Feminist Studies in Religion* 17.2 (2001): 39–55; Stephen J. Davis, "From Women's Piety to Male Devotion: Gender Studies, the Acts of Paul and Thecla, and the Evidence of an Arabic Manuscript," *HTR* 108.4 (2015): 579–93; Ross Shepard Kraemer, "Thecla," in *The Oxford Handbook of New Testament, Gender, and Sexuality*, ed. Benjamin H. Dunning (Oxford University Press, 2019), 485–502.

5. Stevan L. Davies, *The Revolt of the Widows: The Social World of the Apocryphal Acts* (London: Feffer & Simons, 1980); Dennis R. MacDonald, *The Legend and the Apostle: The Battle for Paul in Story and Canon* (Philadelphia: Westminster, 1983); Virginia Burrus, *Chastity as Autonomy: Women in the Stories of the Apocryphal Acts*, Studies in Women and Religion 23 (Lewiston, NY: Mellen Press, 1987).

6. Kate Cooper, *The Virgin and the Bride: Idealized Womanhood in Late Antiquity* (Cambridge, MA: Harvard University Press, 1996), esp. 51–67. For critiques of Cooper's approach, see Matthews, "Thinking of Thecla," 127–52; Stephen J. Davis, *The Cult of Saint Thecla: A Tradition of Women's Piety in Late Antiquity* (Oxford: Oxford University Press, 2001), 18–19; Ross Shepard Kraemer, *Unreliable Witnesses: Religion, Gender, and History in the Greco-Roman Mediterranean* (New York: Oxford University Press, 2011), 127–52. For Cooper's more recent work on Thecla, see Kate Cooper, *Band of Angels: The Forgotten World of Early Christian Women* (New York: Penguin, 2013).

7. Willi Braun, "Physiotherapy of Femininity in the Acts of Thecla," in *Text and Artifact in the Religions of Mediterranean Antiquity: Essays in Honor of Peter Richardson*, ed. Stephen G. Wilson and Michel R. Desjardins, Studies in Christianity and Judaism 9 (Waterloo, ON: Wilfrid Laurier University Press, 2000), 209–30.

8. Rosie Ratcliffe, "*The Acts of Paul and Thecla*: Violating the Inviolate Body

that reconsiders the transgressive nature of Thecla, Mary, and Perpetua, Sarah Parkhouse recognizes that while Thecla rejected her fiancé and the advances of Alexander, she nevertheless consistently pursues another man, Paul.[9] According to Parkhouse, "the catalyst for the entire plot is Thecla's obsessive desire for this man."[10] In my own engagement with *APTh*, I see Thecla primarily as a narrative device that upholds rather than challenges ancient gender norms,[11] certainly a finding that by no means delights!

When writing for a faceless audience of academics, my thinking about *APTh* focuses on how female characters become useful literary devices for expressing the concerns of male writers. Inside the classroom, however, when I come face to face with students who have yet to read *APTh*, I am suddenly confronted with a conundrum: Do I allow students to experience the same excitement I did when I saw Thecla embarrass Alexander, escape death repeatedly, and become a self-baptizing heroine? Or do I pre-emptively stifle this excitement by noting, for example, that Thecla only leaves her fiancé to follow another man who repeatedly dismisses her? Or can we create a space where both Thecla the liberated Christian woman and Thecla the patriarchal literary device can coexist in the classroom? In this essay, I offer some reflections on these questions drawn from both my research and teaching. As I see it, Thecla may not be a fully transgressive figure in her narrative world, but she can become our transgressive accomplice in the classroom if we situate her story properly.

Thecla in the Classroom

My reflections are based in large part on my ongoing research into constructions of women and gender in early Christian literature and on my recent experience of teaching about women and gender in an introductory New Testament course.[12] As I taught, it became clear to me that the Intro-

---

– Thecla Uncut," in *The Body in Biblical, Christian and Jewish Texts*, ed. Joan E. Taylor, LSTS 85 (London: Bloomsbury T&T Clark, 2014), 196.

9. Sarah Parkhouse, "The Fetishization of Female Exempla: Mary, Thecla, Perpetua and Felicitas," *NTS* 63.4 (2017): 574–80.

10. Parkhouse, "The Fetishization of Female Exempla," 580.

11. My forthcoming PhD dissertation, "Lessons, Placeholders, and Delegitmating Devices: The Literary Function of Women in Early Christian Texts," elaborates on this analysis of Thecla and other women in early Christian texts. My perspective aligns most closely with the work of Cooper, *The Virgin and the Bride*; Braun, "Physiotherapy of Femininity in the Acts of Thecla"; Ratcliffe, "*Acts of Paul and Thecla*"; Parkhouse, "The Fetishization of Female Exempla."

12. At my institution, the University of Toronto, the course is titled RLG241 "Early Christian Writings." The absence of "New Testament" in the course title allowed me

duction to New Testament classroom is a very different space than the subfield of women and gender in ancient Christianity. After all, the women that get pushed to the margins in the former (as the final topic for the semester, for example) are at the center of the latter. Because introductory New Testament classes are aimed at providing a survey of literature, instructors cannot go into the depths and nuances that might be the focus of their own research. Nevertheless, the classroom provides an opportunity for us to revisit the excitement we ourselves felt the first time we read these texts. As an instructor, teaching Thecla is one of my favorite parts of the course. After slogging through a first-century man's semi-coherent letters for weeks, discussing the adventures of Thecla escaping death and trolling elite men is a welcome change of scenery (sorry not sorry, Paul). For me, Thecla serves as a counter example to most of the other course readings: the thoughts of men about other men. Thecla is a breath of fresh air in a stale, centuries old, male-dominated discipline.

As much as *APTh* offers a new type of story within the course, it is likely no coincidence that we encounter her in close proximity to that man who receives an author credit in thirteen of the twenty-seven books of the New Testament. It is, after all, the *Acts of Paul and Thecla*, not the *Acts of Thecla* or the *Acts of Thecla and Paul*. Moreover, we should not forget that *APTh* is "embedded within a work designed to emphasize Paul's status, the Acts of Paul," which Rosie Ratcliffe maintains "should naturally make one suspicious" when it comes to the text's treatment of Thecla.[13] Indeed, Thecla is often taught through the lens of the male figure, Paul. For example, many have read *APTh* in conversation with the Pastoral Epistles to demonstrate the different attitudes toward issues such as gender roles and sexual practice.[14] In the Pastorals, women are not allowed to teach or have authority over men but are to remain silent (1 Tim 2.12). Thecla, on the other hand, repeatedly challenges the authority of men by ignoring her fiancé's pleas to stop listening to Paul, or by publicly humiliating the elite man Alexander, when he tries to make advances toward her. For these reasons, *APTh* has become an important counter example to statements about women and gender in New Testament texts.

---

the opportunity to include several non-canonical texts, and I continually stressed the importance of studying texts outside the New Testament in order to get a more complete picture of early Christianity.

13. Ratcliffe, "*Acts of Paul and Thecla*," 185.

14. See for example, Davies, *The Revolt of the Widows*; MacDonald, *The Legend and the Apostle*; Matthews, "Thinking of Thecla," 40–45; Matthijs den Dulk, "I Permit No Woman to Teach Except for Thecla: The Curious Case of the Pastoral Epistles and the 'Acts of Paul' Reconsidered," *NovT* 54. 2 (2012): 176–203.

The method of learning about *APTh* through a canonical, Pauline-centered lens is how I first encountered the text. It is also the same method that I have used with students in the classroom. However, this is where I experience the tension between excitement and betrayal. While I am stoked to introduce another group of young minds to *APTh*, I also feel that I am selling Thecla short. In the context of the New Testament classroom, she is merely an extension of canonical concerns in extra-canonical literature. If framed primarily as a counterpoint to ideas found in the New Testament or as evidence of early Christians' preoccupation with telling more stories about Paul, Thecla is never given a chance to be appreciated on her own terms. Of course, one could argue that this type of approach should be expected in a New Testament classroom given that the course itself focuses on "canonical" literature. I maintain, however, that how we structure our courses should not be guided by the texts themselves but rather what we want to convey *through* these texts. In other words, it may be the case that instructors, depending on their own background and institutional context, necessarily privilege the New Testament over and against other ancient Christians writings. However, for those who want to argue that *APTh* is a text that tells us about the historical situation of early Christianity, it is important to recognize that the ways that we approach the text will affect our interpretations. Failing to read *APTh* on its own merits risks reinforcing the hegemony of the New Testament in the history of Christianity.[15]

The *Acts of Paul and Thecla* is not the only non-canonical text that has been used in the classroom to further debates about canonical texts. The *Gospel of Thomas* (*Gos. Thom.*), sometimes dubbed the "Fifth Gospel,"[16] frequently finds itself among the likes of Mark, Luke, and Matthew. But similar to *APTh*, the inclusion of the non-canonical *Gos. Thom.* in a course on New Testament texts is not surprising. Given the amount of similarity with the Synoptic Gospels, *Gos. Thom.* serves as another witness to the early Jesus traditions.[17] For those who subscribe to the Two Document hypothe-

---

15. For a discussion on how non-canonical texts have traditionally been mined for information regarding New Testament texts, see Annette Yoshiko Reed, "The Afterlives of New Testament Apocrypha," *JBL* 134 (2015): 401–25. For biblical hegemony in the context of Second Temple literature, see Eva Mroczek, "The Hegemony of the Biblical in the Study of Second Temple Literature," *JAJ* 6 (2015): 2–35.

16. Stephen J. Patterson, James M. Robinson, and Hans-Gebhard Bethge, *The Fifth Gospel: The Gospel of Thomas Comes of Age* (Harrisburg, PA: Trinity Press International, 1998); Stephen J. Patterson, *The Gospel of Thomas and Christian Origins: Essays on the Fifth Gospel* (Boston, MA: Brill, 2013).

17. For the connection of *Gos. Thom.* with the Synoptics and Q, see Bart D. Ehrman, *The New Testament: A Historical Introduction to the Early Christian Writings*, 5th ed. (New York: Oxford University Press, 2012), 224–6. The discussion of *Gos. Thom.* and

sis (the existence of Q), the *Gos. Thom.*—a collection of sayings of Jesus—is precisely the type of document Q supporters envisioned.[18] Regardless of whether one posits that the *Gos. Thom.* predates or is dependent on the Synoptic Gospels, it is treated as one of the early sources about Jesus. All of these assets of *Gos. Thom.* are contingent on the implicit hegemony of the New Testament. In other words, the only reason why *Gos. Thom.* is allowed into the New Testament classroom is precisely because it reinscribes several prized features of New Testament literature. In the same way that *Gos. Thom.* encompasses many traditional/historical-critical avenues of exploration within a New Testament-centered course, so too does *APTh* with its Pauline-centered concerns. What *Gos. Thom.* is to the canonical gospels and Jesus, *APTh* is to the Pastoral Letters and Paul. Both of these non-canonical texts are extensions of New Testament-centered concerns.

Thecla in the New Testament Textbook

The tension I experience when preparing my lecture for *APTh* results from coming to terms with the fact that the topics are not those that currently occupy the main discussions in the field about the text. While it certainly was the case that previous research on *APTh* was interested in the text's relationship to the reception of the character of Paul and the Pastoral Epistles, the focus has now shifted to Thecla herself and related questions of gender construction in antiquity. Thecla is rarely read through Paul in more recent scholarship, so why is this not reflected in our classrooms? Part of the issue, as I see it, is the textbook industry for introductory New Testament courses. The most widely used textbook is *The New Testament: A Historical Introduction to the Early Christian Writings*. With the seventh edition published in 2020, this textbook has been a staple in classrooms for over two decades.[19] According to Oxford University Press, the textbook is the "#1-selling New Testament introduction in the U.S."[20] The present analysis uses the fifth edition (2012). My decision to use the fifth edition and not

---

its relationship to the Synoptics and Q is also found in a textbook that does not center New Testament literature. See Nicola Denzey Lewis, *Introduction to "Gnosticism": Ancient Voices, Christian Worlds* (New York: Oxford University Press, 2013), 107–10.

18. Scholars have produced book that compares the sayings of *Gos. Thom.* and Q material. John S. Kloppenborg et al., *Q-Thomas Reader* (Sonoma, CA: Polebridge, 1990).

19. The first edition was published in 1997 Bart D. Ehrman, *The New Testament: A Historical Introduction to the Early Christian Writings* (New York: Oxford University Press, 1997).

20. "The New Testament - Bart D. Ehrman - Oxford University Press," n.d., n.p. [cited 7 August 2020]. Online: https://global.oup.com/academic/product/the-new-testament-9780190909000?cc=ca&lang=en&#.

the most recent is because the fifth edition has been in circulation and use for a longer time. Given that changes from edition to edition are very minor, most instructors allow students to use older editions. And while the seventh edition has 28 chapters instead of 30,[21] the titles of chapters and subsections discussed below remain the same. Thecla's name appears in the title of Chapter 24: "Does the Tradition Miscarry? Paul in Relation to Jesus, James, Thecla, and Theudas." By this point in the textbook, the canonical gospels and Paul's undisputed letters have been discussed and the Deutero-Pauline and Pastoral Epistles are the subject of the next chapter "In the Wake of the Apostle: The Deutero-Pauline and Pastoral Epistles." After this, the topic of women appears in its own chapter entitled "From Paul's Female Colleagues to the Pastor's Intimidated Women: The Oppression of Women in Early Christianity."

There are several details about the chapter titles and chronology alone that reveal the male-centered approach of the textbook. First, Thecla appears in the 24th chapter out of 30. Within the chapters themselves, *APTh* receives a total of a page's worth of text accompanied by a large image of the fifth-century ivory panel depicting Thecla, enclosed in a tower, listening to and gazing at Paul.[22] After providing a summary of *APTh*, the textbook[23] states:

---

21. The reason for this is two chapters, 5 and 6, have been merged into one, "5. From Oral Traditions to Written Gospels," and another chapter "The Historian and the Problem of Miracles," has been downgraded to an "Excursus" in the seventh edition. The order of the chapters remains the same between the fifth, sixth, and seventh editions, with the exception of the chapter discussing the book of Acts. In the fifth edition, it is the 11th chapter immediately after the Gospel of Luke (Chapter 10). In the sixth and seventh edition, the book of Acts is presented after all the Jesus-related chapters and before the Paul chapters (6th ed. Chapter 19; 7th ed. Chapter 17).

22. Ehrman, *The New Testament*, 392–4. This section in the seventh edition remains exactly the same, with the exception of a few minor editorial details (e.g., "1 Cor 7" instead of "1 Corinthians 7"; "hardcore" instead of "hard-core"; and a reference to chapter 24 instead of 26. Bart D. Ehrman, *The New Testament: A Historical Introduction to the Early Christian Writings*, 7th ed. [New York: Oxford University Press, 2020], 433–5). I thank Sara Parks for providing me with access to these pages from the seventh edition.

23. My use of "textbook" rather than the name of the author throughout the analysis is deliberate. By no means am I trying to give a text agency. Rather, my choice to use "textbook" instead of the author's name is to highlight the fact that the textbook genre might not allow for the same type of nuance and caveats that one would expect in other academic writing. There are doubtless other restraints or conventions that the publisher maintains and that might not allow the same flexibility of other monographs. Moreover, in the context of the classroom, it is typical to refer to the "textbook" in discussions rather than the author's name. In a way, the author(s) almost disappear as individuals behind these thick, colorful, image-filled books.

Taking the historian's view, one might ask whether the historical Paul himself would have recognized this version of his own proclamation. Whatever the apostle would have made of it, the stories about Paul and Thecla enjoyed a wide popularity in certain circles, perhaps chiefly, as some scholars have suggested, among Christian women who, as converts, enjoyed a certain liberation from the constraints of marriage and enforced subservience.[24]

The *Acts of Paul and Thecla*, then, as both the chapter title and text itself demonstrate, are centered around how these tales relate to the "historical Paul" and how the second-century text depicts the tradition's preoccupation with this man.

Additionally, in the entire textbook, Thecla is the only named woman in the chapter titles or subsection titles. With the "Woman" chapter following the Pastoral Epistles, this positions the discussion to focus on the "The Oppression of Women in Early Christianity," as the title of the chapter indicates. Chapter 26 of the textbook, which focuses on women, continues to center men. The discussion is framed around themes found in the Pastoral Epistles: "Despite the impression that one might get from such ancient Christian writings as the Pastoral epistles, women were not always a silent presence in the churches," reads the first sentence in the first section of the chapter.[25] The first two sections are titled "Women in Paul's Churches," and "Women Associated with Jesus." Here, women are clearly situated in relation to the two most prominent figures of early Christianity rather than early Christianity more broadly. "Even after the period of the New Testament," the textbook explains, "women continued to be prominent in churches connected with Paul."[26] At the beginning of the section "Women Associated with Jesus," the textbook cautions "[w]e ourselves should not fall into the trap of accepting traditions as historical simply because they coincide with an agenda that we happen to share, feminist or otherwise."[27] I agree that stories such as the one depicted in *APTh* should not be accepted as "historical" because they might "coincide" with our own "agenda." However, in this section, the textbook implicitly draws a distinction between historical-critical scholarship and "feminist" agendas. The hegemony of the historical-critical method looms large in the field of early Christianity, and it is echoed in this introductory textbook. In my estimation, the implied critique of feminist approaches here also results in a refusal to grant agency to women in early Christianity.

24. Ehrman, *The New Testament*, 394.
25. Ehrman, *The New Testament*, 422. The *Acts of Paul and Thecla* are linked to the Pastorals later on this same page.
26. Ehrman, *The New Testament*, 422.
27. Ehrman, *The New Testament*, 423.

This refusal is remarkably common in scholarship on *APTh*. In evaluating critiques leveled against scholars who produced "women-centered" work in their studies of Thecla in the 1980s, Shelly Matthews observes that these "modern critics hurl their insults from their location within the scientific fortress of value-neutrality and objectivity."[28] She recognizes that in the attempt to dismiss the notion that anything resembling resistance by women to patriarchal structures in ancient Christianity, these scholars "employ the interpretive strategy of positing their own scholarly research into the world of early Christianity as objective, scientific, and agenda-free."[29] We see traces of this language in the textbook as it cautions the reader against "accepting traditions as historical," coupled with the allusions to "agendas," "feminist or otherwise." In contrast, "historical" methods and the "historian" are positively portrayed throughout the textbook.[30] The danger here is that students may assume that feminist perspectives in particular have "agendas," while the preferred historical-critical methods are free from agendas or bias.

The Erasure of Ancient Women and Contemporary Women's Scholarship

This textbook is a microcosm of how the field of New Testament studies has treated scholarship about and by women. The trend of marginalizing or ignoring women-related scholarship is so prevalent that it has recently earned itself a term: "The Brooten Phenomenon."[31] The term was coined by Sara Parks who defines it as "the way in which women's scholarship, and scholarship on women, doesn't cross the bridge into what is considered to be 'real' (i.e. male-centred) scholarship."[32] The namesake of this term is Bernadette Brooten, whose monograph *Women Leaders in the Ancient Synagogue: Inscriptional Evidence and Background Issues* (1982) is rarely cited in works on synagogues or Jewish priesthood but rather stays within the "niche" realm of scholarship on women.[33] The lack of engagement with Brooten's book in broader scholarship is just one example of

---

28. Matthews, "Thinking of Thecla," 42.
29. Matthews, "Thinking of Thecla," 46.
30. See especially the subsection "The Historian and the Historical Method" (Ehrman, *The New Testament*, 255–7).
31. Sara Parks, "'The Brooten Phenomenon': Moving Women from the Margins in Second-Temple and New Testament Scholarship," *Bible Crit. Theory* 15 (2019): 46–64.
32. Parks, "'The Brooten Phenomenon,'" 47. For another discussion of scholars dismissing or ignoring Brooten's *Women Leaders in the Ancient Synagogue*, see William E. Arnal, "Gendered Couplets in Q and Legal Formulations: From the Rhetoric to Social History," *JBL* 116. 1 (1997): 75 n. 1.
33. Parks, "'The Brooten Phenomenon,'" 49–50.

this "phenomenon." As Parks contends, there is "an impermeable conceptual wall between [scholarship on women] and what is perceived as 'regular' scholarship."[34] Parks goes on to note that what constitutes "regular scholarship" is linked to what "Elisabeth Schüssler Fiorenza (1999) has dubbed 'malestream' scholarship due to its unspoken patriarchal or kyriarchal assumptions around what constitutes appropriate method and subject matter."[35] Put differently, studies concerning women have become "niche" or specialized areas of study, whereas scholarship topics related to male figures, such as Paul, are assumed to be regular, normative, and mainstream.

The unspoken assumption that male figures ought to be the center around which all other topics orbit is glaringly obvious in *The New Testament: A Historical Introduction to the Early Christian Writings*. Even when women *are* the focus of discussion, it is only because of their relation to Jesus or Paul. Discussions are framed with section titles such as "Women in *Paul's* Churches," "Women Associated with *Jesus*," "*Paul's* Understanding of Women in the Church," and "Women in the Aftermath of *Paul*."[36] Putting this much emphasis on the analysis of chapter and section titles might seem like overkill. However, given that the structure of syllabi and lectures often correspond to the layout of textbooks, these titles influence the way instructors and students situate the material. It is also telling that the names of Jesus and Paul appear a total of thirteen and seven times respectively in chapter titles. It is perhaps fitting that in the only chapter title where a woman's name appears, both Jesus and Paul are named: Chapter 24 "Does the Tradition Miscarry? Paul in Relation to Jesus, James, Thecla, and Theudas." The final four chapters do not have Jesus or Paul in the chapter or section titles. Instead these chapter titles are framed around the term "Christians."[37] This structure reveals two things. First, there are topics related to early Christianity that do not center around Jesus or Paul; and, second, these topics—based on their collective location in the final sixth of the textbook—are of lesser importance.

---

34. Parks, "'The Brooten Phenomenon,'" 47.
35. Parks, "'The Brooten Phenomenon,'" 47.
36. Ehrman, *The New Testament*, 423–8.
37. The chapter titles are as follows: "27. Christians and Jews: Hebrews, Barnabas, and Later Anti-Jewish Literature"; "28. Christians and Pagans: 1 Peter, the Letters of Ignatius, the *Martyrdom of Polycarp*, and Later Apologetic Literature"; "29. Christians and Christians: James, the *Didache*, Polycarp, *1 Clement*, Jude, and 2 Peter"; "30. Christians and the Cosmos: The Revelation of John, *The Shepherd of Hermas*, and the *Apocalypse of Peter*."

Decentering Jesus and Paul

A different and promising way to organize the material in a New Testament textbook is found in *Toward Decentering the New Testament: A Reintroduction* (2018) by Mitzi J. Smith and Yung Suk Kim. In the chapter titles, *Toward Decentering the New Testament* does not center Jesus or Paul by repeatedly inserting their names. In fact, Paul's name appears only twice in the table of contents: once in the section heading "Section III: Pauline Epistles" and a second time in the title of Chapter 15 "Significance of Paul as a Jewish Man in Diaspora."[38] Jesus' name is entirely absent from the chapter titles. Instead, the textbook simply replicates the titles of the texts in the New Testament. While this may seem to "center" rather than "decenter" the New Testament, it deemphasizes the overemphasis of Jesus and Paul in the framework of discussing these texts. Moreover, the authors of the textbook are self-reflective and transparent about their deliberate decisions in structuring the book:

> We have strategically inserted questions throughout each chapter that introduce a biblical book in order to focus readers' attentions on contemporary concerns and interests in dialogue with biblical texts. We have also placed epigraphs or quotations at the beginning of most chapters, primarily from nonwhite, minoritized peoples. This project is intentionally designed to encourage and center an interpretative agenda that prioritizes contemporary issues and critical engagement with minoritized voices and the biblical texts as read by minoritized scholars—an African American female and an Asian-American male.[39]

Including a focus on contemporary concerns and the work of minoritized scholars along with the more "traditional" information one expects from an introductory New Testament textbook is an asset for instructors who are committed to bringing marginalized voices and approaches to the forefront in their classes.

One of the many striking things about *Toward Decentering the New Testament* is that it does not contain a separate chapter on women. Instead, Smith and Kim consistently discuss the role of women as *a part of* not *apart from* the New Testament texts. For example, in the chapter on the Gospel of Mark, the authors note that "with the exception of Jesus' mother Mary and other women named at the empty tomb scene (Mary Magdalene, Mary the mother of James, Salome), the women in Mark are nameless....

---

38. Mitzi J. Smith and Yung Suk Kim, *Toward Decentering the New Testament: A Reintroduction* (Eugene, OR: Cascade Books, 2018), v–vi.
39. Smith and Kim, *Toward Decentering the New Testament*, 5.

Yet, most of these women demonstrate agency."[40] One chapter that particularly stands out is "Intersectionality and Reading Complexity in the New Testament." In it, Smith explains how "intersectionality invites or permits one to critically reflect on what and how social categories such as gender, race/ethnicity, class, sexuality, religious affiliation, dis/ability, and nationality, co-constitute in human experience."[41] As a framework I use in my own research, having intersectionality explained in a manner geared toward undergraduate students coupled with its applications for analyzing biblical texts is a dream come true. What this brief overview of *Toward Decentering the New Testament* highlights is that we have options when it comes to how we teach the New Testament to students. We do not have to make the one lecture devoted to women the only occasion where we discuss them. Nor do we have to limit our theoretical approaches to historical-critical methods. Highlighting the identities and agency of women throughout the semester, rather than lumping women together near the end of the course, brings them from the margins to the center and makes them visible.

Syllabi and Transgressive Pedagogies

Selecting a different textbook for an introductory New Testament course is one step toward counteracting male-centered approaches. Another consideration is how we structure our syllabi. Syllabi do much more than outline the topics and requirements of a course. They also provide glimpses into the mind of the course instructor. For example, sections on course policies related to the use of technology or late penalties can reveal much to students about available supports and the overall learning environment an instructor wants to cultivate. Other sections, such as topics outlined in the course schedule along with the readings/authors selected, can also convey a great deal, even if they appear to be a simple list. Although a list of readings and topics might seem too brief to express anything more than the basics, the chronology of when certain topics are discussed over the course of the term is key. While having male names like Mark, John, and Matthew under the list of readings on the syllabus is unavoidable, there is a way to frame these readings by topics so that a "malestream" approach is not reified in the classroom. For example, rather than framing 1 Corinthians as part of a Pauline corpus, what if we discussed the text as an expression of the *assembly* rather than of *Paul*.[42] In the case of Thecla, instead of reading *APTh* at the end of

---

40. Smith and Kim, *Toward Decentering the New Testament*, 97.
41. Smith and Kim, *Toward Decentering the New Testament*, 53.
42. For an example of this type of approach, see Joseph A. Marchal, ed., *The People*

the term and as the sole text on early Christian women, what if each lecture shone a spotlight on the many women visible in early Christian texts?

Being more cognizant of the way our textbooks and syllabi frame our introductory New Testament classrooms positions us in a way to allow Thecla to *transgress* with us in our pedagogy. In her book *Teaching to Transgress: Education as the Practice of Freedom*, bell hooks outlines the ways in which instructors can cultivate transgressive pedagogies in the classroom.[43] Speaking about her experience at the beginning of her teaching career, hooks comments that "[e]*xcitement* in higher education was viewed as potentially disruptive of the atmosphere of seriousness assumed to be essential to the learning process. To enter classroom settings in colleges and universities with *the will to share the desire to encourage excitement, was to transgress.*"[44]

If, as hooks suggests, "the will to share the desire to encourage excitement" is a means of transgression, perhaps there is a way for Thecla to be transgressive after all. A recent essay by B. Diane Lipsett promotes the use of "signature pedagogy" in teaching *APTh*.[45] Signature pedagogy encourages students to be engaged in the same debates as scholars. "[R]ather than merely offering students the results of scholars' intellectual work," Lipsett explains, signature pedagogy "expos[es] students to 'the way intellectual work in the field is done' by 'engaging them in the conversations, questions, and debates central to what we do professionally.'"[46] Drawing on Lipsett's suggestion to engage students with our own debates and research questions, there seems to be a way to resolve the conundrum I posed at the beginning of the essay: Do I let my students experience the same excitement that I did reading *APTh* for the first time? Or do I point out all the ways that Thecla is not the heroine they think she is at first glance? The third option is to pose this question directly to the students: Is Thecla a transgressive figure in the text? Why or why not? This type of question does not center Paul or the New Testament, and it allows the spotlight to be solely on Thecla. Adopting this approach allows students to (hopefully) experience excitement themselves.

beside Paul: The Philippian Assembly and History from Below, ECL 17 (Atlanta, GA: SBL Press, 2015).

43. bell hooks, *Teaching to Transgress: Education as the Practice of Freedom* (New York: Routledge, 1994).

44. hooks, *Teaching to Transgress*, 8; italics for "Excitement" in the original. Subsequent italics added for emphasis by me.

45. B. Diane Lipsett, "Signature Pedagogies for Ancient Fiction? Thecla as a Test Case," in *Reading and Teaching Ancient Fiction: Jewish, Christian, and Greco-Roman Narratives*, ed. Sara Raup Johnson, Rubén R. Dupertuis, and Christine Shea, WGRW-Sup 11 (Atlanta, GA: SBL Press, 2018), 233–40.

46. Lipsett, "Signature Pedagogies for Ancient Fiction?," 234.

Lipsett notices another benefit to this approach: "As scholarship informs pedagogy, teaching may refresh our own reading practices. One gift of teaching texts such as the Acts of Thecla is witnessing how first-time readers react: amusement and laughter, distress or indignation, perplexity or confusion."[47]

Another related approach that bell hooks advocates is that "[t]he engaged voice must never be fixed and absolute but always changing, always evolving in dialogue with a world beyond itself."[48] Updating our approach to teaching the New Testament "in dialogue with a world beyond itself" is especially true when it comes to issues of women and gender. In the case of teaching the New Testament, it appears that centering our discussions on Paul and Jesus has been "fixed and absolute" for quite some time. Of course, these figures were influential in the development of the tradition but to continually frame our courses through the perspective of these men runs the risk of overlooking other discussions. This type of work is exemplified by Smith and Kim in *Toward Decentering the New Testament*, but it is not limited to their book. Joseph Marchal begins his book *Appalling Bodies: Queer Figures Before and After Paul's Letters* by bluntly stating: "Paul is probably the least interesting thing about Paul's letters."[49] Using queer approaches, Marchal focuses not on Paul but on issues of sex and gender that permeate the letters. In a similar vein, Maia Kotrosits uses *APTh* to critique the so-called "penetration grid" that is frequently used to make sense of ancient conceptions of sex.[50] Kotrosits acknowledges that *APTh* is mostly of interest to scholars of early Christianity. She notes, however, that "[*APTh*] is not distinctly or distinctively Christian in any sense. It is far more productive to view it as an enthralling interlocutor in questions of ancient erotic life: an unusual piece of literature but not an exceptional one."[51] Neither Marchal nor Kotrosits center their work around Paul or the New Testament. Marchal explicitly distances himself from Paul, while Kotrosits does not even rely on the field of early Christianity to situate *APTh* in a broader scholarly conversation. Their approaches reveal that it is possible to escape the gravitational pull of Paul, the New Testament, and the historical-critical method, and that escaping these orbits allows for many ways forward in both teaching and scholarship.

---

47. Lipsett, "Signature Pedagogies for Ancient Fiction?," 238.
48. hooks, *Teaching to Transgress*, 11.
49. Joseph A. Marchal, *Appalling Bodies: Queer Figures before and after Paul's Letters*, electronic resource (New York: Oxford University Press, 2019), 1.
50. Maia Kotrosits, "Penetration and Its Discontents: Greco-Roman Sexuality, the Acts of Paul and Thecla, and Theorizing Eros without the Wound," *JHS* 27.3 (2018): 343–66.
51. Kotrosits, "Penetration and Its Discontents," 357.

It would be naïve of me to think that this essay will convince all instructors to revise their syllabi, lecture notes, or textbook selection. Given the academic job market and the enormous teaching load many adjuncts or sessional instructors face, there is little time for rest let alone planning a new approach to teaching the New Testament. But even if instructors cannot deviate from a curriculum that reinforces a male-centered approach to the New Testament, this does not mean they cannot be transgressive in other ways. bell hooks suggests that instructors be honest and transparent with students: "When professors bring narratives of their experiences into classroom discussions it eliminates the possibility that we can function as all-knowing, silent interrogators. It is often productive if professors take the first risk, linking confessional narratives to academic discussions so as to show how experience can illuminate and enhance our understanding of academic material." Following hooks, I offer a few questions that instructors can pose to themselves and their students at the beginning of the semester. These questions will allow instructors to be transparent about how they developed syllabi and why they chose a certain textbook:

(1) Why are we reading these texts in this course?
(2) Why are we reading the texts in this particular order?
(3) How did the instructor decide on these readings?
(4) Whose perspective are we privileging in these readings?
(5) Whose names appear in the titles of the texts?
(6) Why is the textbook designed the way it is? Additionally, why was this textbook chosen (over others) for the course?

Providing any sort of glimpse into the behind-the-scenes work in this way can create a space for transgression. Instead of being "all-knowing, silent interrogators" or maintaining the veneer of "seriousness," instructors can say things like "I chose this textbook because it contains a great discussion of intersectionality, an approach I use in my own research" or "the textbook compares *APTh* to the Pastoral Letters, but instead I want you to consider this question about Thecla's nature." Gestures such as these, however small, are still tiny pebbles that when thrown into an undisturbed pool of water will create ripples.

Willi Braun's 2000 essay "Physiotherapy of Femininity in the Acts of Thecla," lands on the same ground where I currently find myself: the Thecla of *APTh* is not a socially transgressive character. According to Braun, the fact that Thecla has to minimize or even erase her femininity in order to achieve her quest for ultimate piety is "a testament to the power of androcentric ideology which generally kept women in their place."[52] In the context of a New Testament syllabus, the presence of Thecla's name in the monotonous chorus of Jesus, Paul, and John "succeed[s] in crashing the male club," to borrow Willi's phrasing.[53] Still, Braun cautions that Thecla's disruptive potential may only reinforce "the rules of the dominant game in town."[54] However, this is only if we make Thecla the end point of our transgressive pedagogy. To be clear, I am encouraging us to think of Thecla not as a means to an end but as an invitation to move forward. With our help, Thecla can become the revolutionary who continues to crash the male club and transgress the norms of New Testament classrooms.

Author biography

Anna Cwikla is a PhD candidate in the Department for the Study of Religion at the University of Toronto. Her research focuses on the literary function of women in non-canonical early Christian texts.

Bibliography

Arnal, William E. "Gendered Couplets in Q and Legal Formulations: From the Rhetoric to Social History." *JBL* 116.1 (1997): 75–94. https://doi.org/10.2307/3266747

Braun, Willi. "Body, Character and the Problem of Femaleness in Early Christian Discourse." *RT* 9.1 (2002): 108–17. https://doi.org/10.1163/157430102X00061

—"Physiotherapy of Femininity in the Acts of Thecla." 209–30 in *Text and Artifact in the Religions of Mediterranean Antiquity: Essays in Honor of Peter Richardson*. Edited by Stephen G. Wilson and Michel R. Desjardins. Studies in Christianity and Judaism 9. Waterloo, ON: Wilfrid Laurier University Press, 2000.

Burrus, Virginia. *Chastity as Autonomy: Women in the Stories of the Apocryphal Acts*. Studies in Women and Religion 23. Lewiston, NY: Mellen Press, 1987.

Cooper, Kate. *Band of Angels: The Forgotten World of Early Christian Women*. New York: Penguin, 2013.

—*The Virgin and the Bride: Idealized Womanhood in Late Antiquity*. Cambridge, MA: Harvard University Press, 1996.

Cwikla, Anna. "There's Nothing about Mary: The Insignificance of Mary in the Gospel of Thomas 114." *JIBS* 1.1 (2019): 95–112.

Davies, Stevan L. *The Revolt of the Widows: The Social World of the Apocryphal Acts*. London: Feffer & Simons, 1980.

Davis, Stephen J. "From Women's Piety to Male Devotion: Gender Studies, the Acts of Paul and Thecla, and the Evidence of an Arabic Manuscript." *HTR* 108.4 (2015): 579–93. https://doi.org/10.1017/S0017816015000395

---

52. Braun, "Physiotherapy of Femininity," 222.
53. Braun, "Physiotherapy of Femininity," 222.
54. Braun, "Physiotherapy of Femininity," 222.

—*The Cult of Saint Thecla: A Tradition of Women's Piety in Late Antiquity*. Oxford: Oxford University Press, 2001.

Denzey Lewis, Nicola. *Introduction to "Gnosticism": Ancient Voices, Christian Worlds*. New York: Oxford University Press, 2013. https://doi.org/10.1093/obo/9780195393361-0168

den Dulk, Matthijs. "I Permit No Woman to Teach Except for Thecla: The Curious Case of the Pastoral Epistles and the 'Acts of Paul' Reconsidered." *NovT* 54.2 (2012): 176–203. https://doi.org/10.1163/156853612X628142

Ehrman, Bart D. *The New Testament: A Historical Introduction to the Early Christian Writings*. 5th ed. New York: Oxford University Press, 2012.

—*The New Testament: A Historical Introduction to the Early Christian Writings*. New York: Oxford University Press, 1997.

—*The New Testament: A Historical Introduction to the Early Christian Writings*. 7th ed. New York: Oxford University Press, 2020.

hooks, bell. *Teaching to Transgress: Education as the Practice of Freedom*. New York: Routledge, 1994.

Kloppenborg, John S., Marvin W. Meyer, Stephen J. Patterson, and Michael G. Steinhauser. *Q-Thomas Reader*. Sonoma, CA: Polebridge, 1990.

Kotrosits, Maia. "Penetration and Its Discontents: Greco-Roman Sexuality, the Acts of Paul and Thecla, and Theorizing Eros without the Wound." *JHS* 27.3 (2018): 343–66. https://doi.org/10.7560/JHS27301

Kraemer, Ross Shepard. "Thecla." 485–502 in *The Oxford Handbook of New Testament, Gender, and Sexuality*. Edited by Benjamin H. Dunning. Oxford University Press, 2019. https://doi.org/10.1093/oxfordhb/9780190213398.013.2

—*Unreliable Witnesses: Religion, Gender, and History in the Greco-Roman Mediterranean*. New York: Oxford University Press, 2011.

Lipsett, B. Diane. "Signature Pedagogics for Ancient Fiction? Thecla as a Test Case." 233–40 in *Reading and Teaching Ancient Fiction: Jewish, Christian, and Greco-Roman Narratives*. Edited by Sara Raup Johnson, Rubén R. Dupertuis, and Christine Shea. WGRWSup 11. Atlanta: SBL Press, 2018. https://doi.org/10.2307/j.ctt21h4xx0.19

MacDonald, Dennis R. *The Legend and the Apostle: The Battle for Paul in Story and Canon*. Philadelphia, PA: Westminster, 1983.

Marchal, Joseph A. *Appalling Bodies: Queer Figures before and after Paul's Letters*. Electronic resource. New York: Oxford University Press, 2019. https://doi.org/10.1093/oso/9780190060312.001.0001

— ed. *The People beside Paul: The Philippian Assembly and History from Below*. ECL 17. Atlanta, GA: SBL Press, 2015. https://doi.org/10.2307/j.ctt189tt2d

Matthews, Shelly. "Thinking of Thecla: Issues in Feminist Historiography." *JFSR* 17. 2 (2001): 39–55.

Mroczek, Eva. "The Hegemony of the Biblical in the Study of Second Temple Literature." *JAJ* 6 (2015): 2–35. https://doi.org/10.13109/jaju.2015.6.1.2

Parkhouse, Sarah. "The Fetishization of Female Exempla: Mary, Thecla, Perpetua and Felicitas." *NTS* 63. 4 (2017): 567–87. https://doi.org/10.1017/S0028688517000157

Parks, Sara. "'The Brooten Phenomenon': Moving Women from the Margins in Second-Temple and New Testament Scholarship." *Bible Crit. Theory* 15 (2019): 46–64.

Patterson, Stephen J. *The Gospel of Thomas and Christian Origins: Essays on the Fifth Gospel*. Boston: Brill, 2013. https://doi.org/10.1163/9789004256217

Patterson, Stephen J., James M. Robinson, and Hans-Gebhard Bethge. *The Fifth Gospel: The Gospel of Thomas Comes of Age*. Harrisburg, PA: Trinity Press International, 1998.

Ratcliffe, Rosie. "*The Acts of Paul and Thecla*: Violating the Inviolate Body – Thecla Uncut." 184–209 in *The Body in Biblical, Christian and Jewish Texts*. Edited by Joan E. Taylor. LSTS 85. London: Bloomsbury T&T Clark, 2014.

Reed, Annette Yoshiko. "The Afterlives of New Testament Apocrypha." *JBL* 134 (2015): 401–25. https://doi.org/10.1353/jbl.2015.0017

Smith, Mitzi J., and Yung Suk Kim. *Toward Decentering the New Testament: A Reintroduction*. Eugene, OR: Cascade Books, 2018.

"The New Testament - Bart D. Ehrman - Oxford University Press," n.d. No pages. Cited 7 August 2020. Online: https://global.oup.com/academic/product/the-new-testament-9780190909000?cc=ca&lang=en&#.

Index of Subjects

1 Corinthians 181–2, 195–6, 267
1 Kings 28, 56, 201
1 Peter 63
1 Timothy 259

2 Corinthians 36
2 Esdras 241
2 Samuel 50, 206

Achilles 84, 121
Acts of the Apostles 63, 107, 208
Acts of Paul & Thecla 256–71
Aeschylus 122
Alexander Pope 3, 6
Antiphon 242–244, 247
Apocalypse of John/Revelation 9, 13–30, 235
Apocalypticism 11, 20–21, 23, 29, 116, 210, 221, 231, 235–6, 241, 251
Apostles Creed 108
Aristotle 32–3, 117–18, 138
Authority 9, 31–47, 56, 83, 86, 89, 101, 105–6, 128, 133, 148, 222, 232–3, 259

Babylon 24–5, 28, 72
Baptism 10, 15, 113–30, 181, 188, 195–6, 233, 258
Bethlehem 80
Birds 9–10, 13–30, 48–62
Bull 85–90
Burial 27–8, 182–8, 191, 193–4

Canon 9, 31–47, 64, 69, 76, 102–3, 105, 158, 260–1
Catacombs 80, 85–6, 113
Celsus 16–7

Corinth 11
Crow 56, 128
Crow, the 221–31, 235–6

David (king) 104–7
Day of Atonement 58
Deuteronomy 28, 50, 52–3, 159–60
Demiurge 66
Divination 10, 16, 113, 121–5, 128–9
Dove 9–10, 15–6, 49, 52–3, 59, 72, 87, 90, 113–29, 188, 250

Eagle 8, 19–25, 50–52, 56, 59, 113, 123, 125, 128
Ecclesiastes 123–4
Egypt 53, 63, 80, 118, 124
Elijah 56, 232
Epistemic authority 39–42
Euhemerus 171–3
Executive authority 38–42
Exile 11, 94, 97–100, 104–5, 205, 215–6, 236
Exodus 101, 122, 201
Ezekiel 20, 28, 50–1, 99–100

Funeral 182–96

Galatians 37–8
Galilee 161, 204–5, 209, 236
Genesis 27, 50, 52, 55, 65, 116, 119, 121, 125, 241
Gnostic 66–7, 153
Gospel of Hebrews 117
Gospel of John 69, 83–4, 87, 101–2, 115, 161, 267
Gospel of Luke 1, 10, 15, 18, 28–9, 69, 80, 83–4, 86–9, 93, 107,

114–6, 120, 126, 128, 143, 146, 153–5, 158, 161–3, 260
Gospel of Mark 9, 11, 15, 69–75, 83–8, 107, 113–17, 119, 119, 121, 123, 125–6, 128, 200–37, 242, 246–9, 252, 260, 266–7
Gospel of Matthew 15, 18, 69, 75, 80, 83–4, 87–9, 101, 107, 114–6, 120, 126, 128, 139, 140, 142, 155, 161, 251, 260, 267
Gospel of Thomas 11, 64–9, 234, 233–53, 256, 260

Hebrews 107–8, 206, 208
Herakles 83–4, 88
Herod 80, 89, 106
Herodians 72
Herodotus 124–5
Hezekiah 53–4
Hippocrates 242–5, 247
Holy Spirit 15, 87, 107, 113, 121, 139
Homer 16, 27, 121, 123, 125, 136–7
Hosea 53, 116

Isaiah 20, 51–5, 99–100, 241, 245
Infancy Gospel of James 80
Infancy Gospel of Thomas 15, 82

Jeremiah 16, 72–4, 203, 211
Jerusalem 28, 52–3, 69–72, 74, 86, 105, 201–5, 210, 215, 231–3
Jesus/Christ 1, 3, 9–11, 15, 19, 21, 25–8, 37–8, 63–6, 68–75, 78–91, 101–2, 104, 107–9, 113–16, 120, 123, 126, 128, 135–6, 143, 145, 147, 149, 152–4, 157–63, 166, 182, 189, 195–6, 201, 215, 231–7, 242, 246, 249, 251, 256, 260–3, 265–6, 269, 271
Jewish War with Rome 11, 69–75, 202–5, 216, 231–2, 237
Job 16, 53, 56, 59–60
John the Baptist 87, 114–5, 160
John Chrysostom 109

Jonah 58
Joseph 80, 139–42
Josephus 69–71, 74, 122, 128
Jude 39
Judea 11, 68, 71, 74, 102, 104, 113, 123, 125, 127–8, 161, 204–5, 216, 233, 235–7, 242, 245

Kingdom of God/Kingdom of heaven/Kingdom of the father 15, 27, 65, 102, 108, 206, 208–12, 233, 245, 248–9, 251–2

Lamb 21, 70, 87–8, 90, 127
Lamentations 60
Lazarus 85
Leper 57, 213, 215
Lion 19, 21, 65 187

Magi 81
Marcion 10–1, 152–65
Mary Magdalene 65, 83, 86, 256–8, 266
Mary, Mother of Jesus 80–81, 139–42
Meals 186, 194–5
Menander 134, 136–40, 142, 144, 148–9
Messiah 65, 71, 105–107, 163, 206, 233
Method & Theory in the Study of Religion (*MTSR*) 2, 14
Mithras 10, 78–91
Moses 58, 67–8, 106, 125–7, 195–6, 232
Myth/myth-making 2, 7, 9–10, 66, 78–84, 86–90, 95, 101, 158, 161–3, 176, 200–1, 203, 209, 216, 231, 237–8

New Comedy 10, 131–51
Nicene Creed 108
Noah 55–6, 119, 121, 125, 244
North American Association for the Study of Religion (NAASR) 7

Orthodox Christianity 10, 94, 102–4, 108–19
Ostrich 9, 54, 59–60
Owl 14, 22, 49, 54–5, 61, 123, 128

Paideia 11, 142, 238–253
Parable 15, 72, 86, 175, 211–2, 231, 242, 245–52
Paul 9, 11, 18, 29, 32–42, 75, 104, 107, 207–8, 234–5, 257–63, 265–71
Perpetua 258
Peter 39, 63, 65, 86, 136, 215, 256
Pharisees 72, 114–5, 136, 250
Philo of Alexandria 67–8, 118–9, 125–6, 239, 241–2, 244–5
Pigeon 10, 57, 113–27
Platonism 66–7, 81, 137, 172, 174, 239–40, 242
Pliny 119, 124
Plutarch 67–8, 122, 136
Polybius 190–1
Protagoras 3
Proverbs 56, 59
Psalms 10, 28, 50, 52, 54, 56, 59–60, 74, 93–112, 201, 209–11
Ps. Plutarch 242, 244, 247
Ptolemy 82
Pythagoras 67–8

Quintilian 137, 242–5, 247–8
Qumran 206–7

Raven 22, 56, 59, 87, 90, 125, 128
Redescribing Christian Origins Seminar 7
Ritual 11, 16, 55, 57–8, 78–9, 80–1, 87–9, 119, 176, 181, 185–6, 189, 195–6, 213, 216, 221, 225–5, 236
Romans 70–1, 74–5, 107, 191–3, 233–6
Rome 11, 24, 64, 69–70, 72, 75, 78, 85–6, 169, 231, 233, 235
Ruth 50, 52

Sadducees 72, 114–5
Satan 104, 133–5, 143–9
Sayings Source Q (Q) 7, 10, 152–65, 234, 238–9, 248, 261
Seneca 242–4, 247–8
Sioux, the 224, 227–8, 230
Social Identity Theory 93–7, 108–9
Society of Biblical Literature 7
Song of Songs 58
Study of Religion 2–3, 5–8, 11, 29, 48–9, 128, 179, 220–1
Symbol 14, 49–50, 53, 64, 95, 113, 125
Syrian Dialogue Hymns 131–51

Temple 28, 69–74, 80, 88, 201–12, 215, 231–5
Tertullian 156–7, 163
Tetramorph 20
Thecla 11–12, 256–71
Throne 19–21, 23, 25

Violence 9, 14, 21–2, 24, 26, 28–9, 119, 127
Virgil 24, 27, 121
Voluntary association 196
Vulture 22–5

Zack de la Rocha 44
Zipporah 58

Index of Modern Authors

Ackerman, James S. 100–101
Albright, William F. 97
Allison, Dale C. 114, 116
Alvarez, Francis D. 202, 210, 212
Arnal, William 2–6, 8–9, 157, 202, 205, 207–8, 220, 236, 238–40, 252, 264
Ascough, Richard 33, 37, 196
Attridge, Harold 64, 203
Aune, David 181

Bach, Robert 211
Bailly, Jean-Christophe 13
Bar-Tal, Daniel 95
Barton, Carlin A. 169–71, 174, 176
Bateman, Herbert W. 104
Beasley-Murray, George R. 100, 210
Beck, Roger 87
Becking, Bob 56
BeDuhn, Jason D. 153, 155–6, 162
Bell, Catherine 11, 37, 188–9, 195
Benford, Robert D. 43
Bergen, Doris L. 154
Berner, Christoph 22, 26
Best, Ernest 206
Betz, Hans Dieter 79
Blegen, C. 186–7
Blenkinsopp, Joseph 53
Bloomquist, Gregory L. 5
Bookidis, Nancy 182
Bovon, François 115–16
Boyarin, Daniel 169–71, 174, 176
Braun, Willi 1–12, 14, 16, 29, 31, 32, 48–9, 59–61, 63, 93, 114, 128–9, 131, 156–7, 166–71, 173–9, 205, 220–1, 236, 238–40, 256–8, 270–1
Bremmer, Jan 82–3

Brock, Sebastian P. 132–5, 139–45, 147–9
Brooke, George J. 206, 208–9
Brown, Ian Phillip 11, 240, 256
Brown, Peter 134
Brown, Raymond E. 39, 100, 101, 105–106
Brown, Rupert J. 94–5
Burrus, Virginia 258

Cameron, Averil 132
Cameron, Ron 5, 7, 181, 239, 241–3, 246–7, 252
Capps, Don 213
Caroll, Maureen 193–4
Casadio, Giovanni 82, 88
Charlesworth, James H. 201, 203, 206–7
Chilton, Bruce 209–10
Christian, Michelle 238, 256
Cixous, Hélène 49
Clauss, Manfred 78, 81, 85–8
Collingwood, R.G. 42–3
Collins, Adela Yarbo 181
Conzelmann, Hans 181
Cooper, Kate 257–8
Cotter, Wendy 214
Craffert, Pieter F. 213–14
Crook, Zeba 4
Crossan, John Dominic 214
Crossley, James G. 203, 206–7, 209
Curry, Patrick 121
Cwikla, Anna 11, 240, 256

Dahood, Mitchell 98, 104–5
Damasio, Antonio 50
Davies, Alan T. 154
Davies, W.D. 114, 116, 207

Davies, Stevan L. 257, 259
Davis, Barry C. 104
Davis, Stephen J. 257
DeConick, April D. 246, 250–1
De George, Richard T. 38–40, 42
Deissmann, Adolf 36, 40, 181
Demaris, Richard 181–2, 184
Den Dulk, Mathijs 259
Denzey Lewis, Nicola 262
Desjardins, Michel 5, 257
Dixon, Edward P. 117, 121, 125
Dodd, Charles H. 210
Doody, Aude 241

Edwards, Catherine 194
Egelhaaf-Gaiser, Ulrike 85
Eidevall, Göran 53–5
Ehrman, Bart D. 154, 260–5
Eshleman, Kendra 250
Exum, J. Cheryl 59
Eyl, Jennifer 10, 122

Fairen, Glen J. 10
Feldt, Laura 56
Fewster, Gregory 36
Fichte, Johann Gottlieb 43
Finkelberg, Margalit 121
Finney, Paul Corby 113
Fischer, Peter 43
Flower, Harriet 189–94
Forti, Tova 56
Fossum, J. 55
Fredriksen, Paula 35
Frischer, Bernard 239
Fujita, Shozo 211

Gadamer, Hans-Georg 41, 43
Gaiser, Frederick J. 214
Gamble, Harry Y. 34
Gathercole, Simon 246, 249–51
Gero, Stephen 116–7
Gillmayr-Bucher, Susanne 54–5
Good, Edwin M. 59, 60
Goodacre, Mark 246
Goodfellow, Peter 18, 22, 24, 26–7

Gorak, Jan 33
Gowler, David B. 5
Graham, Emma-Jayne 189
Green, Deborah 183–4
Green, Steven 122
Greenstein, Edward L. 60
Grey, Timothy C. 206, 210
Gruber, Heather Irene Waddell 137
Guenther, Heinz 1, 4
Gunkel, Hermann 104

Harland, Philip A. 4, 33
Harmon, Daniel 194
Hart, H.L.A 39
Hart, Patrick 6, 8, 9, 238
Harvey, Susan Ashbrook 135, 143, 146
Hawley, Richard 137, 146–7
Hay, David M. 106
Haynes, Katharine 138
Hays, Christopher B. 54
Hedrick Charles W. 250–1
Henricksen, Jan-Olav 212, 214
Herzog, William R. 209
Heschel, Susannah 154
Hoffman, R.J. 162–3
Hofstadter, Douglas 50
Holladay, William L. 96, 98, 106
Hollander, David B. 242
hooks, bell 268–70
Hope, Valerie 189–91, 193
Hopkins, Keith 193
Horrell, David J. 40
Hossfeld, Frank-Lothar 97–101
Howarth, W.D. 136
Hübner, Wolfgang 82
Hughes, Dennis 84
Hunter, R.L. 133, 136

Jacobson, Arland Dean 160
Jeffers, Ann 121
Jefferson, Helen Genevieve 104
Jefferson, Lee M. 85–6
Jervell, Jacob 40
Johnston, Sarah Iles 63, 121, 188

Index of Modern Authors 279

Jones, Alexander 82
Juel, Donald 203, 206
Jülicher, Adolf 34
Juschka, Darlene 2, 10

Kant, Immanuel 42
Kaylor, David R. 209
Keck, Leander E. 116
Kee, Min Suc 98
Kennedy, Charles 181, 195
Kierkegaard, Søren 38–9
Kim, Yung Suk 266–7, 269
King, Karen 240, 248, 251–2
Klinghardt, Matthias 153
Klinzing, Georg 207
Kloppenborg, John 1, 4, 33, 152, 155, 158, 159, 234–5, 239–45, 261
Knox, John 154–5
Kotrosits, Maia, 200, 269
Kraemer, Ross Shepard 257
Kraus, Hans-Joachim 98, 104–5
Kronenberg, Leah 241

Landy, Francis 5, 9, 51–2
Larson, Jennifer 81
Last, Richard 37
Lawson, E. Thomas 7
Lear, Jonathan 221–31, 236
Leighton, Albert C. 123–4
Lewis, Sian 118
Lieu, Judith M. 154, 158
Liew, Tat-siong Benny 232
Lightstone, Jack N. 239
Lincoln, Bruce 35, 39–40, 42, 90, 158, 166
Lipsett, B. Diane 268–9
Loader, W.R.G. 104–105, 107
Llewellyn-Jones, Lloyd 118
Lloyd, G.E.R. 82
Lookadoo, Jonathon 202, 207
Lopez, Donald S. 168

MacDonald, Dennis R. 257, 259

Mack, Burton 7, 9, 32, 152–3, 163, 202, 236, 242–3, 246
Malbon, Elizabeth Struthers 201, 205
Marchal, Joseph A. 37, 267, 269
Martin, Luther H. 4, 7, 78–9, 82
Marxsen, Willi 204
Mathews, Shailer 212
Mathews, Thomas F. 81
Matthews, Christopher R. 209
Matthews, Shelly 257, 259, 264
McCutcheon, Russell 2–5, 8, 31, 48, 60, 128, 167, 170–1, 173, 178, 205, 220, 236, 239
McDonald, Lee Martin 34
McEvoy, John A. 210
McGann, Jerome J. 36
McInerny, William F. 201
Merkelbach, Reinhold 81, 85, 89
Merleau-Ponty, Maurice 51
Mettinger, Tryggve N.D. 51
Metzger, Bruce M. 33–4, 195
Mikalson, Jon D. 167–71, 175
Miller, Merrill 5, 7, 181, 202, 205, 208–9
Miller, Patricia Cox 14, 15, 17
Moll, Sebastian 162
Moore, Stephen D. 220, 232–3
Mosser, Carl 100, 103
Mowinckel, Sigmund 98, 104–5
Moxnes, Halvor 209
Mroczek, Eva 107, 260
Muir, Steven 10,
Murphy, Kelly 256
Murray, Gilbert 136
Murray, Robert 132
Mynott, Jeremy 14–7, 21–3, 26, 122

Neyrey, Jerome H. 100–101
Nilüfer, Aydin 43
Nolland, John 114–5
Nongbri, Brent 168–70, 174

O'Collins, Gerald 212–3
Olbricht, Thomas H. 5

Pache, Corinne Ondine 88–9
Pachis, Panayotis 4
Pagels, Elaine H. 239
Palmer, H. 186
Parkhouse, Sarah 258
Parks, Sara 262, 264–5
Parrish, John 5, 11, 181–2
Patterson, Stephen J. 239, 260
Pedersen, Olaf 82
Pendrick, Gerard J. 243
Penny, Donald 40
Perrin, Nicholas 203, 211
Pilch, John J. 213–5
Plisch, Uew-Karsten 249
Pollini, John 191, 193, 195
Porter, Stanley E. 5
Propp, William H. 50
Pryce, F.N. 191

Ratcliffe, Rosie 257–9
Rawson, Beryl 189–90
Raz, Joseph 39, 41
Reed, Annette Yoshiko 260
Reinink, G.J. 132
Robinson, James 153, 158, 160–61, 260
Robbins, Vernon K. 5
Rochford, E. Burke 43
Roetzel, Calvin 40
Rollens, Sarah E. 6, 8–9, 24, 220, 238
Rosen, Ralph Mark 242
Roskam, Hendrika N. 202–203
Roubekas, Nickolas P. 172–4
Roth, Dieter T. 154–6
Ruden, Sarah 78–9
Rutgers, Leonard 183–4

Sahlins, Marshall 224, 229–30
Sandnes, Karl Olav 212, 214
Santrac, Dragoslava 98
Scafuro, Adele 138
Schneemelcher, Wilhelm 34
Scott, Bernard Brandon 38, 246
Segal, Erich 133, 136–8

Shaw, Brent D. 240
Shear, T.L. 185
Sinclair, R.K. 33
Simonetti, Manlio 93
Sluiter, Ineke 242
Smith, Jonathan Z. 2–4, 31, 43, 60, 79, 128, 159, 166, 178, 182–4, 200–1, 203–5, 216, 236, 238–9
Smith, Mitzi J. 266–7, 269
Snow, David 43
Snyder, Graydon F. 153
Stanescu, James K. 15
Stewart, Eric 203–5
Stowers, Stanley 181, 195–6, 207
Sumner, William Graham 95

Taussig, Hal 200
Tajfel, Henri 94–5
Telford, William R. 233
Theissen, Gerd 37, 213
Thibodeau, Philip 241
Toperoff, Shlomo P. 119
Touna, Vaia 11, 176
Toynbee, Jocelyn 189–90, 193–4
Traill, Ariana 133, 138, 141–2, 144–6, 148–9
Tristram, Henry B. 54
Trobisch, David 154
Trotter, James M. 98–101
Tyson, Joseph 154–5, 162

Ueberschaer, Frank 241
Ulansey, David 233–5
Ulrich, Eugene 34
Upson-Saia, Kristi 132–3
Uro, Risto 240

Vaage, Leif E. 4, 153
Van de Beek, A. 34–5
Van der Toorn, Karel 53
Vanstiphout, H.L.J. 132
Vermes, Geza 212
Visser, Margaret 84
Von Wahlde 101
Von Harnack, Adolph 155–6, 162

Walbank, Mary 184–8, 191
Wallis, Roy 96
Walker, M. Justin 53, 55
Walsh, David 78
Walsh, Robyn Faith 10, 116, 207–8
Ware, Timothy 102–103
Watts, James W. 26
Watson, Duane 5
Wenell, Karen J. 201–2
West, Martin L. 89
Wheller, Mark 11, 37
White, Hayden 173

Wiebe, Donald 2–3, 4, 7
Winter, Bruce W. 37, 182, 188
Witherington, Ben 38
Worden, Steven K. 43
Wright, Allan 11

Young, R. 186

Zagagi, Netta 136
Zeichmann, Christopher B. 204–5
Zenger, Erich 97–101

Studies in Ancient Religion and Culture

Series Editors:
Philip L. Tite, University of Washington
Michael Ng, Seattle University
https://www.equinoxpub.com/home/studies-in-ancient-religion-and-culture/

Published:
Critical Theory and Early Christianity
Edited by Matthew G. Whitlock

Death's Dominion: Power, Identity, and Memory at the Fourth-Century Martyr Shrine
Nathaniel J. Morehouse

Social and Cognitive Perspectives on the Sermon on the Mount
Edited by Rikard Roitto, Colleen Shantz, and Petri Luomanen

The Complexity of Conversion: Intersectional Perspectives on Religious Change in Antiquity and Beyond
Edited by Valérie Nicolet and Marianne Bjelland Kartzow

Theorizing "Religion" in Antiquity
Edited by Nickolas P. Roubekas

Worth More than Many Sparrows: Essays in Honour of Willi Braun
Edited by Sarah E. Rollens and Patrick Hart

Forthcoming:
An Embodied Reading of The Shepherd of Hermas: The Book of Visions and its Role in Moral Formation
Angela Kim Harkins

John Cassian and the Creation of Monastic Subjectivity
Joshua Schachterle

www.ingramcontent.com/pod-product-compliance
Lightning Source LLC
Chambersburg PA
CBHW061244230426
43662CB00020B/2418